DATE DUE

# ORGANIZED CRIME

The Allyn and Bacon Criminal Justice Series

# ORGANIZED CRIME

Howard Abadinsky

**Allyn and Bacon, Inc.**

Boston     London     Sydney     Toronto

*To Donna, Alisa, and Sandi*

**Library of Congress Cataloging in Publication Data**
Abadinsky, Howard, 1941–
    Organized crime.
    Bibliography: p.
    Includes index.
    1. Organized crime—United States.    I. Title.
HV6791.A52    364.1'06'073    80–14952
ISBN  0–205–07097–3

*Managing Editor: Robert Roen*
*Series Editor: Jeremy J. Soldevilla*

Printed in the United States of America

# CONTENTS

# Preface

Organized crime in America can be conceived of as one stage along a continuum dating back to the earliest days of our history. Gustavus Myers (1936) reminds us that colonial America exhibited many of the activities currently associated with organized crime—bribery, usury, and monopoly, not to mention the seizure of land by force, indentured servitude, and slavery. Early American adventurers cheated and killed native Americans, and charted pirates, called privateers, plundered the high seas. During the War of 1812, and later during the Civil War, profiteers accumulated fortunes while others suffered and died. The range wars in the West, the frauds, bribery, violence, and monopolistic practices of the "robber barons" are all part of the context in which we must understand modern forms of organized crime.

Organized crime is a fascinating subject for many Americans and for people throughout the world, if we can judge by the popularity of books, articles, and motion pictures on this topic. However, the serious observer is confronted by a paucity of scholarly materials on organized crime. This book is designed to help remedy that situation by presenting a comprehensive and scholarly look at organized crime in the United States.

On the way to better understanding, the reader will be guided through a labyrinth of myth and misinformation so often repeated that it has become part of the popular literature on organized crime; purported "facts" will be revealed as deliberate distortions or exaggerations.

*Chapter One* critiques the host of definitions of organized crime, pointing out their relative strengths and weaknesses. The chapter discusses the bureaucratic/corporate analogy and alternative arguments offered by those who view organized crime as a network of patron-client relationships. The chapter includes the working definition of organized crime used in this book.

*Chapter Two* provides an historical perspective to more recent organized criminal activity by reviewing and discussing the predatory proclivities of earlier "godfathers"—the industrial "pirates" and "robber barons" of the nineteenth and early twentieth centuries. The chapter reviews relevant sociological theory in order to provide an explanation for the existence of modern organized crime, and critiques the "ethnic succession" theory. A cross-cultural perspective is provided by a discussion of organized crime in Japan, Africa, and the Soviet Union, as well as the role of Italians in organized crime with a discussion of the Mafia, Camorra, and Honored Society.

*Chapter Three* begins by pointing out the problems inherent in presenting an accurate historical account of organized crime. Various widely accepted historical inaccuracies are discussed. What follows is a history of organized crime based primarily on activities in Chicago and New York, beginning in the nineteenth century and leading up to the present. Contradictions found in the literature, and they abound, are pointed out.

*Chapter Four* reviews the operations that make organized crime primarily a business enterprise: bookmaking, numbers, loansharking, drug trafficking, labor, and business racketeering, etc. It provides information on the current extent of organized crime involvement in these activities.

*Chapter Five* points out the anomalies inherent in laws directed at prohibiting activities (e.g., gambling) for which there is a widespread demand. There is a review of the political and police corruption that results from these anomalies.

*Chapter Six* discusses the legal strategies and law enforcement tools used to combat organized crime.

*Chapter Seven* reviews the policy options available for responding to organized crime, and presents the author's perspective on organized crime in America.

Throughout this book we will make note of nicknames, not merely to portray persons more colorfully, but because of the importance of nicknames in organized crime. Many organized crime figures know, or are known by, nicknames only—asking for surnames is contrary to criminal "etiquette." Law enforcement agencies often maintain an extensive nickname file so that they can properly identify criminals who are not referred to by their given names. There are actually two categories of nicknames:*

1. Those used by the media, law enforcement officials, and other criminals, and *accepted* by the subject; and
2. Those *not accepted* by the subject.

An example of the former is "Charlie Lucky," also known as "Lucky" Luciano; an example of the latter is "Bugsy" Siegel—a very dangerous name to call a very dangerous person. Nicknames may sometimes help to understand the "nature" of a person, as with "Bathhouse" John Coughlin; sometimes they seem to take on an importance of their own. Prohibition era gang leader Dutch Schultz argued that if he had not acquired his nickname, the newspapers, and hence the public and law enforcement officials, would not have been so interested in him; Arthur Flegenheimer is certainly not an easy name to headline or as catchy as the "Dutchman."

The major shortcoming of any attempt to present a comprehensive look

---

* For an extensive analysis of the phenomenon, see: Morgan, Jane, Christopher O'Neill, and Rom Harré, *Nicknames: Their Origins and Social Consequences.* Boston: Routledge and Kegan Paul, 1979.

at organized crime is the sources of information. There are four basic sources:

1.  Persons who are/were members of, or otherwise engaged in, organized crime;
2.  Law enforcement agencies;
3.  Journalistic (news media) reports; and
4.  Scholarly accounts based on one or more of the above.

This writer has used all of the above, and none is completely satisfying. Accordingly, in this book information from one source will often be tested or weighed against information from other sources. The result will, at best, be "truth," or, at least, informative.

This writer has attempted to maintain the highest scholastic standards, but, inevitably, there will be shortcomings, mainly because while the subject matter is quite large and diverse, available data are actually quite limited. This writer, as one of his "street" friends would say, is "copping out," attempting to "beat the heat" by admitting upfront that he has given this book his "best shot," and asking reader indulgence for the (hopefully) minor errors that might be encountered.

The author wishes to express his thanks for the cooperation he received from the North Carolina Justice Academy, the Federal Bureau of Investigation, the Drug Enforcement Administration, the Internal Revenue Service, the Federal Bureau of Alcohol, Tobacco and Firearms, and the Secret Service.

Special thanks to series editor Jeremy J. Soldevilla and production editor Ken Trani.

# ORGANIZED CRIME

# ONE

# Definition and Structure of Organized Crime

In researching and reporting on organized crime, one is faced with the problem of defining the phenomenon. Oddly enough, a great many works on organized crime avoid this problem, as if the obvious need not be defined. In an issue of the *Annals* (of the American Academy of Political and Social Science 347, March 1963), which contains twelve articles on organized crime, no definition of the phenomenon is offered. In an article dealing with sentencing organized crime figures, William Hogan points out: "The problem to date has been the use of broad, general labels such as 'Organized Crime' without clearly defining the term and setting parameters on what is and what is not organized crime" (1976: 21). Unfortunately, Hogan also fails to provide a definition. Paradoxically, the Organized Crime Control Act of 1970 does not define organized crime.[1]

The lack of an adequate definition is highlighted in a report by the (federal) Task Force on Organized Crime, which noted the inadequacies of state efforts at defining organized crime (1976: 214–215). The inadequacies of these definitions appear quite obvious, or will become obvious as our discussion continues. (It should be noted that Larry Flynt, the publisher of *Hustler* magazine, received a 7- to 25-year sentence under the Ohio "organized crime" statute, although there was no syndicate involvement. Kwitny, 1979: 62.)

**California:** Organized crime consists of two or more persons who, with continuity of purpose, engage in one or more of the following activities: (1) The supplying of illegal goods and services, i.e., vice, loansharking, etc.; (2) Predatory crime, i.e., theft, assault, etc.

Several distinct types of criminal activity fall within this definition of organized crime. The types may be grouped into five general categories:

1. Racketeering—Groups of individuals which organize more than one of the following types of criminal activities for their combined profit.
2. Vice Operations—Individuals operating a continuing business of providing illegal goods or services, such as narcotics, prostitution, loansharking, gambling, etc.
3. Theft/Fence Rings—Groups of individuals who engage in a particular kind of theft on a continuing basis, such as fraud and bunco

schemes, fraudulent document passers, burglary rings, car thieves, truck hijackers, and associated individuals engaged in the business of purchasing stolen merchandise for resale and profit.
4. Gangs—Groups of individuals with common interests or background who band together and collectively engage in unlawful activity to enhance their group identity and influence, such as youth gangs, outlaw motorcycle gangs, and prison gangs.
5. Terrorists—Groups of individuals who combine to commit spectacular criminal acts, such as assassination and kidnapping of public figures to undermine public confidence in established government either for political reasons or to avenge some grievance.

**Delaware:** A group of individuals working outside the law for economic gain.

**Georgia:** The Georgia Organized Crime Prevention Council defines organized crime as: Any group of persons collaborating to promote, or conspiring to engage in, on a continuing basis, criminal activity as a significant source of income or livelihood, or aiding or abetting in the violation of the laws of this State relating to prostitution, lotteries, gambling, illegal drug distribution, illegal trafficking in liquors, illegal distribution of deadly weapons, theft offenses, extortion, arson, lending money at usurious rates of interest, counterfeiting, bribery of law enforcement officers and other public officers, or any other criminal offense for profit (Hand, 1978: 21).

**Hawaii:** Any combination or conspiracy to engage in criminal activity as a significant source of income or livelihood, or to violate, aid or abet the violation of criminal laws relating to prostitution, gambling, loansharking, drug abuse, illegal drug distribution, counterfeiting, extortion, corruption of law enforcement officers or other public officers or employees.

**Kansas:** We use the definition which was first adopted when this office, through the Kansas Bureau of Investigation, applied for a Law Enforcement Assistance Administration grant from the United States Department of Justice to fund a statewide Organized Crime Intelligence Unit. Organized Crime is "a continuing criminal conspiracy organized for power and profit utilizing fear and corruption to obtain immunity from the law."

**Louisiana:** A continuing criminal conspiracy operating legally and illegally in society for a profit motive utilizing the tools of fear and corruption.

**Maryland:** The definition of organized crime used in Maryland would follow that promulgated by the United States Department of Justice at this time. However, in the course of revising the standards and goals of the Committee, a revised definition is being discussed.

**Michigan:** There exists in Michigan, whether characterized as Organized Crime, the Syndicate, the Mafia, or La Cosa Nostra, a loose confederacy among a relatively stable group presently promoting and participating in criminal activity and having a common purpose of extending that criminal activity wherever possible. This group is allied by familial relationships and agreements for mutual support and common action. This confederacy is comprised of individuals of varying degrees of influence and authority within its structure, who jointly establish policies and administer forms of discipline to persons who attempt to interfere with its activities. A substantial cadre of associates is dependent upon and totally subservient to this group, and is directly involved in these illegal enterprises. The core of the criminal activity is in furnishing the illegal goods and services of loansharking, gambling, labor racketeering, and narcotics. But the group's participation is definitely not limited to these enterprises.

**Mississippi:** Two or more persons conspiring together to commit crimes for profit on a continuing basis.

**Missouri:** Organized crime has been defined as a self-perpetuating criminal conspiracy for power and profit, utilizing fear and corruption and seeking to obtain immunity from the law.

**Nevada:** The definition of organized crime is the same definition used by the United States Department of Justice.

**New Hampshire:** 'Organized crime' means the unlawful activities of the members of a highly organized, disciplined association engaged in supplying illegal goods and services, including but not limited to homicide, gambling, prostitution, narcotics, marihuana and other dangerous drugs, bribery, extortion, blackmail and other unlawful activities of members of such organizations. (RSA 570–A:1,XI)

**New Mexico:** Organized crime is defined as "the supplying for profit of illegal goods and services, including, but not limited to, gambling, loansharking, narcotics, and other forms of vice and corruption, by members of a structured and disciplined organization." (Section 39–9–2A., NMSA, 1953 Comp., 1973, P.S.)

The Governor's Organized Crime Prevention Commission of New Mexico ("Commission"), in its 1973 Annual Report, supplemented this statutory definition with the following language, and the Commission has adhered to this supplement in defining and determining its jurisdictional areas of operation:

Where there is evidence of continuing criminal conspiracy, structured according to authority or skills, operating substantially for the purpose of unlawful profit and power, which uses fear, force or corruption, or supplies illegal goods or services, or supplies goods or services illegally, there is evidence of organized crime.

**Ohio:** Organized criminal activity:

(A) When directed by the governor or general assembly, the attorney general may investigate any organized criminal activity in this State. "Organized criminal activity" means any combination or conspiracy to engage in criminal activity as a significant source of income or livelihood, or to violate or aid, abet, facilitate, conceal, or dispose of the proceeds of the violation of, criminal laws relating to prostitution, gambling, counterfeiting, obscenity, extortion, loansharking, drug abuse or illegal drug distribution, or corruption of law enforcement officers or other public officers, officials, or employees.

(B) When it appears to the attorney general, as a result of an investigation pursuant to this section, that there is cause to prosecute for the commission of a crime, he shall refer the evidence to the prosecuting attorney having jurisdiction of the matter, or to a regular grand jury drawn and impaneled pursuant to section 2939.17 of the Revised Code. When evidence is referred directly to a grand jury pursuant to this section, the attorney general and any assistant or special counsel designated by him has the exclusive right to appear at any time before such grand jury to give information relative to a legal matter when required, and may exercise all rights, privileges, and powers of prosecuting attorneys in such cases. (Revised Code Section 109.83.)

**Oregon:** Organized crime is a self-perpetuating, continuing conspiracy operating for profit or power, seeking to obtain immunity from the law through fear and corruption.

**Pennsylvania:** The Pennsylvania Crime Commission's *1970 Report on Organized Crime* cites the description of "organized crime" contained on page 1 of the *Task Force Report: Organized Crime,* President's Commission on Law Enforcement Administration of Justice (1967).

Two Pennsylvania statutes also define the term. Pennsylvania's Corrupt Organizations Act states:

Organized crime is a highly sophisticated, diversified and widespread phenomenon which annually drains billions of dollars from the national economy by various patterns of unlawful conduct including the illegal use of force, fraud, and corruption. (Act of December 6, 1972, No. 334, 18 Pa. C.S.A. Section 911.)

In addition, Pennsylvania's immunity law provides:

'Organized crime' and 'racketeering' shall include, but not be limited to, conspiracy to commit murder, bribery or extortion, narcotics or dangerous drug violations, prostitution, usury, subordination of perjury and lottery, bookmaking or other forms of organized gambling. (Act of November 22, 1968, P.L. 1080, No. 333, 19 Pa. C.S.A. Section 640.6.)

**Puerto Rico:** We have given no special definition to Organized Crime, other than that given by the Task Force Report on Organized Crime of the President's Commission on Law Enforcement and Administration of Justice published in 1967. However, our problem of organized crime in Puerto Rico, up to now has been local in nature. There are four general areas which point out some organization. These are narcotics, gambling, prostitution and automobile theft. There are other areas but these are the most prominent of them.

**Tennessee:** The unlawful activities of the members of an organized, disciplined association engaged in supplying illegal goods and services, including, but not limited to, gambling, prostitution, loansharking, narcotics, labor racketeering, and other unlawful activities of members of such organizations. (T.C.A. Section 38–508.)

**Washington:** Those activities which are conducted and carried on by members of an organized, disciplined association engaging in supplying illegal goods and services and/or engaged in criminal activities in contravention of the laws of this State or of the United States.

**Wisconsin:** The Wisconsin Department of Justice has defined organized crime in the same manner as the Task Force on Organized Crime for the President's Commission on Law Enforcement and the Administration of Justice did in its 1967 report.

The Task Force never comes to grips with the problem of definition, and instead proposes a description that attempts to "(1) explain something of the nature of organized crime activity, and (2) dispel stereotypes surrounding organized crime by indicating *what it is not*" (1976: 7; emphasis added).

The Federal Bureau of Alcohol, Tobacco, and Firearms provides a definition of organized crime, the key elements of which are a) self-perpetuation, b) structure and discipline, and c) use of graft and corruption. To fill the obvious gaps in its definition, the Bureau also provides a description of organized crime "characteristics":

> "Organized Crime" refers to those self-perpetuating, structured, and disciplined associations of individuals, or groups, combined together for the purpose of obtaining monetary or commercial gains or profits, wholly or in part by illegal means, while protecting their activities through a pattern of graft and corruption.
>
> Organized crime groups possess certain characteristics which include but are not limited to the following:
>
> 1. Their illegal activities are conspiratorial;
> 2. In at least part of their activities, they commit or threaten to commit acts of violence or other acts which are likely to intimidate;
> 3. They conduct their activities in a methodical, systematic, or highly disciplined and secret fashion;
> 4. They insulate their leadership from direct involvement in illegal activities by their intricate organizational structure;
> 5. They attempt to gain influence in Government, politics, and commerce through corruption, graft, and legitimate means;
> 6. They have economic gain as their primary goal, not only from patently illegal enterprises such as drugs, gambling and loan sharking, but also from such activities as laundering illegal money through and investment in legitimate business.

Whether the purpose is scholarly research or crime control, the first problem that requires attention is: "How are we to recognize organized crime?" We cannot attend to this question without adequately defining organized crime in a way that permits us to classify particular behavior that is deemed criminal [2] as "organized crime" or *not* "organized crime." Michael Maltz points to a problem of semantics: we can call a specific behavior or act organized crime, although when we refer to organized crime in the generic sense, we usually mean an entity, a group of people (1976: 339). He offers a "tentative" definition of organized crime (1975: 76):

> A crime consists of a transaction proscribed by criminal law between offender(s) and victim(s). It is not necessary for the victim to be a complainant or to consider himself victimized for a crime to be committed. An organized crime is a crime in which there is more than one offender, and the offenders are and intend to remain associated with one another for the purpose of committing crimes. The *means* of executing the crime include violence, theft, corruption, economic power, deception, and victim collusion or participation. These are not mutually exclusive categories; any organized crime may employ a number of these means.

The *objective* of most organized crimes is power, either political or economic. These two types of objectives, too, are not mutually exclusive and may coexist in any organized crime.

There are a number of *manifestations* the objectives may take. When the objective is political power, it may be of two types: overthrow of the existing order, or illegal use of the criminal process. When the objective is economic power, it may manifest itself in three different ways: through common crime (*mala in se*), through illegal business (*mala prohibita* or "vices"), or through legitimate business (white-collar crime).

This definition is quite broad—it fails to provide a basis for distinguishing between the James Gang (of Wild West fame) and the Capone organization (of Prohibition fame). While our predilections permit us to accept Al Capone as an "organized crime" figure, Jesse James does not seem to fit the conventional stereotype. Perhaps, then, what is needed is a definition that includes Al Capone while excluding Jesse James.

Alfred Lindesmith (1941) and Clifford Shaw and Henry McKay (1942) focus on the *organizational* nature of organized crime. Lindesmith observes that organized crime "involves the co-operation of several different persons or groups for its successful execution. Organized crime is usually professional crime. The organization may be loose and general, or informal, or it may be definite and formal, involving a system of specifically defined relationships with mutual obligations and privileges" (1941: 119). Shaw and McKay (1972: 173): "In this type of organization can be seen the delegation of authority, the division of labor, the specialization of function, and all the other characteristics common to well-organized business institutions wherever found." William Whyte, writing about numbers gambling in a Boston ghetto during the Depression, noted the businesslike approach; he quotes one observer (1961: 120):

They got their representative in every city, and you can't write numbers unless you belong to the organization. The racket is organized like a big business. Everybody has his own job to do. They got the con men, smart talkers —they can convince you that black is white. Then there's the muscle men. They muscle in to take over a business. There ain't much work for them now. There's the strong-arm men, they protect the business when it gets going. There's the killers. And then there's the bookkeepers, because they got plenty of accounts to figure every day. All them men get paid every week, and maybe for some of them there won't be no work for fifty-one weeks out of the year, but for that other week, there's plenty they got to do.

## THE CORPORATE/BUREAUCRATIC ANALOGY

Donald R. Cressey, writing for the Federal Task Force on Organized Crime, uses a business analogy: ". . . in 1931 organized crime units across the United States formed into monopolistic corporations, and these corporations, in turn, linked themselves together in a monopolistic cartel" (Task Force on Organized Crime, 1967: 31). Alan Block challenges this view that syndicate criminals restructured organized crime during the early 1930s "casting aside its informal, parochial structure and transforming it into a slick, modern bureaucracy" (1975: 228). He presents "numerous examples of haphazard recruiting, ineffective administration, insistent bickering and disputes, probable double-crosses within criminal syndicates, along with the continual shifting of syndicate criminals from enterprise to enterprise" as proof of the limitations of the bureaucratic-corporate interpretation of organized crime (Ibid.: 199).

Donald R. Cressey, writing as a member of the Federal Task Force on Organized Crime, presented his version of the structure of each organized crime unit, the "monopolistic corporation" called the *family* (1967: 8–9):

Each family is headed by one man, the "boss," whose primary functions are maintaining order and maximizing profits. Subject only to the possibility of being overruled by the national advisory group [the *Commission*] ... his authority in all matters relating to his family is absolute. [The boss is also called a *capo*.]

Beneath each boss is an "underboss," the vice president or deputy director of the family. He collects information for the boss; he relays messages to him and passes his instructions down to his own underlings. In the absence of the boss, the underboss acts for him. [The underboss in Italian is called *sottocapo*.]

On the same level as the underboss, but operating in a staff capacity, is the *consigliere,* who is a counselor, or adviser. Often an elder member of the family who has partially retired from a career in crime, he gives advice to family members, including the boss and underboss, and thereby enjoys considerable influence and power.

Below the level of the underboss are the *caporegime,* some of whom serve as buffers between the top members of the family and the lower-echelon personnel. To maintain their insulation from the police, the leaders of the hierarchy (particularly the boss) avoid direct communication with the workers. All commands, information, complaints, and money flow back and forth through a trusted go-between. A *caporegima* fulfilling this buffer capacity, however, unlike the underboss, does not make decisions or assume any of the authority of his boss.

Other *caporegime* serve as chiefs of operating units. The number of men supervised in each unit varies with the size and activities of particular families. Often the *caporegima* has one or two associates who work closely with him, carrying orders, information, and money to the men who belong to his unit. From a business standpoint, the *caporegima* is analogous to plant supervisor or sales manager.

The lowest-level "members" of a family are the *soldati,* the soldiers or "button" men who report to the *caporegime.* A soldier may operate a particular illicit enterprise, e.g., a loan-sharking operation, a dice game, a lottery, a bookmaking operation, a smuggling operation, on a commission basis, or he may "own" the enterprise and pay a portion of its profit to the organization, in return for the right to operate. Partnerships are common between two or more soldiers and between soldiers and men higher up in the hierarchy. Some soldiers and most upper-echelon family members have interests in more than one business.

Beneath the soldiers in the hierarchy are large numbers of employees and commission agents who are not members of the family and are not necessarily of Italian descent. These are the people who do most of the actual work in the various enterprises. They have no buffers or other insulation from law enforcement. They take bets, drive trucks, answer telephones, sell narcotics, tend the stills, work in legitimate businesses.

According to Cressey, organized crime in America is "a nationwide alliance of at least twenty-four tightly knit 'families' of criminals." The members are all Italian or of Italian descent, "and those on the Eastern Seaboard, especially, call the entire system 'Cosa Nostra' [Our Thing]. Each participant thinks of himself as a 'member' of a specific 'family' and of Cosa Nostra (or some equivalent term)" (1969: x). Cressey states that the families are connected "by understandings, agreements, and 'treaties,' and by mutual deference to a 'Commission' made up of the leaders of the most powerful of the 'families' " (1969: xi).

Ralph Salerno, a former police officer with the New York City Police Department's Central Intelligence Bureau, who, like Cressey, was a consultant to the Task Force on Organized Crime, also provides a corporate analogy (Salerno and Tompkins, 1969: 84–85):

> The major difference between the diagram of an organized crime family and the chart of a major corporation is that the head of the enterprise—the Boss —does not have a box over him labeled "stockholder." Many of the other boxes are paralleled in the underworld. The Underboss serves a function similar to that of executive vice-president. The Counselor off to one side is much like a vice-chairman of the board or a special assistant. He is an adviser but has no command authority. He is available to everyone for advice—but in his advice he always reflects the Boss's wishes. He also serves as confidant of the Boss and as an oral historian. Ostensibly, he is a referee; impartial, he is not.
>
> The lieutenants or captains farther below are the equivalent of divisional vice-presidents or general managers. There are different staff jobs corresponding to personnel director, public relations manager, general counsel, security officer, and the like, but they are not assigned permanently to any one man and they do not appear on the chart. (See Fig. 1-1.)

## ORGANIZED CRIME
## AS KINSHIP NETWORKS

In contrast with the above views, Francis Ianni argues that organized crime, or at least the Italian-American version, is a traditional social system "organized by action and by cultural values which have nothing to do with modern bureaucratic virtues" (1972: 108). Instead, he maintains that Italian-American crime syndicates are better explained through an examination of kinship networks; the subtitle of the Ianni book is *Kinship and Social Control in Organized Crime* (1972). The kinship network is made quite vivid by Gay Talese (1971) who, in a study of the crime family of Joseph Bonanno, points out

**An Organized Crime Family**

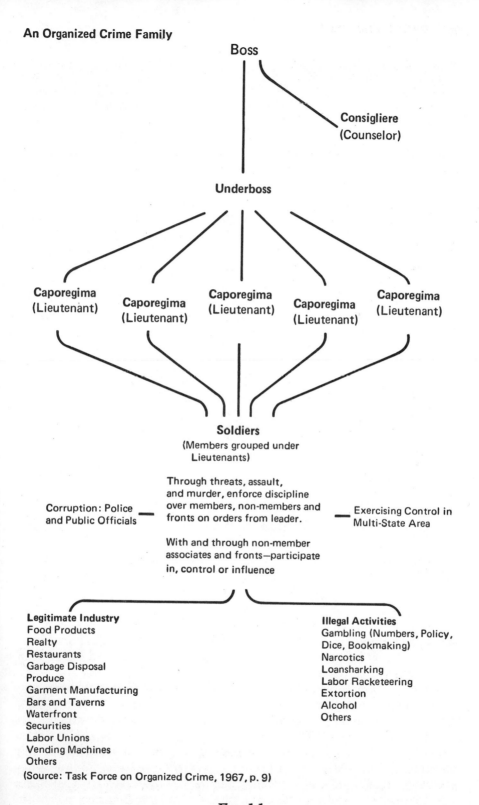

(Source: Task Force on Organized Crime, 1967, p. 9)

FIG. 1-1.

some of the family (in the literal blood sense) ties of the leading organized crime figures in the United States. For example, Salvatore ("Bill") Bonanno, son of Joseph, is married to Rosalie Profaci, the niece of Joseph Profaci, the "Olive Oil King" and boss of another crime family. Stefano Magaddino, Buffalo crime family boss, is Joseph Bonanno's cousin, and two of Joseph Profaci's daughters married into the Joseph Zerrilli and William Toco crime families of Detroit. The daughter of the reputed "boss of bosses," Carlo Gambino, is married to the son of Thomas Lucchese, another leading crime boss. In addition to ties by blood and marriage, there must be added *compareggio* or *comparatico,* which Ianni describes as "the practice of establishing fictitious kin roles in conjunction with rites of passage," e.g., godparents (1972: 19). Ianni notes, "They are products of ritual kinship, but the mutual rights and obligations established are real and binding" (1972: 19).

Randall Collins contrasts the patrimonial type of organization, which is found in organized crime, with the modern bureaucratic organization (1975: 65fn):

> Patrimonial organization, most characteristic of traditional societies, centers around families, patrons and their clients, and other personalistic networks. The emphasis is on traditional rituals that demonstrate the emotional bonds among men; the world is divided into those whom one can trust because of strongly legitimated personal connections, and the rest of the world from whom nothing is to be expected that cannot be exacted by cold-blooded bargaining or force. In modern bureaucratic organization, by contrast, personal ties are weaker, less ritualized, and emotionally demonstrative; in their place is the allegiance to a set of abstract rules and positions. The different class cultures in patrimonial and bureaucratic organizations are accordingly affected. Patrimonial elites are more ceremonious and personalistic. Bureaucratic elites emphasize a colder set of ideals.

Block goes so far as to criticize the "corporate code" of organized crime with respect to punishing informants. He argues that while many are killed, still others are not harmed. "The dynamics of informing and murder indicate that homicide in these instances was more a reaction to stress than a function of a system of justice" (1975: 210). Annelise Anderson studied the Benguerra crime family (a pseudonym) which at the time had seventy-five members. (She used official government sources.) Her conclusion about this group, one of the twenty-four that Cressey refers to, is that it "is not as complex as that of any large corporation"; however, it is "more defined and formal than Ianni claims" (1979: 36).

At this juncture we should note the important ramifications of the corporate analogy. Ianni states that its use "may arise from honest attempts to explain syndicate organization in terms that are familiar to the public." However, he notes a suspect motive: "The 'national conspiracy' theory demands the existence of a national organization with a set of goals aimed at corrupting and subverting the American way of life" (1972: 110). That a widespread belief in such an organization can enhance law enforcement budgets is obvious.

Dwight Smith argues that "proving" the existence of an organized crime syndicate operating as a national corporation justifies the use of certain law enforcement techniques that otherwise might be severely limited if not curtailed, e.g., wiretapping and eavesdropping (1975: 88). Richard Quinney, writing from a Marxist viewpoint, argues that the "war" against organized crime "further extends the power of the government over the lives of citizens, overturning even constitutional protections" (1974: 104).

Interestingly, probably the single most important event tending to support the existence of a national syndicate involved unconstitutional police activity. New York State Police Sergeant Edgar Croswell became suspicious of the activities at the home of Joseph M. Barbara, an "organized crime figure," who resided on an estate in Apalachin, New York. The sergeant had discovered a number of expensive automobiles with out-of-state license plates parked at the Barbara estate. "There was nothing Croswell could legally do about Barbara's visitors, but by Saturday, November 14, 1957, with what he figured to be as many as 70 guests assembled, Croswell no longer could stifle his curiosity. He organized what few deputies he had and conducted a raid on Barbara's home, one merely, as he explained later, to see if anything criminal was going on or if Barbara's guests were wanted on outstanding warrants" (Brashler, 1977: 144). Salerno and Tompkins state that "within minutes dozens of well-dressed men ran out of the house and across the fields in all directions." Using road blocks and reinforcements, the police took sixty-three men into custody (1969: 298). Frederic Sondern reports: "One by one they were summoned to Sergeant Croswell's office, gave their names and addresses, took off their shoes, emptied their pockets as troopers searched and watched" (1959: 36). The rest is history—leading crime figures from areas throughout the country were identified as guests at the Barbara estate.

The episode was dramatic and received extensive media coverage. It is offered as "conclusive" proof that a national syndicate exists (Sondern, 1959: 49–50; Cressey, 1967: 32), but another aspect tends to be discounted if not disregarded—the obviously illegal activity of the police. Sondern reports: "While all this was going on, Croswell and his superiors up the line had been racking their brains for something they could do about the extraordinary assemblage. The attorney general's office in Albany went into high gear. But there was absolutely no ground for arrest or even fingerprinting" (1959: 39). The people at the Barbara estate were taken into custody, detained, and searched without "probable cause" that a crime had been committed.

Giovanni Schiavo maintains that the Apalachin incident was exactly what the guests present said it was: "In all sincerity, it is our firm conviction that the men who went to Apalachin told the truth when they said that they went over to pay a call on their sick friend in order to cheer him up" (1962: 128). This strains credulity; it totally discounts the timing of the "visit," less than one month after the murder of Albert Anastasia. It must also completely dismiss the revelations of Joseph Valachi (1968: 260–266) and a report of a government tape of a telephone conversation between two leading organized crime figures, Sam Giancana of Chicago and Stephen Magaddino of Buffalo (Brash-ler, 1977: 185–186, paper edition):

GIANCANA: "I hope you're satisfied. Sixty-three of our top guys made by the cops" (apparently alluding to Magaddino's arranging the meeting in Apalachin).

MAGADDINO: "I gotta admit you were right, Sam. It never would have hap-pened in your place."

GIANCANA: "You're fuckin' right it wouldn't. This is the safest territory in the world for a big meet."

## ORGANIZED CRIME AS A PATRON-CLIENT RELATIONSHIP

The most serious criticism of the bureaucratic analogy comes from Joseph Albini. He states that as a bureaucratic entity, the structure described by Joseph Valachi, who left school at age fifteen, and "interpreted" by Donald Cressey, who holds a Ph.D., actually adds up to a structure less complex than that of the Boy Scouts (1971: 221). Indeed, the structure of the Boy Scouts of America is quite complex:

- A national council with headquarters in New Jersey;

- A regional center in each of the six regions in the United States;

- Each of the six regions is divided into councils; the Southeast Region, for example, has seventy-two councils;

- Each council is divided into districts in which there are packs and troops that have their own troop leaders and other officers.

Albini argues that organized crime actually consists of a number of syndi-cates in a "loose system of power relationships in contrast to a rigidly organ-ized secret society" (1971: 229). He defines organized crime "as any activity involving two or more individuals, specialized or non-specialized, encompass-ing some form of social structure, with some form of leadership, utilizing cer-tain modes of operation, in which the ultimate purpose of the organization is found in the enterprises of the particular group" (1971: 37). This broad defi-nition permits Albini to subdivide organized crime and to differentiate it from "syndicate crime": organized crime is not necessarily syndicate crime—the former subsumes the latter. Thus, organized crime may include: a) the politi-cal: Ku Klux Klan or Molly Maguires;[3] b) mercenary: theft-oriented organi-zation like the Jesse James gang; c) in-group: outlaw motorcycle gangs, e.g., Hell's Angels (1971: 38–47). *Syndicate* organized crime "differs from other types of organized crime primarily because it provides goods and/or services that are illegal, yet for which there is a demand by certain elements of society" (1971: 47).

The different forms of organized crime proposed by Albini are problematic.* If providing "goods and services" is crucial, we may have to move Hell's Angels into the "syndicate" category since they are reputedly involved in drug distribution networks.[4] Jesse James, on the other hand, was viewed as a political actor by midwestern farmers "because he typically limited his exploits to the robbery of banks and railroads—institutions hated by Jesse's worshipers" (Inciardi, Block and Hallowell, 1977: 73).

Harold Lasswell and Jeremiah McKenna distinguish between organized crime and *politically-oriented* organized crime; organized crime is non-ideological in its perspectives (1972: 24). We will see in Chapter Two that this is not the case in Japan, where organized crime is highly ideological and political. We must also note that syndicate criminals have often engaged in predatory crime such as hijacking and bank robbery (for which the prominent New York syndicate criminal John ("Sonny") Franzese received a long prison sentence). The Campisi crime family of northern New Jersey (which is also a family in the sense that at least eight of its members are blood relatives) operated numbers, bookmaking, and dice-games, and was involved in narcotics trafficking. These ventures were financed by more than one hundred *armed robberies* ("Nine Men Linked to Organized Crime Go On Trial Today in Eight Murders," *New York Times,* Sept. 16, 1974: 75). In 1970, the late Carlo Gambino, alleged *Capo di Tutti Capi* ("Boss of Bosses") was arrested for his alleged part in a scheme to rob armored trucks carrying millions of dollars. Gambino was accused of offering to finance the operation by supplying such items as cars, and he would arrange for the disposition of the "hot" money for sixty cents on the dollar (Meskil, 1973: 11). On December 11, 1978, six men robbed the Lufthansa Airlines cargo terminal at Kennedy International Airport in Queens, New York, of money and jewels valued at $5.8 million. The *New York Times,* hereafter referred to as the *NYT,* reports that the robbery gang is responsible for numerous thefts and hijackings in Queens and Brooklyn and is reputedly associated with Paul Vario of the Lucchese crime family (now headed by Anthony Corallo). The *NYT* reports that "current theory is

---

* Some sociologists (Inciardi, 1975; Clinard and Quinney, 1967; Gibbons, 1977) emphasize typologies that present various criminal types as distinct from one another. In particular, they distinguish between "professional" and "organized" crime. While at one time (prior to the Prohibition era) such distinctions may have been relevant, they now appear to be artificial constructs that do not adequately "classify and organize events in the world so that they can be placed in perspective" (Turner, 1974: 2). As the examples presented below indicate, and as the history of organized crime presented in Chapter Three tends to prove, these criminal types interact and are connected to each other in a network of reciprocal services that defy typological distinctions.

Clinard, Marshall B. and Richard Quinney
    1967  *Criminal Behavior Systems: A Typology.* New York: Holt, Rinehart, and Winston.

Gibbons, Don C.
    1977  *Society, Crime, and Criminal Careers.* Englewood Cliffs, N.J.: Prentice-Hall.

Inciardi, James A. (see bibliography)

Turner, Jonathan H.
    1974  *The Structure of Sociological Theory.* Homewood, Ill.: Dorsey Press.

that the robbers would have to pay Mr. Vario and associates for the privilege of committing the robbery" ("A Den of Thieves Robbed Lufthansa," *NYT,* Feb. 25, 1979: E6). Doug Feiden reports, however, that the *NYT*'s account is not accurate. Rather than merely "licensing" the robbery (which he states was the largest cash haul in United States history—$5.8 million in unmarked, untraceable bills [1979: 37]), Vario arranged the operation. He instructed his associates to have James ("Jimmy the Gent") Burke, a Vario associate, engineer the operation (Ibid.: 39). Burke is a bookmaker and cargo thief who has a reputation as a "tough-guy." At the time Vario reputedly ordered the operation, Burke was awaiting release from a federal prison where he was incarcerated as the result of a loansharking conviction (Ibid.). Inside information required for the robbery was supplied by a Lufthansa employee who was in debt to a syndicate bookmaker (Ibid.).

Federal officials have told this writer that the first Federal Strike Force effort against organized crime occurred in Buffalo, New York, where members of the Magaddino family were prosecuted for conspiracy to commit bank robbery. James Henry ("Blackie") Audett provides an historical perspective to the interlocking relationship between organized and "professional heavy crime" (Inciardi, 1975). Audett was an armed robber during the Prohibition era, and he reports that he was given a "license" to practice his trade in Chicago, Detroit, and Kansas City, Missouri. In Chicago the "okay" came from Al Capone, and in return Audett performed such chores as delivering bootleg whiskey (1954: 93–94). When Audett made himself "hot" by being identified in a Cedar Rapids, Iowa, bank robbery, Capone ordered him out of Chicago (Ibid.: 99). In Detroit Audett reports that he "got the okay to operate from the old Purple gang" (Ibid.: 94). In Kansas City Audett received the "nod" from the Pendergast organization: "The nod was simply the privilege of doing most everything you wanted to do without fear of getting pinched" (Ibid.: 120). In return Audett provided a vital service—looking up vacant lots (Ibid.: 120):

> I looked them up, precinct by precinct, and turned them lists in to Mr. Pendergast—that's Tom Pendergast, the man who used to run Kansas City back in them days. When we got a precinct all surveyed out, we would give addresses to them vacant lots. Then we would take the addresses and assign them to people we could depend on—prostitutes, thieves, floaters, anybody we could get on the voting registration books. On election days we just hauled these people to the right places and they went in and voted—in the right places.

Albini states, correctly, that the rigid and bureaucratic system alleged by law enforcement officials would be easy to move against: "All that would be necessary to destroy it would be to remove its top echelon" (1971: 285). Instead, he points out, the real power is in the amorphous quality of the syndicate: "If a powerful syndicate figure is incarcerated, all that has really been severed is his position as a patron to his clients. If it so happens that another individual is in a position to assume this role, the clients may continue in this enterprise." The alternative is to find a new patron, "boss" or "family," or to develop their own enterprises (1971: 285).

The patron-client relationship is a superior description of organized crime. Eric Wolf states that when the social exchange relationship (see Homans, 1961; Blau, 1964) becomes unbalanced, we have a patron-client relationship: the patron "provides economic aid and protection against both the legal and illegal exactions of authority. The client in turn pays back in more intangible assets," e.g., esteem and loyalty. He may also offer political or other important support, thus making the relationship reciprocal (1966: 16–17). The patron may act as a power-broker between client and the wider society (Wolf, 1966: 18), both legitimate and illegitimate. Wolf also points out that the patron relationship can also be incorporated into the kinship pattern (1966: 18), as noted in Ianni's writings.

Jeremy Boissevain points out that every person is embedded in a social network: "The chains of persons with whom a given person is in contact" (1974: 24). Since contact can be through a chain of persons, an individual can send "messages" to far more people than he or she actually knows on a direct basis. These are the "friends of friends" (Ibid.: 25). In addition: "Every individual provides a point at which networks interact. But not everyone displays the same interest in and talent for cultivating relationships with strategic persons for profit" (Ibid.: 147). The organized crime figure, if successful, displays this interest and talent. He uses his position to act as a patron, having certain resources as well as strategic contacts with people who control other resources directly or who have access to such persons (Ibid.). The patron can "place you in touch with the right people." He can bridge communication gaps between the police and criminals, between businessmen and syndicate connected union leaders; he can transcend the world of business and the world of the illegitimate entrepreneur. He is able to perform important favors and be rewarded in return with money or power. Boissevain and Henner Hess refer to this network as *partito*—a surrounding circle of dyadic relationships whereby most clients have no relations between each other except through the patron (Hess, 1973: 82).

Boissevain (1974: 157) notes that a patron needs a great deal of time to manage his network adequately, to develop and maintain contacts, provide services that enhance power, and keep well-informed. Since organized crime figures usually do not have to maintain conventional schedules, they are free to "chat," to "hang around," to pick up and disseminate information.

An organized crime patron may dominate a particular geographic area or industry. He will have available a network of informants and connections, e.g., with police and other officials, as well as specialized operatives such as *papermen,* who convert stolen "paper," e.g., securities and checks, into cash, and *enforcers.* He will act as a center for information, "license" criminal activities, and use his position to assist criminals in linking up for specialized operations. Criminal activities in his territory or industry that are not under his patronage are "outlaw" operations, and the participants act without his "grace." If they are arrested, he will not intervene; if their activities conflict with those under his patronage, police raids or violence will result. Professional criminals who are not necessarily part of organized crime will often pay financial tribute to the patron, indicating *rispetto,* a word that literally means respect, but that inclines toward meaning protection. This show of *rispetto* enables a criminal to secure vital information and other assistance, and ensures that other criminals will not jeopardize his operations.

In his study of "Racketville," a pseudonym for a largely Italian neighborhood, Irving Spergel noted that the patron exercised dominant power over both criminal activities and the conventional structure of the area. Relatives of the racketeer are accorded high status and respect, and the racketeer maintains neighborhood peace. A settlement house worker used his friendship with the racketeer to keep youngsters "in line" (1964: 18–19). Several years ago, in a New York City neighborhood noted for the extent of its patron control, several criminals burglarized a famous restaurant that had no connections with organized crime. The burglary was not "authorized," and was thus an affront to the powerful local patron—the burglars were executed.

In Chicago, a high ranking member of organized crime, William ("Willie Potatoes") Daddano, provided a unique service for several bank robbers under his patronage. Through his connections with Richard Cain (real name Scalzetti), chief investigator for the Cook County Sheriff's Office, a lie-detector test was administered to all of the bank robbers to determine which one had informed on the robbery. The tests were apparently "successful," and one of the robbers was executed. For his role, Daddano received a fifteen-year prison sentence (Peterson, 1969: 55–63).

Michael Raymond, a convicted confidence man, provides an inside view of organized crime as *catalytic agent.* Testifying before a congressional committee in 1971 investigating stolen securities, Raymond stated (quoted in Yeager, 1973: 57–58):

> In this thing, you have to have somebody to act as catalyst. The catalyst is the organized crime procurer because he has the contacts on the other side to dispose of these securities. He may not himself be able to do it, but he certainly knows the people that can do this.

## ORGANIZED CRIME: PERPETUITY AND MONOPOLY

The Task Force Report (1967: 1) points to additional dimensions of organized crime: *time* and *monopoly.* "Its actions are not impulsive but rather the result of intricate conspiracies, carried on *over many years* and aimed at gaining *control over whole fields of activity* in order to amass huge profits" (emphasis added). It is the *time* dimension that we stress in the definition provided by the Oyster Bay Conference on Organized Crime, 1965 (cited in Philcox, 1978: 3–4):

Organized crime is the product of a *self-perpetuating* criminal conspiracy to wring exorbitant profits from our society by any means—fair or foul, legal and illegal. It survives on fear and corruption. By one or another means, it obtains a high degree of immunity from the law. It is totalitarian in organization. A way of life, it imposes rigid discipline on underlings who do the dirty work while the top men of organized crime are generally insulated from the criminal act and the consequent danger of prosecution. (Emphasis added)

The ITT Research Institute and the Chicago Crime Commission, in their *Study of Organized Crime in Illinois,* 1971 (cited in Maltz, 1975: 94), note the important element of *time:*

Organized crime consists of the participation of persons and groups of persons (organized either formally or informally) in transactions characterized by:
1. An intent to commit, or the actual commission of, substantive crimes;
2. A conspiracy to execute these crimes;
3. *A persistence of this conspiracy through time (at least one year) or the intent that this conspiracy should persist through time;*
4. The acquisition of substantial power or money, and the seeking of a high degree of political or economic security, as primary motivations;
5. An operational framework that seeks the preservation of institutions of politics, government and society in their present form." (ITT Research Institute and the Chicago Crime Commission, *A Study of Organized Crime in Illinois,* 1971) (Emphasis added)

*Monopoly* is also a goal of organized crime activities. As Whyte notes (1961: 117), there is a need to limit competition: "The syndicate operates to stifle outside competition." This is done by superior organization, which means the ability to purchase police and political protection, or the exercise of "muscle"—coercion through violence, including murder (Ibid.: 120). Ianni notes that the crime family he studied, the "Lupollos" (a pseudonym), controls gambling in sections of Brooklyn and Long Island, New York: "In gambling the territorial control is complete, and no 'independent' can operate very long without some difficulty from either the police or the Lupollos, or both" (1972: 98). Salerno states that the most valuable advantage of organized crime "is a thing that ordinary businessmen dream about, and sometimes go to jail for trying to arrange: the absence of competition." He points out that the "essence of organized crime is, of course, monopoly." Thus, when "a member persuades all the bars in town to use his beer, or all the restaurants to take his linen service, or controls the local garbage collections, he has a monopoly and is in a position to raise prices because there is no competition." Salerno notes that organized criminals do not gain a monopoly by greater efficiency: "He has a monopoly because he has coerced or bribed his way into it, and he keeps it by the threat of violence" (1969: 186). Thus, in his characterization of organized crime, James Inciardi notes the "dependence upon the threat of, and/or use of, force and violence to maintain discipline, restrain competition, and secure cooperation" (1974: 104).

In its definition of organized crime, the International Association of Chiefs of Police (IACP) Organized Crime Committee adds a dimension—crimes that "produce high profits and entail relatively little risk" (1975: 1.1/1–1.1/2). The IACP definition of organized crime (1975: 1.1/1–1.1/2):

> Organized crime is an illegal enterprise possessing four major characteristics:
>
> - *Structured Organization.* A formally organized and disciplined group insulates its top leadership from direct personal involvement in criminal acts and, at the same time, insures organizational permanency and form in the event of the jailing, death, or other removal of any of the leading members.
> - *Profit Continuity.* Although organized criminals may occasionally commit such highly visible individual crimes as kidnapping or bank robbery, their primary source of income stems from the ongoing supply of illegal goods or services, such as drugs, gambling, usury, prostitution, or other activities catering to human weakness. These *so called* "victimless crimes" generally produce high profits and entail relatively little risk.
> - *Monopoly.* Monopoly or near monopoly in the supplying of marketable goods or services guarantees high profits. Organized criminal elements clearly realize that the maintenance of a monopoly position can be most effectively achieved through intimidation or corruption.
> - *Immunity.* Apathy or ignorance is the foundation upon which organized criminal immunity is built. Once either of these basic requirements is met, bribery or intimidation can be used most effectively against victims or witnesses. Thereafter, the corruption of police, prosecutors, judges, legislators, other elected officials, or prison and parole officials may be attempted.

The IACP also provides indicators for recognizing the presence of organized crime (1975: 1.2/1–1.2/2):

> First, note whether traditional organized criminal activities are occurring. Gambling, prostitution, and narcotics addiction are among the most obvious manifestations. Of course, these danger signs *do not necessarily* prove the existence of an organized criminal operation, since gamblers, prostitutes, and street-level drug dealers can all be independent operators.
> Second, determine if the tools of organized crime—intimidation and corruption—are being used to promote and strengthen the basic ingredients of organized crime: organization, profit continuity, monopoly, and immunity.
> Affirmative answers to the following questions are good indicators of structured organized criminal activity:
> —Are unreported assaults occurring?
> —Are there a series of unexplained arsons involving marginal businesses?
> —Is there a reluctance by witnesses or victims to testify?
> —Does the criminal activity continue after the arrest of persons who appear to hold key positions?
> —Do patterns emerge in the setting or posting of bail?
> —Are high priced attorneys defending persons whose level of operation would apparently preclude their ability to pay for such service?

—Is testimony by police and witnesses vague or uncertain?

—Do patterns of light sentences or lack of vigorous prosecutions emerge in the prosecution of certain persons?

—Does the income of the families of incarcerated persons appear to continue?

Although this list of indicators could be expanded, an affirmative answer to the following basic question is an absolute indication of the existence of organized crime: *Is there a structured group using force, fear, or corruption in your community to obtain or maintain monopoly and immunity for a continuing criminal enterprise?*

Let us now review and consolidate the salient items that add up to organized crime:

1.  The organization is hierarchical, based on either kinship or a deliberately rationalized structure, which exhibits a division of functions, e.g., enforcer, fixer, loanshark, etc. These need not be mutually exclusive, and any one "member" may have more than one specialty.
2.  The organization has permanency, exists through time, and is not dependent on any person or persons for its continued existence.
3.  It strives for monopoly over certain activities on an "industry" or territorial basis.
4.  It engages in illicit activities that yield high profits relative to risk.
5.  It uses force and/or bribery whenever necessary.

## RECRUITMENT IN ORGANIZED CRIME

The only item vital to organized crime activity that we have not considered is *recruitment.* Ianni (1974: 157) points out that childhood gangs in the ghetto are sources of organized crime membership. Salvatore Giangana, more widely known as Sam Giancana, the "Don" of Chicago organized crime, began his criminal career as a leader of the "42 Gang" in the Italian ghetto of Chicago known as "The Patch." This gang of youngsters made a reputation for being quite wild and violent (Brashler, 1977: 55). Salerno (1969: 94–96) reports that recruiting into organized crime involves the careful study of neighborhood youngsters by those who control membership. A potential recruit must exhibit a recognition for the authority of the organization and a willingness to perform various (usually minor at first) criminal functions with skill and daring.

Robert Woetzel points out that "the standards and values of the teenage gang from which the potential criminals come are the same as those of an adult conspiracy": a code of loyalty and exclusive "turf." The gang boy may also have a criminal record and an antisocial attitude which indicate that he is a "stand-up" kid, the proper credentials for a career in organized crime. "Much of the recruitment for criminal activity goes on in neighborhoods where persons with such backgrounds can be found" (1963: 3). Raymond Martin, a former ranking officer with the New York City Police Department, describes why recruitment is made easy in certain neighborhoods (1963: 61):

On so many street corners in Bath Beach; in so many luncheonettes and candy stores in Bensenhurst, boys see the mob-affiliated bookies operate. They meet the young toughs, the mob enforcers. They hear the tales of glory recounted—who robbed what, who worked over whom, which showgirl shared which gangster's bed, who got hit by whom, the techniques of the rackets and how easy it all is, how the money rolls in. What wonder is it that some boys look forward to being initiated in these practices with the eagerness of a college freshman hoping to be pledged by the smoothest fraternity on campus. With a little luck and guts, they feel, even they may someday belong to that splendid, high-living band, the mob.

Those unfamiliar with the Brooklyn neighborhoods mentioned by Martin might easily imagine a ghetto slum. While New York has its share of such areas, neither of these neighborhoods qualifies. Both are heavily Italian, with a strong Jewish representation, and contain mostly well-kept two-family private homes. The streets are neat and clean. The families in these neighborhoods are far from wealthy; neither, however, are these youngsters fighting their way out of deprivation.

Ianni (1974: 158) reports that "prisons and the prison experience are the most important locus for establishing the social relationships that form the basis for partnerships in organized crime, both among blacks and among Puerto Ricans." Both California and Illinois are experiencing the impact of black and Hispanic street gangs in their prison systems. Scholarly and popular literature has reported on the activities of such groups as the "Mexican Mafia," "La Nuestra Familia," "Black Guerrilla Family," "Black P. Stone Nation," and the "Latin Kings," to mention a few. These gangs have extended their turfs to include ghetto streets and correctional institutions; there they often rule more effectively than prison officials (Adams, 1977; California Board of Corrections, 1978; Jacobs, 1977). Ianni notes that the "Italians do not form their criminal partnerships in prison, both because they do not go to jail as often as blacks and Puerto Ricans do now and because they form their organized crime networks on the Mafia-oriented basis of kinship" (1974: 158).

Thus, the last item is recruitment. The organization limits its membership, and recruits come primarily from the ranks of youthful gangs, fellow prison inmates, or on the basis of kinship.

## ORGANIZED CRIME: AUTHOR'S DEFINITION

We are now ready to propose a definition of organized crime:

A non-ideological enterprise that involves a number of persons in close social interaction, organized on a hierarchical basis for the purpose of securing profit and power[5] by engaging in illegal, and legal, activities which yield high profits while offering relatively low risks. Positions may be assigned on the basis of kinship or rationally assigned according to skill. The positions are continuous and not dependent on the individuals occupying them at any particular time. Permanancy is assumed by the members, who strive to keep the enterprise integral and active in pursuit of its goals. It eschews competition and strives for monopoly over particular activities on an industry or territorial basis. There is a willingness to use violence and/or bribery to achieve ends or to maintain discipline. Membership is restricted, although non-members are involved on a contingency basis.

It should be noted that the above definition may be unique to the American situation. J. A. Mack, for example, points out that organized crime has a different meaning in Europe, where *organized* "takes in all criminal operations, however small-scale, in which more than one person participates and some rudimentary role-differentiation occurs" (1973: 103). Thus, in Europe one does not have *organized crime,* but, instead, criminals with varying degrees of organization, ranging from the *primitive* to the *hierarchical* (Ibid.). He points out that taken literally, the two words "organized crime" cover "anything other than spur-of-the-moment crime" (Ibid.: 104). Mack also reports that the "U.S. model" of organized (syndicated) crime is not to be found outside of North America (1973: 107).

## ENDNOTES

1.  Organized Crime Control Act of 1970, at 1073.
    The Congress finds that (1) organized crime in the United States is a highly sophisticated, diversified, and widespread activity that annually drains billions of dollars from America's economy by unlawful conduct and the illegal use of force, fraud, and corruption; (2) organized crime derives a major portion of its power through money obtained from such illegal endeavors as syndicated gambling, loan sharking, the theft and fencing of property, the importation and distribution of narcotics and other dangerous drugs, and other forms of social exploitation; (3) this money and power are increasingly used to infiltrate and corrupt legitimate business and labor unions and to subvert and corrupt our democratic processes; (4) organized crime activities in the United States weaken the stability of the Nation's economic system, harm innocent investors and competing organizations, interfere with free competition, seriously burden interstate and foreign commerce, threaten the domestic security, and undermine the general welfare of the Nation and its citizens; and (5) organized crime continues to grow because of defects in the evidence-gathering process of the law inhibiting the development of the legally admissible evidence necessary to bring criminal and other sanctions or remedies to bear on the unlawful activities of those engaged in organized crime and because sanctions and remedies available to the Government are unnecessarily limited in scope and impact.
        It is the purpose of this Act to seek the eradication of organized crime in the United States by strengthening the legal tools in the evidence-gathering process, by establishing new penal prohibitions, and by providing enhanced sanctions and new remedies to deal with the unlawful activities of those engaged in organized crime.

2. There are also problems inherent in defining crime or criminals in the generic sense. See Sutherland (1973: 44–98) and Schwendinger and Schwendinger (1977).

3. The Molly Maguires were a secret organization of Irishmen working in the coal mines of Scranton, Pennsylvania, in the latter part of the nineteenth century. To further their efforts against the mining companies, they often used violence. There are a number of books on the Molly Maguires; for example Coleman (1969) and Lewis (1964).

4. Federal and local law enforcement officials have informed this writer that motorcycle gangs have been used as "muscle" for organized crime groups. In Durham, North Carolina, members of the Hell's Angels motorcycle gang have gained a monopoly over the sale and distribution of certain drugs, and local officials have told the writer that a recent attempt to break this monopoly resulted in a murder. In 1979, eighteen members of the Hell's Angels, which is nationwide in scope, were indicted in San Francisco for conspiracy to violate federal drug laws. The indictment alleges that the gang trafficked extensively in heroin, cocaine, LSD, and "speed" (methamphetamine). The regional director of the Drug Enforcement Administration, Jerry Jenson, is quoted as saying: "The club's bylaws clearly spell out that members will engage in distribution of drugs of a specified quantity and quality in order to remain members." The DEA maintains that the Hell's Angels controlled up to 90 percent of the "speed" trade in northern California ("Hell's Angels: Some Wheelers May Be Dealers," *Time*, July 2, 1979: 34). See also Wallace Turner, "U.S. Drug Investigation Brings a Round of Arrests for Hell's Angels," *NYT*, June 18, 1979: 14. It is apparent that motorcycle gangs such as Hell's Angels have the potential to be important organized criminal groups.

5. *Power* is another term that presents problems of definition. See, for example, Bachrach and Baratz (1962); Dahl (1957 and 1968); Nagel (1968); and Wrong (1968). To maintain internal consistency with our quest for a definition of organized crime, we will use the following definition of power: "The probability that one actor within a social relationship will be in a position to carry out his own will despite resistance, regardless of the basis on which this probability rests" (Weber, 1968: 53).

# TWO

# Explaining Organized Crime

Max Weber reminds us that scientific inquiry requires that we "see uncomfortable facts and the realities of life in all their starkness" (1949: 58), while Daniel Bell states, "The most shameless political deals (and 'steals') have been rationalized as expedient and realistically necessary" (1964: 116). Of particular interest for our subject is the use of methods (often illegal) by "captains of business," methods that bear so close a resemblance to those used by "captains of crime" that we can refer to them as the historical antecedents of organized crime.[1]

## THE HISTORICAL ANTECEDENTS OF ORGANIZED CRIME

In Chapter Four we will discuss in detail the *scam* or *bust out*—essentially a scheme for deliberately bankrupting a business for illegal profit. For now, however, it is sufficient to note that Jay Gould, a famous "financier" of the late 19th century, "made his several fortunes not by catering to the public, but by deliberate mismanagement of whatever he touched" (Holbrook, 1953: 100). Gustavus Myers (1936: 70–75) explains how Russell Sage diverted money from his railroad holdings and used it for usurious loans (called loan-sharking when committed by "captains of crime"). Richard O'Connor, who refers to Sage as a loanshark, notes that he had $27 million invested in usurious loans—even his (not so moral) peers detested him (1962: 135).

Let us briefly review some of the activities of America's foremost families so that we will have the proper perspective from which to view other "families" more closely related to the topic of this book.

One of the earliest American fortunes was amassed by John Jacob Astor. His money was originally gained through lawlessness and violence committed by his agents against Indians in the Western fur trade—"J.J." was at the time living in New York City, a respectable businessman (Myers, 1936: 104). This money was used for real estate speculation in New York City where easily corrupted officials helped Astor become the richest person in America (Ibid.: 128, 145). He crowned his successful business career by becoming one of America's greatest "slumlords," extracting money from the poor for the privilege of living in the vilest of tenement housing (Ibid.: 166–67). These slums were the spawning ground for organized crime.

While in the context of our current society we express horror over the narcotics trade, particularly the smuggling of heroin by organized crime, John McConaughy (1931: 220) helps place this in a better historical perspective: "In 1807, it became a capital offense to import slaves into these United States. Wherefore the pious New Englanders who bought and stole Negroes along the African coast raised the price of slaves to the Southern gentlemen, and the trade went on as usual."

The methods of the captains of business could, and perhaps did, serve as a training manual for the captains of crime. Consider, for example, the use of "muscle." In 1855, C. K. Garrison and Charles Morgan took on Cornelius Vanderbilt. They financed an insurrection in Nicaragua where Vanderbilt's Accessory Transit Company had its charter. On October 13, 1855, the revolutionary forces backed by Garrison and Morgan achieved a significant victory; on February 18, 1856, the Vanderbilt charter was revoked, and the property of Accessory Transit was seized (Andrews, 1941: 54–55). Vanderbilt responded in the summer of 1856 by persuading the governments of Honduras, San Salvador, and Costa Rica to form an alliance against Nicaragua. Then, on his orders, two Americans, Sylvanus Spencer and William Webster, led an invasion of Nicaragua. By the end of 1856 the invasion force was progressing quite well; however, the Nicaraguans counter-attacked.` Vanderbilt thwarted the offensive by calling on the State Department, which then sent in the United States Marines. They succeeded in deposing the revolutionary government and restored the Vanderbilt charter (Ibid.: 60). Even Mario Puzo's *Godfather* of fiction fame did not operate on this scale.

### The "Erie War"

The Erie Railroad ran from Jersey City to Lake Erie. In 1866, the line was in financial trouble and borrowed $3.5 million from Daniel Drew, treasurer of the Erie. Drew received 28,000 shares of unissued common stock and $3 million in convertible bonds as security for the loan. The stock had been entrusted to him only as security, and was not to be sold. Drew converted the bonds into 30,000 more shares, and began selling short (speculating that the price of the stock would go down). To ensure a financial "killing," Drew dumped all 58,000 shares and realized a profit of $48 a share (Andrews, 1941: 122–123). Drew had already gained notoriety for his comments on the advent of Civil War: "Along with ordinary happenings, we fellows on Wall Street now have in addition the fortunes of war to speculate about, and that always makes great doings on the stock exchange. It's good fishing in troubled waters" (O'Connor, 1962: 51).

Drew then moved to double-cross Cornelius Vanderbilt, who had a financial interest in the line. Drew teamed up with Jay Gould and Jim Fisk, and the trio began to grind out shares of watered stock at a rate that was draining Vanderbilt's attempt to dominate the Erie (Andrews, 1941: 123–125). Vanderbilt secured an injunction against the issuance of any further shares, which was disregarded by the trio (Ibid.: 130), costing Vanderbilt $7 million (Ibid.: 131). To avoid being arrested for violating the injunction, the trio, which had become known as the "Erie Ring," fled to New Jersey. (Six decades later the prominent Prohibition era gangster Dutch Schultz would also flee from New York to New Jersey to avoid arrest.) In Jersey City the ring maintained a stronghold at the Taylor Hotel; "Fort Taylor" it was called in the newspapers. There they were guarded by members of the Jersey City Police Department (O'Connor, 1962: 71).

The "war" shifted from the stock exchange and the courts to the New York State Legislature where the ring spent more than a million dollars to legalize its issuing of the watered stock (Ibid.: 76–77). When Vanderbilt tired of the bribery and withdrew from the legislative contest, the price of a vote fell from $5000 to $100 (Andrews, 1941: 136). The ring was assisted by William Marcy Tweed, "Boss Tweed," who was appointed a director of the Erie (Ibid.: 141). Eventually a favorable settlement was made with Vanderbilt, and the ring, consisting of only Gould and Fisk, gained complete control, legal and otherwise (Ibid.).

Gould gathered his early fortune by systematically embezzling money from his employer, and used the money to establish a private bank (O'Connor, 1962: 36). He continued to divert other people's money for his own private use on a grand scale, buying into railroads with the purloined funds (Ibid.: 40–49). He and Jim Fisk siphoned off so much money from the Erie Railroad that no funds were available for improvements on the line; the serious wrecks that resulted killed and injured a great many persons. Under Gould's guidance, $53 million worth of watered stock was issued and about 10 percent was used for its stated purpose, improvements to the line (Ibid.: 113). Between 1866 and 1872, when he turned thirty-six years of age (Ibid.: 126), Gould's systematic rape of the Erie and his gold market speculations enriched him by more than $22 million. W. A. Swanberg concludes that Gould and Fisk "had stolen the Erie Railway, bribed judges and legislators to make the robbery legal, and since then had milked millions out of the road and its stockholders" (1959: 2).

## Pinkertons and Private Police

In the first chapter of this book, the definition offered for organized crime noted a willingness to use bribery and violence to further entrepreneurial interests. We have already reviewed some instances of bribery by the captains of business, and more will be presented shortly. Now let us turn to the violence—or in the parlance of organized crime, the "muscle"—used by the captains of business.

The "Hill-Harriman War," which lasted from 1901 to 1916, saw the extensive use of "muscle" by the captains of business. James Jerome Hill of the Great Northern Railroad took on Edward H. Harriman of the Union Pacific. What began in the stock exchange moved to the courts and finally to pitched battles and killings by thugs from both sides (Holbrook, 1953: 190–201). More often, however, the captains of business used private and public police and the American military as their *enforcers:* Pinkertons, private and public police, and federal troops were used extensively in the nineteenth and twentieth centuries to protect the interests of the captains of business. In 1865 Pennsylvania gave the railroads the power to employ their own police, who had the same powers as publicly employed law enforcement officers, and a year later this power was extended to "any colliery, furnace or rolling mill," creating the "coal and iron police" (Friedman, 1973: 507). Private police existed in other states as well, and they were often used as strikebreakers. Not until the 1930s were they abolished in Pennsylvania (Ibid.: 507–508). Texas continues to have a similar system of private ranch police.

In one historic incident in 1894, workers struck when the Pullman Railroad paid out an 8 percent stock dividend while refusing to restore recent cuts in wages for its workers. The strike paralyzed the nation's rail lines. President Grover Cleveland responded by ordering out federal troops to break the strike, while the Attorney General had Eugene V. Debs, the union leader, jailed for interfering with the business of the railroads (Ibid.: 488; Holbrook, 1953: 91–94). The "Battle of Homestead," Pennsylvania, in 1892 was the result of an attempt by the Carnegie Steel Company to provoke the union into a strike that would break its power. Carnegie declared a unilateral lowering of wages. To back up this action, Henry Frick, Carnegie's agent at Homestead, brought in 300 Pinkertons who proved insufficient to the task of helping guard the plant and suppressing the strike. Federal troops were then sent in and fourteen persons were killed and 163 seriously wounded (Ibid.: 83–86). With able assistance from the government, Carnegie won and for thirty-four years there were no unions in American steel mills where workers put in twelve-hour days, seven days a week. Carnegie's biographer, Joseph Frazier Wall, states: "And Carnegie went on giving to libraries and wondering why so few adults made use of his magnificent gifts" (1970: 579). It is of some historical interest that Carnegie had earlier gained control over a more efficient steel competitor by sending to railroads throughout the country a libelous circular warning that his competitor's product was unsafe. This lie enabled Carnegie to buy out his rival at bargain prices, a purchase that would pay for itself six times over (Ibid.: 498).

In the anthracite mining region of northern Pennsylvania, miners rebelled at the misery and death that were their daily experience. In 1894 446 men had been killed (Novak, 1978: 8). Mining companies flagrantly ignored labor laws that required miners to be paid every other week and, instead, paid them at the end of the month. This increased the debts the miners incurred at the company store, which also cheated them, and for company housing and company doctors (Ibid.: 18–19). On August 11 or 12, 1897, a mining superintendent made a decision that would require mule drivers for the mines to work longer hours without any additional pay. The drivers went on strike: the superintendent attacked one of the strikers with a crowbar and was himself badly beaten. The incident triggered a wider strike, and in 1897 strikes were rampant throughout the northern minefields (Ibid.: 25–26).

The miners held mass meetings and marches, often intimidating those who refused to join the strike. An organizing official of the United Mineworkers Union entered the area and counseled nonviolence, so when miners marched to the Lattimer mine on September 10, 1897, they were armed only with two American flags (Ibid.: 105). What the marchers did not know was that the mine owners had provided money for the sheriff to raise a posse (Ibid.: 88): "The owners wanted the strike broken and operations resumed. How the Sheriff accomplished this was up to him. They had put him in office and they would hold him responsible" (Ibid.: 90).

The marching miners reached Lattimer with only one flag; the other had been seized and ripped to shreds by deputies who also assaulted several miners. At Lattimer 150 heavily armed deputies were arrayed against the marchers who ignored the sheriff's order to disperse. Without orders from the sheriff, the deputies opened fire. The miners began to flee and were pursued by the deputies who fired at them until nineteen were dead and more than thirty-nine wounded (Ibid.: x, 104–131). To continue the maintenance of peace and order —i.e., to protect the mines—the National Guard was ordered into the area.

## Rockefeller–Morgan–Du Pont–Ford

In 1872, John D. Rockefeller, head of Standard Oil, attempted to form an oil trust, the Southern Improvement Company (SIC), in order to drive out competition, a goal also familiar to the type of organized crime we are studying. In a conspiracy with the railroads, it was agreed that oil freight rates would be doubled, but the SIC increase, as well as the increases collected from competitors, would be returned ("kicked back") to the SIC (Lloyd, 1963: 17–18; Josephson, 1934: 115–120). The plot was thwarted, not by legal action, but by the threats of violence on the part of the small oil producers who threatened to rip out the rail lines (Lloyd, 1963: 25).

In 1878, however, Rockefeller was more successful. His Standard Oil, the largest producer in the country, was given special discount railroad rates to transport oil. When the Tidewater Pipeline Company threatened to break this tactic by its superior efficiency, the oil trust, led by Rockefeller, joined in support of "cutthroat" railroad prices designed to drive Tidewater into bankruptcy. Tidewater was quite efficient and held out. In the best tradition of the captains of crime, its pipelines were plugged up, its financial credit attacked in the money market, and corrupt judges enjoined its bonds. Tidewater capitulated and was bought out by the National Transit Company, which was owned by the oil trust (Lloyd, 1963: Chapter 8; Josephson, 1934: 111–114).

J. Pierpont Morgan was successful in driving independent coal producers out of business and then driving up the price of coal during the latter part of the nineteenth century (Myers, 1936: 75–76). Morgan also profited directly from the government. During the Civil War he avoided conscription and bought defective carbines from the government. Still defective, they were then resold to the government at enormous profit (Myers, 1936: 548–550). Morgan was able to secure the ownership of railway systems, constructed largely with public funds, using tricks of finance—e.g. bankruptcy and squeezing out creditors and small stockholders (Myers, 1936: 577). He milked the government out of millions through gold bond manipulations made possible by a conspiracy of national and international bankers (Myers, 1936: 578). The *Godfather* would turn green with envy.

Later we will see how the captains of crime involve themselves in the political arena, for example, by using "goons" to strong-arm voters. If they were students of history, the captains of crime could have learned the technique from the Du Ponts of Delaware. E. I. Du Pont de Nemours & Co. was the largest producer of gunpowder in the United States. During the War of 1812 the company made huge profits. However, as the election of 1813 neared, some candidates in Delaware openly opposed the continuation of the war. The Du Pont brothers formed their workers into militia companies and used them to forcibly register alien voters in favor of pro-war candidates. Angry Delaware voters, however, became incensed and attacked the Du Pont militiamen. As a result of these activities the Delaware Legislature passed laws prohibiting private militia (Zilg, 1974: 20–21). The captains of industry often did not involve themselves in the petty activities of election politics; they bought entire legislatures (Holbrook, 1953: 29–34; Lloyd, 1963: Chapter 27; Josephson, 1934: 348–349; Myers, 1936: 460) and had their own way with Congress (Myers, 1936: 455–460). Gerard Zilg reports: "From a corrupt Congress and state governments, over 325 million acres of some of the most fertile land in America—common land belonging to all the American people, and worth close to a billion dollars—were given as gifts to Jay Gould and other railroad magnates for their own profits" (1974: 64).

The Du Ponts, who made vast fortunes during the Civil War, arranged for the formation of a cartel of gunpowder manufacturers, the "Powder Trust," after the Civil War. Competitors were driven out of business by cutthroat pricing. When that did not work, bribes and sabotage were used, and gunpowder companies disappeared in mysterious explosions (Zilg, 1974: 64–68).

Lest we think of the "robber barons" as unique to the East, Wayne Moquin and Charles Van Doren (eds., 1976) remind us that the West spawned its own (cattle) barons and land grabbers who were not above using any means at their disposal to achieve their ends, as is evidenced by such sensational escapades as the "Lincoln County War" in New Mexico (1876–78) and the "Johnson County War" in Wyoming (1891–92). William H. Bonney, born Henry McCarty, better known as Billy the Kid, began his murderous career during the "Lincoln County War."

The gap between the captains of business and the captains of crime was breached when the former began employing the latter for assistance in dealing with American labor movement. Henry Ford provided a philosophical basis for this partnership: "There is something sacred about big business. Anything which is economically right is morally right" (Sinclair, 1962: 369). In this spirit Ford hired ex-pugilist Harry Bennett as "Director of Services," and Bennett employed a small army of thugs, gangsters, and ex-convicts. "Men were fired without reason, terrorized and beaten, and there were stories of actual disappearances" (Herndon, 1969: 66). Bennett's army of thugs and spies kept the workers in line: "Any suspicion of union sympathy brought retaliatory action from Bennett's men. Men were beaten up on the job, in their own homes and in their own neighborhoods." This terror extended to Ford plants throughout the country (Ibid., 171).

On May 26, 1937, Walter Reuther, head of the United Auto Workers, and other union men arrived at the Ford Rouge plant, armed with a permit from the city of Dearborn to distribute handbills. Bennett's men attacked, and Reuther and the other union men and women were severely beaten, while newsmen stood by recording the event for history. After they finished with the union, Bennett's men attacked the reporters, and they retaliated with a graphic expose of the event. Ford won the "Battle of the Overpass," as the incident became known, but he lost the "war": the United Auto Workers unionized the Ford Company (Ibid., 172–173).

## Conclusion

The lesson to be learned from the story of the men we have discussed in this chapter would not be complete without indicating another aspect of their legacy; that is, those things we as the public most closely associate with these illustrious names. For Daniel Drew, for example, we have Drew University in Madison, New Jersey; for Carnegie we have the Carnegie Corporation, Carnegie Endowment for International Peace, the Carnegie Institute of Technology in Pittsburgh, and the Carnegie Institution of Washington; Pierpont Morgan is the name of a world-famous library; John D. Rockefeller founded the Rockefeller Foundation and the Rockefeller Institute (now known as Rockefeller University); both Ford and Russell Sage have important foundations named after them, and there is Russell Sage College in Albany, New York; and for Cornelius Vanderbilt we have Vanderbilt University in Nashville, Tennessee. If, as some observers maintain, history tends to repeat itself, we may yet experience the Meyer Lansky Foundation and Carlo Gambino University.

## ACCOUNTING FOR
## ORGANIZED CRIME

At the beginning of this chapter was a quotation by Daniel Bell whose appellation for crime in America is quite fitting: "The Queer Ladder of Social Mobility" (1964: 115). Crime, he argues, is an American way of life. He states that the captains of business, those pioneers of early American capitalism, did not graduate from the Harvard School of Business Administration, but gathered their fortunes "by shady speculations and a not inconsiderable amount of violence" (1964: 134). Ironically, he points out, "This has not prevented them and their descendents from feeling proper moral outrage when, under the changed circumstances of the crowded urban environments, latecomers pursued equally ruthless tactics" (1964: 134).

Ianni (1974: 14) tells us: "Organized crime as an American way of life persists and transcends the involvement of any particular group and the changing social definitions of what is illegal and what is not." It provides a "queer ladder" for social mobility, "an integral part of the American social system that brings together a public that demands certain goods and services that are defined as illegal, an organization of individuals who produce these goods and services, and corrupt public officials who protect such individuals for their own profit or gain" (Ianni, 1974: 15). Bell points to some structural variables effecting the growth of organized crime: "At the turn of the century the cleavage developed between the Big City and the small town conscience. Crime as a growing business was fed by the revenues from prostitution, liquor, and gambling that a wide-open urban society encouraged and that a middle-class Protestant ethos tried to suppress with a ferocity unmatched in any other civilized country" (1964: 116).

In 1938, *Robert Merton* provided a theoretical basis for the contradictions we have discussed in this chapter: "There may develop a disproportionate, at times, a virtually exclusive, stress upon the value of specific goals, involving relatively slight concern with the institutionally appropriate modes of attaining these goals" (1938: 673). He called this situation *anomie,* a term used by Emile Durkheim (1951) to describe socio-cultural conditions that predispose towards deviance, in particular suicide. Merton states that the sacrifices engendered by conformity to the normative order must be compensated by "socialized rewards." When the socialized rewards are not forthcoming, we have deviance: "Aberrant conduct, therefore, may be viewed as a symptom of dissociation between culturally defined aspirations and socially structured means" (1938: 674). Merton explains why crime is an American way of life: "The extreme emphasis upon the accumulation of wealth as a symbol of success in our society mitigates against the completely effective control of institutionally regulated modes of acquiring a fortune. Fraud, corruption, vice, crime, in short, the entire catalogue of proscribed behavior, becomes increasingly common when the emphasis on the culturally-induced success-goal becomes divorced from a coordinated institutional emphasis" (1938: 675–676). American society dangles the carrot of success, but for some the only available way to reach it is by climbing the "queer ladder," which Merton refers to as *innovation* (1938: 676): "the use of conventionally proscribed but frequently effective means of attaining at least the simulacrum of culturally defined success —wealth, power, and the like" (1938: 678). Taylor, Walton, and Young (1973: 97) summarize *innovation:* "The 'American Dream' urges all citizens to succeed whilst distributing the opportunity to succeed unequally: the result of this social and moral climate, inevitably, is innovation by the citizenry—the adoption of illegitimate means to pursue and obtain success."

*Albert Cohen* points to the importance of "reference groups" in accounting for innovation: "The level of goal attainment that will seem just and reasonable to concrete actors, and therefore the sufficiency of available means, will be relative to the attainment of others who serve as reference objects" (1965: 6). Thus, when we see others whom "we define as legitimate objects of comparison" doing better than us by "innovating," we are faced with a "sense of strain," which has important implications for future normative conformity (1965: 6).

What is the factor that decides whether we move toward continued conformity or innovation? According to *Edwin Sutherland*'s theory of *differential association,* criminal behavior is learned in interaction with other persons and thus depends on the strength or intensity of criminal associations. Crime results when there is "an excess of definitions favorable to violation of law over definitions unfavorable to violation of law" (1973: 5). Sutherland also points to the need to evaluate the variable "susceptibility"—incomplete criminality. "If a person has a high degree of susceptibility [e.g., lives in abject poverty], it will take relatively little more association with criminal patterns to make him engage in overt crime; if he has relatively low susceptibility, it will take a great deal of association with criminal patterns to make him deal overtly in crime" (1973: 42–43).

The socioeconomic stratification of our society relegates persons to an environment wherein they experience "a sense of strain" and "differential association." In the environment that has traditionally spawned organized crime, this "strain" is intense. Conditions of severe deprivation, with extremely limited access to ladders of legitimate success, are coupled with readily available success models that are innovative: pimps, racketeers, drug sellers. *Richard Cloward and Lloyd Ohlin* explain that "many lower-class male adolescents experience desperation born of the certainty that their position in the economic structure is relatively fixed and immutable—a desperation made all the more poignant by their exposure to a cultural ideology in which failure to orient oneself upward is regarded as a moral defect and failure to become mobile as proof of it" (1960: 106–107). That innovation should result is as natural and American as slums and ghettos. However, Cloward and Ohlin point out that illegitimate means of success, like legitimate means, are not equally distributed throughout society: "Having decided that he 'can't make it legitimately,' he cannot simply choose among an array of illegitimate means, all equally available to him" (1960: 145). They conclude (1960: 148):

> Only those neighborhoods in which crime flourishes as a stable indigenous institution are fertile criminal learning environments for the young. Because these environments afford integration of different age-levels of offender, selected young people are exposed to "differential association" through which tutelage is provided and criminal values and skills are acquired. To be prepared for the role may not, however, ensure that the individual will ever discharge it. One important limitation is that more youngsters are recruited

into these patterns of differential associations than the adult criminal structure can possibly absorb. Since there is a surplus of contenders for these positions, criteria and mechanisms of selection must be evolved. Hence a certain proportion of those who aspire may not be permitted to engage in the behavior for which they have prepared themselves.

Nicholas Gage also notes that *The Mafia Is not an Equal Opportunity Employer* (1971: 113): "No door is more firmly locked to blacks than the one that leads to the halls of power in organized crime." He states that Jewish, Irish, and Italian mobsters tend to hire and promote from within their own ethnic groups, although there is also a great deal of cooperation between them (1971: 115). In the ethnically stratified society of organized crime, the dominant group has always been white and has always strictly used its monopoly of resources to reserve the better positions for themselves. In New York, federal and local law enforcement officials have told this writer that blacks cannot move into such lucrative crime areas as labor racketeering and loansharking because of racial prejudice. One federal official noted that even Chinese criminals preferred to deal with Caucasians rather than blacks in such areas as gambling, drugs, and loansharking. Ianni, who in his *Black Mafia* (1974) argues that blacks and Hispanics *are* moving into and taking over organized crime in certain areas, also notes: "It is difficult to imagine that most white Americans would deal with a black salesman pushing stolen goods or even more difficult to envision whites borrowing from black loan sharks" (1974: 143). Salerno and Tompkins state that prejudice has been used by organized crime which takes advantage of the conservative attitudes of many police officers who resent blacks (1969: 332). Since the police are often vital in organized crime activities, prejudice can stymie black efforts at innovation.

Based on their extensive Chicago area research originally published in 1942, *Clifford Shaw* and *Henry McKay* formulated a theory of the "cultural transmission" of crime through generations living in the same ecological niches. "It was found that some members of each delinquent group had participated in offenses in the company of other older boys, and so on, backward in time in an unbroken continuity as far as records were available" (1972: 175). They conclude: "This means that delinquent boys in these areas have contact not only with other delinquents who are contemporaries but also with older offenders, who in turn had contact with delinquents proceding them, and so on back to the earliest history of the neighborhood. This contact means that the traditions of delinquency can be and are transmitted down through successive generations of boys, in much the same way that language and other social forms are transmitted" (1972: 174). Gerald Suttles adds an additional dimension, a "strong sense of history." He states (1968: 111): "Locally [in Chicago], many of the members in the street groups can trace their group's genealogy back through the Taylor Dukes, 40 [sic] gang, Genna Brothers, and the Capone Mob. Actually, there is no clear idea of the exact order of this descent line; some persons include groups that others leave out. Moreover, there is no widespread agreement on which specific group is the current successor to this lineage. Nonetheless, there is widespread agreement that the groups on Taylor Street have illustrious progenitors. On some occasions this heritage may be something of a burden, and on others a source of pride. In any case, it is unavoidable, and usually the Italian street groups preface their own name with the term 'Taylor' " as in Taylor Dukes.

While the sons of Jewish immigrants played a vital role in organized crime, by the third generation the Jews moved out and organized crime was dominated by the Italians. Jackson Toby provides an explanation by comparing the cultural differences between the Jewish and southern Italian immigrant (1958: 548):

> Jews and Italians came to the United States in large numbers at about the same time—the turn of the century—and both settled in urban areas. There was, however, a very different attitude toward intellectual accomplishment in the two cultures. Jews from Eastern Europe regarded religious study as the most important activity for an adult male. The rabbi enjoyed great prestige because he was a scholar, a teacher, a logician. He advised the community on the application of the Written and Oral Law. Life in America gave a secular emphasis to the Jewish reverence for learning. Material success is a more important motive than salvation for American youngsters, Jewish as well as Christian, and secular education is better training for business and professional careers than Talmudic exegesis. Nevertheless, intellectual achievement continued to be valued by Jews—and to have measurable effects. Second-generation Jewish students did homework diligently, got high grades, went to college in disproportionate numbers, and scored high on intelligence tests. Two thousand years of preparation lay behind them.
>
> Immigrants from Southern Italy, on the other hand, tended to regard formal education either as a frill or as a source of dangerous ideas from which the minds of the young should be protected. They remembered Sicily, where a child who attended school regularly was a rarity. There, youngsters were needed not only to help on the farm. Equally important was the fact that hard-working peasants could not understand why their children should learn classical Italian (which they would not speak at home) or geography (when they would not travel in their lifetime more than a few miles from their birthplace). Sicilian parents suspected that education was an attempt on the part of Roman officials to subvert the authority of the family. In the United States, many South Italian immigrants maintained the same attitudes. They resented compulsory school attendance laws and prodded their children to go to work and become economic assets as soon as possible. They encouraged neglect of schoolwork and even truancy. They did not realize that education has more importance in an urban-industrial society than in a semi-feudal one. With supportive motivation from home lacking, the second-generation Italian boys did not make the effort of Jewish contemporaries. Their teachers tried to stuff the curriculum into their heads in vain. Their lack of interest was reflected not only in low marks, retardation, truancy, and early school leaving; it even resulted in poor scores on intelligence tests. They accepted their parents' conception of the school as worthless and thereby lost their best opportunity for social ascent.
>
> Some of these youngsters did not reconcile themselves to remaining on the bottom of the heap; they rebelled.

Walter Miller, who studied adolescent groups over a period of years, concludes that delinquent gang behavior is "the product of a distinctive cultural system which may be termed 'lower class' " (1958: 6). Miller states that this distinctive cultural system emphasizes such items of behavior as "toughness" and "smartness" (gaining money by one's wits) (1958: 7), and the movie gangster is often a role model (1958: 9). Donald Goddard reports that the Brooklyn gangster Joseph ("Crazy Joey") Gallo at age sixteen "would stand on a corner like George Raft, endlessly flipping a half-dollar and talking to himself without moving his lips." Gallo later prided himself on looking like Richard Widmark in his role as the vicious Tommy Udo in *Kiss of Death* (1974: 36). Miller points out some of the qualities of the adolescent street corner group that correlate well with the prerequisites for organized crime: "The activity patterns of the group require a high level of intra-group solidarity; individual members must possess a good capacity for subordinating individual desires to general group interests as well as the capacity for intimate and per-sisting interaction" (1958: 14). Status is achieved by "toughness" and "smart-ness," which add up to one's reputation—"rep"—while the routine patterns of these groups include law-violating behavior (1958: 16–17).

In his classic study of Chicago street gangs originally published in 1927, Frederic Thrasher notes, "Experience in a gang of the predatory type usually develops in the boy an attitude of indifference to law and order—one of the basic traits of the finished gangster" (1968: 270). He points out, "If the younger undirected gangs and clubs of the gang type, which serve as training schools for delinquency, do not succeed in turning out the finished criminal, they often develop a type of personality which may well foreshadow the gang-ster and gunmen" (Ibid.: 273). Thrasher observed that in the Chicago of that era, there was "no hard and fast dividing line between the predatory gangs of boys and criminal groups of younger and older adults. They merge into each other by imperceptible graduations, and the latter have their real explanation, for the most part, in the former" (Ibid.: 281). Thrasher also points out, how-ever, that some of the men in organized crime "have a different genesis from that of the ordinary gang boy." He notes that in some cases "they seem to be men of questionable character or easy ethics who come from presumably reputable or well-to-do families, but who have been drawn into the activities of organized crime . . ." (Ibid.: 286). The writer has encountered several of the types that Thrasher is referring to—men who did not run with adolescent gangs, who were not "street persons," whose families were legitimate and financially comfortable. Nevertheless, these men became organized crime fig-ures. The most glaring example, historically, is Arnold Rothstein, who will be discussed in the next chapter.

One area for further research is the degree to which organized crime figures encourage their offspring to enter into syndicate activities, to follow in their "footsteps." There are some well-known father-son criminals in organized crime, e.g., Anthony and Joseph Paterno of New Jersey; Joseph Colombo, Senior and Junior; and Joseph and Bill Bonanno. However, there appear to be many more important organized crime figures whose children are apparently not involved in criminal activities. For example, the sons of Meyer Lansky and Thomas Lucchese both graduated from West Point as commissioned officers.

## Conclusion

What does all this add up to; what are we to conclude? First, we must understand that the United States, as the Eisenhower Commission* pointed out, is quite a violent country. Violence in both the figurative (e.g., "financial piracy") and literal sense (e.g., the use of gunmen, thugs, private police, law enforcement agents, and the military) has played an important part in the development of America. With the Western frontier closed, with the wealth of the "robber barons" now institutionalized and their progeny firmly in control of the economy, there has been little opportunity for the poor but ambitious of our urban frontiers, except to innovate—not on the grand scale of the Goulds, the Vanderbilts, and the Rockefellers, but in a manner more consistant with available opportunity.

Among the financial pirates of an earlier century we can see the strength of the so-called "Protestant Ethic" (Weber, 1957) distorted out of its theological origins and twisted into a savage temporal credo. In later day pirates, our contemporary gangsters, can be seen the remnants of a primitive culture that gave strength to the now dominant group in American crime, the Italians.

## ITALIANS AND ORGANIZED CRIME

The debate over the extent of Italian involvement in organized crime is often a sparring match over the existence of the "Mafia" or the "Camorra" in America. These two groups and the *Onorate Società* all arose in southern Italy, referred to as the *mezzogiorno*. About 90 percent of the Italians who came to America from 1875 until 1920 came from the mezzogiorno (Gambino, 1974: 3). The history of southern Italy is the history of political, social, and economic repression; a succession of foreign rulers culminated in a revolution in 1860 that eventually united Italy. For people in the south, however, little changed. Instead of foreign repression, the *contadini* (peasants) of the south were repressed by Italians from the north.

This southern experience dates back 700 years, and it led to the development of a culture that stressed the variables necessary for survival in a hostile environment. The only basis of loyalty is the family, *sangu de me sangu* (blood of my blood). Richard Gambino describes the family of southern Italy (1974: 3):

> The *famiglia* was composed of all of one's blood relatives, including those relatives Americans would consider very distant cousins, aunts and uncles, an extended clan whose genealogy was traced through paternity. The clan was supplemented through an important custom known as *comparatico* or *comparaggio* (godparenthood), through which carefully selected outsiders became to an important (but incomplete) extent members of the family.

* National Advisory Commission on Causes and Prevention of Violence, 1969.

Gambino notes that the family patriarch, *capo di famiglia,* arbitrated all ambiguous situations, and the family was organized hierarchically. "One had absolute responsibilities to family superiors and absolute rights to be demanded from subordinates in the hierarchy" (1974: 4). Luigi Barzini describes the dynamic qualities of the southern Italian family (1977: 36):

> The family, first source of power, had to be made prosperous, respected, and feared with antlike tenacity; it was enlarged (like dynasties of old) by suitable marriages, strengthened by alliances with families of equal status, by negotiated submission to more powerful ones, or by establishing its domination over weaker ones.

The southern Italian developed an ideal of manliness, *omertà,** which included noncooperation with authorities, self-control in the face of adversity, and the vendetta in which any offense or slight to family must be avenged no matter what the consequences or how long it takes. Out of this history and culture developed the famous "secret societies" of southern Italy.

## Mafia

David Chandler traces the origins of the Mafia to fifteenth-century Spain and a secret criminal society called the *Garduna* (1975: 6). Spanish kings ruled Naples during most of the years between 1504 and 1860, and Chandler argues that the Garduna reached Naples in the 16th century where it took the form of the *Camorra* (1975: 14–15). The Italian revolutionary Giuseppe Mazzini had a close relationship with the Camorra, and Chandler states that he brought it to Sicily in the form of a secret revolutionary society (1975: 26–27). The name, Chandler argues, by which it became known was derived from the initials of *Mazzini Autorizza Furti, Incedi, Avvelenamenti* (Mazzini authorizes theft, arson, poisoning), the slogan of his organization.

James Inciardi disputes this account (1975: 112–113, reference deleted):

> A scholarly analysis of the Italian language during these periods, combined with an examination of Sicilian history, suggests that such derivations represent little more than pure fiction. More laudable explanations of *Mafia* come from Sicilian historical and literary works that link its root and meaning to elements prevailing within Sicilian culture. *Mafia* is seemingly Sicilian-Arabic, descending from the etyma *hafa:* to preserve, protect, and act as guardian; from *mo'hafi:* friend or companion; from *mo'hafah:* to defend; and from *mo'hafiat:* preservation, safety, power, integrity, strength, and a state that designates the remedy of damage and ill. That the Arabic *mo'hafiat* became *mafiat* by elision, and *mafia* by apocope, can be drawn from [Giuseppe] Pitre who described *mafia* as a dialect term common in pre-1860 Palermo. It expressed "beauty and excellence," united with notions of "superiority" and "bravery"; in reference to *man,* it also meant: "the consciousness of being a man," "assurance of the mind," "boldness" but never "de-

---

* Omertà is derived from the word *uomo* (man) and refers to "behaving like a *man.*"

fiance," and "arrogance" but never "haughtiness." Thus, both Arabic-Sicilian references and common Palermitani usage contributed to *Mafia*'s meanings: protection against the arrogance of the powerful, remedy to any damage, sturdiness of body, strength and serenity of spirit, and the best and most exquisite part of life.

Barzini separates mafia (lower-case), referring to a state of mind and a philosophy of life, from Mafia, the illegal secret organization. The former, he notes, is shared by all Sicilians, the honest and the criminal—"they must aid each other, side with their friends and fight the common enemies even when the friends are wrong and the enemies are right; each must defend his dignity at all costs and never allow the smallest slight to go unavenged; they must keep secrets and always beware of official authorities and laws" (1965: 253–254). Barzini points out that the two (Mafia and mafia) are closely related, that Mafia could not flourish without mafia (1965: 256).

Michael Pantaleone, to whom Ianni refers as one of the most "careful students" of the Mafia in Sicily (1972: 30), states that the Mafia evolved out of the companies of private guards (*compagnie d'armi*) on the manorial estates in Sicily. Out of these eventually developed the *gabellotto,* Mafia, who ruled and eventually came to own the estates. The Mafia controlled the families living on the land, thus their votes and the politics of the area. Political control enabled the Mafia to gain immunity for criminal activities (1966: 32–33). The Mafia eventually moved from its rural base into urban areas, and "by the beginning of this century the Mafia was very [sic] flourishing in all the urban centres, particularly in western Sicily" (1966: 34). (Actually, Mafia never developed in the eastern end of the island.) However, Henner Hess points out that the urban mafia has more in common with the American urban gangster, whose pattern the new mafiosi copied, than with the mafia of rural Sicily (1973: 162–163).

Gambino states that the term Mafia or mafiosi was seldom used in Sicily; instead, members of the society were *gli uomini qualificati* (qualified men) or *gli amici degli amici* (friends of friends) (1974: 296). He also reports that the Mafia leaders, *padrini* (godfathers), formed a confederation by the late 19th century, and a *capi di tutti capi* (boss of bosses) emerged (Ibid.: 297). This is scoffed at by Hess who argues that "*Mafia* is neither an organisation nor a secret society, but a method" (1973: 127). A "method" does not have a "boss of bosses." In Sicily "a *mafioso* is simply a courageous fellow who won't stand any nonsense from anyone" (Ibid.: 1). These mafiosi, "men in whom the *mafioso* attitude is particularly strong come together in a kind of instinctive solidarity in order to support one another mutually in the pursuit of their aims" (Ibid.: 10). They form "small clique-like associations which are independent of each other but maintain relations with one another" (Ibid.: 11). The mafioso succeeds because he commands a *partito,* a network of relationships whereby he is able to act as an intermediary providing services which include votes and violence for the holders of institutionalized power (Ibid.: 12). Thus, he gains immunity to carry out his activities.

Each mafia clique (*cosca*) concentrates its activities in a particular endeavor —extortion involving the sale of agricultural products or livestock, kidnapping, robbery, etc. This enables them to avoid competition that can easily result in a blood-feud. The feud between the *stoppaglieri cosca* and the *fratuzzi cosca* lasted from 1872 until 1878 and claimed many lives (Pantaleone, 1966: 34–35).

Anton Blok (1974) provides a comprehensive look at the Sicilian *mafia* (he always uses the lower case and italics). Blok studied the *mafia* of a Sicilian village from the years 1860 to 1960. An anthropologist, he lived in the small rural village, and his analysis shows great insight into the phenomenon. Blok notes that the *mafia* is not a *secret* society, but an entity that developed from an association between violent peasant entrepreneurs who were charged with maintaining order and security on the large estates of absentee landlords and Sicilian bandits. These entrepreneurs came to represent a class of intermediaries between the aristocracy and the peasants—"individuals who operate in different social realms and who succeed in maintaining a grip on the intrinsic tensions by means of physical force" (1974: xxviii). As intermediaries, the *mafiosi* exploit communication gaps between the peasant and the wider society, and they maintain their position as intermediaries through the systematic application of force, physical and political (Ibid.: 8).

The men hired by the landlords, *gabelloti,* and the men they hired, *campieri,* earned *rispetto* because of their capacity for violence and their ability to provide access to resources, particularly land, for their followers (Ibid.: 62). On one level of society they kept the peasants in line, while at a higher level they lent political support to any government that provided them with enough freedom to continue operating in western Sicily (Ibid.: 75–76).

The Bourbon government depended on private groups to maintain law and order in the rugged terrain of Sicily. These private groups, *compagnie d'armi,* mixed with bandits and the *gabelloti.* "To a large extent what was later called *mafia* coincided with these associations of armed strong men and their followers who exercised jurisdiction on the local level in conjunction with formal authority" (Ibid.: 94). Blok notes that although they date back to the early 19th century, the term *mafia* was not used until 1868 (Ibid.: 95).

In contrast with Eric Hobsbawm's (1959) view of the outlaw as a *social bandit,* a pseudo-revolutionary, Blok points out, using the *mafia* as an example, that outlaws are more often in concert with the aristocratic class to whom they pose no serious threat (Ibid.: 102). Thus, they represent a conservative, if not reactionary, position, as borne out by the *mafia's* continuing battle with left-of-center parties in southern Italy.

Each village in western Sicily has its own *cosca* (clique), larger ones have two, and collectively these *cosche* are referred to as the *mafia,* although there has never been one *mafia.* While *mafiosi* maintain relationships with *amici* from other villages, in opposition to Gambino (1974: 297), Blok states that there has never been one hierarchical organization of *mafiosi* throughout Sicily (1974: 145). One becomes a member of a *cosca* gradually, and "not through any kind of formal initiation." Hess argues that "the *cosca* is not a group to which initiation would be possible," being too informal a structure (1973: 80). He concludes, "The *cosca* is not a group with a rigid organization, let alone a societá—'friends of friends,' that is an exact description of the fluctuating, oscillating bonds along the relationship lines described" (Ibid.: 88).

## Camorra

The term "Camorra" comes from the Castillian *kamora,* meaning "contestation," and was imported into Naples during the years of Spanish domination (Serao, 1911a: 722). The forebears of the Neapolitan Camorra were the Spanish brigands of the Sierras known as the *gamuri.* Ernest Serao reports (1911a: 723):

> Not a passer-by nor a vehicle escaped their watchful eye and their fierce claws, so that traveling or going from one place to another on business was impossible for any one without sharing with the ferocious watchers of the Sierras either the money he had with him or the profits of the business that had taken him on his journey.

The Camorra developed in the Spanish prisons during Bourbon rule of the Two Sicilies, early in the 19th century. The members of this criminal society eventually moved their control of the prisons into Naples proper. Eric Hobsbawm notes that they were "rather tightly, centrally and hierarchically organized" (1959: 55). John McConaughy reports (1931: 244):

> The Camorra in Naples was organized as openly and carefully as a public school system, or an efficient political machine in one of our own cities. Naples was divided into twelve districts, and each of these into a number of sub-districts. Although burglary and other remunerative felonies were not neglected, extortion was the principal industry; and the assassination of an inconvenient person could be purchased by any one with the price. In the case of a friend in need, a murder could be arranged without any cost—a simple gesture of affection.

One English diplomat in Naples (quoted in Hibbert, 1966: 181–82) during the 1860s observed:

> There was no class, high or low, that had not its representatives among the members of the Society which was a vast organised association for the extortion of blackmail in every conceivable shape and form. Officials, officers of the King's Household, the police and others were affiliated with the most desperate of the criminal classes in carrying out the depredations, and none was too high or too low to escape them. If a petition was to be presented to the Sovereign or to a Minister it had to be paid for; at every gate of the town *Camorristi* were stationed to exact a toll on each cart or donkey load brought to market by the peasants; and on getting into a hackney *carrosel* in the street, I have seen one of the band run up and get his fee from the driver. No one thought of refusing to pay, for the consequences of a refusal

were too well known, anyone rash enough to demur being apt to be found soon after mysteriously stabbed by some unknown individual, whom the police were careful never to discover.

Ianni states that after 1830 "they were more efficiently organized than the police, and set up a parallel system of law in the typical southern Italian style" (1972: 22). When Garibaldi became active in the Two Sicilies, the Bourbon king actually turned police power over to the Camorra, and those in jail were set free. The Camorra constituted not only the de facto but also the legally constituted police power in Naples (McConaughy, 1931: 245). The Camorra welcomed Garibaldi, and after his success their power increased. Gambino states that the Camorra was at the peak of its power from 1880 until 1900 (1974: 292). "If they so decided, there would not be, in some regions, a single vote cast for a candidate for the Chamber of Deputies who was opposed to their man" (Ibid.: 246).

In contrast with the mafia, the Camorra was highly organized and disciplined. Serao provides a look at the organizational structure (1911a: 724):

> There is a *capo'ntrine*—a sectional head—and a *capo in testa,* or head-in-chief of the Camorra, a kind of president of the confederation of all the twelve sections into which Naples is divided and which are presided over by the *capi'ntrini.*

The society has its own judicial structure (Ibid.: 725–726). The Cammorista must avenge all wrongs and slights that he may have suffered,

> ... to avenge the offense with one's own hands, if possible, after having first laid the complaint before the natural judges or the Camorra Tribunal. Whoever transgresses this all-important rule loses his right to have recourse to the Social Tribunal, which must decide as to the punishment.
>
> The Tribunal is manyfold and there is a high and low judicature. The meetings of the judges may take place anywhere; either in the towns to condemn Camorrists who are free, or in the prisons to judge imprisoned associates. ...
>
> The low judicature Tribunal is composed of three members, presided over by the Camorrist of highest rank among them, and deals with cases implying only a small penalty.
>
> The high judicature Tribunal is constituted of twelve high-rank Camorrists only, presided over by a *capo in testa,* and it deals with cases implying an attempt against the safety of the Society, the betrayal of the secrets of the association, denunciations, habitual theft from the social funds, etc., all punishable by death, and it appoints the executioner or executioners.

The lowest or entry level of the Camorra is the *picciutto,* which requires an act of daring and often simply a bloody deed, including "very dreadful crimes committed against very peaceful and quiet people ..." (Serao, 1911b: 781). The *picciutto* (Ibid.):

> ... has no share in the social dividend. If he wishes to live on other people's money, he must do the best he can by stealing, cheating, or swindling whom

he can, giving, however, to his superiors of the Camorra proper *shruffo* or proportionate percentage.

Only the regular Camorrist participates in the social dividends. In the prisons, when there are *picciuotti* and Cammorists, the former must make the beds and wait upon the latter, collect the dues from the non-associates and give them to the *cuntaiuola,* treasurer, who will pass the amount to his superiors. The *cuntaiuolo* must produce every Saturday a balance-sheet giving an account of all the dues collected during the week. As before said, the *picciuotti* do not receive anything as "right of Camorra," but their superiors usually let them have something in view of their assiduous and diligent attentions, and this optional profit is called the *sgarro.* Thus the imprisoned Camorrists often send out to their families handsome sums of money. These families enjoy just the same the "right of Camorra" (*shruffo*), and the wives and children of the Camorrist receive every week from the *cuntaiuola* of the gang to which he belonged the sum of money which would have been due to him had be been at liberty.

Below the *picciuotti* are specialized associates of the Camorra such as the *basista*—a person who can plan burglaries because of his access to the homes of wealthy persons. The Camorra also has its own authorized fences, usually dealers in second-hand goods, who arrange for the auction of stolen goods (Ibid.: 780):

Out of the proceeds of the sale so much is due to the *basista,* so much to the Camorrist who had knowledge of the burglary and patronized it, so much to the sectional chief of the society, and, when the burglary is a very important one, a small offering—"a flower," as it is called—is sent to the Supreme Head of the Camorra; the remainder, which is usually a meager thing, is divided among the material executors of the deed.

Gambino argues that there were actually "two Camorras"; that as noted above, the Camorra was quite stratified. The "low" Camorra did the actual physical work, while the "high" Camorra gave the orders and acted as patrons, intermediaries between institutionalized power and the "lower" Camorra. The men of the "high" Camorra, he states, were often lawyers, doctors, college professors, members of Parliament, and Cabinet Ministers (1974: 246).

Ianni states that the Camorra did not survive Mussolini, since, like the Mafia, it requires weak governmental control (1970: 7). In 1931, McConaughy wrote that the Camorra welcomed the Fascists as they had Garibaldi; there is not a Camorra: "They are all Fascists, and everything they do is legal" (1931: 248). While there are still criminals operating in Naples identified as being the Camorra, Ianni states that they have no direct links to the Camorra of an earlier era (1970: 7).

## Onerate Società

The Honored Society or 'Ndrangheta (Brotherhood) of Calabria was actually several bands that were collectively referred to as the "Brotherhood." They grew out of government repression and gained popular support because of their political stance against the central government (Gambino, 1974: 290). These bands mixed political insurrection with banditry and were supported and romanticized by the repressed peasants. Hobsbawm notes, however, that the Brotherhood had no positive social program; its sense of social justice was basically *destructive* (1969: 56):

> In such circumstances to assert power, any power, is itself a triumph. Killing and torture is the most primitive and personal assertion of ultimate power, and the weaker the rebel feels himself to be at bottom, the greater, we may suppose, the temptation to assert it.

Ianni reports that the Brotherhood was apparently still operating in Calabria as late as 1970 (1970: 7).

## MAFIA IN NEW ORLEANS

Chandler reports that the Mafia reached the United States in the latter part of the nineteenth century when members of the society arrived in New Orleans and New York and began to organize a new society of criminals. In New Orleans, Chandler reports, a feud between two rival Mafia factions developed (1975: 75). Ianni maintains that the feud was merely between "rival gangs of Sicilian and Neapolitan stevedores who found themselves in competition for business" (1972: 1). The feud was between Joe and George Provenzano, whom Ianni identifies as Neapolitans, and Charles Matranga, a Sicilian (Ibid.).

Herbert Asbury reports that the "Stoppagherra Society" (he apparently meant Stoppaglieri), a branch of the Sicilian Mafia, established itself in New Orleans in 1869 (1936: 406). This Mafia group eventually came under the leadership of Charles and Anthony Matranga (Ibid.: 407). The Mafia invaded the territory of the Provenzanos—George, Joe, and Peter—who held a monopoly on unloading fruit ships from South America. "The Provenzanos were rich and politically influential and, so far as was ever known, had no connection with the Mafia." As a result of attacks by the Mafia, the Provenzanos gave up their business to the Matrangas (Ibid.: 409–410). However, Asbury reports, when the Provenzanos opened a grocery store, the Mafia again drove them out of business. In desperation, he points out, the Provenzanos hired gunmen and fought back. During this time David Hennessey was appointed chief of police in New Orleans (Ibid.: 410).

In 1890 Anthony Matranga and two of his men were shot, and Joe and Peter Provenzano were arrested, along with three of their men, for the shootings. Hennessey, "who had been a friend of George and Peter Provenzano for many years," actively intervened on their behalf (Ibid.: 410–411).

Hennessey was appointed chief of police in 1888 by a reform mayor, Joseph A. Shakespeare. Richard Gambino argues that the extent of his "reform" was to drive out all gambling houses and bordellos owned by the "wrong people," while those owned by the "right people," the mayor's friends, were permitted a monopoly over vice (1977: 63–64). Hennessey had been a policeman until 1881, when he was involved in a gun fight with the chief of detectives, who had been feuding with Hennessey's cousin Mike. Mike was wounded in the fight and his rival was killed. Both Hennesseys were tried and acquitted, but David Hennessey was dismissed from the force (Asbury, 1936: 405). In 1886, Mike was killed in Houston, and until his appointment in 1888, David was employed as a private detective (Ibid.: 406).

In an effort to aid the Provenzanos, Hennessey announced that he had sent a letter to the head of the Rome police for the names and photographs of several Matranga men he believed were fugitives from the Italian authorities. On the night of October 15, 1890, before he had received the information, Hennessey was ambushed and severely wounded. Despite his wounds, he drew his pistol, ran after the gunmen, and fired two shots at them. These rounds missed and were later recovered; a third shot that he fired was not recovered (Gambino, 1977: 3). The newspapers reported that one police officer had been grazed on the head by a shot that Hennessey fired, and another had been shot in the ear. These wounds were never explained, and Gambino notes, suspiciously, "All references to their wounds soon disappeared from the accounts of the murder night" (Ibid.: 10).

The *NYT* alluded to the possibility that the murder was in retaliation for Hennessey's arrest and the eventual deportation of the Italian bandit Giusseppe Esposito ("Shot Down at His Door," Oct. 17, 1890: 1). Asbury identifies Esposito as a fugitive member of the Sicilian Mafia who, when he arrived in New Orleans, became the head of that city's Mafia (1936: 407–408). Gambino reports that Esposito was a member of a notorious gang in Sicily, not a *mafioso,* who had escaped from Italian custody and made his way to New Orleans where he worked as a fruit peddler (1977: 32). Despite the severity of his wounds, Hennessey was lucid and alert, with opiates easing his pain. Hennessey, and those attending him, believed that he would recover (Ibid.: 6). Gambino notes, accusingly: "Although it was well known that Hennessey knew by sight virtually every Italian criminal in New Orleans, and knew all the prominent Italians in the city personally, no one had asked him directly if he could name any of his assailants—or if they were in fact Italians" (Ibid.: 8).

Hundreds of Italians were arrested, and later several were indicted for the murder, the "true assassination squad," according to Chandler (1975: 88) and Asbury (1936: 415–416)—innocent victims according to Gambino (1977) —although Ianni (1972: 2) and Dwight Smith (1975: 38) are not sure. Seventeen persons were to stand trial for the murder, nine as principals and eight as accessories. Legal technicalities and quashed indictments led to new indictments, and on March 1, 1891, the front page of the *NYT* reported that nineteen were on trial, nine for murder and ten for being accessories. On March 12, 1891, the case went to the jury which returned a verdict on March 13. On March 14, 1891, the front page of the *NYT* reported "Six Persons Acquitted" and a mistrial was declared for three defendants. The accessories had not been tried.

Asbury reports, "The Italian colony received the news of the verdict with great rejoicing" (1936: 416). This reaction should have been, but was not, deserving of comment—only pages before Asbury had stated that the Mafia "kept the Italian colony of New Orleans in a state of terror for more than twenty years, and grew rich and powerful upon the proceeds of robbery, extortion and assassination, most of the victims being fellow-countrymen who failed to pay the sums demanded by the Mafia leaders" (Ibid.: 407). Why would the victims of Mafia crime, the Italian community, rejoice over the freeing of their tormentors?

In any event, the verdict outraged the non-Italian citizenry of New Orleans. Asbury reports that the evidence had been conclusive and the acquittal was the result of jury tampering (Ibid.: 416). The *NYT* reported: "So strong a case had been made by the State, the evidence had been so clear, direct, and unchallenged, that the acquittal of the accused to-day came like a thunder clap from a clear sky." The *NYT* noted that the defendants were returned to the Parish Prison on a related charge, lying in wait to commit murder, but indicated that they would not be tried on this charge since it would constitute double jeopardy.[2] Mass meetings were held and cries for "action" appeared in some newspapers. On March 14, 1891, a mob stormed the prison and eleven of the defendants were lynched ("Chief Hennessey Avenged," *NYT*, March 15, 1891: 1). Mayor Shakespeare is quoted as having stated, "I do consider that the act was—however deplorable—a necessity and justifiable" (Asbury, 1936: 421). Asbury reports that other officials made similar comments (Ibid.). Several newspapers denounced the lynchings, "but as a whole New Orleans greeted the action of the mob with approval" (Ibid.: 420), and "No investigation of the lynchings was ever made" (Ibid.: 422).

Giovanni Schiavo discounts this version of what occurred in New Orleans. He argues that the lynchings were not spontaneous, but rather were part of a plot that began before the trial ended. He maintains that only twenty persons, and not a "mob," took part in the assault on the prison and the lynchings that followed. (Asbury reports that there were sixty-one; they had all signed a notice calling for a public meeting. The sixty-one who actually entered the prison were supported by a cheering crowd which Asbury reports numbered in the thousands [1936: 417–419]). Schiavo claims that Chief Hennessey was a business associate of George Provenzano, that they were partners in a club that specialized in gambling and prostitution (1962: 151–152). He argues that the "real culprits" involved in the Hennessey murder could have been apprehended; "but neither the mayor nor *his gang* was interested in justice. All they wanted was to get rid of their rivals"[3] (Ibid.: 145, italics added). Unfortunately, Schiavo provides no evidence for his conclusion.

Dwight Smith points out that after the lynchings, "the New Orleans Mafia society ceased to be a public issue, and no further effort was made to combat a local Mafia" (1975: 38). According to Asbury none was needed: "After the fearful slaughter in the Parish Prison the Mafia was never again a power in the New Orleans underworld" (1936: 420).

## THE MAFIA IN NEW YORK

The Mafia is mentioned in the *NYT* on October 21, 1888, when New York City Police Inspector Thomas Byrnes stated he had discovered that the murderer of one Antonio Flaccomio "is Carlo Quarteraro, an Italian fruit dealer and a member of a *secret society* to which Flaccomio also belonged." (Byrnes had apparently forgotten that George Washington also belonged to a *secret society*—indeed, an international secret society: *The Fraternal Order of Free and Accepted Masons*).[4] Byrnes went on to report that the *secret society* is known as the *Mafia,* and the persons involved in the killing are fugitives from Sicily. The inspector noted, "There are two principal headquarters of this society in this country—one in this city and the other in New Orleans—so that members of the society who commit a serious crime in this city find refuge among friends in the South and vice versa" ("By Order of the Mafia," *NYT,* Oct. 22, 1888: 8; emphasis added). Chandler, who misquotes Inspector Byrnes, agrees that this was a Mafia killing (1975: 110), although it appears that Flaccomio was actually killed because of an altercation over a card game. According to follow-up stories in the *NYT* no evidence was presented linking either the deceased or the accused to the Mafia.

New York, without doubt, did have *La Mano Nero,* the Black Hand, and it is the subject of a great deal of controversy. Francis Ianni states: "The Black Hand activities were the work of individual extortionists or small gangs, and there is no evidence which suggests that there was any higher level of organization or any tie with the *Mafie* in Sicily, or the Camorra in Naples" (1972: 52).

Thomas Pitkin and Francesco Cordasco present a different version. They note that the leaders of a prominent Black Hand group, Ignazio Saietta (called "Lupo the Wolf"; *lupo* means wolf in Italian) and Giuseppe Morello, "maintained affiliations with Mafia chiefs on their home ground in Sicily" (1977: 188). When Morello was arrested in 1909 by United States secret service agents (he and Saietta were also counterfeiters), correspondence was found linking him to Vito Cascio Ferro, or Don Vito as the prominant Mafioso was known in Sicily. It is also believed that Don Vito spent some time in the United States at the turn of the century (Ibid.: 131–132).

Arthur Train, writing in 1911, points out that the Camorra and the Mafia have never been transferred to the United States (1922: 287). Indeed, he argues that many immigrants who were involved with these groups in Italy became quite honest and respectable in the United States: "The number of south Italians who now occupy positions of respectability in New York and who have criminal records on the other side would astound even their compatriots" (Ibid.: 290). Train states, however, that there are Mafia and Camorra gangs in New York headed by a *capo:* "Each *capo maestra* works for himself with his own handful of followers who may or may not enjoy his confidence, and each gang has its own territory held sacred by the others" (Ibid.:

287). Train points out that these gangs "rarely attempt to blackmail or ter-rorize any one but Italians" (Ibid.: 288). Occasionally an important *capo* from Italy arrives, and local "friends" must "get busy for a month or so, rais-ing money for the boys at home and knowing they will reap their reward if they ever go back." The most popular method of collecting the money is to hold a banquet at which all "friends" must be present: "No one cares to be conspicuous by reason of his absence and the hero returns to Italy with a large-sized draft on Naples or Palermo" (Ibid.: 301).

In 1895, Giuseppe (Joseph) Petrosino, a New York City police officer, was put in charge of a special squad of Italian detectives and assigned the task of investigating "Italian crime," in particular "Black Hand" extortion. The latter flourished in Italian ghettos until Prohibition began to offer greater criminal opportunities. Italian families with varying amounts of wealth would receive a crude letter "signed" with a skull or black-inked hand. The letter requested money with dire threats offered as an alternative. These threats, often bombings, were sometimes carried out. Petrosino and his squad were quite successful in their work. Petrosino was eventually sent to Italy to check judicial records for lists of criminals about to be released, or recently released, from Italian prisons so that these men could be picked up on arrival in the United States and returned to Italy (Ibid.: 109–110). Petrosino left New York on February 9, 1909; on March 12, 1909, he was shot down on a Palermo street. Chandler states that Don Vito as well as leaders of the Camorra and the New York Mafia took credit for the Petrosino murder (1975: 122). The ac-tual murderer(s) was never caught.

Arrigo Petacco reports that Ferro, who was born in Palermo on January 22, 1862, arrived in New York City in 1901. Based on his reputation in Sicily, Ferro assumed the leadership of the gang headed by Saietta and Morello. In 1903, Don Vito Ferro, Morello, Saietta, and five others, were arrested by Petrosino and charged with murder. Shortly thereafter, Petacco reports, Ferro fled to New Orleans, and on September 28, 1904, sailed for Sicily (1974: 93–95). Upon his return, less than two years later, Ferro succeeded in assuming control of all the Mafia bands in the Palermo area (Ibid.: 95). Petacco states there is no doubt that Ferro was responsible for Petrosino's murder, and that he was probably the actual executioner. The motive was apparently prestige (Ibid.: 187). In 1926, Prefect Cesare Mori, acting under the unlimited police powers of the Fascist government of Benito Mussolini, began a drive against the Mafia. Ferro was arrested and held in detention for four years. On July 6, 1930, he was sentenced to nine years in solitary confinement (Ibid.: 194). Petacco states that he succeeded in establishing the date of Ferro's death— 1943 at age eighty-one. In that year prison authorities abandoned the institu-tion in the face of the Allied invasion; Don Vito was forgotten and starved to death in his solitary cell (Ibid.: 195).

Chandler reports that in New York, a "war" began in 1889 between the Mafia and the Camorra. Ianni notes that Enrico ("Erricone": Big Henry) Alfano, a leader of the Camorra in Naples, was arrested in New York in 1907 (1972: 52), but Ianni maintains: "These vendetta-like feuds grew out of the inter-group hostility among Italian immigrants—and do not seem to have been associated with any Mafia-Camorra war" (1972: 53).

Joseph Valachi, born in New York of Neapolitan parents, confirms the great enmity between New York Sicilians and Neapolitans. His information, Valachi states, came from Alessandro Vollero, "a member of the Camorra" (Maas, 1968: 74fn). Vollero is quoted as having said to Valachi: "If there is one thing that *we who are from Naples* must always remember, it is that if you hang out with a Sicilian for twenty years and you have trouble with another Sicilian, the Sicilian that you hung out with all that time will turn on you" (Maas, 1968: 74–75; emphasis added). Vollero, however, is identified by Pitkin and Cordasco, in their well-documented book, as a *Sicilian* allied with Brooklyn Neapolitans. These Brooklyn Neapolitans came to be identified as the Camorra (1977: 207). During Vollero's trial for murder several witnesses "spoke of having been initiated into the *society*." Pitkin and Cordasco conclude that very few of these early Sicilian and Neapolitan criminals "were the product of American slums but brought their criminal habits, or at least proclivities, with them from elsewhere" (1977: 209). "That they were and remained largely unorganized seems clear. That there was a tendency toward coalition and considerable continuing contact with Old World criminal societies, which they sought to emulate, is equally clear" (Ibid.: 228).

What is also clear is the strong anti-Italian feeling of the period. Arthur Train, a former Manhattan Assistant District Attorney, writing for *McClure's Magazine* in 1912, states that southern Italians "are apt to be ignorant, lazy, destitute, and superstitious. A considerable percentage, especially of those from the cities, are criminal" (1912b: 83). Ironically, in 1912 Manhattan gambling and prostitution was well-organized under the able leadership of Tammany Hall; the southern Italian was not part of this Irish-Jewish cabal.

## LUCIANO AND
## THE SICILIAN MAFIA

The final great episode in American "Mafia history" occurred during World War II. In 1942, Lucky Luciano, christened Salvatore Lucania, the most prominent gangster in New York, was serving a thirty-to-fifty-year sentence for compulsory prostitution. He had been successfully prosecuted by then Special Prosecutor Thomas E. Dewey, who in 1942 was governor of New York. The story, which had been widely reported but not documented, concerns a visit by Naval Intelligence officials to Luciano. They wanted his cooperation, some say to help with possible espionage or labor problems on the waterfront where his associates held sway; others maintain that the Navy wanted more. Luciano was to arrange for the Sicilian Mafia to assist the American invasion of that island in 1943. The ties between American organized crime and the Sicilian Mafia, according to Pantaleone, date back to the early twentieth century and Don Vito Cascio Ferro, the chief of the Mafia in Sicily before Mussolini's campaign against the Mafia: "Men schooled by Don Vito Cascio Ferro founded and organized gangsterism in America fifty years ago" (1966: 39). As we will soon see, this is a gross exaggeration, if not an out-right distortion of the history of organized crime in the United States. Pantaleone, and others (e.g., Chandler, 1976) report that the Mafia, then under Don Calogero Vizzini, did indeed help in the invasion effort, and they believe that it was because of Luciano (1966: 58–60). Vizzini, the illiterate son of a poor farmer, died on July 12, 1954, leaving an estate worth several million dollars (Ibid.: 80).

Rodney Campbell reports that between January 28 and September 17, 1954, the New York State Commissioner of Investigation, William B. Herlands, conducted a confidential inquiry into the "Luciano affair." Campbell's book, based on Herland's heretofore "secret report," states that by May 1942, 272 ships had been sunk by German submarines operating in American coastal waters. It was suspected that information on American shipping was being leaked to the Germans by people working in eastern ports. It was also suspected, incorrectly, that German submarines were being supplied by American fishing boats. The spectre of sabotage was also raised when the luxury liner *S.S. Normandie,* refitted for use as a naval vessel, rolled over in flames while harbored in the Hudson River.

Desperate naval intelligence officials in New York turned to organized crime for help. Joe ("Socks") Lanza, czar of the Fulton Fish Market, Meyer Lansky, Frank Costello, and other prominent syndicate figures, acting under orders from Luciano, cooperated with naval intelligence. According to Campbell, in addition to ordering port workers and fishermen to "keep alert," these crime figures helped to place intelligence operatives in key areas by supplying them with union cards and securing them positions on the waterfront, in fishing boats, and in waterfront restaurants. They also provided another important service. At the request of naval officials they prevented strikes and other forms of labor unrest that could interrupt wartime shipping.

While Campbell provides documentation of Luciano's domestic role during the war, his role in the invasion of Sicily is tenuous. Elements in the *mafia* apparently aided the American invasion, but as Barzini notes, there is no organizational connection between the *mafia* in Sicily and organized crime in the United States. Indeed, Barzini explains how the exiled Luciano was swindled by the *mafia* when he arrived in Palermo (1965: 271). It does seem logical, however, that the *mafia* would support the American effort. Mussolini had empowered Cesare Mori with unlimited police authority in his drive against the *mafia*—and Mori had been quite successful. Many *mafiosi* fled to the United States, while others who escaped imprisonment and execution went "underground" or joined the Fascists. They lay dormant until the American invasion. Schiavo argues that it died forever, that whatever *mafia* exists in Italy has merely usurped the name and not the traditions (1962: 74–75). Pantaleone states, however, that collusion between the American Intelligence Service and *mafia* "was responsible for the regrettable rebirth of the Onorata Societa in the post-war period and for the strengthening of its power in the traditional

Mafia area" (1966: 61). Pantaleone reports that in addition to the reemergence of the (old) *mafia*, a "New Mafia" has developed, and it is working with American gangsters in drug smuggling operations.

In 1945, Governor Dewey received a petition for executive clemency on behalf of Luciano. On January 3, 1946, he announced that Luciano would be released from prison and deported to Italy. Luciano left the United States on February 9, 1946.

While nobody denied that Luciano was a leader of organized crime his conviction for compulsory prostitution has been a source of controversy. Allegations of fabricated evidence and perjured witnesses abound. Indeed, the case that led to his conviction has incredible elements that raise questions about the "real" motivation for Luciano's pardon prior to Dewey's narrow loss to Truman in 1948.

## THE AMERICAN MAFIA

By early 1900 there were about 500,000 (mostly southern) Italians in New York City, living in the most deprived social and economic circumstances. The Italian immigration "made fortunes for speculators and landlords, but also it transformed the neighborhood into a kind of human antheap in which suffering, crime, ignorance and filth were the dominant elements" (Petacco, 1974: 16). The Italian immigrants provided the cheap labor vital to the expanding capitalism of that era.

Robert Merton states that "functional deficiencies of the official structure generate an alternative (unofficial) structure to fulfill existing needs somewhat more effectively" (1967: 127). Randall Collins (1975: 463) states that "where legitimate careers are blocked and resources are available for careers in crime, individuals would be expected to move in that direction." Thus, the prominance of Italian-Americans in organized crime "is related to the coincidence of several historical factors: the arrival of large numbers of European immigrants from peasant backgrounds who demanded cultural services that the dominant Anglo-Protestant society made illegal; the availability of a patrimonial form of military organization that could be applied to protecting such services; and the relatively late arrival of the Italians in comparison with other ethnic groups (e.g., the Irish) who had acquired control of legitimate channels of political and related economic mobility" (1975: 463). Luigi Barzini adds: "In order to beat rival organizations, criminals of Sicilian descent reproduced the kind of illegal groups they had belonged to in the old country and employed the same rules to make them invincible" (1966: 273). Gambino concludes that although southern Italian characteristics do not dispose men toward crime, "where the mode of life has been impressed onto organized crime it has made it difficult to combat effectively the criminal activity" (1974: 304). Gambino argues that Italian criminals "totally corrupted and perverted traditional codes of la famiglia and vendetta" (Ibid.: 297).

Humbert Nelli reports that there were Mafia gangs in every American city that had a sizable Sicilian population—"feeding off the common laborer's honest toil and claiming to serve as a means of easing adjustment to American society" (1976: 136). Hobsbawm states that the Mafia "was imported by Sicilian immigrants, who reproduced it in the cities in which they settled, as a ritual brotherhood consisting of loosely linked but otherwise independent and uncoordinated 'families' organised [sic] hierarchically" (1969: 686). Nelli points out that Mafia organizations "served important social as well as financial functions. The group produced a sense of belonging and of security in numbers. This function was achieved at least in part through the use of initiation ceremonies, passwords and rituals, and rules of conduct with which members must abide" (1976: 138). Hobsbawm notes that the Sicilian immigrants found the American environment quite different from their native island; this called for some adaptation. "The Chicago Mafia, for instance, appears to have abandoned the traditional initiation ritual quite a while ago" (1969: 686).

Nelli notes that at various times the influence of Irish political-criminal leaders such as John Powers, boss of Chicago's largely Italian Nineteenth Ward, was greater than that of a *Capo Mafioso* like Anthony D'Andrea. The battle for control of the "Bloody Nineteenth," 1915 to 1921, is called by Nelli an Italian revolt against Irish rule. This "revolt" is referred to in Chapter Three as the "Alderman's War" and was won by John Powers; D'Andrea was murdered in 1921 (1976: 135). One of Ianni's informants describes a Mafia gang operating in Brooklyn in 1928 (1972: 57):

> ... all the old Sicilian "moustaches" used to get together in the backrooms of the club—it was a *fratellanze* [brotherhood] and they used to call it the *Unione Siciliana*. They spent a lot of time talking about the old country, drinking wine and playing cards. But these were tough guys too, and they were alky cookers [bootleggers] and pretty much ran things in the neighborhood. They had all of the businesses locked up and they got a piece of everything that was sold.

## L'UNIONE SICILIANA

Both historical and contemporary perspectives on organized crime in America suggest that *L'Unione siciliana* was an outgrowth of the Sicilian or American *Mafia,* or that the *Mafia* and *L'Unione* were synonymous. However, further analysis of the historical structure of organized crime indicates differences between these groups. *L'Unione siciliana* emerged in late nineteenth-century New York as a lawful fraternal society designed to advance the interests of Sicilian immigrants. The *Unione* provided its members with life insurance and additional social benefits, and was energetic in the eradication of crime within Sicilian-American communities. Its prominent opposition to the festering evil of the Black Hand was designed to improve the unfavorable images shared by the immigrants from southern Italy and Sicily. Early in the twentieth century emigration from southern Europe increased, with some 3.2 million coming from Italy during the first two decades. Additional branches of *L'Unione siciliana* were chartered wherever new colonies of Sicilians expanded. The Chicago area, for example, contained *L'Unione*'s largest chapter, which was composed of thirty-eight lodges and more than forty thousand members by the 1920s.

The respectability and benevolence of the *Unione* declined as Prohibition approached. First in New York and later in distant city branches, cadres of gangsters began to infiltrate and pervert the association. *L'Unione siciliana* acquired a dual character: it was open and involved in good works among needy Sicilians, yet it was hidden and malevolent, dealing in theft, murder, and vice. With an expanding criminal front, leaders of this "society" became natural catalysts for any racketeers seeking to widen their influence and profit potentials. *L'Unione* membership included old and clannish *Mafia* types who stressed maintenance of the cultural traditions of the Sicilian *Società onorata*. To these were added the younger Americanized factions that were anxious to increase their operations through cooperative agreements with a greater variety of criminal groups, even with those not of their blood. The *Unione* of the 1920s became the object of power struggles, with both orientations contending at local, regional, and national levels for the more advantageous posts. This struggle terminated in 1931 in the Castellammarese war. (Inciardi, 1975: 115)

## The Castellammarese War

In 1930, there were two major factions in Italian organized crime, one headed by Giuseppe ("Joe the Boss") Masseria, and the other by Salvatore Maranzano. The struggle for power between the two became known as the Castellammarese War since many of the Maranzano group came from a small Sicilian coastal town, Castellammarse del Golfo. Masseria was a Neapolitan and his group included other non-Sicilians: Vito Genovese, Joseph ("Joe Adonis") Doto, and Frank Costello (christened Francesco Castiglia or Francesco Seriglia), and they were allied with non-Italians such as Meyer Lansky and Benjamin ("Bugsy") Siegel. The Maranzano faction consisted mainly of Sicilians, especially the "moustaches." As the war turned against Masseria, five of his leading men—Genovese, Luciano, Ciro Terranova, Frank Livorsi, and Joseph ("Stretch") Stracci—went over to the Maranzano camp. On April 15, 1931, "Masseria drove his steel-armored sedan, a massive car with plate glass an inch thick in all its windows, to a garage near the Nuovo Villa Tammaro at 2715 West Fifteenth Street, Coney Island, and parked it. Then he went to the restaurant" ("Racket Chief Slain By Gangster Gunfire," *NYT,* April 16, 1931: 1). As he ate, Masseria was murdered by three of his lieutenants and the war ended (Ianni, 1972: 59).

On September 10, 1931, four men carrying pistols entered a suite at 230 Park Avenue, the Grand Central Building in New York City. "One of them ordered the seven men and Miss Frances Samuels, a secretary, to line up against the wall. The others stalked into the private office of Salvatore Maranzano. There was a sound of voices raised in angry dispute; blows, struggling, and finally pistol shots, and the four men dashed out of the suite." Maranzano was found with "his body riddled with bullets and punctured with knife wounds" ("Gang Kills Suspect in Alien Smuggling," *NYT*, Sept. 11, 1931: 1). More about this incident appears in the next chapter.

This incident can be called the final chapter in American "Mafia" history. After 1931 a loose confederation of syndicates was established in the United States, and many members of these syndicates were not Italians. The term "Mafia," however, began to be used as a synonym for organized crime as Italians became the dominant ethnic group in the American syndicates.

## The "Mafia" in America Today

The research of Peter Reuter and Jonathan Rubinstein indicates the existence of a "Mafia," although it may be referred to by different names: "It is clear that membership confers certain rights and obligations, but there is disagreement over whether it is better to be a member or a close associate; associates appear to enjoy most of the rights and incur none of the obligations" (1978: 63). Vincent Teresa, a New England syndicate associate, states: "The associates were guys who worked for the made men [syndicate members] and the bosses to make money, but weren't accepted in the Office [syndicate] as members. First of all, to be a member you had to be an Italian" (1973: 96). Teresa explains why he never became "made." "When you're made by the Office, they own you, body and soul. They more or less own you as long as you're on the street working for them anyway, but at least you have a chance to refuse to do something if you're not made." The "something," as Teresa explains, is that when a close friend or even a close relative "is out of line," you have to assist in his murder, usually by "setting up" the victim for mob enforcers or "hit men" (1973: 97). "Which family one joins has relevance only in cases of disputes. There are no restrictions on whom one does business with, but if there is a dispute each member is required to align with his own family" (Reuter and Rubinstein, 1978a: 63). This situation is highlighted in a conversation (secured by means of an unauthorized FBI electronic interception; see below) between Angelo Bruno, a Philadelphia crime boss, and Sam ("The Plumber") de Cavalcante, a New Jersey crime boss. De Cavalcante is complaining about Jimmy Christy, his partner in a numbers operation and a member of Bruno's crime family. Bruno reminds de Cavalcante that if the situation goes to *arguimendo* (arbitration), "I have to represent Jimmy whether I want to or not. . . . You understand, that we have to represent him and we have to represent him to the best of our ability. . . ." (Volz and Bridge, 1969: 127–128).

During the 1960s the Federal Bureau of Investigation "bugged" the office of de Cavalcante for almost four years. On June 10, 1969, some of the results of the bugging were made public, a move that generated a great deal of publicity—the electronic interception had been done without court authorization. The material released is over 2000 pages, and covers the period May 7, 1964, until July 12, 1965, with some material from 1962. Known as the "De Cavalcante tapes," it is actually a document based on transcripts of conversations overheard by four microphones and summarized by FBI agents. Some of what was overheard, however, was quoted verbatim, and throughout the "tapes" there are references to "being made" (a member of a crime family) and the "Commission," a type of national board of organized crime. Reuter and Rubinstein state: "There may be a 'national' Mafia Commission. If there is, it has very limited powers, perhaps only to mediate high level disputes" (1978: 63). Teresa states: "Over everyone was the Commission, a ruling council of bosses from different areas who made decisions on rules and policy involving mobs across the country. They didn't interfere in local affairs unless it was something like the Gallo-Profaci war, and even then they only gave advice" (1973: 96). Raymond Martin, a former ranking police official in New York City who investigated the Gallo-Profaci war, states that the Commission sat as a court and decided not to intervene, that it was a local matter (1963: 108). Gay Talese, in his study of the Bonanno crime family, notes that Joseph Bonanno was removed as head of the family by "the Commission" (1971: 86–87), and de Cavalcante was recorded discussing his role as a mediator between the Commission and Bonanno (Volz and Bridge, 1969: 149–185). Both of these incidents will be discussed in the next chapter.

Reuter and Rubinstein report that the one distinctive *service* provided by the Mafia that is not available from other hierarchical criminal organizations is arbitration. "In an economy without conventional written contracts, there is obviously room for frequent disagreements. These are hard to resolve. Many bookmakers make payments to 'wise guys' to ensure that when disputes arise they have effective representation" (1978: 64). However, the syndicate provides important services to both legitimate and illegitimate operations—it restricts otherwise unlimited competition. Private garbage carting concerns, for example, can be protected from potential cut-throat competition by belonging to a trade association often operated by or with the approval of organized crime. Illegitimate operations are likewise protected.

Being a "made" member, as opposed to associate status, has two advantages:

1.  Prestige, which can often be converted into financial profits; many (even legitimate) businessmen prefer to deal with someone having the status (and thus "connections") of a syndicate member; and
2.  Having a greater degree of status means that you can be trusted; a member is an insider, which means he has access to information, e.g., stock thefts, narcotic shipments, that can generate profits.

Syndicate members also provide another "service." Albert Seedman, former chief of detectives in New York City, taped a conversation between "Woody," who had swindled $500,000 from Mays Department Store in Brooklyn, and Carmine ("The Snake") Persico, a Brooklyn syndicate enforcer with a reputation for violence. Woody wanted to know why he was being asked to pay a rather large share of the money he had stolen to Persico who had played no part in the scheme. Persisco replied (in this edited version):

When you get a job with the telephone company, or maybe even Mays Department Store, they take something out of every paycheck for taxes, right?
Right. (Woody responds).
Now why, you may ask, does the government have the right to make you pay taxes? The answer to that question, Woody, is that you pay taxes for the right to live and work and make money at a legit business. Well, its the exact same situation—you did a crooked job in Brooklyn [in the territory of the crime family to which Persico belongs]. You worked hard and earned a lot of money. Now you have got to pay your taxes on it just like in the straight world. Why? Because *we* let you do it. We're the government (1974: 70–74).

## Skepticism and the "Mafia"

There are apparently some who do not believe, or are at least skeptical, that a "Mafia" (used here as a popular synonym for organized/syndicate crime) exists. With this in mind, on May 24, 1979, New Jersey Attorney General John J. Degnan announced "the first indictment anywhere in the United States formally alleging the existence of a nationwide criminal organization used by its members to commit crimes and maintain power over rivals and victims." Degnan was referring to a New Jersey Grand Jury indictment (SGJ 49–78–77) against eight organized crime figures in the New Jersey branch of the Vito Genovese crime family then headed by Frank Tieri. (In the indictment Tieri is not named, but is referred to by his nickname "Funzi.")

The twenty-four count indictment alleges, among crimes such as murder and extortion, the existence of a nationwide criminal organization—"This Thing of Ours" (*La Cosa Nostra*). Throughout the indictment, which runs sixty-three pages, there are references to "being made" (a member), the ordering of an "authorized hit" (murder) by a *caporegime* (which was carried out), and some discussion of the crime family's structure.

The information contained in the indictment appears to be based on electronic surveillance and the testimony of an unindicted co-conspirator, Patrick J. Pizuto, who became a state witness. At the time of his involvement in the alleged conspiracy, which includes his admitted participation in a murder, Pizuto had been "proposed" for family membership and was on "probation." According to the indictment, actual initiation was being held up because Pizuto had charges pending against him in a prior case. These charges apparently made him a security risk.

## ETHNIC SUCCESSION IN ORGANIZED CRIME

Ianni reviews ethnic succession in organized crime (1973: 1):

The Irish were the first immigrant groups to become involved in organized crime on a large scale in the United States, and early Irish gangsters began to climb up the social ladder. As more Irish came to American cities and as the Irish gangsters became successful in organized crime and therefore money began flowing into Irish-American communities, the Irish began to acquire political power. As they eventually came to control the political machinery of the large cities, the Irish won wealth, power and respectability by expanding their legitimate business interests and gaining control of construction, trucking, public utilities and the waterfront. The Irish were succeeded in organized crime by the Jews . . . [who] dominated gambling and labor racketeering for a decade. The Jews quickly moved into the world of business as a more legitimate means of gaining economic and social mobility. The Italians came last and did not get a commanding leg up the ladder until the late thirties.

However, once established in organized crime, the Italians made significant social progress. Ianni reports that in one Italian crime family, the "Lupollos," in the fourth generation "only four out of twenty-seven males are involved in the family business organization. The rest are doctors, lawyers, college teachers, or run their own businesses" (1972: 193). Ianni argues that ethnic succession in organized crime continues, as the more recent urban immigrants, blacks and Hispanics, move into organized crime: "We shall witness over the next decade the systematic development of what is now a scattered and loosely organized pattern of emerging black control in organized crime into the Black Mafia" (1974: 12). Let us examine Ianni's view.

Ianni is not convincing. Gus Tyler (1974) notes that Ianni's evidence "consists of a pimp with a stable of seven hookers, a dope pusher, a fence who dabbles in loan sharking and gambling, a con man who gets phony insurance policies for gypsy cabs, and a numbers racketeer, etc." Tyler points out that although these activities are "organized," they are not in a class with white organized crime either qualitatively or quantitatively (1975: 178). Indeed, early in his book (1974) Ianni reports that the brother and partner of the aforementioned "dope pusher," actually a large-scale dealer in Paterson, New Jersey, was found sans his genitals—a "message" from the "White Mafia."

The Kerner Commission (National Advisory Commission on Civil Disorders) stated that timing has had a negative impact on blacks (1968: 278–279): "The Negro migrant, unlike the immigrant, found little opportunity in the city; he had arrived too late, and the unskilled labor he had to offer was no longer needed." The Commission also noted that reform groups were beginning to attack the urban political machines that had aided immigrant mobility: "The machines were no longer so powerful or so well-equipped to provide jobs and other favors" (1968: Ibid.). Timing continues to play negative tricks on blacks. In a humorous, yet extremely perceptive article, Russell Baker (1977) turns down the job of being the new "Mafia Godfather" because of the poor economic conditions currently associated with certain organized crime activities: "So the Mafia developed the bookmaking industry and cleaned up. What happened? states [sic] like New York, seeing a chance for a killing, legalized bookmaking and took the gravy for themselves." Baker, quoting a "Mafia representative," states: "Our problem is that we are hard-pressed for new revenue sources. Every time we develop a rich new field of vice, governments move in on us and take it over" (1977: 8). Several days after the article appeared, the State of Connecticut began operating a legal numbers game, and the following year New Jersey opened legalized casino gambling in Atlantic City. (That the "White Mafia" has not been hurt by the latter event is made clear by Michael Dorman (1978), and Howard Blum and Jeff Gerth (1978).)

Ironically, black and Hispanic mobsters are beginning to take over, or franchise from white organized crime, various numbers operations in the ghetto. However, as lotteries, off-track betting, and casino gambling become increasingly available legally, this "takeover" may not be meaningful. From 1963 to 1978, for example, fifteen states began operating lotteries (Marshall, 1978: 20).

## The Road to Ethnic Succession
## Is Paved with Drugs

Ianni has noted that the one sector of organized crime activity that seems to offer some possibility for black and Hispanic innovators to expand beyond the ghetto is drug trafficking: "Narcotic and drug traffic have the same pattern of relationship which surrounded alcohol and bootlegging during the prohibition era" (1974: 143). David Durk states that if anything can be said for the drug business, it is that it has become an equal opportunity employer (1976: 175).

However, some observers maintain that black opportunity in this area has been due in large part to the movement of white organized crime out of narcotics. Ralph Salerno and John Tompkins state that the passage of the Federal Narcotics Control Act in 1956 resulted in significant action against organized crime drug activity. Such important crime figures as John Ormento and Vito Genovese drew long prison sentences—Ormento received forty years, and Genovese died in prison. "At that point, when the scales of value tipped against them, the Confederation began its slow and halting withdrawal from narcotics, a business that had become its quickest moneymaker since the repeal of prohibition" (1969: 294).

Joseph Valachi reported that on the agenda of the aborted "Apalachin Conclave" (discussed in Chapter Three) was the question of what to do about narcotics. "The prevailing mood was to outlaw drug traffic for all families, with death the penalty for disobedience; while realistically it would have the same effect on some elements in the Cosa Nostra as Prohibition had for the nation, it was considered worth trying as a deterrent" (Maas, 1968: 262). This is corroborated in a taped conversation released by the Federal Bureau of Investigation. In the conversation between two New Jersey syndicate members, Anthony ("Little Pussy") Russo and Sam ("The Plumber") de Cavalcante (sometimes spelled DeCavalcante), the latter, head of a small New Jersey crime family, refers to the syndicate ban against dealing in drugs (Volz and Bridge, 1969: 98).

After the death of crime boss Carlo Gambino in 1976, syndicate operations in drugs resumed at an accelerated pace (they had never actually stopped). This meant confronting black and Hispanic crime figures who had set up their own drug networks. Paul Meskil reports that since the syndicate moved back into drugs, black and Hispanic drug dealers have been "swatted like flies" in the ghetto areas of New York and New Jersey. Carmine Galente, who was murdered in 1979 after his release from federal prison in 1974 where he served twelve years for narcotic violations, "sent his troops to recapture drug markets that had been abandoned over the years to other ethnic groups that lived in the neighborhoods involved" (1977: 32). Lucinda Franks reports, however, that Galente came to terms with Leroy ("Nicky") Barnes, who, though now in federal prison, is reputed to have been Harlem's biggest drug dealer (1977: 34). Fred Ferretti reports that Barnes used Italian suppliers and was allowed to establish control over manufacturing and distribution throughout the metropolitan New York-New Jersey area (1977: 106).

One major black operator, Charles Lucas, began working in numbers and moved into heroin wholesaling. He apparently had no connection to the white syndicate and had established his own pipeline to suppliers in an area of Laos, Burma, and Thailand called the "Golden Triangle." He was reportedly the first black operator to do so. The Lucas organization is primarily made up of his relatives from North Carolina (Schumach, 1977: 37) and a few trusted non-kin members. Lucas supplied his brothers Shorty and Larry, who operated in Northern New Jersey and the Bronx. He also supplied drug rings in Chicago, Los Angeles, and North Carolina (his birthplace). Lucas had seventy-five persons working for him with pick-up and delivery men earning $500 a week. Rudy Langlais provides a description of how Lucas imported his heroin from Southeast Asia (1978: 14, edited):

A Lucas (importer's) agent leaves Kennedy Airport for Thailand in 1974 carrying $600,000 in brand new 50s and 100s. (This is already a violation of federal law which requires that all amounts over $5000 entering or leaving the United States be declared). In Bangkok he checks into a hotel and telephones the overseas source's agent. He offers a password and is given instructions on where to deliver the money. At the money drop he is informed of the shipping arrangements by an Oriental. The next day the importer's agent returns to New York and reports to Lucas. Shortly afterwards 150 kilos of heroin (retail value more than $50 million) is smuggled into Georgia in the footlocker and trunks of a soldier returning to Fort Gordon.

The heroin is transported into New York by automobile with two back-up vehicles fore and aft. In New York it is secreted ("stashed") in one of the apartments rented throughout the city for this purpose. Lucas then arranges for the cutting and distribution. The Lucas operation runs all the way to the street level where his "salesmen" offer heroin marked with his own distinctive "Blue Magic" logo.

The Lucas downfall came in 1975 as the result of the trust he placed in a nonkin member of his organization, who subsequently became a government informer and eventually a murder victim (Ibid.: 13). Lucas is serving a forty-year federal sentence.

Black opportunity is highlighted by the story of Frank Matthews. Matthews was born in Durham, North Carolina, on February 13, 1946 (Goddard, 1978: 104). He started his criminal career as a chicken thief and moved to New York City where he began working for a syndicate numbers operation. With money he earned from the numbers, he entered the drug market by purchasing heroin from the same syndicate family that ran the numbers. He also dealt in cocaine which he purchased from Hispanic operators. In the space of three years he developed an organization that spanned twenty states (Ibid.: 104–121). Matthews ruled his empire from a fortified headquarters in Brooklyn. In 1971, he convened a conference of black drug dealers in Atlanta that was reportedly attended by more than forty prominent figures of the "black mafia." The agenda dealt primarily with ways of breaking the white syndicate's domination of heroin importation. Nixon's "war on drugs" had hurt the syndicate and paved the way for the "black mafia" to deal directly with the Corsicans who controlled the international trade at the time (Ibid.: 121–122).

Matthews exhibited many of the characteristics of a figure of an earlier era, Al Capone. Like Capone, Matthews was flamboyant, displaying wealth and power that was more appropriate for the Chicago of the 1920s. In the New York of the 1970s it was reckless. In addition to expensive homes, cars, and a yacht, he used two credit cards in his own name for extensive purchases. The result was inevitable; he attracted attention and was indicted for income tax evasion and drug violations. Matthews spent his twenty-ninth birthday in federal custody. In 1973, he was released on bail; his whereabouts, as of this writing, are unknown.

## ORGANIZED CRIME: CUBAN AND COLOMBIAN *

When Castro took control of Cuba, American gangsters who worked under Meyer Lansky and operated extensive gambling casinos in Havana were expelled. Many of their Cuban associates fled to the United States and settled in New York and Miami where they began to look for new areas of income. Many Cuban exiles were organized and trained by the Central Intelligence Agency to dislodge Castro. After the 1961 Bay of Pigs debacle, they were supposed to disband and go into legitimate business. However, as Donald Goddard points out, they *"had no lawful business"* (1978: 44). Elements in these exile groups (they sometimes overlapped) began to enter the drug market.

Until the early 1970s, the importation of marijuana, cocaine, and counterfeit Quaaludes into the United States continued to be a largely Cuban opera-

---

* The information in this section is from a variety of sources, including the Drug Enforcement Administration, the Internal Revenue Service, and the *Miami Herald*. Reporters Carl Hiaasen and Al Messerschmidt have been covering the Colombian drug situation in south Florida.

tion whose source was Colombia. The Colombians harvest marijuana, import cocaine paste, which they process into crystals, from Bolivia and Peru, and manufacture imitation Quaaludes.* During the later half of the 1960s, Colombians began migrating to the United States in numbers sufficient to establish communities in New York, Miami, Los Angeles, and more recently in Chicago. Many were illegal immigrants brought in through the Bahamas and carrying false documents, Puerto Rican birth certificates or immigration papers of high quality. The Colombians became highly organized, both in the United States and at home. By 1973, independent foreign nationals were no longer able to "deal drugs" in Colombia. In 1976 the Colombians became dissatisfied with their Cuban agents in the United States. The latter were reportedly making most of the profits and shortchanging the Colombians. Enforcers, young men from the Guajira Peninsula of Colombia, were sent in, and Cubans were executed in New York and Miami. According to government officials, the Colombians now dominate both importation and distribution.

Officials report that currently five major Colombian "families" dominate the importation of marijuana, cocaine, and Quaaludes into the United States. The Cubans have apparently become aligned with these "families." Each "family" is an extended kinship group; the one hundred to two hundred members in each family are related by blood, marriage, or godparenthood. Each family is ruled by a patriarch and is hierarchical. Until late 1978, the five "families" exhibited a great deal of cooperation. For example, if 500 tons of marijuana were needed to effect a deal with a wholesaler, they would pool their resources. Financing was often cooperative, and the "families" even shared couriers and used the same enforcers. The latter are quite feared in the Latin community. One enforcer known as "El Loco" strikes such fear that prospective witnesses turn away when shown his photograph. Their favorite weapon is a lightweight submachine gun, although smaller weapons and slit throats are not uncommon.

Officials report that the Colombian "families" are doing a business estimated at $8–12 million per month, although opinion differs as to what they are doing with this wealth. According to Internal Revenue Service sources, most are not filing income taxes (they may be illegal aliens) and are merely hiding the money here or in Colombia. Luxury housing is often purchased by men who can barely speak English and who pay in cash delivered in shopping bags. Other sources reveal that some "families" have patrons in Colombia who are legitimate, sophisticated international businessmen. As a result, drug profits are funneled to the nearby Antilles, where investment corporations controlled by the Colombians "launder" the money and invest it in legitimate businesses, particularly real estate and housing in south Florida. This investment has reportedly been responsible for greatly inflating the cost of housing in the area.

---

* Quaaludes are a brand name for a sedative (methaqualone) used to treat insomnia when barbiturates are medically contraindicated or have failed. Despite earlier beliefs to the contrary, addiction can develop to methaqualone as easily and as rapidly as with barbiturates. Its effects are similar to barbiturates, except there is a greater loss of motor coordination, which explains why it is sometimes referred to as "wallbanger."

The Colombians are operating internationally, supplying cocaine to Europeans as well as North Americans. There is some indication that they may be connected to overseas Chinese; this could mean involvement in heroin trafficking.

At the end of 1978, for a reason not clear as of this writing, the cooperation between the Colombian "families" was replaced by internecine warfare that parallels Chicago of the Prohibition era. Estimates of those killed (the exact number is unknown) range from twenty-seven to forty as of July 1979. In one incident, a delivery van drove into a crowded Miami shopping mall. Two men exited and walked into a liquor store where they opened fire with submachine guns. Two persons were killed and two wounded as the killers easily escaped in the pandemonium that followed. One of the dead men was the head of a Colombian "family." Inside the abandoned van the police found several submachine guns and revolvers with silencers attached. In that same month New York City police and federal agents raided the residence of a Colombian leader in Forest Hills, Queens. The nearby neighborhoods of Elmhurst and Jackson Heights contain a Colombian community of several hundred thousand. In addition to forty-four pounds of cocaine, the raiders found forty firearms, many with silencers attached, and a machine gun. The size of the weapons cache may indicate that the "war" raging in south Florida is expected to move north (Judith Cummings, "44 Lb. of Cocaine Seized Along With Arms Cache," *NYT*, July 31, 1979: B1).

## Colombian and Italian Organized Crime

There has been some relationship between the Colombian crime families and established Italian crime syndicates. The latter have financed some Colombian operations and have purchased cocaine, and more recently marijuana, from the Colombians. In 1979 the *NYT* reported that the crime family once headed by Joseph Profaci is involved in a multi-million-dollar marijuana operation: "It is believed to be the first time that a major New York organized crime faction has branched out into extensive marijuana trafficking" (Raab, 1979: 4). Presumably, the syndicate had ignored marijuana because it seemed less lucrative than heroin. One Italian organized crime figure attempted to deal directly with suppliers in Bogotá, avoiding United States-based Colombians. He apparently did not realize that the Colombians in the United States and those in Bogotá are part of the same families. As a result, he lost his five expensive vessels without importing any cocaine or marijuana. Drug Enforcement Administration sources state that no friction has been reported between the Colombian families and the Italian syndicates, while an article in *Time* indicates that there has been some conflict ("The Colombian Connection," *Time*, Jan. 29, 1979: 28). The Colombians appear to be satisfied to deal in marijuana, cocaine, and Quaaludes (in addition to counterfeiting American money), and have not sought to move into areas of traditional interest to Italian crime syndicates—gambling, loansharking, and racketeering.

There are some rather striking similarities between the two groups. In both, the nuclear family unit is patriarchal, with the father or oldest male having absolute authority. In the Colombian family, however, in the absence of the father, the mother may occupy this position. This might account for the dramatically different roles that women play in Italian crime families and their Colombian counterparts. For the southern Italian, organized crime is strictly a man's business, excluding traditionally female roles in prostitution and related enterprises. However, two Colombian crime families are reputedly headed by women; one is said to be a beautiful woman of about twenty-eight. Like the southern Italian, the Colombian family is extended by ritual godparenthood (*compadrazgo*), and duty to family, including *compadres* (ritual kinsmen), is *the* primary responsibility. The Colombian stresses *dignidad,* which is inadequately translated as dignity. It actually shares some kinship with the Italian concern with *rispetto.*

In the Colombian crime families, a division of labor has emerged that parallels roles in Italian-American crime families. Roles such as "enforcer" and "corrupter" have been identified by enforcement agencies. The latter role is of prime importance in Colombia where the "cooperation" of officials is vital to drug operations. In the United States, where the Colombian community in general and the crime families in particular, have been impenetrable, the position is not as important. Enforcers, however, are necessary in both Colombia and the United States. They have tended to come from the Guajira Peninsula, where Colombia's northern coast juts out into the Caribbean Sea. An area of desperate poverty, hot, dry, remote, and primitive, it has few natural resources besides a marijuana crop and access to the sea and border with Venezuela. The area has a large native Indian population and has traditionally been a smuggler's paradise. About twenty-five years ago, Levantine traders moved into the Gaujira and married into powerful Indian families. They organized and developed the smuggling trade into a sophisticated business enterprise (Aschmann, 1975: 37). Because the Gaujiro Indians identify with the upper strata rather than the lower classes of Colombian society (Ibid.), they have been able to relate easily to the cocaine businessmen of Bogotá. Secret airstrips now service planes transporting cocaine, marijuana, Quaaludes, and counterfeit money, as part of the smuggler's trade in the Guajira. The area has also achieved a reputation for violence, and "Guajiro" is a term sometimes used to indicate a "tough" or "wiseguy," much as the term "mafioso" might be used in southern Italy.

The Italians and Colombians took advantage of the relatively easy immigration, legal and illegal, into the United States, and elements in each group found innovative-based opportunity in substances which, although illegal, were in great demand.

## Other Developments in "Ethnic Succession"

There are two developments that could affect ethnic succession in organized crime. The first is the smuggling of illegal aliens, in this case Sicilians by

Italian-American crime families. These aliens often serve in the numerous pizza parlors and Italian restaurants that proliferate in the New York metropolitan area. While often working for substandard wages, these Sicilians stand available as "muscle" when the occasion arises. Paul Meskil states that these Sicilians are reminiscent of earlier immigrants from that island with their *mafia* ways. He quotes a United States Department of Justice official who refers to them as "animals on a leash" (1973: 252–253; see also Pileggi, 1972). When crime family boss Carmine Galente was slain in 1979, two of the men dining with him, reputedly members of his crime family, had come to the United States several years earlier from Castellammarse del Golfo (Thomas Raferty and Paul Meskil, "2 Who Saw Galente Die Surrender to DA," *New York Daily News,* Aug. 1, 1979: 5).

A second development, contrary to Ianni's observations, is the continued entry of young Italian-Americans into organized crime. This activity is highlighted by the rise of a gang of young Italians in the Pleasant Avenue section of Harlem, a syndicate stronghold, dubbed the "Purple Gang," apparently after the murderous Detroit mob of Prohibition days. The Purple Gang is reputedly supplying the heroin network of the imprisoned Nicky Barnes, with syndicate approval (Blum, 1977: D12). The money secured from the lucrative narcotics business appears to have already provided a basis for the gang to move into other activities. They are alleged to have formed an investment company that invested $300,000 in a firm that had a state-granted monopoly on vending machine sales of New York State Lottery Tickets. The owner of this firm was shot to death in 1977; the reason has not been determined (Seigel, 1977: 27). Mark Schorr reports that the Purple Gang is being used as "muscle" and as executioners for the syndicate. They have allegedly been responsible for a series of gangland murders, and their reputation for violence has apparently made them quite useful (1979: 44): "No one wanted to mess with them. Informants began to grow forgetful when they remembered the man who informed on the Purple Gang and was found with fourteen stab wounds and two bullet holes in his body—or another suspected informant who lost his head, literally, by the Grand Central Parkway."

## A CROSS-CULTURAL PERSPECTIVE

Most Americans have heard of the Mafia, Lucky Luciano and Frank Costello, and their "soldiers," but what about the Yamaguchi, Kazuo Taoka and Hideomi Oda and their yakuza (pronounced YAHK-za)? Florence Rome introduces us to the *Tattooed Men* (1975) of the Japanese criminal syndicate. The Yamaguchi, the largest criminal organization in Japan, has 11,000 members (Kirk, 1976: 61), has been in existence more than 300 years, and goes back to the Tokugawa period when Japan was united under a central system of government, a situation that put an end to the employment of many samurai, the knights of the earlier feudal period (Rome, 1975: 47–48). The yakuza view themselves as modern samurai, maintaining exotic rituals including extensive tattooing that virtually covers the entire torso down to the ankles, and clipped fingers that have been self-amputated with a short sword as a sign of contrition for mistakes.

Like their American counterparts, the Yamaguchi members "were born into poverty and graduated from juvenile delinquency into organized crime" (Kirk, 1976: 93). The "Al Capone" of Japan, Kazuo Taoka, was like Capone, born into poverty. Taoka began his criminal career as a bouncer in Kobe (Rome, 1975: 96), much as Capone filled the same capacity in Brooklyn before going to Chicago (Kobler, 1971: 31). Taoka, like Capone, played a major role in the gang conflict of the day, and both men rose to prominence because of their talents with violence and organization.

There are other important similarities between American and Japanese organized crime. The politics of both tend to be to the right. The yakuza have always been allied with right-wing politics in Japan (Kirk, 1976: 91), and Rome states that she was "well-briefed on the ultra-conservative political views of the yakuza" (1975: 44). Ianni reports of the "Lupollos": "Politically they are ultra-conservative and express very strong support for 'Americanism.' " They are hawks on matters of foreign policy and very anti-communist (1972: 84), like the Yamaguchi who exclaim: "We are united in our opposition to Communism" (Kirk, 1976: 91).

The major difference is that in Japan the "sense of belonging" is intense: tattooes and clipped fingers, banners and insignias worn on coats and jackets —membership is flaunted (Kirk, 1976: 116). The *NYT* reports that recent efforts at fighting organized crime in Japan are also uniquely Japanese (Malcolm, 1977: 8). One method is social ostracism. Malcolm points out that social acceptance and influence of the yakuza have been so pervasive that the police find it difficult to fight them. A series of gang-related murders, however, resulted in a public outcry, and the police reacted accordingly. They put up a 24-hour barricade around a yazuka leader's home, closing the streets to vehicles, questioning and searching every pedestrian passing the house. In addition, the police are subjecting crime leaders to ridicule: "The leader is forced to sit alone in a simple wooden chair surrounded by policemen denouncing him and urging the gang's dissolution." Malcolm also reports: "With official encouragement, including the loan of a police band for protest meetings, neighborhood groups have begun forming crime prevention associations." Shades of "old Chicago" and the Chicago Crime Commission, a citizen's group formed to combat organized crime during Prohibition.

On January 14, 1979, the NBC television program *Weekend* presented the yakuza who, they noted, are 110,000 strong and divided into twenty-five gangs. Loyalty is described as absolute, and a gang leader is viewed as a "father figure." The yakuza usually describe themselves as modern versions of Robin Hood, although at least one older member was critical of the modern yakuza preoccupation with making money and exhibiting prosperity. (Yakuza usually drive Cadillacs or Mercedes, and they are quite open about their membership.)

*Weekend* noted the fanatical right-wing politics of the yakuza, and this would seem to tie in well with two of their profitable enterprises—strike breaking and providing "muscle" to prevent any opposition at corporate stockholders meetings. In addition, the yakuza are involved in more conventional organized crime activity—drug trafficking, bookmaking (on bicycle, horse and, especially, motor boat racing), prostitution, and pornography. *Weekend* alleged that the yakuza have been moving into Hawaii and Las Vegas. Paralleling the extensive interest in organized crime in America, *Weekend* pointed out that films and books about the yakuza are extremely popular in Japan.

## "Organized Crime" in the Soviet Union

Vallery Chalidze reports that while the Soviet Union does not have organized crime in the American pattern, it does have a "professional underworld." This is the *vorovskoy mir,* the "thieves' world," which has its own code of ethics and cohesion (1977: 34). The so-called "regulars," Soviet equivalent to a "made man," is the *vory v zakone,* literally "thieves professing the code" (Ibid.: 45). Like organized crime in the United States, valid information on the *vorovskoy mir* is difficult to secure. "Its real members so appreciate its unique and esoteric character that they are most unlikely to write memoirs or otherwise enlighten observers about its nature and activities" (Ibid.: 35).

Chalidze reports that the code does not permit a member to return to a law-abiding life without the consent of his fellows; violations are punished by death (Ibid.: 42). On occasion they hold a congress to deal with disputes between gangs over territories and with upholding the code (Ibid.: 45). Information on the structure of these gangs is incomplete, but there are at least three levels: the elite, the rank and file, and apprentices aspiring to full membership. One often becomes a member as a result of being born into a thieve's family—a "born thief" (Ibid.: 53). In addition, there is a category of associates who form a link between the underworld and normal society, e.g., receivers of stolen goods. The thieve's code stresses detachment from normal society, and the most serious conflict in the underworld was the result of thieves who served in the military during World War II; they were considered traitors by those who did not serve (Ibid.: 49). The code disapproves of avarice and accumulation (Ibid.: 50). In the underworld, the role of women is completely servile, taking the form of a master-slave relationship between husband and wife (Ibid.: 52).

## Organized Crime in Africa

James Opolot (1979) reports that the most prevalent form of organized criminal activity in Africa is smuggling. This activity involves a variety of commodities: coffee, cocoa, ivory, gold, and diamonds. Smuggling is an effort to avoid customs or to find a black market for goods on which government controls restrict profits. Opolot notes that tribal formations transcend the national boundaries established by colonial powers without regard for tribal structures. A single tribe may actually dwell in two or more countries with contiguous boundaries. This facilitates smuggling, as a person in one country "visits" a relative in another, crossing national borders as part of an active smuggling operation.

Opolot reports that certain tribes have tended, historically, to monopolize smuggling activities; they were usually those involved in commerce, e.g., cattle herders and fishermen. Modern Africans in these tribes organize their more primitive brethren, using them to carry out the smuggling physically. The operations are quite sophisticated, with goods being channeled into legitimate commercial enterprises on an international basis.

Opolot states that "crime is almost part of life" in Nigeria, and research conducted by William Chambliss tends to confirm this observation. He reports that corruption in Nigeria (at least at the time of his study, 1967–68) was rampant and blatant (1973: 17). Prostitution and gambling were organized, and gangs of professional thieves operated with official protection (Chambliss, 1973: 17–18).

## ENDNOTES

1.  Smith argues that the activities of organized crime "represent, in virtually every instance, an extension of a legitimate market spectrum into areas normally proscribed. Their separate strengths derive from the same fundamental considerations that govern entrepreneurship in the legitimate marketplace: a necessity to maintain and extend one's share of the market" (1978: 164).
2.  Chandler reports that eighteen of the nineteen defendants held a victory party in the jail: "For their own protection they had not yet been released" (1975: 92).
3.  The problem of historical accuracy, discussed in Chapter 3, is highlighted by a reference to this incident in a book produced under the scholarly imprint of Purdue University. Homer states that "At least half of the jury was intimidated or bribed . . ." (1974: 31). Homer's footnote offers the source of this information as Maas, 1968: 56–57. Maas, however, provides *no* source at all for this information.
4.  Inspector Byrnes was eventually promoted to Chief Inspector, based on his real "specialty": providing city policemen for the private protection of Wall Street moguls (O'Connor, 1962: 219).

# THREE

# History of Organized Crime

The task of presenting a history of organized crime in the United States is insurmountable. This is not for lack of material, for these are abundant. But quantity cannot replace quality, and the latter is the major problem. Alan Block (1978: 470) notes that there is a reliance on unsubstantiated accounts of informers or the ideological preconceptions of law enforcement agencies. John Galliher and James Cain (1974: 69) point out a lack of scholarly material relating to organized crime, with the dominant literature being journalistic, and tending toward sensationalism, or government documents: "There are two troublesome aspects to this reliance on such sources, one empirical, the other political. In arriving at conclusions and statements of fact, the journalist or political investigator is not bound by the canons of scientific investigation as is the social scientist" (1974: 73). These authors also refer to the journalist's need to produce exciting copy even at the expense of "careful accumulation and sifting of information characteristic of scientific investigation" (Ibid.). Anthony Villano, an FBI agent for twenty-three years, who specialized in organized crime, states that the bureau regularly "leaked" false reports to the press to stir up dissension among organized crime figures (1978: 246–247).

Dwight Smith points to an American preoccupation with conspiracy, from the "Bavarian Illuminati" of 1798 to the "Red Scare" of 1919. One of the conditions required for an "alien conspiracy" theory is a set of "facts" or assumptions that can be constructed into evidence supporting a conspiratorial explanation (1975: 77). These "facts" often make fascinating reading, they sell newspapers and books, and, Smith argues, they provided the Federal Bureau of Narcotics with an explanation for failure: "The notion of total suppression of illegal narcotics use through importation control was a self-proclaimed mission, and it had not been attained. How better to explain failure (and, incidentally, to prepare the ground for increased future budgets) than to argue that, dedicated though it might be, the bureau was hard pressed to overcome an alien, organized, conspiratorial force which, with evil intent and conspiratorial methods had forced its ways on an innocent public?" (1975: 85).

That the federal drug agency, now called the Drug Enforcement Administration, is still capable of such activities is made obvious by a 1977 episode. In one week major stories (Meskil, 1977; Franks, 1977) appeared revealing that Carmine Galente, a 67-year-old mob leader, was emerging as the new *capo di tutti capi,* the "boss of bosses." Paul Meskil (1977: 30), an investigative reporter, stated that law enforcement officials say that Galente's immediate goal is to bring all five New York crime families under his direct control and, according to these officials, he will succeed: "Soon, federal agents predict, Carmine Galente's peers on the Mafia Commission, will elect him boss of all bosses" (1978: 28). Lucinda Franks, a *NYT* crime reporter stated: "Officials say that Mr. Galente is moving to merge the five New York crime families under his own leadership and aims to become a national chieftain who would try to restore the Mafia to a position of power it has not held in at least 20 years" (1977: 34). Jerry Capeci reports, however, that the *real* "Godfather" is Frank ("Funzi") Tieri, a 74-year-old Brooklyn mob leader. He notes that Carmine ("Lilo") Galente was being proclaimed boss of all bosses as "the result of a well-planned 'leak' by the Drug Enforcement Administration of a 'confidential' report by its Unified Intelligence Division" (1978: 28). Capeci adds: "It turns out now that the report was based on quite old information and was leaked in self-interest by the drug agency" (Ibid.). Galente was ordered returned to federal prison for violating his parole.

Peter Reuter and Jonathan Rubinstein state: "The difficulty the government had in obtaining accurate information on the reserves of energy-producing companies in the wake of the 1973 oil boycott should serve as a sober reminder of how difficult it is to collect accurate information even from legitimate organizations operating in a highly regulated environment. The challenges are immeasurably greater in collecting information about people who are consciously involved in illegal activities" (1978: 57). They report on a United States Department of Justice effort to determine the amount of illegal gambling revenues; the department frequently asserts that organized crime derives its major income from that source. After noting the totally unscientific basis for the final estimate, they conclude: "In truth, we suspect that the real failing of the estimate was that no one really cared precisely how it was developed, but only that it produce a large number. The assumption that the details of the calculations would not be subjected to any scrutiny led to a cavalier use of the available data. Also, the estimate had no possible consequences; it was produced for rhetorical purposes and has served these purposes very well" (1978: 62). Unfortunately, baseless estimates of organized crime income continue to abound in the literature. In a book published in 1979, August Bequai, a former Justice Department official, states that the untaxed profits of organized crime "may average as much as $600,000 per hour" (1979: 1).

In 1974, a book by Gosch and Hammer appeared, which purported to be *The Last Testament of Lucky Luciano*: "Dictated by Charles 'Lucky' Luciano himself during the final months of his life." The book's introduction (1974: v) explains that Luciano made a decision in 1961 to provide the details of his life as a crime boss to Martin A. Gosch, an award-winning author and former reporter for the *NYT*. According to the introduction, the syndicate, acting on orders from Meyer Lansky, vetoed a movie that Gosch was producing titled *The Lucky Luciano Story*. Luciano, who was living in exile in Italy, was to be technical advisor, and now he was angry. However, according to Gosch, who died of a heart attack before publication, Luciano extracted a promise that his autobiography not be published earlier than ten years after his death; he died in 1962. The book earned more than one million dollars before it was even published, and paperback rights were auctioned for an additional $800,-000 (Gage, 1974: 1).

On December 17, 1974, in a front page article, Nicholas Gage of the *NYT* questioned the authenticity of the book by pointing to numerous errors of fact: "It is widely known that Mr. Gosch met on a number of occasions with Mr. Luciano on the aborted film project, and presumably the gangster recounted some of his experiences during these meetings. But contradictions and inaccuracies in the book raise questions to the claim that Mr. Luciano told his whole life to Mr. Gosch and that everything in the book attributed to Mr. Luciano actually came from him" (Gage, 1974: 28).

The problem inherent in presenting an accurate history of organized crime is highlighted by another episode. On September 10, 1931, Salvatore Maranzano, the self-appointed "boss of bosses," was killed by mobsters dispatched by Meyer Lansky and Benjamin ("Bugsy") Siegal at the request of Luciano —an historic event in interethnic cooperation. Cressey reports (1969: 44): "On that day and the two days immediately following, some forty Italian-Sicilian gang leaders across the country lost their lives in battle." Fred Cook refers to this episode as the "Purge of the Greasers" (1972: 107–108): "Within a few short hours, the old-time crime bosses who had been born and reared in Sicily and were mostly illiterate—the 'Mustache Petes' or 'the greasers,' as they were sometimes called—were liquidated by the new breed of Americanized, business-oriented gangsters of the Luciano-Costello-Adonis school." Cook adds: "Beginning on September 11th and lasting through the next day, some thirty to forty executions were performed across the nation . . ." (Ibid.). A special publication of *New York* magazine (Plate, 1972) adds to the story: "During the bloodbath nearly 40 of the Old Guard were executed in various *ingenious ways*" (1972: 45; emphasis added). As late as August 21, 1978, this incident was being reported as *historical fact*—"the 'Night of the Sicilian Vespers,' so named because Luciano had not only engineered the slaughter of Salvatore Maranzano for the night of September 10, 1931, but had gone ahead and wiped out 40 of the 'Mustache Petes' across the country" (Capeci, 1978: 26). The last quotation is from Jerry Capeci, the journalist who would not be "duped" by the Drug Enforcement Administration.

Alan Block surveyed newspapers in eight major cities, beginning with issues two weeks prior to Maranzano's death and ending two weeks after, looking for any stories of gangland murders that could be connected, even remotely, with the Maranzano case. He reports: "While I found various accounts of the Maranzano murder, I could locate only three other murders that might have been connected" (1978: 460). As he notes, three murders do not make a "purge."[1] Block observes that "it is by no means clear why so many scholars have bought a story which so grossly violates historical respectability" (Inciardi, Block, and Hallowell, 1977: 100). James Inciardi and Lyle Hallowell, along with Block, note (1977: 13): "The history of crime contains many valid representations of past events, but in addition, it also includes much that has become clouded by legend and folklore and generational distortions unreclaimed by rigid historical analysis." This creates *the* problem in reconstructing the important events of organized crime history.

The remainder of this chapter contains a history of organized crime that represents a summary of the available literature on this topic. When the literature conflicts, the divergence of opinion will be noted. Otherwise, the material will be presented as "history," although we have already seen the weaknesses inherent in much that passes for the history of organized crime. *Caveat emptor.*

Tyler notes that organized crime in America "is the product of an evolutionary process extending more than a century." He points out that the roots of organized crime can be found in such cities as Chicago and New York decades before Prohibition (1962: 89). Our historical review will focus on these two cities, since only in the cases of Chicago and New York do we find sufficient information for an historical analysis of organized crime (Albini, 1971: 177).

## ORGANIZED CRIME IN
## CHICAGO AND NEW YORK

In both these cities we see a similar pattern: The saloonkeeper, gambling house operator, and politician were often the same person. The saloon was a center of neighborhood society, an important social base for political activity, and saloonkeepers became political powers in both cities. They were in a position to deliver the votes of their wards (Chicago) or districts (New York), often with the help of the street gangs that proliferated in the ghetto areas. The politician employed the gangs for such legitimate purposes as distributing campaign literature, hanging posters, and canvassing for votes; they were also used as "repeaters" who voted early and voted often, and as sluggers who attacked rival campaign workers and intimidated voters. The "ward healer," however, was usually a popular figure who in the days before social welfare programs provided important services to his loyal constituents—jobs, food, assistance with public agencies including the police and the courts. All that he asked for in return for his largesse were votes and a free hand to become wealthy in politics. To the impoverished and powerless ghetto dweller, this was a small price to pay for services that would otherwise not be available.

Robert Merton notes (1967: 128):

> The political machine does not regard the electorate as an amorphous, undifferentiated mass of voters. With a keen sociological intuition, the machine recognizes that the voter is a person living in a specific neighborhood, with specific personal problems and personal wants. Public issues are abstract and remote; private problems are extremely concrete and immediate. It is not

through the generalized appeal to large public concerns that the machine operates, but through the direct, quasi-feudal relationships between local representatives of the machine and voters in their neighborhood.

The very personal nature of the machine is highlighted by McConaughy, writing in 1931: "In the midst of the current depression, an Irish alderman named Moriarity distributed unleavened bread [matzah] to hundreds of Jewish families in his district, so that they might keep the feast of Passover. This will not cost him any votes" (1931: 319).

Harold Gosnell highlights the interdependence of machine politics and gangsters. He notes that the immunity that gangsters receive is dependent on the money and the votes they deliver (1937: 42):

> When word is passed down from the gangster chiefs all proprietors of gambling houses and speak-easies, all burglars, pick-pockets, pimps, prostitutes, fences, and their like, are whipped into line. In themselves they constitute a large block of votes, and they frequently augment their own value to the machine by corrupt election practices.

In return for "delivering the vote," the ward boss was rewarded with patronage and was recognized as lord of his district in a system that resembled feudalism. He appointed, directly or indirectly, the police officials in his area; thus he was in a position to protect vice activity (gambling and prostitution) which he "licensed," growing wealthy from the "fees."

Prohibition brought this system to an end. The gang leaders grew wealthy, and with their army of sluggers and gunmen *they* controlled the votes and elected the politicians. The politicians became the servants of the gangsters.

In both New York and Chicago both employers and labor unions turned to gangsters for help, only to find themselves dominated by these thugs-turned-"businessmen." The gangsters, who historically worked as lackies for the politicians, the employers, and the unions, began to dominate all three.

In both cities we see a pattern of corruption–reform–corruption–reform, often interspaced with investigations and widely reported hearings. It is important to recognize the political motivation, and not an insignificant amount of hypocrisy, behind many of these exposés. In New York investigations were often initiated by upstate, rural, Protestant Republicans against downstate (New York City), urban, Catholic and Jewish Democrats. The upstate Republicans were able to dominate state legislatures in New York (and elsewhere) by gerrymandering districts in a most outrageous manner—a practice eventually declared unconstitutional by the United States Supreme Court in 1962 in the landmark "one-man, one-vote" decision (*Baker v. Carr*, U.S. 186). The threat of investigation and public disclosure was used to secure the support of city politicians for legislation favored by more rural interests. Corruption was real and often rampant, but many of the efforts purporting to deal with it were just as corrupt, morally if not legally.

This is exemplified by legislation passed as the result of the efforts of New

York Governor Charles Evans Hughes—it banned betting on horses and book-making. In 1909 the law was rigidly enforced during the metropolitan racing season, that is when horses ran in the New York City metropolitan area. In Saratoga, an upstate city just north of the state capital, a Republican strong-hold, gambling continued unabated; the racetrack in Saratoga was "big busi-ness," an important tourist attraction (Katcher, 1959: 49–50). Historically, in Illinois and New York, the urban masses had to place a bet illegally with a bookmaker, while their more affluent brethren enjoyed the "sport of kings" in the sunshine of the great outdoors, at the racetrack where they could bet legally.

Even so-called "reform" mayors showed a not inconsiderable amount of hypocrisy. New York's Mayor La Guardia moved vigorously against Frank Costello, a Democrat, but did not bother racketeers in East Harlem where his Republican protege, Congressman Vito Marcantonio, held sway. In Brooklyn, Joe Adonis was equally untouchable until 1937, when he switched his sup-port to La Guardia's opponent. La Guardia had the police drive him out of New York, and Adonis stayed in New Jersey until 1945, the year La Guardia's term ended (Repetto, 1978: 184). "Nucky" Johnson, the racketeer overlord of Atlantic City, New Jersey, was a Republican stalwart. As such, he avoided prosecution until Franklin Roosevelt became President, at which time he was convicted and imprisoned for tax evasion. (Treasury agents counted the num-ber of towels sent to the laundry from local brothels. They were thus able to determine the number of customers and hence Johnson's income.) (Ibid.: 281)

While the tax weapon was used freely against Roosevelt's political enemies, "Nucky" Johnson as well as Tom Pendergast, James Michael Curley of Bos-ton, and Huey Long, friendly politicians, Frank Hague of Jersey City, and Chicago's Kelly and Nash escaped criminal sanctions (Ibid.: 282).

Chicago and New York were not just isolated cases. In New Orleans Thomas C. Anderson was the saloonkeeper political boss of the Fourth Ward. He was a two-term member of the state legislature and the proprietor of several bor-dellos. Herbert Asbury reports that when Prohibition arrived, instead of en-tering into bootlegging and speak-easies, Anderson went into the oil business, prospered, and was eventually bought out by Standard Oil (1936: 435). In Kansas City, Missouri, James Pendergast began his political career as a sa-loonkeeper (Dorsett, 1968: 4). He became a dominant power in the First Ward, and his ability to "deliver the votes" enabled him to provide police protection to organized gambling by 1895. The police acted on behalf of the gambling combine, forcing independent operators to join or be raided out of business (Ibid.: 23). Lyle Dorsett reports that between 1900 and 1902, Pendergast named 123 of the 173 policemen on the K.C. force (Ibid.: 32). The Pendergast machine, under brother Tom, received the support of the gang bosses, and they in return secured police protection (Ibid.: 128). Like many gangsters, Tom Pendergast was imprisoned for tax evasion in 1939 (Ibid.: 135).

The most significant event in the history of organized crime in the United States is Prohibition.

# PROHIBITION

Herbert Packer reminds us that people do not necessarily respond to new criminal prohibitions by acquiescence. He points out that resistance can be fatal to the new norm, and moreover, when this happens, "the effect is not confined to the immediate proscription but makes itself felt in the attitude that people take toward legal proscriptions in general" (1968: 263). Thus, primary resistance or opposition to a new law, e.g., Prohibition, can result, secondarily, in disregard for laws in general, *negative contagion.* Andrew Sinclair notes what occurred during Prohibition: "A general tolerance of the bootlegger and a disrespect for federal law were translated into a widespread contempt for the processes and duties of democracy" (1962: 282).

The Eighteenth Amendment to the Constitution, ratified by the thirty-sixth state, Nebraska, on January 16, 1919, provided:

> *Section 1.* After one year from the ratification of this article the manufacture, sale, or transportation of intoxicating liquors within, the importation thereof into, or the exportation thereof from the United States and all territory subject to the jurisdiction thereof for beverage purposes is hereby prohibited.
> *Section 2.* The Congress and the several States shall have concurrent power to enforce this article by appropriate legislation.
> *Section 3.* This article shall be inoperative unless it shall have been ratified as an amendment to the Constitution by the legislatures of the several States, as provided in the Constitution, within seven years from the date of the submission hereof to the States by the Congress.

Ten months after ratification, over the veto of President Wilson, Congress passed the National Prohibition Act, usually referred to as the Volstead Act after its sponsor, Congressman Andrew Volstead of Minnesota. The Volstead Act strengthened the language of the amendment and provided for federal enforcement; the Prohibition Bureau, an arm of the Treasury Department, was created. The bureau soon became notorious for employing agents on the basis of political patronage, persons who were untrained and often unfit. In addition to being inefficient and corrupt, they ran up a record of being killed (by 1923 thirty had been murdered) and for killing hundreds of civilians, often innocent women and children. The bureau was viewed as a training school for bootleggers because agents often left the service to join their wealthy enemies. The Treasury Department was headed by Secretary Andrew Mellon, a man who had millions invested in the liquor trade before Prohibition and was not interested in enforcing the new laws (Sinclair, 1962: 184–189).

In the ninety days preceding the date when the Eighteenth Amendment became effective, $500,000 worth of bonded whiskey was stolen from government warehouses, and afterwards it continued to disappear (Sinclair, 1962: 176). Thomas Coffey reports that less than one hour after Prohibition went into effect, six armed men robbed $100,000 worth of whiskey from two Chicago boxcars (1975: 7). He also notes that in February of 1920, a case of whiskey purchased in Montreal for ten dollars could easily be sold in New York City for eighty dollars (1975: 22–23). In fact, the Canadians began making so much money from American Prohibition, that provinces that had similar laws soon repealed them (Sinclair, 1962: 197–198).

William Chambliss states that Prohibition was accomplished by the political efforts of an economically declining segment of the American middle-class: "By effort and some good luck this class was able to impose its will on the majority of the population through rather dramatic changes in the law" (1973: 10).* Sinclair states: "In fact, national prohibition was a measure passed by village America against urban America" (1962: 163). Coffey writes: "The nation's smaller towns observed the end of legal liquor with more celebration in the churches than in the saloons. Thousands of Protestant churches held thanksgiving prayer meetings. To many of the people who attended, prohibition represented the triumph of America's towns and rural districts over the sinful cities" (1975: 7). Most dramatically, Prohibition pitted a white Protestant rural population against the Catholics, Jews, and blacks that populated America's urban areas.

While America had organized crime before Prohibition, it "was intimately associated with shabby local politics and corrupt police forces"; there was not organized crime activity "in the syndicate style" (King, 1969: 23). The "Great Experiment" provided a catalyst of opportunity that caused organized crime, an especially violent form, to blossom into an important force in American society. Herbert Block and Gilbert Geis note: "There is rather complete agreement that organized crime became a significant phenomenon on the American scene in 1920, after the advent of Prohibition" (1962: 222).

## Chicago

Humbert Nelli traces the origins of organized crime in Chicago to the election of 1873 in which Michael Cassius McDonald backed Harvey Colvin (1969: 383): "In the mayoralty election of 1873, Mike McDonald, the gambling boss of Chicago, demonstrated that under effective leadership the gamblers, liquor interests, and brothel keepers could be welded into a formidable political power" (Peterson, 1963: 31). The excesses permitted under Colvin resulted in the election of a reform mayor in 1876, Republican Monroe Heath. McDonald reorganized, and in 1879 Democrats were swept back into office with Carter Henry Harrison being elected mayor (Smith, 1962: 142). Peterson states that in the years that followed, Chicago's first real political machine was created, and "crime became organized as never before" (1963: 31).

"King Mike" McDonald was a prosperous gambling entrepreneur, who, in addition to controlling the bookmaking syndicate in Chicago (Smith, 1962: 142), owned "The Store," which offered not only gambling but politics. The

* On December 5, 1933, Utah became the thirty-sixth state to vote for the Twenty-First Amendment which repealed Prohibition.

"King" controlled mayors, senators, and congressmen; his newspaper, the *Globe,* often influenced elections, and he also owned the elevated railroad line in Chicago (Wendt and Kogan, 1943: 27). McDonald's "Store" was located in the Levee, Chicago's notorious vice district in the First Ward. The "Lords of the Levee," originally with McDonald's approval, were the "Mutt and Jeff" team of John ("Bathhouse") Coughlin, a powerfully built six-footer, and Michael ("Hinky Dink") Kenna, a diminutive organizational genius. Born in 1860, Coughlin began his career as a rubber in the exclusive Palmer House baths, where he met the wealthy and the powerful. These contacts helped him when he opened his own bathhouse, and soon others (Wendt and Kogan, 1943: 16–18). Among his friends and customers were politicians, and he soon became a Democratic captain. On April 5, 1892, he was elected alderman from the First Ward, one of thirty-five into which the city was divided (Wendt and Kogan, 1943: 19). The city council into which "Bathhouse," a nickname he enjoyed, entered was literally selling out the city of Chicago. The "boodles," schemes through which city privileges were "sold," made the three-dollar-a-meeting alderman's position quite lucrative (Wendt and Kogan, 1943: 34–35).

Coughlin joined up with "Hinky Dink" Kenna, who was nicknamed after the waterhole he swam in as a youngster. Kenna was born in the First Ward in 1858, and from being a hard-working newsboy succeeded as a successful saloonkeeper and politician (Wendt and Kogan, 1943: 75). Kenna was responsible for establishing a defense fund to which brothel keepers and gamblers contributed to secure the services of Kenna's lawyers, who were on retainer (Ibid.: 79). Eventually, as their power grew, it was necessary to be "licensed" by the Kenna-Coughlin team to do business in the Levee. Their ability to deliver votes was a mainstay—whether it was for their favorite mayoral candidate or for themselves; Kenna eventually joined Coughlin as an alderman in the council. In 1897 the pair skillfully engineered the Democratic nomination for Carter Henry Harrison (the younger) whose father had been killed while he was mayor by a disgruntled job-seeker. In the First Ward, the team delivered a five-to-one vote for Harrison (Ibid.: 169). Their election techniques included the use of the Quincy Street Boys, a gang of vicious thugs who provided election day "services." Kenna was also something of a humanitarian; he provided food and lodging to men made destitute during a depression. During election campaigns these thankful men were brought into the First Ward where they registered and voted for the Kenna-Coughlin candidates (Ibid.: 91; 102–108).

Despite reform efforts in Chicago, Mayor Harrison left the First Ward alone, that is until Kenna and Coughlin balked at supporting some of his candidates. Harrison then authorized a special Morals Squad which invaded the Levee (the local police were ruled by Kenna). His move against the First Ward did not put Kenna and Coughlin out of business, but it did cost him reelection in 1915, a year when William Hale ("Big Bill") Thompson, a Republican, was elected mayor (Ibid.: 325–327).

The rise of Kenna and Coughlin coincided with the decline of McDonald. He had grown rich, and by the time he died in 1907 his interest in ward politics had dwindled. Mont Tennes, who had dominated gambling on Chicago's North Side, took over McDonald's bookmaking operations.

## MONT TENNES

In 1929, John Landesco, an investigator for the Illinois Association for Criminal Justice, a civic organization, wrote: "The complete life history of one man, were it known in every detail, would disclose practically all there is to know about syndicated gambling as a phase of organized crime in Chicago in the last quarter century. That man is Mont Tennes" (1929: 45). In 1907, Tennes secured control of the wire service that transmitted race results, and every bookmaker depended on the service. Without the wire service a bookmaker is vulnerable to "past–posting"—placing a bet after the race is already over and the winner determined. The swindler sets up a relay system that transmits the results of a race to a confederate, who quickly places a bet on a horse that has already won. The bookmaker accepts the bet because regular channels have not informed him that the race has even started.

When some bookmakers balked at paying Tennes for the service, an outbreak of violence and police raids ensued. While walking with his wife, Tennes was attacked and badly beaten. Bombings and police raids on gamblers who refused to pay Tennes followed. By January 1909, Tennes had an absolute control over race track gambling and hand books in Chicago. "The Tennes ring at this time established systematic exclusion. Anyone wishing to enter the gambling business had to apply to the ring. The man and the location would be investigated, the leading gamblers in the city would be asked to approve the applicant, and if disapproved he would be placed upon the 'dead list' " (Landesco, 1929: 54). Tennes paid the Payne Telegraph Service of Cincinnati, politicians, and the police, and gamblers who paid Tennes received race results and protection from raids. The Tennes syndicate paid half of the money lost to bettors who won from bookmakers and received fifty percent of net receipts after racing sheets were balanced each day. Tennes agents made the rounds of subscribers checking betting sheets (1929: 50–51). When Tennes encountered legal difficulties, he was represented by Clarence Darrow (Ibid., 71).

In 1911, a struggle ensued between the Payne News Service and a company founded by Tennes, the General News Bureau. Disclosures resulting from this feud revealed that Tennes "had risen from king of the Chicago gamblers to czar of all the race track gambling in the United States and Canada" (Landesco, 1929: 59). His combine had a grip on the police in twenty American cities and enforced its dictates with dynamite. Cities from New York to San Francisco, Detroit to San Antonio paid for the Tennes wire service, which involved eighteen telephone and telegraph companies (Landesco, 1929: 59).

With the advent of Prohibition, the level of violence in organized crime increased dramatically. Tennes sold his service to both George ("Bugs") Moran and his rival Alphonse ("Scarface Al") Capone. In the end he became an associate of Jimmie Mondi, the Capone organization spokesman for gambling matters. Tennes eventually withdrew from this "shotgun marriage" and finally retired in 1929 (Landesco, 1929: 81–83) a multimillionaire (Smith, 1962: 146). Smith says he retired in 1927.

The election of Big Bill Thompson significantly changed the relationship between politics and organized crime in Chicago. Thompson had promised a "wide-open city," and he delivered—vice operations were permitted throughout the city. Political brokers such as Kenna and Coughlin were no longer needed; the gamblers and brothel keepers dealt directly with city hall (Wendt and Kogan, 1943: 329).

James ("Big Jim" or "Diamond Jim") Colosimo took over in the Levee. Colosimo had arrived from Calabria in 1895 at age seventeen. As a street sweeper in the First Ward, he organized his fellow sweepers into a successful political bloc. He became a power among the Italians in the ward and a precinct captain under Kenna and Coughlin (Nelli, 1969: 385). He later became a "bag man" (collector of bribes) for Kenna and Coughlin, and eventually a successful "white slaver" with a string of brothels and gambling houses (Kobler, 1971: 38–39). In addition, he owned the nationally known restaurant called Colosimo's Cafe which attracted luminaries from society, opera, and the theater —such persons as George M. Cohan and Enrico Caruso (Nelli, 1969: 385).

JOHNNY TORRIO

In 1909, Colosimo brought John Torrio, age 32, to Chicago. John Kobler refers to Torrio as Colosimo's nephew (1971: 46), while Jack McPhaul reports that he was a distant cousin of Victoria Colosimo, Jim's wife and a former madam. She invited Torrio to Chicago to help Jim deal with black hand extortion threats (1970: 74). Torrio did not smoke, gamble, drink, or consort with women (Ibid.: 37); he was, however, the head of the notorious James Street Boys, an affiliate gang of Paul Kelly and his Five Pointers (Ibid.: 42–45). Torrio was also a partner of Frankie Yale (real name Uale) in the saloon business (Ibid.: 51).

Torrio was apparently the right man for the job; shortly after his arrival three black handers were lured into an ambush and shot to death (Ibid.: 79). Torrio began running a brothel for Colosimo and encountered trouble when a white slave victim agreed to testify against him under the recently passed Mann Act, which made it a federal crime to transport someone over a state line for immoral purposes. White slavers had been luring young girls to Chicago with promises of legitimate employment. Upon their arrival they were provided with knock-out drops and removed to brothels. If they objected, they were raped and brutalized; some took their own lives (Ibid.: 94–101). The potential witness against Torrio was in FBI custody when she was murdered (Ibid.: 101–102).

When public opinion in Chicago turned against the red-light district of the Levee, the mayor, Charles Carter Harrison, ordered the police to close the brothels. Torrio moved the Colosimo operations into Burnham, a township of one thousand persons. The mayor and the police chief were put on the payroll (Ibid.: 114–117). Torrio was able to open a series of roadside brothels by bribing both public officials and residents where the brothels were located (Ibid.: 120).

In New York, at a saloon owned by Frankie Yale, nineteen-year-old Alphonse Capone worked as a bouncer. Capone,[2] a Five Pointer, was prone to be somewhat over-exuberant in carrying out his duties—a man died and Yale sent Capone to Torrio in Chicago (Ibid.: 121). Kobler reports that Torrio was actually a godfather to Capone's first child (1971: 32). Capone continued to work as a bouncer, this time at the Torrio Four Deuces, a saloon–gambling house–brothel (McPhaul, 1970: 121). Shortly after his arrival in Chicago, Torrio sent him to teach some etiquette to someone who had had the temerity to slap an important but physically unimposing Torrio aide, Jake Guzik. Temerity turned to outright stupidity; Capone too was insulted, and another man died. Capone fled to Burnham until the witnesses could be convinced of their mistaken identification (Ibid.: 127–28). Torrio began to run Colosimo's operations and gave Capone important responsibilities (Ibid.: 144). Colosimo divorced his wife, and on April 17, 1920, he married Dale Winter (Ibid.: 148).

PROHIBITION

With "the coming of Prohibition, the personnel of organized vice took the lead in the systematic organization of this new and profitable field of exploitation. All the experience gained by years of struggle against reformers and concealed agreements with politicians was brought into service in organizing and distribution of beer and whiskey" (Landesco, 1929: 43). Colosimo, however, was fearful of federal enforcement efforts and wanted to stay away from bootlegging (McPhaul, 1970: 144). On May 11, 1920, he was shot to death. The murderer and the reason for his murder remain unknown. Speculation about the former centers on Frankie Yale. Infatuation with a young bride made Colosimo neglect business, and his murder has been ascribed to a reluctance to take full advantage of the new avenues of profit offered by Prohibition. A second speculation concerns his ex-wife acting out the role of a "woman scorned." McPhaul, however, reports that Victoria had remarried and at the time of Colosimo's death was in Los Angeles visiting her new in-laws (Ibid.: 150). The pallbearers and honorary pallbearers at Colosimo's funeral included ten aldermen, three judges, a congressman, and the Democratic leader of the state legislature (Wendt and Kogan, 1943: 341).

Nelli notes, "After Colosimo's death, Johnny Torrio succeeded to the first ward based Italian 'syndicate' throne, which he occupied until his retirement in 1925. An able and effective leader, Torrio excelled as a master strategist and organizer and quickly built an empire which far exceeded that of his predecessor in wealth, power and influence" (1969: 386). This power is highlighted by an incident in 1921, when he was arrested as a result of the white slavery activities of one of his lieutenants, Jake ("Greasy Thumb") Guzik (also spelled Cusick). Guzik advertised for a housemaid, whom he subsequently imprisoned, had raped, and forced into working in a brothel. She was able to inform her brothers, who rescued her, and Guzik and Torrio were prosecuted. Before a verdict could be reached, the two were pardoned by Governor Len Small. Small had been indicted shortly after he took office, only to be saved by a Torrio enforcer who bribed and intimidated the jurors. The pardon was a reward for Governor Small's acquittal (Kobler, 1971: 72–73).

Other gangs ruled over sections of Chicago, where they combined politics and crime into wealth and power. On Chicago's Northeast Side were the 42nd and 43rd Wards. There Dion O'Banion's gang, which controlled the Irish vote much as Colosimo controlled the Italian, held sway. Despite a sordid background, including several shootings in public view, a banquet was held in O'Banion's honor by the Chicago Democratic Party in 1924. It seems that O'Banion had decided to switch his loyalty to the Republicans; the Democratic mayor at the time was a reformer who actively enforced laws against many of O'Banion's activities. The Democrats made speeches in his honor and even presented him with a platinum watch. It didn't help; O'Banion and the votes of the 42nd and 43rd Wards went to the Republicans (Coffey, 1975: 150). O'Banion was a regular churchgoer and loved flowers. This led him to purchase a florist shop and became "gangdom's" favorite florist.

Landesco points out that the O'Banion gang "lacked the racial cohesion which bound together the dominant element in the Capone gang. O'Banion was Irish; Nails Morton was Jewish; Vincent Drucci was an Italian and Hymie Weiss was a Pole" (1929: 183). Other parts of Chicago also had their gangs: William ("Klondike") O'Donnell and his brothers Myles and Bernard were on the West Side (Landesco, 1929: 86); on the South Side were another group of O'Donnells, Steve, Walter, Thomas, and Spike (Ibid.); also on the West Side were the Druggan-Lake or Valley gang headed by Terry Druggan (Kobler, 1971: 89–90). The Saltis-McErlane gang of the Southwest Side was headed by Joe Saltis and Frank McErlane. The latter was a "compulsive killer," and Saltis is noted for having introduced the Thompson Submachine Gun ("tommy gun") into Chicago. Until the late 1920s, the tommy gun could be freely purchased by mail or in sporting goods stores (Kobler, 1971: 90–92).

On the South Side were Ragen's Colts, whom Landesco selects as examples "of the genuine popularity of the gangster, homegrown in the neighborhood gang, idealized in the morality of the neighborhood" (1929: 169). The gang began as a baseball team with Frank and Mike Ragen as star players. As the Morgan Athletic Club, they participated in amateur football, baseball, and rugby and stood high in their respective leagues. Around their activities centered many of the neighborhood's social events—picnics, dances, and an annual ball supported by business and professional men throughout the neighborhood. In 1908 the club's name was changed to the Ragen Athletic Association, and Frank Ragen remained president. He became a respected political leader and county commissioner and eventually announced his separation from the club. In 1917, the club's New Year's Eve party was attended by over 5000 people. The group prided itself on its patriotism, and 500 members went into the armed forces during World War I. They also participated in race riots.

The Colts became "election specialists" during the years of Prohibition and were used for strong arm work throughout Chicago. They eventually split into factions when various members joined opposite beer-running gangs that were then at war in Chicago. On August 4, 1927, the twelve remaining members met and voted to disband and sell their club headquarters (Landesco, 1929: 169–175).

In the "Little Italy" of Chicago's South Side were the "Terrible Gennas," six brothers known for their brutality but who, like O'Banion, were regular churchgoers (Kobler, 1971: 81–82). Prohibition had enabled them to become quite prosperous by organizing the Italian home stills that proliferated, or were encouraged by the Gennas, in Little Italy, and distributing the spirits with police and political protection (Kobler, 1971: 81–86). Just where politics ended and crime began was not always clear in Chicago, as the history of the "Alderman's War" points out.

## ALDERMAN'S WAR

John Powers ("Johnny de Pow") was the ruler of the Nineteenth Ward since 1888, when the area was predominantly Irish. The influx of Italian immigrants changed the ethnic makeup of the ward; by 1916 the Italians held a majority of votes in the Nineteenth. In that year, Anthony D'Andrea announced that he would oppose Alderman James Bowler, Powers' candidate. D'Andrea was educated at the University of Palermo and was an accomplished linguist. He was president of the International Hod Carriers' Union, and later business agent for the Macaroni Manufacturer's Union as well as president of the Unione Siciliana in Chicago. On February 21, 1916, Frank Lombardi, a Powers ward boss, was shot to death (the Gennas were suspected) in a Taylor Street saloon. D'Andrea lost the election to Bowler, but the war had begun.

In March 1920, in an effort to secure Italian support, Powers had D'Andrea elected in his place as Democratic Committeeman from the Nineteenth Ward. The Supreme Court of Illinois, however, voided the election and Powers regained the post. On September 28, 1920, a bomb exploded on Powers' porch. In 1921, D'Andrea announced that he would seek Powers' post of alderman. Numerous bombings and killings followed as sluggers and gunmen from both sides patrolled the streets. In the end, Powers defeated D'Andrea by 435 votes, but the violence continued. A Powers supporter was shot to death on March 9, 1921, and another was murdered a short time later. The "bloody Nineteenth" remained an armed camp. D'Andrea renounced any further political ambitions in the Nineteenth Ward, but the war went on. Shooting incidents broke out throughout the ward, and finally on May 11, 1921, D'Andrea was shotgunned to death. After his death, two friends who had vowed vengeance for D'Andrea's murder were themselves murdered (Landesco, 1929: 120–125; Kobler, 1971: 85–89).

By 1923 Torrio had expanded his beer operations well beyond his South Side stronghold. He moved out into the Cook County suburbs, and when a location was decided upon, the neighborhood people were canvassed. If they were agreeable, Torrio's agents would provide rewards—a new car, a house redecorated or repaired. The local authorities were then approached and terms were arranged (Allsop, 1968: 45–46). In the suburban city of Cicero (population 50,000), the saloons were associated with Klondike O'Donnell, and the only gambling was with slot machines owned by a local politician. The O'Donnells were opposed to prostitution (at that time), so when Torrio opened a brothel in Cicero, it was promptly raided. He opened a second, and it too was raided. Two days later, at Torrio's direction, a posse of deputy sheriffs entered Cicero and confiscated the slot machines—no whores, no slots! An arrangement was made whereby the slot machines were returned, the O'Donnells continued to handle bootlegging, and Torrio was allowed to operate his bordellos and gambling houses (Ibid.: 58–59).

In 1923, reform hit Chicago and the mayoralty went to a Democrat, William E. Dever, a judge and "by Chicago standards a decent man" (Royko, 1971: 34). He ordered the police to move against the rampant vice in Chicago, but corruption was too deeply engrained to be pushed aside. Kenneth Allsop states that "sporadically and trivially" Dever harassed some liquor deliveries and effected an occasional police raid. Although he was not corrupt, Dever accomplished very little (1968: 201). However, with the Democrats in control of Chicago, the Republicans were fearful of a reform wave that would loosen their hold on the suburban areas of the county. A local Republican leader made a deal with Capone when Torrio was on vacation. In return for helping the Republicans win re-election in Cicero, Torrio would be given a free hand in the city (Ibid.: 59).

### "WHEN YOU SMELL GUNPOWDER YOU'RE IN CICERO"

In the Cicero election of April 1924, the Capone brothers, Al and Frank, led a group of some two hundred Chicago thugs into Cicero. They intimidated, beat, and even killed Democrats who sought to oppose their candidates. Some Cicero officials responded by having a county judge deputize seventy Chicago policemen, who entered Chicago and engaged the Torrio gangsters. The police saw the Capone brothers, Dave Hedlin, and Charley Fischetti standing by the polls with guns in their hands ushering voters inside. In the ensuing shootout Frank Capone was killed, but Joseph Z. Klenha, the Capone candidate, was re-elected mayor of Cicero (Kobler, 1971: 104–114).

Capone moved his headquarters from Chicago and took over the Hawthorne Inn in Cicero, courtesy of Myles O'Donnell and a gunman named James J. Doherty—they opened fire on the owner "while shopping housewives and local tradesmen threw themselves behind cars and into doorways in the horizontal position that was becoming an identifiable posture of Cicero citizens" (Allsop, 1968: 62–63). At the Hawthorne Inn, Capone ruled Cicero with an iron hand. When Mayor Klenha failed to carry out one of his orders, Capone went to city hall where he knocked "His Honor" down the steps and kicked him repeatedly as a policeman strolled by (Ibid.: 64). Mike Royko states that since the Capone organization took over Cicero, it has never completely let go: "It still has its strip of bars where gambling and whoring are unnoticed. The only thing they won't tolerate in Cicero are Negroes" (1971: 34).* The Torrio organization expanded its suburban operations into Forest View, where they intimidated village officials into leaving. With their own chief of police in control, the Torrio organization turned Forest View into one large brothel and gang headquarters (Kobler, 1971: 114–116).

Reform in Chicago had an unexpected consequence; it created an unstable situation that encouraged competitive moves by various gang interests. When Thompson lost to Dever, the system of protection broke down and in the ensuing confusion the South Side O'Donnells began to move. They encroached on Torrio territory, terrorizing saloonkeepers into buying their beer. On September 7, 1923, the O'Donnell sluggers entered the saloon of Joe Kepka and began threatening him. The lights went out, shots rang out, and by the time the police arrived, the O'Donnells were short one young tough. Ten days later two more O'Donnell men were dispatched and the O'Donnells stopped bothering Torrio (Landesco, 1929: 87). This was apparently a wise move. Allsop reports that Capone had under his command an army of 700 men and among them were some of the most proficient gunmen in the country (1968: 57). By 1924 Torrio was the head of a combine of Chicago gang leaders who included:

| | |
|---|---|
| Louie Alterie | Frank McErlane |
| Al Capone | Dan McFall |
| Terry Druggan | Dion O'Bannion |
| Genna Brothers | West Side O'Donnells |
| Frankie Lake | Walter Stevens |
| Dan McCarthy | Hymie Weiss |

John Landesco reported that in a feudal arrangement bootlegging was divided among the gangs, and Torrio acted as an arbitrator in cases of disputes. The South Side O'Donnells were not included, and they began to move into the territory of the McErlane-Saltis gang, just as they had tried to move in on Torrio several years before (1929: 92).

During the *South Side Beer War* that ensued, the "take 'em for a ride" technique was inaugurated with the murder of Thomas ("Morrie") Keane by McErlane-Saltis men. The war continued into 1928 as Joe Saltis gave his machine gun a "work out," and the O'Donnells suffered most of the losses. Edward ("Spike") O'Donnell escaped several near misses until October 17, 1928, when he was machine gunned to death and the O'Donnells were beaten ("Machine Gun Kills Chicago Mobster," *NYT*, Oct. 18, 1928: 32).

WEST SIDE BEER WAR

In 1924 O'Banion began to feud with the Gennas. Allsop reports that the Gennas moved in on O'Banion territory (1968: 79–80); Kobler reports that

* In 1965 Dr. Martin Luther King, Jr. stated: "We can walk in outer space, but we can't walk in the streets of Cicero without the National Guard." Jim Bishop, noting that shortly after entering Cicero the National Guard retreated, stated: "It was worse. Blacks couldn't march in Cicero *with* the National Guard" (Bishop, 1971: 444).

O'Banion started to sell liquor in Genna territory (1971: 118). In that same year O'Banion swindled Torrio and Capone by selling them his share of a brewery that they all owned jointly for $500,000. O'Banion knew that the Sieben Brewery was about to be raided (Allsop, 1968: 74). Emboldened by the lack of a response from Torrio, mistaking caution for fear, O'Banion went around boasting about what he had done to Torrio.

On November 10, 1924, Albert Anselmi and John Scalise, hired killers, and Mike Genna entered the O'Banion flower shop. O'Banion was busy preparing floral arrangements for the funeral of Mike Merlo, president of the Unione Siciliana, who had died two days before. What the florist did not know was that Merlo had been exerting his influence to keep the Gennas and Torrio from moving against O'Banion. Kobler reports that Merlo abhorred violence and also got along well with O'Banion (1971: 119). Before O'Banion could reach for any of the three guns he always carried, he was shot to death (Allsop, 1968: 86). The war that ensued lasted over four years, ending on St. Valentine's Day, 1929.

The O'Banion forces, under the leadership of Hymie Weiss (real name Earl Wajciechowski), struck back, and in 1925 they narrowly missed killing Capone. Afterwards Capone travelled in a specially built armored Cadillac limousine. To avoid the battle, Torrio pled guilty to a bootlegging charge and was sentenced to a nine-month term to begin five days from sentencing. On January 24, 1925, before he could begin serving the sentence, Torrio was critically wounded by O'Banion gunmen. He recovered from his wounds and retired from Chicago, leaving his organization to Capone (Kobler, 1971: 132).

During the war four of the Genna brothers were killed, three by rival gangsters and one by the police. The remaining brothers fled Chicago (Kobler, 1971: 148–151). While Capone was fighting with Weiss, other problems arose. The West Side O'Donnells began to move in on Capone operations in Cicero (Allsop, 1968: 101). On April 27, 1926, William H. McSwiggin, a twenty-six-year-old assistant state's attorney, stood in front of a Cicero saloon with two members of the West Side O'Donnells. Shortly afterwards a car drove up and a machine gun killed the three men. The murderers were never caught, but Capone was suspected. McSwiggin's reason for being with the gangsters in Cicero has never been determined (Landesco, 1929: 9–23). His murder, however, resulted in a public outcry and raids on Capone's suburban empire by both police and vigilantes. Capone became a fugitive from a federal grand jury, although he eventually surrendered and avoided prosecution (Kobler, 1971: 162–164). On October 11, 1926, Weiss was shot down. Weiss, at age twenty-eight, left an estate of $1,300,000 (Allsop, 1968: 113).

In the midst of the mayhem and murder, a truce was called, and the principals met at a Chicago hotel; according to Allsop (1968: 118) and Kobler (1971: 182) it was the Hotel Sherman. Allsop states that it was on October 20, 1926; Kobler states it was October 21. Landesco states that it took place on October 21 at the Morrison Hotel (1929: 102). Allsop and Kobler agree that the meeting was initiated by Saltis who had pledged loyalty to Capone but was secretly allied with Weiss—and Capone had discovered this double-cross. Capone, however, wanted peace more than revenge, and the meeting, quite extraordinary even for Chicago, took place. The gang chieftains divided up the city of Chicago. Receiving the largest shares were the Capone organization and the O'Banion gang, now headed by Vincent Drucci and George ("Bugs") Moran. Drucci was killed shortly afterwards by the police as they were driving him to the station house for "questioning" (Landesco, 1929: 102–103). Also present were representatives of the McErlane-Saltis gang (both were in jail) and the Sheldon gang now allied with Capone (Ibid.).

The truce lasted seventy days, until a member of the Sheldon gang was killed on orders from Saltis (Allsop, 1968: 121). Sheldon went to Capone to complain; two Saltis men were shot to death in their car. Peace prevailed (Ibid.: 122).

In 1927, running on a pledge to let the liquor flow again in Chicago, Bill Thompson was swept back into office for a third term: "As much as Chicagoans wanted reform, they wanted their bootleg gin more, so after four years of Dever, they returned Thompson to power" (Royko, 1971: 35). During the election campaign the peace treaty of October 21 came apart; there were a number of killings and an attempt on Capone's life. Four hired killers from out-of-town were themselves killed while trying to collect a $50,000 bounty that had been placed on Capone's head by his rivals. They were machine gunned only hours after arriving in Chicago (Kobler, 1971: 194).

The Republican primary election of April 10, 1928, for State's Attorney became known as the "Pineapple Primary" because of the numerous instances of bombings and other forms of violence. In order to guarantee an orderly general election, Frank Loesch, president of the Chicago Crime Commission, a citizen's group, had to appeal to Capone at his headquarters in the Lexington Hotel. Capone rented several entire floors that were lavishly refurnished and stocked with rare wines and liquors, and where the food was prepared by a famous chef (Dobyns, 1932: 5).

> . . . the president of that Commission knew that it would be useless to appeal to the Mayor, the Chief of Police, the State's Attorney or the Sheriff to prevent "hoodlums and cutthroats" from controlling the election of a State's Attorney . . . (Ibid.: 3).

He realized that only Al Capone "had the power to prevent a reign of terror and permit the people to cast their votes without being molested . . ." (Ibid.: 3–4). The appeal was successful; Capone ordered his men away and had the police round up and detain potential "trouble-makers" until the election was over. Loesch reported: "It turned out to be the squarest and the most successful election day in forty years. There was not one complaint, not one election fraud and no threats of trouble all day" (Ibid.: 3). Fletcher Dobyns notes (Ibid.: 4):

> The orderly election and the success of the candidate in whom Mr. Loesch was interested created not a ripple of excitement in Chicago's gangland. It was understood that whatever his intentions might be, he would be powerless. Capone knew this when he agreed to permit the people to elect him.

Prohibition had enabled Capone to rise from the ranks of common thugs to a place in the *Guinness Book of World Records*—highest gross income ever achieved by a private citizen in a single year, $105,000,000 in 1927. During the Depression Capone used some of this money to open soup kitchens where he fed thousands of people daily.

Harold Seidman points out that until 1929, labor racketeering was only a sideline for top gangsters like Capone. However, as the sale of liquor fell off with the onset of the Depression, gang leaders were faced with a restless army of young and violent men who were receiving anywhere from $100–$500 per week (1938: 112). McPhaul reports that Capone also recognized in 1928 that Prohibition would probably only last a few more years; new sources of income would be needed (1970: 241). Capone moved into racketeering on a grand scale. He took over the many rackets then prevalent in Chicago—extortion from Jewish butchers, fish stores, construction industry, garage owners, bakeries, laundries, beauty parlors, dry cleaners, theaters, sports arenas, even bootblacks. In 1928 the state's attorney had listed ninety-one Chicago unions and business associations under gangster control; these gradually came under the control of the Capone organization (Kobler, 1971: 222–223). The gangsters who had controlled racketeering proved no match for the Capone forces in Chicago. It was the same in other cities; in Detroit, for example, the Purple Gang took over labor racketeering through a reign of terror (Seidman, 1938: 117).

In 1928, Capone clashed with Frankie Yale. Kobler states that Capone had discovered that Yale, his one-time boss and president of the Unione Siciliana, and the person responsible for protecting Capone's liquor shipments as they were trucked west to Chicago, was actually behind a series of hijackings. According to Kobler, Yale had also become friends with Capone's enemies, the Aiellos (1971: 213). McPhaul provides a different version. He reports that Capone had been cheating some New York gangsters, especially Yale, over his beer shipments. Both Kobler and McPhaul agree that Yale was responsible for killing a Capone aide sent to spy on Yale in New York, James De Amato. On July 1, 1928, two weeks after De Amato's murder, a black sedan began following Yale's new Lincoln as it moved down a Brooklyn street. As the sedan drew near, shots were fired, and Yale sped off with the sedan in pursuit. The end came with a devastating burst of gunfire that filled Yale's head with bullets and buckshot ("Gangster Shot in Daylight Attack," *NYT*, July 2, 1928: 1). Yale was thirty-five years old (Ibid., 1928: 3).

## ST. VALENTINE'S DAY, 1929

In 1929, while the peace was in effect, at least in theory, Bugs Moran had been hijacking Capone's liquor, which was owned jointly with the Purple Gang. In addition, Pasqualino Lolardo, "a harmless old codger," who had been made president of the Unione Siciliana through Capone's efforts, was murdered by the Aiellos, who were allied with Moran (McPhaul, 1970: 248). Capone gave the orders and went off for a Florida vacation. While Capone was on his vacation, on St. Valentine's Day, seven of Moran's men were lured into a warehouse to await shipment of a load of hijacked liquor. In the meantime, five men, two wearing police uniforms, lined the seven up against the warehouse wall and systematically executed them with machine guns. Moran was not in the warehouse at the time, although the "St. Valentine's Day Massacre" had been arranged in his honor (Coffey, 1975: 255–257). The killers were never caught; it was suspected that they were brought in from Detroit or St. Louis where Capone had ties with Egan's Rats. The affair was apparently arranged by a Capone gunman, "Machine-gun Jack" McGurn (real name James De Mora) (Allsop, 1968: 140). (On St. Valentine's Day seven years later, Mc-Gurn was himself machine gunned to death in a Chicago bowling alley. The killers left a Valentine card.) For a long time it was generally believed that *real* policemen were the actual killers (Kobler, 1971: 235–242). In any event, while the wrath of Bugs Moran continued, his gang withered. Moran returned to more conventional crime; in 1946 he was sent to prison for robbing a tavern employee of $10,000 near Dayton, Ohio. He was released after ten years, and several days later was arrested for bank robbery. On February 26, 1957, the *NYT* reported that Moran died while serving his sentence in the federal penitentiary in Leavenworth, Kansas (" 'Bugs' Moran Dies in Federal Prison," *NYT,* Feb. 26, 1957: 59). (Less than two months later, Johnny Torrio suffered a heart attack while in a barber's chair in Brooklyn, and on April 16 he died. His death went unnoticed by the media until May 8 when the *New York Times* ran the story. The *NYT* noted that Torrio had been sentenced for income tax fraud in 1939, and had been released from prison in 1941. At the time of his death he was described as a real estate dealer. "Johnny Torrio, Ex-Public Enemy 1, Dies; Made Al Capone Boss of the Underworld," *NYT,* May 8, 1957: 32.)

McPhaul reports that gangsters in New York resented the activities of Capone, activities that generated a great deal of media coverage and governmental scrutiny; the murder of Frankie Yale was a final outrage (1970: 228). Johnny Torrio, acting on behalf of a syndicate of eastern gangsters, "ordered" Capone to a meeting in Atlantic City, New Jersey. The meeting included Frank Costello, Lucky Luciano, Bugsy Siegel, Meyer Lansky, Joe Adonis, and Longy Zwillman (Ibid.: 252). At the meeting Capone was "ordered" to take the "heat" off by going to jail. McPhaul states that it was not fear of the important gangsters arrayed against him that caused Capone to comply, but his respect for Torrio (Ibid.). This is the version reported in the *Chicago Tribune* which had Jake Lingle, a Capone intimate, as a reporter. Jake also served as an intermediary between gangsters and officials, a lucrative but dangerous business. On June 9, 1930, he was shot to death while wearing a diamond-studded belt buckle given to him by Capone (Ibid.: 256). Kobler reports that the meeting, which took place from May 13 through May 16, 1930, was attended by more than thirty gangsters—in addition to those already mentioned were Nitti, Rio, McErlane, and Saltis of Chicago; Max ("Boo Boo") Hoff, Sam Lazar, and Charles Schwartz of Philadelphia; Dutch Schultz of New York; and from Atlantic City itself, Enoch J. ("Nucky"—short for "Knuckles") Johnson

(1971: 246). Hank Messick adds the following (1973: 38, 59): Lepke Buchalter, Larry Fay, and Frank Erikson of New York; Lou Rothkopf and Moe Dalitz of Cleveland; Joe Bernstein of Detroit; King Solomon of Boston; Nig Rosen of Philadelphia; and John Lazia of Kansas City. Kobler maintains that going to jail was Capone's idea, to let things "cool off" in Chicago. In either event, Capone arranged to be arrested in Philadephia for possessing a firearm. He received an unexpectedly long sentence, one year, and was released, with time off for good behavior, on March 17, 1930 (Kobler, 1971: 251).

Out of this meeting we could anticipate the development of a national confederation, or "syndicate," "cabal"; or later when the ethnic make-up of organized crime changed significantly, "Mafia" and "Cosa Nostra."

### CAPONE'S DOWNFALL

The Depression severely reduced the income of the Capone organization. In addition, a special team of federal investigators headed by Elliot Ness and dubbed the Untouchables, began moving against Capone distillaries, breweries, and liquor shipments (Kobler, 1971: 253). The most important event for Capone, however, was a United States Supreme Court decision (*United States v. Sullivan* 274 U.S. 259), handed down in 1927, that stated that even unlawful income was subject to income taxes, the Fifth Amendment guarantee against self-incrimination notwithstanding. The Internal Revenue Service began to move against Capone and his organization. His brother Ralph was convicted of income tax evasion and received a three-year prison sentence; Frank ("The Enforcer") Nitti received an eighteen-month sentence; Sam Guzik received one year, while brother Jake was sentenced to a term of five years (Horne, 1932).

In 1931, Big Bill Thompson lost to Anton ("Tony") Cermak, an immigrant who had been born in Prague and had worked in the coal mines of Illinois. Cermak moved to Chicago where he obtained a job as a railroad brakeman, and became active in politics. He was elected to the legislature, the City Council, bailiff of the Municipal Court, president of the Cook County Board, and by 1929 he was head of the Democratic organization of Cook County and a wealthy man. Mike Royko notes that Cermak, political leader of the Bohemian community in Chicago, "had sense to count up all the Irish votes, then he counted all the Italians, Jews, Germans, Poles and Bohemians." Cermak concluded that the Irish domination of Chicago politics did not make numerical sense. He organized, instead, an ethnically-balanced slate of candidates and put together "the most powerful political machine in Chicago history" (Royko, 1971: 36). That machine still dominates Chicago politics. Harold Gosnell reports that Cermak was deeply involved with bootlegging interests, and Allsop states that while Thompson's organization was corrupt, Cermak "systematized grand larceny" (1968: 217). Fletcher Dobyns reported that Cermak reached his position of wealth and power by joining with a group of men who "organized the denizens of the underworld and their patrons, political job holders and their dependents and friends, those seeking special privileges and immunities, and grafters of every type; they engaged in political sabotage and entered into bipartisan deals and alliances" (1932: ix).

With Prohibition coming to an end and Capone standing trial for income tax evasion, the time was opportune: "So while the Federal authorities were bending all their energies to rid Chicago of Capone, the city's mayor, with other gang bosses and political leaders, was plotting to fill the vacuum created with an even more efficiently organized gambling syndicate" (Allsop, 1968: 219). Capone, who had supported Thompson, found himself the target of city enforcement efforts (Kobler, 1971: 306). The police acted as "muscle" for gangster Ted Newberry who allegedly offered $15,000 for the killing of Frank Nitti, Capone's second-in-command. Two detectives, apparently trying to collect the bounty, raided Nitti's office. In an exchange of gunfire that followed, Nitti and one detective were wounded. During subsequent legal proceedings Nitti went free, and a detective, who had been tried and acquitted, was fired from the police force (Allsop, 1968: 220). Newberry was not as fortunate; his body was discovered in a ditch in Indiana (Ibid.).

On February 15, 1933, Cermak was sitting with President-elect Roosevelt on a Miami speaker's platform. Guiseppe Zangara, an Italian immigrant residing in Hackensack, New Jersey, opened fire at the platform. He managed to discharge five rounds before being seized. Five persons were wounded, including Cermak, who died several days later. Zangara was quoted as saying, shortly after he was arrested, "I'd kill every president." On his clothing he had several local newspaper clippings announcing Roosevelt's visit to Miami (Hagerty, 1933: 1). Investigations into the incident revealed no evidence tying Zangara with any group, and it is generally believed that Roosevelt was the assassin's real target. Roger ("The Terrible") Touhy (1959), a Chicago bootlegger, maintains that it was not Zangara, but a Capone gunman, firing at the same time, who killed Cermak. August Bequai states that on his deathbed Zangara "told the authorities that the syndicate had ordered the mayor's assassination" (1978: 38). Royko refers to Zangara as a would-be "mad" presidential assassin, and this is the generally accepted view (1971: 36).

The tax evasion case against Capone originated in 1929. The Special Intelligence Unit of the Treasury Department was formed by Elmer Lincoln Irey in 1920, when he was 31 (Spiering, 1976: 44–45). It was a low-key agency as contrasted with the publicity-seeking FBI. In 1929, Secretary of the Treasury Andrew Mellon, acting under pressure from President Hoover, directed Irey to investigate Capone, since J. Edgar Hoover was apparently unwilling to take on Capone—the risk of failure was too high (Ibid.: 45–46). Frank Wilson, a nearsighted Special Agent who never carried a firearm, was put in charge of the Capone investigation; he brought Capone down with a pencil. Agents engaged in an extensive investigation, interviewed hundreds of persons, scanned bank records (Capone did not have a personal account) and Western Union records which revealed that while in Florida, Capone was receiving regular payments from Jake Guzik. "Some of the more daring investigators actually joined gangs controlled by Capone in Chicago, Cicero and elsewhere" (Horne, 1932). Capone stood trial for having a net income of $1,038,654 during the years 1924 to 1929. On October 17, 1931, he was found guilty of income tax evasion and received sentences totalling eleven years. On May 3, 1932, his appeals exhausted, Capone entered the federal prison in Atlanta. He was released from prison in 1939, as a result of time off for good behavior, suffering from what is believed to have been an advanced case of venereal disease. On January 26, 1947, the *NYT* reported: "Capone Dead at 48; Dry Era Gang Chief." The story, on page seven, stated that Capone's death was attributed to apoplexy; he had been an invalid for many years before his death.

Al Capone was the subject of a great deal of public admiration and even hero worship. He emphasized the "service" aspect of his activities, proclaiming, "All I do is to satisfy a public demand" (Nelli, 1969: 389). Kobler states, "Ordinary citizens throughout the country tended to accept his own estimate of his activities" (1971: 292).

CAPONE IN PERSPECTIVE. Gosnell states that dishonest, corrupt, and inefficient government was actually promoted by the business and important economic interests in Chicago: "All factions, Republican and Democratic, were the handmaidens of the business interests..." (1937: 8). Dobyns, reporting in 1932, states, "Populous and efficient as the underworld is, it could not wield the influence it does if it were not for its financial and political alliance with the inhabitants of Chicago's upper world."

> The vast sums of money which gangsters use to control elections and bribe public officials are poured into their hands by the patrons of gamblers, prostitutes, dope sellers, bootleggers, smugglers, and racketeers. Gangsters, job hunters, from mayor to day laborer, and grafters, from millionaire social leaders seeking franchises, contracts and escape from taxation, down to the pettiest parasites, are organized into an invincible, political army, the object of which is to elect public officials who will permit each of its members to carry on his particular racket unmolested.
>
> The deal is that the underworld shall have a "liberal government" and a "wide open town" and its upper world allies shall be permitted to plunder the public treasury and appropriate wealth belonging to the people. (1932: 15)

Allsop concludes that the enormity of the piracy by public officials and businessmen in Chicago, businessmen such as Samuel Insull and Charles T. Yerkes, placed the bootlegger and the gangster "in a state of relative grace" (1968: 244).

CHICAGO AFTER CAPONE

Frank Nitti succeeded Al Capone and, with the assistance of Jake Guzik, Al's brothers Ralph and Matt, his cousins Charles and Rocco Fischetti, Murray ("The Camel") Humphreys, Anthony Capezio, Paul De Lucia (better known as Paul "The Waiter" Ricca), and Anthony ("Joe Batters") Accardo, ran the Capone organization. In 1943, Nitti, fearing prosecution for extortion, apparently committed suicide. He had been involved in a scheme with Willie Bioff and George Browne extorting money from theater chains.

Bioff was a Chicago racketeer who had specialized in shakedowns of kosher butchers. He went into partnership with Browne, a local official of the International Alliance of Theatrical Stage Employees (IATSE) whose members also included motion picture projectionists and other movie theater employees. The two began extorting money from theater chains under the threat of labor trouble. Nitti soon "muscled in" on the racket as a 50 percent and eventually 75 percent partner (Nelli, 1976: 248). In 1932, Browne had unsuccessfully run for the presidency of the international union. In 1934, with the backing of Nitti, Browne received help from Lucky Luciano and Lepke Buchalter of New York, and Longie Zwillman of New Jersey; he was elected president (Nelli, 1976: 249). Malcolm Johnson states that the convention in Louisville that elected Browne was pervaded with "such an atmosphere of intimidation that opposition wilted" (1972: 329). Browne appointed Bioff to a union position and the two increased their extortion activities, this time on a nationwide scale. They were able to extort money from Hollywood film studios such as Twentieth Century-Fox and RKO under the threat of closing down theaters throughout the country (Johnson, 1972: 332). The scheme came to an end when federal investigators succeeded in prosecuting Bioff for income tax evasion, and eventually Browne and Bioff for extortion. Bioff received a ten-year sentence and Browne was sentenced to eight years. While in prison, both provided evidence against Nitti, Ricca, and other Capone organization members who were convicted and imprisoned [3] (Ibid.: 332–333).

After Nitti's death and Ricca's imprisonment, leadership was assumed by Anthony Accardo, who was joined by Ricca after the latter was paroled in 1947 (Kefauver, 1968: 54–55). His parole, and those of other organization members involved in the Bioff-Browne scheme, was the subject of an investigation by the United States Senate Crime Investigating Committee. The results of the investigation led the Committee Chairman, Estes Kefauver of Tennessee,[4] to declare the paroles as a "shocking abuse of parole powers" (Ibid.). Ironically, in 1978 several aides of Tennessee Governor Ray Blanton were convicted of selling paroles.

WIRE SERVICE WAR.    In the years before, during, and just after the Second World War, another episode in organized crime history occurred, and the picture is not altogether clear. The Nation-Wide Wire Service, owned by Moses ("Moe") Annenberg of Chicago provided racing results that were telegraphed through circuits leased from Western Union. Annenberg had taken over the wire service from Mont Tennes. Jack Lynch, an associate of Tennes, fought the takeover, but eventually sold his share for $750,000. Messick notes that Frank Nitti was paid by Annenberg for "services" rendered in the dispute (1967: 192–193). In 1939, Annenberg was sentenced to federal prison for income tax fraud, and Nation-Wide went out of business. In its place Arthur B. ("Mickey") McBride, a multimillionaire with connections to the Cleveland syndicate,[5] began the Continental Press (Kefauver, 1968: 36–37). Kefauver reports: "Instead of selling 'news' direct to bookies, as National-Wide had done, Continental set up regional 'distributors' to whom it sold this service . . .

Continental gathered the racing news through an elaborate nationwide system and telegraphed this information to its distributors." They in turn provided it to bookmakers (1968: 38). Kefauver maintains that the distributors were merely dummy operators designed to protect Continental from federal prosecution (1968: 39), while William Moore argues that the Kefauver Committee was not able to prove that this was the case (1976: 111–113). In 1942, McBride sold Continental to James Ragen and his son, and sometime later bought back a one-third interest as an investment for his son (Kefauver, 1968: 39).

At this point history becomes a bit clear. Kefauver states that the "Capone mob" wanted to take over Continental, but it was rebuffed by Ragen, "a tough, irascible Irishman who wouldn't play the game. He refused to be 'muscled' " (1968: 40). Moore notes that Kefauver painted a picture of Ragen as an embattled businessman besieged by Capone mobsters. However, Moore notes that the Kefauver Committee received information that Ragen himself was "a tough operator bent on expansion" (1974: 110). In fact, Ragen sought help from the Cleveland syndicate through his ties with McBride (Ibid.: 11). Messick reports that Ragen had good reasons for wanting the help of the Cleveland syndicate. In return for their help in forcing Lynch out of the wire service, the Chicago "Outfit" used the Continental Wire Service free of charge. Ragen wanted them to pay (1967: 195–196). His first move was against bookmaker Hymie Levin, from whom Ragen demanded all profits; he would put Levin on salary. Levin offered 60 percent, and Ragen cut off the wire service. Shortly afterwards, on March 20, 1946, the "Outfit" opened its own wire service, the Trans-American Publishing and News Service. Levin secured the wire service from Trans-American (Ibid.: 196).

Messick states that what eventually cost Ragen his life was not his competition with Trans-American, but a critical breach of criminal etiquette. He "squealed" on a former employee, Patrick J. Burns, who had quit Ragen to work for Trans-American. Burns was actually a fugitive who had fled while on trial for assault and robbery (Ibid.: 196–197). According to Kefauver, Ragen also provided information about the "Outfit" to the FBI and prepared an affidavit, to be opened in the event he met an untimely death, for the State's Attorney (1968: 41). On June 24, 1946, Ragen was shotgunned to death on a Chicago street (Ibid.: 44). In May 1947, McBride bought back controlling interest in Continental, and one month later Trans-American went out of business—the "war" was over. Kefauver concluded that McBride had made a deal with the "Outfit" (Ibid.: 44–45).

ENTER SAM GIANCANA.    Virgil Peterson (1962) provides some background on Anthony Accardo. The former bodyguard for Al Capone was born in Chicago in 1906. A member of the Circus Cafe Gang, which later became affiliated with the Capone syndicate, Accardo was successful in avoiding any serious difficulties until 1955, when the Internal Revenue Service expressed dissatisfaction with his tax returns. Since 1940, Accardo had reported over 43 percent of his income as coming from "gambling and miscellaneous sources." The IRS considered this too vague, and prosecution was initiated for income tax violations. Accardo was eventually convicted, but the conviction was later reversed on appeal. Fearing further federal prosecution, Accardo and his aging partner, Paul Ricca, looked for someone else to take over the day-to-day operations of the "Outfit." They turned to Sam Giancana.

Born Gilormo Giangona on May 24, 1908, Giancana was called "Mooney" and "Momo" by law enforcement officials and fellow criminals, an apparent reference to his "crazy" behavior as a young man (Brashler, 1977: 16). Giancana was raised by his immigrant parents in the notorious "Patch," where he became a member of the 42 Gang, a group that even other criminals of that day viewed as crazy (Ibid.: 55). Fellow members of the "42s," such as Sam ("Teets") Battaglia, Felix ("Milwaukee Phil") Alderisio, and Marshall Caifano (legally changed to John M. Marshall), would also gain prominence in the Chicago Outfit (Demaris, 1969: 5). While the gang was periodically involved in politics and union organizing as "muscle," its primary activities centered around conventional and often reckless crime (Brashler, 1977: 56–60). Deaths, via the police or rival criminals, and imprisonment eventually brought an end to the "42s"; Giancana was imprisoned for burglary (Brashler, 1977: 63–66).

Giancana's specialty was being a "wheelman," driving a getaway car. This eventually earned him a position as a chauffeur for Paul Ricca (Brashler, 1977: 72–73). Despite this connection with the Outfit, in 1938 Giancana was convicted of bootlegging and sentenced to Terre Haute. There he met Eddie Jones, a black numbers operator. In 1942, Giancana was released from prison, and Jones financed his entry into the jukebox racket (Brashler, 1977: 97–98). Giancana eventually double-crossed Jones; he had him kidnapped and muscled in on his numbers operation. In 1949, using his connection with Ricca, Giancana influenced the Outfit to take over the Jones' numbers operation and place him, Giancana, in charge. One black numbers operator, Terry Roe, held out, killing several syndicate "torpedoes" (killers) in the process. Eventually, the Outfit succeeded—Roe was killed in a shotgun ambush in 1952: Giancana's control was complete (Brashler, 1977: 106–111).

Money from numbers enabled Giancana to branch out into other enterprises, and his organizational skills allowed him to prosper. Accardo and Ricca, both fearful of federal investigations, placed Giancana in charge of syndicate operations. Brashler comments: "The Chicago outfit had always been run more like a corporation than like a family" (1977: 258). Giancana represented Chicago syndicate interests at the aborted Apalachin conference in 1957.

Giancana lived a rather public social life, something that had become an anathema for the now modernized leaders of organized crime. He had a highly publicized romance with Phyllis McGuire (of the singing McGuire Sisters), a public friendship with Frank Sinatra, and he generated a great deal of publicity by securing an injunction against the FBI's intensive surveillance of his activities. In 1965 he refused to testify in front of a Grand Jury after being given immunity from prosecution, and was imprisoned for contempt from July 1, 1965, until May 31, 1966 (Peterson, 1969: 56). After his release he went into self-imposed exile in Mexico where he remained until he was expelled in 1974. His subsequent return to Chicago was apparently not welcomed by the Outfit; on June 19, 1975, he was shot to death in his home by someone he apparently knew and obviously trusted.

The death of Sam Giancana created a great deal of public interest because of his involvement with the Central Intelligence Agency (CIA). The CIA had apparently contacted Giancana and an associate, John Roselli (who was murdered the following year), in a bizarre plot to use the syndicate to assassinate Fidel Castro (Horrock, Nicholas M., "Roselli Describes His Role in a CIA Plot on Castro," *NYT*, June 25, 1975: 1).

## New York

On September 9, 1923, the *NYT* reminisced about the old breed of gang with its twisted sense of valor, as compared to the current (1923) gang style with "the calculation and efficiency of an industrial tool for breaking strikes or wrecking factories" ("New Gang Methods Replace Those of Eastman's Days," *NYT*, Sept. 9, 1923: Section 9, p. 3). The *NYT* was referring to the demise of the Shirt Tails, Dead Rabbits, Plug Uglies, Bowery Boys, Hudson Dusters, Cherry Hill Gang, Gophers, Five Pointers, and the Whyos. The last gang used printed price lists for mayhem commissions—e.g., punching $2; leg or arm broken $19; murder $100 and up (Asbury, 1928: 227–229). Before he left for Chicago, Al Capone was a member of the Five Pointers, as was Lucky Luciano. These gangs were used by the politicians as "repeaters" and "sluggers," a situation that led the notorious ape-like gang leader Monk Eastman (real name Edward Osterman) to utter: "Say, I cut some ice in this town. Why, I make half the big politicans" ("New Gang Methods"). Andy Logan notes that gangs such as the Whyos were so useful on election day that the politicians made natural alliances with them: "To keep gang members in funds between elections, the politicians found jobs for them in the off-season months." They worked as lookouts, steerers, and bouncers—resident thugs for the gambling houses (1970: 56).

On November 8, 1909, the *NYT* decried the use of gangs for "hired mayhem" and murder, and pointed to their election day "specialties" (White, 1908: 9). Herbert Asbury noted that early in the twentieth century several gangs operating with protection from Tammany Hall (the Manhattan Democratic Party) controlled various city neighborhoods (1928: 252–253). The Five Pointers had 1500 members and was led by Paul Kelly, real name Paolo Vaccarelli. Kelly eventually left the mayhem of lower Manhattan for Harlem (in uptown Manhattan) where he founded the Harlem Branch of the Paul Kelly Association. One of the highlights of New York gang history was the feud between the Kelly and Eastman gangs over a small piece of Manhattan real estate that each claimed as their "turf." When their political patrons insisted that they cease the bloodshed, Kelly and Eastman fought it out in a fracas that lasted two hours and ended in a draw. Eastman was eventually imprisoned, but after his release, served with distinction in the First World War. During that time his gang faded. Because of his performance in the war, Governor Alfred E. Smith re-enfranchised Eastman. He was eventually shot and killed by an old crony after a petty quarrel that followed a Christmas Eve drinking bout. His friend, who at the time was a Prohibition Agent, received a 3–10 year sentence by alleging self-defense—he thought the unarmed Monk Eastman was reaching for a gun (Lee, 1963: 53–54). Kelly eventually became a labor organizer, and with the help of some of his Five Pointers, was made vice-president of the International Longshoreman's Association, a respected public figure.

In Manhattan, New York's richest borough, organized criminal activities were presided over by a three-man board: a representative of Tammany Hall, the police, and Frank Farrell, the bookmaking czar, represented gambling interests. Logan points out that during the years prior to the First World War, the New York City Police Department was more or less a branch of Tammany (1970: 85); indeed, to secure a job as a policeman, a fee of $250 to Tammany was required. Promotions were handled in the same manner (Logan, 1970: 105–106). The police not only tended to be corrupt, but were brutal toward the poor and helpless, as the story of "Clubber" Williams highlights. This vicious and corrupt officer, who rose to the high rank of inspector, told his recruits: "Boys, there's more justice in the end of this nightstick than there is in all the courts in the land" (Ibid.: 106). For $15,000 he effected a transfer to the midtown Manhattan area where lucrative graft was available from gambling establishments and brothels. He told a newspaper reporter: "I've had nothin' but chuck steak for a long time, and now I am going to get a little of the tenderloin" (Connable and Silberfarb, 1967: 215), as this Manhattan section soon became known. Williams was eventually dismissed from the force by Theodore Roosevelt, then a New York City Police Commissioner (Logan, 1970: 107).

Leo Katcher points out that at this time, prior to the First World War, gangsters were merely errand boys for the politicians and the gamblers; they were at the bottom of the heap. The gamblers were under the politicians who were "kings" (1959: 74–75). Gambling was "licensed" by Tammany State Senator Timothy Sullivan with the support of Police Chief "Big Bill" Devery. When Devery's post was abolished by the state legislature, Sullivan notified the city Democratic leader, "Boss" Richard Croker of Tammany Hall, that unless Devery was reappointed to head the police "ten thousand gamblers in the Sullivan-Devery syndicate would make no further campaign contributions to Tammany." Devery was reappointed (Connable and Silberfarb, 1967: 224). When a Tammany alderman, Paddy Divver, opposed brothels in his district, Sullivan organized a primary election fight against him. With Tom Foley as his candidate, Sullivan sent in Monk Eastman and Paul Kelly to beat and intimidate Divver voters; Foley won by a margin of three-to-one (Ibid.: 224–239).

In addition to the likes of Eastman and Kelly, Sullivan used Charles Becker, a New York City police lieutenant in charge of Special (Vice) Squad No. 1, to "muscle" uncooperative gamblers (Ibid.: 250). Sullivan eventually became insane, was committed, escaped, and died on some railroad tracks in Westchester County, New York (Ibid.: 251). In 1911, while Sullivan was ill, Lieutenant Becker moved to take over (Katcher, 1959: 76–77). This takeover ended on July 15, 1912, the day Herman ("Beansy") Rosenthal was murdered. Rosenthal was a well-known gambler and an associate of Tim Sullivan. When his gambling establishment was raided by the ambitious Becker, Rosenthal went to the newspapers and implicated Becker as his partner. He claimed the raid was a "double-cross." This brazen violation of the "code of silence" resulted in the inevitable—Rosenthal's murder. The four gunmen, "Gyp the Blood" Horowitz, "Lefty" Louis Rosenberg, "Whitey" Lewis, and "Dago" Frank Cirofici, were convicted and electrocuted ("Conviction of Becker," *NYT*, Jan. 1, 1913: 12). ("Whitey Lewis" was actually Jacob Seidenscher, a Jew who, like Rosenthal, Horowitz, and Rosenberg, reflected the then current ethnic make-up of organized crime.) Becker was convicted of ordering the murder and became the only American policeman ever put to death by the state (Logan, 1970: 329), and Logan concludes that he was actually innocent, while Katcher (1959) disagrees.

Charles Murphy, another former saloonkeeper, became the Tammany boss. Murphy changed operations: open gambling and prostitution were ended; total immunity for gangsters was withdrawn. He also moved to cut down the power of the police who, like Becker, had challenged the politicians (Katcher, 1959: 95–96). Murphy "concluded that the use of members of the police as major graft collectors was an antiquated concept" (Logan, 1970: 340). Modern organization was needed—a conduit between the politicians and the gamblers who would be organized into a dues-paying trade association as were the brothel owners. Arnold Rothstein was selected as the conduit (Ibid.).

ARNOLD ROTHSTEIN

"A.R." or the "Brain," as Damon Runyon called him, was born in New York in 1882 and served as the inspiration for Meyer Wolfsheim in F. Scott Fitzgerald's *The Great Gatsby* and for Nathan Detroit in the musical *Guys and Dolls*. His father, an Orthodox Jew of immigrant parents, became a successful and respected businessman. Arnold Rothstein was also successful and respected, but his "business" was gambling, bootlegging, drug smuggling, labor racketeering, etc. (Katcher, 1959).

Rothstein worked in poolrooms* and became a "shark," an expert player. The money that he earned was used for usurious loans, and Monk Eastman was employed as a collector (Katcher, 1959: 22–23). He would later employ Waxie Gordon and the Diamond brothers, "Legs" and Eddie (Ibid.: 239). Rothstein began running his own dice games and worked as a collector for a

---

* Poolrooms were places where lottery (pool) tickets were sold. The drawings were held in the evenings, and the owners installed billiard tables to help customers pass the time while waiting for the lottery results (Katcher, 1959: 21).

bookmaker. By 1902 he was booking bets himself (Ibid.: 24–38) and was the owner of a gambling house. For protection he associated with Tim Sullivan (Ibid.: 51–52). Eventually he went into the bail bonds business (Ibid.: 101), insurance, and real estate. He also became the "bookmaker's bookmaker"; by 1914 he handled lay-off bets from other bookmakers (Ibid.: 117, 151). He contracted a crew of thugs for the unions, using a gang led by "Little Augie" Orgen who employed, among others, "Lepke" Buchalter and "Gurrah" Shapiro (Ibid.: 282).

Rothstein also fenced stolen bonds and securities (Ibid.: 165) and when Prohibition arrived organized the importation of liquor from England and Canada. At the same time, he had diamonds and drugs, heroin and cocaine, smuggled in on his whiskey boats, and he established an international drug-smuggling network. His buyers overseas shipped the drugs into the United States where they were distributed to organizations in several states—in Chicago to Torrio-Capone, in Philadelphia to "Nig" Rosen, in Boston to "King" Solomon, and in New York to Buchalter and Lucky Luciano (Ibid.: 293). His power was enormous, as an incident in 1919 indicates. Rothstein had never been convicted of a crime; in 1919 a floating dice game was raided, but someone, apparently Rothstein, fearing that the raiders were actually hold-up men, opened fire and wounded several policemen. The evidence against Rothstein was not very strong, but the case was pursued. New York City Police Inspector Dominick Henry, an honest man working for anti-Tammany mayor John F. Hylan, presented his evidence to a grand jury. The grand jury failed to indict Rothstein, but Inspector Henry was indicted for perjury (Ibid.: 161–62). Needless to say, the police became rather reluctant to tangle with Arnold Rothstein.

Rothstein continued to play the role of "middleman," this time for two of New York's political-crime factions. One faction was headed by James J. Hines, a Tammany renegade with ties to Ownie Madden, Dutch Schultz, Bill Dwyer, Vannie Higgens, and Larry Fay. The other was headed by Albert C. Marinelli, a port warden and Tammany stalwart with ties mainly to Italian gangsters Joe Masseria, Lucky Luciano, Frankie Yale, Frank Costello, Frank Marlow, and Albert Anastasia (Ibid.: 260–264). Alfred Connable and Edward Silberfarb report that during Prohibition nearly half of the Tammany Democratic Clubs were controlled by gangsters (1967: 309). Rothstein was tied to both factions, and did favors for both sides—pistol permits, bail bonds, fencing of stolen merchandise, financing illegal operations, etc. (Ibid.: 264–265). Rothstein is perhaps best remembered by the general public for his alleged involvement in the "Black Sox Scandal," the fixing of the 1919 World Series.

On Sunday night, November 4, 1928, Arnold Rothstein was found staggering in the service entrance of the Park Central Hotel where he resided; he had been shot once in the abdomen with a small caliber gun. Rothstein died without naming the person who shot him, and the murder was never solved. It has been attributed to Rothstein's refusal to pay a gambling debt in excess of $300,000—he maintained that the card game was rigged ("Gamblers Hunted in Rothstein Attack," *NYT,* Nov. 6, 1928: 1). After his death, federal officials opened many of his files. Papers found in his apartment linked Rothstein to what Charles H. Tuttle, the United States Attorney, called "the largest drug ring in the United States" ("Unger Indicted in Drug Conspiracy," *NYT,* Dec. 11, 1928; see also "$4,000,000 Narcotics [cocaine] Seized Here, Traced to Rothstein Ring," *NYT,* Dec. 19, 1928: 1). Tuttle, in 1930, became the Republican candidate for governor of New York. He lost to Franklin Delano Roosevelt primarily because of the issue of Prohibition (Sinclair, 1962: 383). Rothstein left a public estate appraised at $1,757,572; his hidden assets, of course, are not known (Sherwin D. Smith, "35 Years Ago: Arnold Rothstein Was Mysteriously Murdered and Left a Racket Empire Up for Grabs," *NYT Magazine,* Oct. 27, 1963: 96).

## PROHIBITION IN NEW YORK

Andy Logan notes that Prohibition turned gangs into empires (1970: 341). The *NYT* points to the transition made by Arthur Flegenheimer, better known as Dutch Schultz. In 1919 he was sentenced to imprisonment for unlawful entry; by 1933 he was "a wealthy man with widespread interests." He "is the beer baron of the Bronx, with an ambitious eye on the more lucrative territory south of Yorkville that until recently was the undisputed territory of the Madden clique. He owns several speakeasies now, as far down as Seventy-sixth Street on the West Side." In addition, he "is the backer of the bail bonds business, an enterprise which he took over when he found the fees required to get his helpers out of jail was running into real money. He also owns an architectural firm, whose chief business is the reconstruction of abandoned breweries" ("Schultz Product of Dry Law Era," *NYT,* Jan. 22, 1933: 23).

Schultz received protection through Jimmy Hines, especially for his extensive numbers operation: "Hines supplied protection for $1000 a month, but all contacts between Schultz, the numbers bankers, and Hines were made through key intermediaries, like 'Dixie' Davis, Schultz's attorney. When Schultz was killed, Hines ran the numbers banks directly" (Blakey, 1967: 93). The prosecution of Hines was made possible through the use of telephone wiretaps, and his case is cited by G. Robert Blakey as an example of the need for wiretapping in efforts against organized crime (Ibid.). Hines was a key figure in the Democratic party in New York City which was then under the administration of James J. Walker, "Beau James," the playboy mayor. On August 26, 1930, the Appellate Division of the New York State Supreme Court chose Judge Samuel Seabury to investigate the Magistrates (criminal) Courts in the boroughs of the Bronx and Manhattan, the territory of Dutch Schultz. On March 28, 1931, Governor Franklin D. Roosevelt appointed Seabury to head an inquiry into charges against Thomas T. C. Crain, the Manhattan District Attorney. On April 8, 1931, the Joint Legislative Committee to Investigate the Affairs of New York City elected Seabury as its counsel. From 1930 to 1932 Seabury, in these three capacities, held hearings that revealed widespread corruption in New York City government. On September

1, 1932, Mayor Walker resigned. In 1933, reform came to New York City in the guise of Mayor Fiorello La Guardia. However, William Copeland Dodge, Jimmy Hines' handpicked candidate, with the muscle and money of the Schultz organization, was elected Manhattan District Attorney.

At the beginning of Prohibition, Schultz worked for Otto Gass who went from the trucking into the beer business. In 1928 Schultz became a partner with Joe Noe when they became owners of a Bronx speakeasy. They soon bought trucks and garages and became major beer distributors. With a vicious crew of gunmen including John T. Nolan, better known as Legs Diamond, Joseph Rao, the Weinberg brothers, Bo and George, and the Coll brothers, Vincent ("Mad Dog") and Peter, they began to expand into the territory of rival beer producers. In the case of Joe Rock, the Schultz-Noe crew kidnapped him, beat him severely, hung him by his thumbs, and eventually blinded him —a message that was not lost on other recalcitrant racketeers. Rao, however, was gunned down on October 15, 1928.

Schultz expanded into Harlem and Midtown Manhattan until he ran into the area controlled by Irving Wexler, better known as Waxey Gordon. In 1933, warfare finally broke out as Schultz gunmen made an unsuccessful attempt on Gordon's life ("2 Women Wounded As Gangs Open Fire in Upper Broadway," *NYT,* May 25, 1933: 1).

Gordon was another Prohibition success story. In 1933, the *NYT* cited him as an outstanding example of "what the golden opportunities of the prohibition era could do for a man without scruples and anxious to get ahead" ("Gordon Made By Dry Era," *NYT,* Dec. 2, 1933: 6). Born in 1889 in New York's teeming Lower East Side, the son of poor tenement dwellers, Gordon took to the streets (Ibid.). On October 5, 1905, he was arrested for practicing his specialty, picking pockets, and sent to the Elmira Reformatory. He received other convictions for this crime, and finally was sent to Sing Sing Prison for robbery; he was released in 1916 ("Gordon Says He Got Up to $300 a Week," *NYT,* Dec. 1, 1933: 14). Gordon had married the daughter of a rabbi, but his future looked dim ("Gordon Made By Dry Era"). Then came Prohibition, and Gordon teamed up with Max Greenberg, hijacker and member of the St. Louis gang known as Egan's Rats. The two soon had a fleet of rum ships riding the seas and making them rich. Despite Greenberg's murder, Gordon was able to control the beer business in New Jersey and much of New York City. He owned breweries and was one of the largest liquor importers in the East. As befitting a multimillionaire, Gordon lived in a castle, complete with a moat, in southern New Jersey. He owned extensive property in New Jersey and Philadelphia, as well as night clubs and gambling casinos. However, he paid an average of only $33 a year in income taxes from 1928 to 1930 (Schnepper, 1978: 90–91). A second mistake was his apparent feud with Meyer Lansky, who reputedly fed information to the Internal Revenue Service about the sources of Gordon's enormous income (Hammer, 1975: 150–151).

In 1931, apparently worried about federal efforts to prosecute gangsters for tax violations, Gordon paid $35,000 in federal taxes. It was too little, too late. Elmer Irey, head of the Treasury Department's Special Intelligence Unit and the man responsible for heading the successful investigation of Al Capone, began to work on Gordon. Thomas E. Dewey had been appointed interim United States Attorney for the Southern District of New York. Based on Irey's investigation, on November 20, 1933, Gordon was brought to trial; Dewey personally prosecuted the case. Among other items that Dewey was able to prove was that Gordon had spent $36,000 to install a bar in his $6000-a-year apartment; this was during the Depression (Schnepper, 1978: 90–91). It took the jury 51 minutes to find Gordon guilty, and on December 1, 1933, he was sentenced to ten years imprisonment ("Waxey Gordon Guilty; Gets 10 Years, Is Fined $80,000 for Tax Evasion," *NYT*, Dec. 2, 1933: 1).

After Gordon's release from federal custody, Prohibition was over, and Gordon looked for other areas of profit. During the war he was convicted for black market operations (Hammer, 1975: 153), and following the war he was active in heroin trafficking. In 1952 he was one of twenty-three persons indicted in a nationwide narcotics case. On December 13, 1951, he was sentenced in a New York State court for narcotics violations. Under New York's Baume's Law, as a fourth offender, Gordon was sentenced to a term of twenty-five years to life. On April 10, 1952, a federal detainer brought him to Alcatraz to await trial on the federal narcotics charges. On June 24, 1952, while at Alcatraz, Gordon became ill and died in the hospital ("Waxey Gordon Dies in Alcatraz at 63," *NYT*, June 25, 1952: 1).

### THE SCHULTZ-COLL WAR

Schultz took over the numbers in Harlem from several independent black and Hispanic operators, as well as some white numbers bankers. The takeover was apparently engineered by Dixie Davis, who had served as a criminal lawyer representing the numbers operators. With his guidance, Schultz offered political and physical protection, as well as money (several operators had a run of costly bad luck). Eventually, the operators were reduced to being employees of the Schultz organization (Sann, 1971: 150–163). Schultz also moved into labor racketeering, and on January 31, 1934, the *NYT* reported an alliance between officials of the restaurant workers union and the Schultz organization —employees and employers paid for "protection" ("Gang Linked to Union Charged at Trial," *NYT*, Jan. 31, 1934: 8).

In 1931, the Coll brothers moved against Schultz, killing off his drivers and payoff men: "His band of killers would wake the Schultz employees in their homes at the dead of night and kill them in their own bedrooms" (Berger, 1935: 17). In a five-month period in 1931, seven Schultz men were murdered ("Schultz Aid Slain; 7th in Five Months," *NYT*, June 22, 1931: 2). Schultz responded by placing a $50,000 "contract" on Coll and began to return the gunplay ("Woman, 2 Men, Slain As Gang Raids Home in Coll Feud," *NYT*, Feb. 2, 1932: 1). During this feud Coll received his nickname, "Mad Dog." His men opened fire at Joe Rao as he was standing in the street near a group of playing children. Rao escaped injury, but a five-year-old was killed and four other children lay on the ground wounded. Coll was arrested as one of the shooters, but his attorney, Samuel J. Leibowitz, who later became a New York State Supreme Court Judge, disclosed that the witness to the shooting had a criminal record and a history of providing false testimony. Coll went free (O'Connor, 1958: 228).

Another important Prohibition figure would soon play a role in the Schultz-Coll feud. Owen ("Ownie the Killer") Madden was born in England and began his career as head of the Gophers, a notorious and widely feared gang that controlled the area of Manhattan appropriately named "Hell's Kitchen" (O'Connor, 1958: 217). In 1915, Madden was sentenced to Sing Sing Prison for ordering the murder of one of his rivals. In 1923 he was paroled and became a partner with George Jean ("Big Frenchy") de Mange, a bootlegger and speakeasy owner who saw the need for the services that Madden and his Hell's Kitchen stalwarts could provide (O'Connor, 1958: 221–223). Madden became a millionaire during Prohibition, and he continued his operations until 1932, when he was arrested for parole violation and returned to prison. A year later he was reparoled and retired to Hot Springs, Arkansas. There he married and lived out his days in comfort. On April 24, 1965, the front page of the *NYT* reported that Madden, an ex-gangster who gave big contributions to charity, died of chronic emphysema.

In need of money to help finance his campaign against Schultz, Coll kidnapped de Mange and demanded ransom from Madden, who turned over $35,000 for de Mange's safe return (O'Connor, 1958: 226–227). Coll then tried to extort money from Madden by threatening to kidnap him. Instead, Madden joined forces with Schultz in an all-out war against Coll; they divided the city into zones and dispatched their gunmen to find the "Mad Dog." Madden then fled to Florida while Schultz barricaded himself in a bordello surrounded by bodyguards. Finally, one of Coll's bodyguards "fingered" him. On February 8, 1932, Coll stepped into a drugstore phone booth and made a call. As he was busy on the telephone his bodyguard left and two men entered; one carried a tommy gun. They ordered the customers to remain calm and several bursts of machine gun fire entered the phone booth; Coll was almost cut in half by the fire (Ibid.: 229).

With Coll out of the way, Schultz began to experience a new problem, the same one that plagued Capone—the Internal Revenue Service. Schultz went into hiding; he stayed in Harlem watching over business for eighteen months. Paul Sann reports that despite the fact that Schultz was readily available, the wanted man remained at liberty until Henry Morganthau, Jr., Secretary of the Treasury, contacted J. Edgar Hoover and began to pressure Mayor La Guardia: "There was nothing left for Dutch Schultz to do except come in and get it over with" (1971: 212). On November 29, 1934, the front page of the *NYT* reported: "Dutch Schultz Surrenders." He subsequently succeeded in a change of venue, based on his New York City notoriety. His case was moved to Syracuse where the trial ended in a hung jury. The next trial was moved to a small upstate community, Malone, New York. Schultz travelled to Malone in advance of his trial, bought candy and flowers for the children he visited in the hospital, held a grand ball to which he invited the entire town, and generally endeared himself to the good people of Malone. Schultz was acquitted. The presiding judge referred to the verdict as one that "shakes the confidence of law-abiding people in integrity and truth" (Ibid.: 235).

Schultz could not return safely to New York City. The federal government had one or more counts of the original indictment held in abeyance, and to avoid possible double-jeopardy problems, also had Schultz indicted for a series of misdemeanors. In addition, New York State had a warrant outstanding for income tax evasion; Schultz reportedly owed $36,937.18 in back taxes. It was understood that if Schultz could be arrested in New York City, the authorities would be able to institute a prohibitive bail and thus keep him in custody. Schultz travelled to New Jersey and eventually surrendered to authorities. His bail was set at an amount that enabled him to remain at liberty (Ibid.: 236–243). The *NYT* reported that Schultz could not return to New York City "because of Mayor La Guardia's warning that he would be arrested if he returned here" "Schultz Succumbs to Bullet Wounds Without Naming Slayers," Oct. 25, 1935: 1). La Guardia often made outrageous public statements—poor "civil liberties," good politics. Schultz set up headquarters in a Newark tavern.

A SYNDICATE IS FOUNDED

During the eighteen months that Schultz was hiding, a group of important New York and New Jersey gang chieftains formed a combine, possibly under the guidance of Chicago exile Johnny Torrio. (Torrio died in 1957 at age 75.) The *NYT* referred to the combine as the "Big Six," and they were listed as:

Charles Luciana (Lucky Luciano)

Charles "Buck" Siegel (probably Bugsy Siegel)

Meyer Lansky (born Maier Suchowljanky)

Louis "Lefty" Buckhouse (apparently Lepke Buchalter)

Jacob "Gurrah" Shapiro

Abe "Longie" Zwillman (Abner Zwillman of Newark)

The same front page story reported that Johnny Torrio was the new "ruler" of the "Big Six" ("7 Gangsters Seize Dutch Schultz Rackets," *NYT,* Oct. 26, 1935: 1). The list contains many errors in names and associations: Lansky and Siegel operated together as the "Bug and Meyer" gang; Buchalter and Shapiro also worked together, and it is highly unlikely that the members of the new combine would recognize any one person as ruler.

Burton Turkus, an Assistant District Attorney whose prosecutions sent seven members of Murder, Inc. to the electric chair, presents a more accurate list of the "Big Six," and he includes two important figures who were omitted from the *NYT*'s:

Lucky Luciano

Joe Adonis (real name Doto)

Lepke Buchalter and Gurrah Shapiro

Meyer Lansky and Bugsy Siegel

Longie Zwillman and Willie Moretti

Frank Costello (real name Francesco Castiglia) along with Frank Erikson and "Dandy Phil" Kastel

Turkus states that in 1934 Torrio approached the Big Six with the idea of syndication; each boss remained in control of his own territory or rackets, and any disagreements between members would be settled by the combined group sitting as a commission (Turkus and Feder, 1951: 99).

Turkus reports that criminal groups throughout the country followed the lead of the New York-New Jersey syndicate, and "all flocked to the confederacy of crime until it was nationwide" (Ibid.). Hank Messick reports that in 1934 a "national association did emerge." The exact year, he states, can be fixed with accuracy "not because stool pigeons whispered about a meeting in New York or Atlantic City or Miami—but because things began to happen and other things stopped happening" (1967: 140).

The gang wars stopped,* and territories were assigned. "Meyer Lansky was assigned Florida and the Caribbean. His partner Bugsy Siegel, got the Far West, including Nevada." Messick states that assignments were also made according to specialties: Frank Costello received the slot machines, Lepke Buchalter the garment center, Luciano narcotics and prostitution, and Mike ("Trigger Mike") Coppola numbers. The Cleveland syndicate headed by Moe Dalitz, Morris Kleinman, Sam Tucker and Louis Rothkopf were given the Middle West, outside of Illinois where the Capone organization ruled (1967: 142). Messick also adds to the list of New York syndicate members Irving ("Waxey Gordon") Wexler and Bill Dwyer (1967). Dwyer was sent to prison in 1926 as the "alleged head of a $25,000,000 liquor syndicate" ("Dwyer Loses Plea to Delay His Trial," *NYT,* July 7, 1926: 27). On August 13, 1928, he was paroled after serving most of his two-year sentence "for health reasons" ("Dwyer Is Released from Federal Prison," *NYT,* Aug. 14, 1928: 40).

The federal government added other names to the list: Joseph Weiner and the Herbert brothers, Charles and Arthur, the Salinsky brothers, Abe, Frank and Ike, and Ciro Terranova ("Federal Men List Racket 'Big Shots' in Tax Drive Here," *NYT,* May 20, 1935: 1). Terranova, who was known as the "Artichoke King," was a Bronx gangster in the tradition of the "mustaches," although he was nontraditional enough to work with such non-Italians as

---

* Support for this contention is provided by a compilation of statistics on Chicago gangland murders. They indicate a dramatic reduction in the number of gang-related murders in Chicago after 1934 (Peterson, 1969: 131): 1920–1924, 194; 1925–1929, 318; 1930–1934, 229; 1935–1939, 50; 1940–1944, 39; 1945–1949, 37; 1950–1954, 19; 1955–1959, 29; 1960–1964, 47.

Dutch Schultz. Prior to Prohibition he cornered the market on artichokes, a flower-like vegetable widely used in Italian cooking. He was one of the men directly involved in the murder of "Joe the Boss" Masseria. On February 17, 1935, at the age of 46, Terranova was arrested for violating a section of the New York State Penal Code that made it a crime for anyone with a criminal record to associate with another person with a criminal record for unlawful purposes; proving the "unlawful purpose" was the law enforcement problem. However, the law was frequently used to harass organized crime figures and to give the public the impression that the police were active in their efforts against organized crime. As usual, the case against Terranova was dismissed a few hours after his arrest. In the meantime he was forced to participate in a police lineup and questioned about his occupation. The *NYT* noted that Terranova was "dressed nattily in a light blue suit under a Chesterfield overcoat, and he wore a new light blue hat and gray spats." This was during the Depression, and the police noted that he lived in a mansion in the Pelham Manor section of the Bronx. In response to the police query about his occupation, Terranova replied, "None at the present time" (" 'Artichoke King' Seized and Freed," *NYT*, Feb. 17, 1935: 27).

Whatever its original makeup, the syndicate was moving in on Schultz's operations during his trouble with the federal government; it apparently believed that he would be convicted and imprisoned. His return was problematic.

Turkus reports that at Schultz's request the commission, of which Schultz was not a member, held a meeting to discuss the appointment of Thomas E. Dewey whom Schultz considered his nemesis. No decision was made, but at the "Dutchman's" insistence an assassination plan was developed. The "contract" on Dewey went through Albert Anastasia, ganglord of the Brooklyn docks and the patron of a special detail of syndicate killers later dubbed by the newspapers Murder, Inc. However, the commission, following the recommendation of Lepke Buchalter ("The Judge") decided against killing Dewey; killing a prosecutor, it was reasoned, would generate too much "heat." Schultz was incensed and announced that *he* would take care of Dewey (1951: 135–140).

## MURDER, INC.

The killers assigned to prepare for the murder of Dewey were part of a Brooklyn-based ring that worked under a retainer from the syndicate; Albert Anastasia was their steward, and murder contracts were usually passed through him. The ring, which the newspapers eventually called Murder, Inc., originated in 1930 when a gang headed by Abe ("Kid Twist") Reles, with Martin ("Bugsy") Goldstein, joined their former rivals, a gang headed by the Maione brothers, Harry ("Happy") and "Duke." Together they moved against the Shapiro brothers, Meyer, Irving, and Willie, who controlled organized criminal activities in the East New York and Brownsville sections of Brooklyn. In his early moves against the Shapiros, Reles did not do well; he and Goldstein were ambushed and wounded, and a third member was killed. Meyer Shapiro then abducted Reles' girlfriend, whom he beat and raped (Turkus and Feder, 1951: 110–111). The ring grew in strength, however, with persons such as Harry ("Pittsburgh Phil") Strauss, a psychopathic killer, Frank ("Dasher") Abbandando, and Vito Gurino.

During 1930 and 1931 eighteen attempts were made on the life of Meyer Shapiro; all failed. On the nineteenth, Meyer was killed. Then brother Irving, and later Willie, was abducted, severely beaten, and buried alive (Turkus and Feder, 1951: 118–119). The ring took over gambling, loansharking, and prostitution in the East New York, Brownsville, and Ocean Hill sections; their major specialty, however, was contract murder. The "boys from Brooklyn" were used as staff killers by the newly formed syndicate with assignments from all over the country. Their methods were quite efficient—full dress rehearsals; getaway routes checked; a "crash car" followed the stolen vehicle containing the actual killer (in the event of police pursuit); guns were rendered untraceable, although ice picks and ropes were also used. One of the ring's members, who became a government witness, described the contract system (Berger, 1940: 5): "They don't tell you what the job is. Only the top men know the contract." The killer ("trooper") is merely directed to take a plane, car, or train to a certain place to meet "a man." The man points out ("fingers") the victim for the trooper, who kills him when it is convenient. He then leaves town immediately, and when local hoodlums are questioned, their alibis are perfect.

In 1940 several ring members were indicted for the 1933 murder of Alec ("Red") Alpert. The nineteen-year-old had been "convicted" of talking to the authorities. Quite to the surprise of Burton Turkus, chief of the Homicide Bureau in the Brooklyn District Attorney's Office, one of the ring members who agreed to become a government witness was the toughest of the boys from Brooklyn. Abe Reles, upon being granted immunity from prosecution, began to disclose the sensational details of Murder, Inc.

ALBERT ANASTASIA

The conduit between the syndicate and the boys from Brooklyn was born Umberto Anastasio in Tropea, Italy, on September 26, 1902. Anastasio, who entered the United States in 1919, reportedly changed his name to save his family some embarrassment as a result of his 1921 arrest for murdering a fellow longshoreman (Freeman, 1957: 12). His brother, Anthony ("Tough Tony") Anastasio became the official ruler of the Brooklyn waterfront as head of Local 1814 of the International Longshoreman's Association; Albert became the unofficial ruler of these same docks. He was widely feared even among his associates, and reportedly enjoyed the title "Executioner" (Berger, 1957).

In 1923, Anastasia was sentenced to two years imprisonment for possessing a firearm, and in 1955 he served a one-year sentence for income tax evasion. His most serious legal involvement, however, arose when Abe Reles began to inform, and a "perfect case" * was developed against him. That case literally went out the window on November 12, 1941, when Reles fell to his death from the sixth floor of a hotel where he was under "constant police guard." His death remains unexplained, as does the 1951 disappearance of Vincent Mangano, whose position as head of one of New York's crime families Anastasia "inherited."

Anastasia lived in a home along the Palisades in Fort Lee, New Jersey— a home with a seven-foot barbed wire fence, Doberman pinschers, and a bodyguard. On October 25, 1957, Anastasia was in a barber shop getting his hair cut (some accounts say it was a shave). His bodyguard was conveniently absent when two gunmen entered the barber shop, and the "Executioner" was executed. The *NYT* noted that the barber shop was located in the Park Sheraton, which in 1928 was known as the Park Central, the hotel where Arnold Rothstein was killed.

## LEPKE BUCHALTER

The man who vetoed the murder of Thomas E. Dewey was Louis ("Lepke") Buchalter, born February 12, 1897. His father died when Lepke was thirteen, and his destitute mother sent him to live with his older sister. Lepke was arrested and imprisoned several times for burglary. After his release from Sing Sing Prison in 1922, he teamed up with Jacob ("Gurrah") Shapiro, and the two became industrial racketeers. The team worked for "Little Augie" Orgen, whom Shapiro subsequently killed on October 15, 1927 (Turkus and Feder, 1951: 336–337). Buchalter revolutionized industrial racketeering: "Instead of using his sluggers and gunmen to terrorize labor unions during strike periods, Lepke worked them directly into the unions. By threat and by violence they controlled one local after another" (Berger, 1944: 30). Meyer Berger pointed out that the manufacturers who had hired Lepke to deal with the unions "soon found themselves wriggling helplessly in the grip of Lepke's smooth but deadly organization. He moved in on them, as he had on the unions" (Ibid.).

Until 1940 Lepke was the head of an organization that extorted wealth from the garment, leather, fur, baking, and trucking industries in New York City (Ibid.). Turkus estimated his income at between five and ten million dollars annually (1951: Turkus and Feder: 332–346). The death of Salvatore

---

* Mockridge and Prall argue that there was no "perfect case" against Anastasia. They state that then Brooklyn District Attorney William O'Dwyer, in fact, had nothing at all; he never moved against important organized crime figures, even while his office successfully prosecuted lower-echelon Murder, Inc. gunmen (1954: 62–64). Mockridge and. Prall state that Anastasia served in the stateside United States Army during the Second World War while actually a fugitive. The wanted cards and police records on Anastasia were lifted from police files by O'Dwyer's assistant, James J. Moran (1954: 62). O'Dwyer, a former policeman, was elected mayor of New York, according to Mockridge and Prall, with the assistance of Frank Costello (Ibid.: 80). He eventually resigned amid scandal and served as Ambassador to Mexico under President Truman. Moran went to prison for eleven years for a host of criminal charges.

Maranzano, discussed in Chapter Two, was related to Lepke's operations. Maranzano had leased his services to a labor faction opposing a Lepke affiliated group; Lepke called on Luciano, who had Maranzano killed[6] (Turkus and Feder, 1951: 346). Berger notes: "All through the Prohibition era, when other mobsters were splashing headily in alcoholic wealth and getting their names in headlines with a series of competitive killings that strewed urban and suburban landscapes with untidy corpses, Lepke went his quiet way" (1940: 30).

Alan Block presents a slightly different picture of Buchalter's operations. While he notes that Buchalter and Shapiro had their share of successes, they also experienced dramatic setbacks. In 1932, for example, Buchalter and Shapiro were invited into the fur industry where the Protective Fur Dressers Corporation was attempting to put an end to the cutthroat competition that was hurting the businessmen. Buchalter and Shapiro were informed when dealers, dressers, or manufacturers were not "cooperating." Bombings, assaults, acid, and arson were the responses (1975: 93–97). However, the duo had more difficulty dealing with the fur union, and this led to their sudden exit from the fur industry. On April 24, 1933, Buchalter and Shapiro had their thugs stage an attack on the headquarters of the fur workers' union, where a membership meeting was taking place. Although heavily armed, the gangsters were driven out into the street by the irate workers where they were joined by other workers as news of the attack spread. A number of men were killed and several gangsters were severely beaten. Seven gangsters were convicted of felonious assault, and this ended Buchalter's activities in the fur industry (Ibid.: 102–103).

In 1935, at the request of an investigative grand jury, Governor Herbert Lehman, a Democrat, appointed Thomas E. Dewey, a Republican, as a special prosecutor. Dewey began to move against Buchalter, and by 1937 Lepke was in hiding, leaving Emanual ("Mendy") Weiss in charge. In an effort to remove all possible witnesses, Buchalter ordered a murder rampage; the number of persons killed at his direction is estimated at between sixty and eighty (Berger, 1940: 30). Turkus reports that the murder binge backfired, the terror of the killings turned loyal Lepke men into terrified informers seeking police protection (1951: 350). Lepke surrendered on August 1, 1937, according to a prearranged plan, to columnist Walter Winchell and J. Edgar Hoover. There was a $50,000 reward for Buchalter, and reportedly pressure on the syndicate had grown as efforts to capture Lepke intensified. Berger reports that when one of his gunmen killed the wrong person, an innocent music publisher, there was a great public outcry and demand for Buchalter's apprehension (1940: 30). Turkus states that Buchalter had been misled into believing that a deal had been arranged with the authorities, that he would only have to stand trial for federal and not state charges (1951: 360). On January 2, 1940, Buchalter was convicted in federal court of antitrust and narcotic law violations and sentenced to fourteen years. (Block [1975: 179–184] reports that Buchalter's involvement in narcotics was limited to declaring himself in for half the profits of a lucrative narcotics smuggling business, extortion.)

To Buchalter's dismay, he was subsequently turned over to New York authorities and prosecuted by Dewey for extortion, for which he received a sentence of thirty years to life. Then in 1941, he was prosecuted by Turkus for murder, along with Mendy Weiss and Louis Capone. The three were convicted, and after a protracted legal battle, were electrocuted on March 4, 1944. Buchalter has the dubious distinction of being the only major organized crime figure to be executed by the state.

### FRANK COSTELLO

The death of Albert Anastasia has been linked to an attempt on the syndicate's "Prime Minister" (Grutzner, 1969: 29), a title the news media bestowed on Frank Costello. On May 2, 1957, Vincent ("The Chin") Gigante, an easily identified, obese ex-pugilist, fired a revolver at Frank Costello in the lobby of his apartment house. The bullet hit Costello in the head, but caused only a superficial wound. The attempt on Costello was reportedly ordered by Vito Genovese as part of his plan to recapture the largest of New York's crime families. The family had been headed by Lucky Luciano and subsequently Genovese until the latter fled to Italy before World War II (Ibid.). The murder of Anastasia was viewed as an attempt to thwart a retaliatory gang war; he had been a close ally of Costello (Ibid.). At the demise of Anastasia, Costello announced his retirement (Ibid.).

Costello, born January 26, 1891, in the Calabria district of Italy, was christened Francesco Castiglia ("Frank Costello Dies of Coronary at 82; Underworld Leader," *NYT,* Feb. 19, 1972: 1, 21). Like several other Italian criminals, he affected an Irish surname, something that was certainly no hindrance in New York City where the Irish dominated politics. In 1915, he served a ten-month sentence for carrying a concealed weapon. By 1923, he was a successful bootlegger working for Bill Dwyer, an ex-longshoreman turned rumrunner, who brought liquor from Canada across the Great Lakes in armored speed boats (Talese, 1965: 67–68). Costello moved into gambling and eventually became a successful (and legitimate) real estate dealer.

Costello was known as the "King of the Slots" (i.e., slot machines; "one-armed bandits"), and operated extensively in New York City until Mayor Fiorello La Guardia went on a highly publicized campaign to rid New York of "that bum." Many sources (e.g., Talese, 1965) report that Costello was then invited to move his slot machines into New Orleans by the political boss of Louisiana, United States Senator Huey P. Long. Though Costello did move into New Orleans, where he placed Philip ("Dandy Phil") Kastel in charge, Long's connection seems questionable. T. Harry Williams, in his extensively researched biography of "The Kingfish," a name by which Long referred to himself, states that the story is implausible, if not impossible. Costello had informed a federal grand jury that Long had invited him into New Orleans to set up one thousand slot machines for a fee of thirty dollars per machine annually. However, such a set up would require police protection, and Long could not provide it in a city that in 1935 was controlled by Semmes Walmsley, a bitter enemy of the Kingfish. Williams points out that the police in New Orleans "would have rushed to confiscate any machine operating under Long sponsorship" (1969: 865–866).

Costello was noted for his political influence. In one widely reported incident in 1943, a telephone wiretap revealed Thomas A. Aurelio thanking Costello for securing for him the Democratic nomination as a New York Supreme Court judge from Manhattan. Aurelio pledged "undying loyalty" to which "Francesco" responded: "When I tell you something is in the bag, you can rest assured" ("Frank Costello Dies of Coronary at 82," p. 21). Despite a grand jury probe, Aurelio was elected and served with distinction, without any hint of favoritism toward organized crime. Costello, it appears, was motivated more by ethnic than criminal interests. He had broken Irish domination over judicial appointments in Manhattan.

In 1949, Costello was asked to serve as vice-chairman of a Salvation Army fund raising drive. He gladly accepted and held a fund raising party at the Copacabana to which judges and other leading political figures were invited. The party raised $3,500; Costello added $6,500 and sent a check to the Salvation Army for $10,000. However, the newspapers found out about the party, and public reaction was indignant (Talese, 1965: 75).

In 1951, Costello appeared before the Kefauver Committee and was exposed on national television as a major crime figure. For the television viewing audience, however, only Costello's hands were seen; his lawyer had insisted that Costello not be televised. His evasive responses, coupled by a dramatic walkout, eventually led to an eighteen-month term for contempt of the Senate. In 1952, the federal government moved against him for income tax evasion, for which he received a sentence of five years imprisonment in 1954. In 1956, his attorney, the noted criminal lawyer Edward Bennett Williams, proved that the conviction had been based on illegal wiretaps, and Costello was freed (Ibid.: 80–81).

On February 19, 1972, at the age of eighty-two, Costello died of a heart attack. In its obituary, the *NYT* reported that his power continued despite his imprisonment. While on a prison visit, Edward Bennett Williams had mentioned to him that he wanted, but had been unable to purchase, tickets for the hit Broadway musical *My Fair Lady*. Williams reported that that same day, after he had returned home, his doorbell rang: "A broad-shouldered man thrust an envelope in his hands and disappeared"; it contained four tickets for that evening's performance.

## VITO GENOVESE

The man who allegedly ordered the bungled attempt on Costello was described by the news media as the "Boss of Bosses." Vito Genovese was born near Naples on November 27, 1897. At age fifteen he arrived in New York and lived with his family in the Little Italy of downtown Manhattan. Beginning as a street thief, Genovese graduated to working as a collector for the Italian lottery and eventually became an associate of Lucky Luciano. It was Genovese and Luciano who were suspected of arranging the murder of "Joe the Boss" Masseria in 1931.

When his first wife died of tuberculosis in 1931, Genovese stated his intention of marrying Anna Petillo, who was already married. Twelve days after Mr. Petillo was strangled to death, Genovese married the widow Petillo. After twenty years of marriage, however, Anna Genovese sued him for support and denounced Vito in court as a racketeer with a huge income.

Genovese was becoming a power in the syndicate and was making large profits from narcotics. In 1934, however, there was a bungled murder, that of Ferdinand ("The Shadow") Boccia, and Genovese was forced to flee to Italy with $750,000. There he became a confidant of Benito Mussolini until the American invasion. At that time he successfully gained the confidence of the American military authorities for whom he acted as an interpreter. His position enabled him to become a major black marketeer, until he was identified as an American fugitive and returned to the United States. However, a key witness was poisoned while in protective custody, and Genovese went free.

The conclave at Apalachin was reportedly called to discuss the Genovese attempt on Costello and murder of Anastasia—violations of the syndicate Commission rules (Maas, 1969: 261). While the state police raid may have interfered with the order of business, the syndicate bosses apparently took no action against Genovese. The federal government, however, did act. On April 14, 1959, Genovese, along with fourteen others, was sentenced to fifteen years for conspiracy to violate narcotic laws. At the time, Genovese was described as the behind-the-scenes director of a multimillion-dollar drug ring. Vincent Gigante, the man who bungled the attempt on Costello, received a five-year sentence as a Genovese co-defendant (Feinberg, 1959: 1, 15). While serving his fifteen-year sentence, Genovese died on February 14, 1969, at age seventy-one.

SCHULTZ IS MURDERED

On the evening of October 23, 1935, Dutch Schultz entered the Palace Chop House and Tavern in Newark where he had established his headquarters "in exile." With him were his bodyguards Bernard ("Lulu") Rosenkrantz and Abe Landau, as well as Otto ("Abbadabba") Berman, the financial wizard of the Schultz organization. Schultz left the group and entered the men's room; two men suddenly entered the tavern—Charles ("Charlie the Bug") Workman, top killer from Murder, Inc., and the second man believed to be Emanuel ("Mendy") Weiss. The pair opened fire with handguns and a shotgun, and the Schultz men were mortally wounded. Workman went into the men's room and shot Schultz, who died about twenty hours later (Sann, 1971: 23). Less than two hours after the Newark attack, a top Schultz aide, Martin Krompier, was shot and severely wounded in a Manhattan barbershop. Paul Sann states that Krompier handled the numbers and did other important jobs for Schultz (1971: 37–38). The *NYT* reported that the Krompier shooting was connected to the takeover of loansharking operations in Schultz's territory by Luciano,

Buchalter, and Shapiro ("Usury Racket Stirred Gang War," *NYT*, Oct. 25, 1935: 17).

Workman was tried for the Schultz murder six years later, and during his trial suddenly entered a guilty plea. The thirty-four-year-old "Bug" received a life sentence; he was paroled in 1964 and permitted to return to New York under parole supervision. He worked in the garment center for several years until age and illness overcame him. As of this writing he is an invalid in a Long Island nursing home. Despite his condition, the New Jersey parole authorities have refused to discharge Workman from supervision. Weiss was electrocuted with Louis Capone (no relative of Al) and Lepke Buchalter on March 4, 1944. His last words before his execution were "Give my love to my family, and everything" (Feinberg, 1944: 1).

ITALIAN DOMINATION OF ORGANIZED CRIME

As the Second World War drew to an end, the Italian domination of organized crime in New York became quite apparent. The Irish and Jewish criminals of an earlier era were no longer important forces in organized crime. The Italian syndicate in the New York City area was now made up of five families whose lineage could be traced back to the 1930s and the following crime figures:

Lucky Luciano, whose family leadership went to Vito Genovese, Frank Costello, and back to Genovese;

Vincent Mangano, whose disappearance made way for the leadership to pass to Albert Anastasia;

Gaetana Gagliano, who died of natural causes in 1953, with family leadership going to Thomas Lucchese;

Joseph Bonanno, whose leadership ended during the "Banana War," to be discussed shortly; and

Joseph Profaci, whose leadership was challenged by the Gallo brothers, to be discussed shortly, and who was succeeded by Joseph Colombo when Profaci died of cancer in 1962.

Each "boss" has been replaced by other Italians, and "family" continuity appears to be basically intact, although even "new" leadership often qualifies for Social Security. However, as we noted in Chapter Two, younger Italians are moving into positions in organized crime. Some of these men are Sicilian immigrants, and some are "Young Turks," such as the Purple Gang in New York.

AFTER THE WAR

In the years following World War II, many changes took place in the leadership of organized crime in New York. Luciano was deported in 1946, and shortly afterwards he left Italy for Cuba. In 1947, American pressure caused the Cuban government to expel the exiled syndicate leader. Bugsy Siegel was no longer on the New York scene; in 1937 (according to Turkus and Feder, 1951: 270) or 1933 (according to the *NYT*) he went to the Far West and established himself in a host of racket and legitimate gambling activities. With syndicate financing Siegel built the Flamingo Hotel in the only state where gambling was legal. In California he gained control of the union that represented movie extras and began extorting money from the movie industry. Turkus reports that syndicate units in Cleveland, Chicago, and New York sent men to join the Siegel organization, one of the more notorious being Mickey Cohen* (Turkus and Feder, 1951: 272–273). The West Coast gang figure Jack Dragna worked for Siegel, and together they took over the California branch of the Trans-American Wire Service. When the Capone organization took over the wire service from James Ragen, Trans-American was supposed to go out of business. However, Siegel balked and defied his former associates who had financed his Western "expedition" (Turkus and Feder, 1951: 283–288). At midnight, June 20, 1947, patience apparently ended; the *NYT* reported that Benjamin Siegel, one of the "Big Six" in New York, at age forty-two, was hit "by a fusillade of bullets fired through the living room of a Beverly Hills house [home of Virginia Hill] where he was staying" ("Siegel, Gangster, is Slain on Coast," *NYT*, July 22, 1947).

In 1956, Joe Adonis voluntarily accepted deportation and died in Italian exile in 1972. Luciano, likewise, died of a heart attack in Italian exile on January 26, 1962. Adonis had received his start working for the "bootlegger's bootlegger," Bill Dwyer. At the end of Prohibition, Adonis was a millionaire and a power in the syndicate. Born near Naples in 1903, Adonis was the "gentleman of the mob," a handsome, soft-spoken, yet respected boss of a wide variety of criminal and legitimate interests. The latter included the Automatic Conveying Company, a trucking concern that handled 50,000 Ford motor vehicles manufactured at the company's Edgewater, New Jersey, plant. The Adonis firm was the only trucker to which the Interstate Commerce Commission had granted a license to haul cars in the Edgewater area (Turkus and Feder, 1951: 221).

## Meyer Lansky

Despite the distinct ethnic shift in organized crime one key Jewish figure apparently remained influential throughout the periodic shifts and turmoil in

---

* Cohen, in his autobiography, confirms that he was sent to California by Lou Rothkopf of the Cleveland syndicate: "When I was told to come out here and that Benny was out here, I actually wasn't told that I was *fully* under Benny's arm" (1975: 35). Cohen states that he went out to Los Angeles in 1936 or 1937. He reports that Jack Dragna, who had been in charge of California, was not running things well: "The organization had to pour money on to help Dragna at all times. So Benny come out here to get things moving good" (Ibid.: 41).

organized crime. Meyer Lansky was born Maier Suchowljansky in Grodno, at times part of either Poland or Russia, in either 1902 or 1904. His first recorded arrest was on October 24, 1918. Up until that time the various popular sources report he was an honest and hardworking tool and die maker. On that date in 1918 he was arrested for assaulting Lucky Luciano with a crowbar. According to Hank Messick, Lansky was returning home from work, tools in his hand, when he came upon Luciano beating a woman in an alley, as the young (age twelve to fourteen, depending on the source) Benjamin Siegel feebly attempted to stop him; Meyer and the crowbar succeeded. They were all arrested, and Lansky was fined two dollars for disorderly conduct (1973: 20). The judge is reported to have stated to Siegel and Lansky, "You boys have bugs in your heads." Messick notes that Siegel not only kept the nickname, but lived up to it (Ibid.).

Siegel and Lansky became friends and partners. Lansky, to supplement his income as a tool and die maker, and Siegel organized floating dice games. As these grew successful, the duo surrounded themselves with other "starkers" (Yiddish for tough guys); men such as Phil ("Little Farvel") Kovolick, described as a "hulking brute" (Nash, 1975: 195). The "Bug and Meyer" operation came to the attention of one of Joe Masseria's men who unsuccessfully tried to "muscle in." The altercation that followed resulted in Lansky's second arrest and conviction for disorderly conduct; again a two-dollar fine (Messick, 1973: 21). At this point, apparently admiring the feistiness of these Jews, Luciano intervened—he was at the time working for Joe Masseria—and reconciled the differences between the Jewish and Italian gangsters. Throughout his criminal career, Luciano was apparently able to act as an intermediary between Jewish and Italian gangsters, a position that enabled him to gain important stature in organized crime.

Lansky, who had mechanical skills, went into the used car business, servicing and selling stolen vehicles. With the onset of Prohibition, these cars and trucks were used to haul bootleg whiskey, and the "Bug and Meyer" gang supplied the gunmen necessary to protect these valuable shipments. The gang was made up of an impressive group of sluggers and gunmen (Ibid.: 24–26) who were available for various assignments, such as the murder of Salvatore Maranzano.

Lansky, as well as Johnny Torrio and Lucky Luciano, has been credited with being the "father" of a national crime syndicate. While this is still a point of contention, it is clear that at some time in his criminal career, Lansky became noted for his brains as opposed to his brawn. (Physically, Lansky is short and of slight stature.) From head of the notorious "Bug and Meyer" gang, he was elevated to the financial wizard and money-mover for organized crime.*

Lansky's activities in Florida and Cuba have been widely reported. In the

* Donald Cressey states that a "money-mover" is a vital position in the division of tasks in organized crime, "a kind of treasurer;" the money-mover "is an expert who goes into a vague kind of partnership with any family member who needs his expertise." The money-mover is skilled in finances, legal and otherwise (1967: 53–54).

1930s he was able to arrange with Fulgencio Batista for the syndicate to control gambling in Havana. This domination was not broken until Fidel Castro booted both Batista and the syndicate out of Cuba. Lansky moved syndicate gambling interests into the Bahamas and Haiti.

In 1970, fearing an indictment for income tax evasion, Lansky fled to Israel. Pressure on the Israeli government resulted in Lansky's return to the United States in 1972. He continues to remain free, as of this writing, on bail and is considered too ill to stand trial. As late as 1978 Lansky was described "as the most dangerous underworld figure in organized gambling today" (Dorman, 1978: 42). In that same year, however, Jack Anderson reported in his syndicated column on October 11 that "Lansky is an aged relic of a bygone criminal era." His "day is past," and "doctors who examined him at the behest of the Justice Department found him to be in poor physical condition."

PROFACI-GALLO "WAR" *

Joseph Profaci was born in Palermo on October 2, 1897; he came to the United States in 1921 and, until his death from cancer on June 7, 1962, never served a prison term in this country. However, he did manage to owe the United States $1,500,000 in income taxes ("Profaci Dies of Cancer, Led Feuding Brooklyn Mob," *NYT,* June 8, 1962: 32). Profaci owned numerous (at least twenty) legitimate businesses, and was the largest single importer of olive oil in the United States. In addition to his modest Brooklyn home, he owned a luxurious house in Miami Beach and a hunting lodge.

Of the remaining old-line bosses, Profaci was clearly a "mustache," faithful to old world traditions. He was a devoted family man, devoid of any apparent extramarital romantic interests. A religious man, his profession not withstanding, Profaci was a faithful churchgoer, a friend of the pastor, and a large contributor to church charities. One of the churches in the Bensenhurst-Bath Beach section where Profaci lived, had a statue adorned with a crown of jewels worth several thousand dollars. Some reports state that Profaci had been the contributor of this crown. In any event, James ("Bucky") Ammino decided to steal the crown—an outrage that Profaci ordered "corrected." Although the crown was returned, three diamonds were missing; the body of Bucky Ammino was subsequently found, and lest the meaning of his death be misinterpreted, a set of rosary beads was wrapped around his neck.

Profaci's traditionalism was viewed as despotic by some members of his "family"; he demanded a big percentage of all their illegal profits, and he placed "blood" and old friendships above business; old friends and relatives receiver larger shares than the younger men in his ranks. In 1959, a policy

---

* Information in this section not specifically cited is from the following sources: Martin, 1963; Salerno and Tompkins, 1969; the *NYT*; and the author's personal knowledge of the Red Hook section of Brooklyn.

bank owner, Frank ("Frankie Shots") Abbatemarco was murdered on orders from Profaci. The contract was carried out by Joseph ("Joe Jelly") Gioielli, a short, obese, but vicious killer, and a stalwart of the Gallo brothers, a Red Hook gang that was part of the Profaci family. The brothers, Lawrence ("Larry"), Albert ("Kid Blast"), and "Crazy Joey," expected to receive a large share of Abbatemarco gambling interests. Instead, Profaci divided it up among his friends and relatives. The Gallos fumed until February 1961. Then, in one twenty-four-hour period they abducted four of Profaci's closest associates, but Profaci himself evaded capture. What transpired afterwards would rival the Roman plots in the days of the Caesars. Profaci agreed to be more generous with the Gallo faction, However, several Gallo men went over to the Profaci side, and on August 20, 1961, they lured Larry Gallo to the Sahara Lounge in Brooklyn. At an early hour in the morning, before the lounge had opened for business, Carmine ("The Snake") Persico and another man placed a rope around Larry's neck and proceeded to strangle him. A police sergeant came into the lounge apparently only moments before Larry would have expired; he had already lost control of his bowels and bladder. The officer noticed Larry's feet sticking out behind the bar, and he saw two men dash out a side door. His patrolman driver waiting outside attempted to stop them and was shot in the face.

On that same day, Joe Jelly was "put to sleep with the fishes"—his coat was dumped onto the street wrapped around several fresh fish. The "war" was on, but it was a rather one-sided affair; at least twelve men were killed, mostly Gallo loyalists. The gang "took to the mattresses," that is they took refuge in their Red Hook headquarters at 49–51 President Street, a block away from the Union Street 76th Police Precinct House. A special squad of New York City detectives was assigned to maintain surveillance of the area, and it was the police who probably saved the Gallos from being completely wiped out by Profaci gunmen.

In 1962, Profaci died, and his place was taken by Joseph Magliocco, his brother-in-law. Magliocco died of natural causes in December 1963, and was succeeded by Joseph Colombo, Sr. A truce was finally arranged between the two factions in 1964. Ralph Salerno reports that one condition of the truce was that several top Gallo men were "made" (inducted as) members of the "Cosa Nostra" [7] (Salerno and Tompkins, 1969: 143).

During the period when they were "holed up," the Gallos were responsible for saving several neighborhood youngsters from a fire. They became local heroes, and the news media reported extensively on their exploits. On May 11, 1961, in an effort to replenish a dwindling income caused by the "war," Joey Gallo attempted to extort money from the owner of several bars. The victim refused, so Joey performed his best "Richard Widmark," explaining to the businessman that he could meet with an unfortunate "accident." It was no accident that two detectives were in the bar and Gallo received a lengthy prison sentence. In 1968 Larry Gallo died of cancer.

While in prison, Joey continued to "raise hell." He so annoyed fellow inmates in Attica that several of them threw him off a tier. Transferred to another prison, Joey befriended many black inmates, several of whom he recruited for his Brooklyn organization. In May 1971 he was released from prison, and the intrigue reached new heights.

## JOSEPH COLOMBO

There appears to be general agreement over how Joseph Colombo was chosen to succeed Magliocco as head of the Profaci family. There was a plot to kill two other family chieftans, Carlo Gambino (boss of the Anastasia family) and Thomas Lucchese ("Three-Finger Brown," boss of the Gagliano family), and Colombo informed Gambino of the plot. Some accounts say that Colombo was the person who was supposed to effect the murders. Salerno reports that Magliocco and Bonanno were behind the plot (Salerno and Tompkins, 1969: 142), while Gay Talese places responsibility on Magliocco and reports that Bonanno played no part (1971: 89).

In either event, Colombo emerged as boss of the Profaci family. In 1970, he founded the Italian-American Civil Rights League and led in the daily picketing of the New York FBI headquarters, generating a great deal of publicity. Colombo and the League succeeded in having all references to the Mafia or Cosa Nostra deleted from the script of *The Godfather* and the television series *The FBI,* and Attorney General John Mitchell and Governor Nelson Rockefeller ordered their employees to refrain from using such references.

The League raised large sums through dues and testimonial dinners, and held an "Annual Unity Day" rally which drew tens of thousands who listened to speeches by prominent political figures. Reports state that other family bosses did not look favorably on the activity of Colombo and the League, either because Colombo failed to share the financial fruits, or because they themselves resented the publicity—perhaps both. On June 28, 1971, at the Second Annual Unity Day rally, in view of thousands, a lone black man wearing a camera and apparently presenting himself as a newsman, approached Colombo, pulled out a gun, and shot him. The gunman, Jerome A. Johnson, was seized immediately and brought to the ground where he was shot to death. Colombo survived the shooting, but barely. He remained paralyzed until his death.

Interest focused on Jerome Johnson. He was never connected to organized crime, although he had a criminal record and was known as a violent person. The person or persons who shot him are not known (at least to this author). However, suspicion about who was behind the murder immediately centered on Joey Gallo, well-known friend of black criminals. The day after Colombo was shot the *NYT* stated: "When Joseph Gallo was released in May he was reported to have complained that the lot of his faction within the family had not improved much in his absence. He was also said to have questioned Colombo's involvement in the Italian Civil Rights League as drawing undue attention to the family" (Gage, 1971B: 21). Some observers speculate that the entire scenario was part of a script directed by Carlo Gambino as a way of "killing two birds with one stone"; on April 7, 1972, three Colombo family gunmen entered Umberto's Clam House in Lower Manhattan and shot Joey Gallo to death as he was eating with family and friends.

### JOSEPH BONANNO

Salvatore Bonanno left his home in Castellammare del Golfo in 1906 with his wife and son Joseph, who had been born the year earlier. They lived in New York until 1911, when Salvatore was asked to return to Sicily by his brothers in Castellammare. So, at age six, Joseph returned with his family to Sicily where his father was one of the *amici* (mafioso). In 1915, Salvatore died of a heart attack. In 1924, Joseph fled from Mussolini with five *amici,* reached France, and eventually made his way to the United States (Talese, 1971: 84–85).

In the United States Bonanno worked in the Italian lottery and was involved in bootlegging. He joined with Salvatore Maranzano and other Castellammarese in the struggle aganst Joe Masseria. The Bonanno family had been allied with the Maranzano family in Sicily, and young Joseph continued the alliance in America. Talese states that *after* Maranzano's death (Valachi states it was *before*), the top men in Italian crime, Mangano, Gagliano, Profaci, Luciano, and Bonanno, agreed on the establishment of five separate families as part of a syndicate; Bonanno was the youngest "Don" (Ibid.: 194).

In 1963 came the plot against Gambino and Lucchese. In February 1964, while Bonanno was in Canada (he sought, but was denied, Canadian citizenship), the Bonanno family captains elected his son Salvatore (called Bill; born 1932) *consigliere*. The elevation of young Bonanno was opposed from within and without the Bonanno family. This coupled with the plot against Gambino and Lucchese and resulted in a "summons" for Joseph Bonanno to appear before the national commission, of which he was one of the nine members; Bonanno declined (Ibid.: 208–210). On October 21, 1964, Bonanno and his attorney were standing in front of a luxury apartment house in Manhattan when two gunmen forced Bonanno into a car and fired a warning shot at the attorney. Some reports maintain that the abduction was ordered by the commission; others, including federal authorities, declared it a hoax, an effort to avoid appearing before a grand jury investigating organized crime.

During his absence the "Banana War," actually a revolt within the Bonanno crime family, broke out. On January 28, 1966, in an effort to reestablish unity, Bill Bonanno and several family members loyal to his father went to Troutman Street in Brooklyn to meet with Gasper Di Gregorio. Di Gregorio, with the encouragement of the commission, was leading the revolt. The unity meeting turned out to be an ambush, and young Bonanno narrowly escaped (Ibid.: 142–147). On May 18, 1966, Joseph Bonanno reappeared and the war raged on. Di Gregorio eventually withdrew, and the commission turned the family over to Paul Sciacca (Salerno and Tompkins, 1969: 146), who apparently retired a year after the Banana War ended. Talese reports how it ended in 1969: "The feuding factions became so splintered that nobody knew who was on which side. Disillusioned, the elder Bonanno returned to his winter home in Arizona, and Bill settled his family in San Jose" (1971: 478).

## CARMINE GALENTE IS MURDERED *

The ranking member of the Bonanno family at the time of Joseph's forced retirement was Carmine Galente. Galente, however, was serving a twenty-year sentence for narcotics violations. In 1974, Galente was released from federal prison and became boss of the Bonanno family, which officials estimate to have about two hundred members; it is the smallest of the five Italian crime families in New York.

Galente was born on February 21, 1910, in the East Harlem section of New York City. In his younger days he was a street gang member and served a sentence for armed robbery. While on parole in 1943, he was implicated in the murder of Carlo Tresca, a radical, antifascist publisher. Although Galente was never convicted of the crime, speculation at the time was that Vito Genovese, living in self-imposed exile in Italy (he was wanted for murder in the United States), ordered the "hit" at the behest of Mussolini.

On July 12, 1979, while in the back of a restaurant owned by his cousin in the Bushwick section of Brooklyn, Galente, age 69, was shot to death. Three masked men entered the restaurant while a fourth remained in front with a shotgun waving off potential customers. The three gunmen moved within six feet of Galente and fired nineteen rounds from a shotgun and handguns. Galente and two others at his table were killed instantly. A fourth man was severely wounded. The killers escaped. At the time of his death, Galente was appealing a Federal Board of Parole ruling, ordering him back to prison for violating the conditions of his release by associating with known criminals.

In view of the fact that no retaliatory murders have been linked to the Galente slaying, his execution had apparently been "authorized." The police believe that he was killed because he got too greedy, was demanding more than the usual cut, and was encroaching on the operations of other crime families.

## HISTORY, NOW

In Chapter Two we noted that many areas of social and economic mobility that had been available in the nineteenth century were no longer available in the twentieth. By the time the great waves of Jewish and Italian immigration reached America, the West had been settled, the railroads built, and the great family fortunes already established. Instead of a land of opportunity, these immigrants found urban ghetto squalor. In this chapter we reviewed the history of some of these immigrants and their offspring who *innovated* their way up the "queer ladder" into the wider prosperous American society. Thus, Ianni

---

* The information in this section is from news reports that appeared in the *New York Daily News, New York Post, NYT, Village Voice, New York Magazine, Time,* and *Newsweek* immediately after Galente's murder.

can report in 1972 that by the fourth generation the Lupollo family has only four of twenty-seven males in the "family business."

A new wave of immigrants and emigrants, Hispanic and black, have moved into America's urban ghettoes, and they are also in search of the American Dream. However, as the twentieth century closes, avenues of success available earlier in the century are not now available; gambling, liquor, and even certain narcotics (e.g., methadone) are available under state-owned or -regulated monopolies. The political machine that was an integral part of organized crime is a thing of the past; labor unions have lost their zeal for organizing and union membership in private employment sectors has declined. There has been some innovative activity in government health and welfare (poverty) programs, but this is quite an uncertain "market." In short, available avenues for innovation have been barricaded or no longer exist for the ambitious but impatient among the new "immigrant" class of our urban areas. Is there still a "queer ladder" worth climbing?

## ENDNOTES

1.  Nelli (1976: 182) states that the "purge" believed by New York criminals to have taken place nationwide "applied only to that city and [the murders] were not repeated elsewhere." He notes: "In the Maranzano case the message stated clearly that any oldtimers still permitted to live had better accept and adjust to the new order." Indeed, the murder of some thirty to forty top Sicilian gangsters within a forty-eight-hour period seems quite outrageous on its face for several reasons:
    1.  It took at least four men to kill Maranzano (and he was unarmed), and many more had to know of the plot. To kill forty tough Sicilian gangsters who were often armed, cautious, and accompanied by trusted bodyguards, would have required a conspiracy involving hundreds of persons.
    2.  If only one person informed, the "purge" would have been aborted, the proposed victims would have gone into hiding or barricaded themselves, or perhaps they would have struck preemptively at the assassins.

    The *NYT* did not note the apparent significance of the Maranzano murder. Although it was a front page story on September 11, 1931, the focus was on alien smuggling. The article, "Gang Kills Suspect in Alien Smuggling," reported that the murder has resulted in "startling disclosures regarding the operators of a nationwide ring of alien smugglers."
2.  Al Capone's place of birth is the subject of debate; in addition to Brooklyn, various parts of Italy, other than Sicily, are mentioned (Albini, 1971: 7). Allsop maintains that he was born in Castel Amara, near Rome, on January 6, 1895 (1968: 40). The *NYT* states that he was born in Naples on January 17, 1899 ("Capone Dead at 48; Dry Era Gang Chief," Jan. 26, 1947: 7).
3.  Bioff changed his name to William Nelson and eventually settled in Phoenix, Arizona. There he gained public notice as a result of his friend-

ship with Senator Barry Goldwater. On November 4, 1955, Bioff was killed when the dynamite bomb wired to the starter of his pick-up truck exploded. The murder has never been solved (Reid and Demaris, 1964: 42–43).

4.  The "Kefauver Committee" lasted from May 10, 1950, until May 1, 1951, and held well-publicized and televised hearings. Although they proved popular and entertaining, and helped make the obscure senator from Tennessee a national figure, the hearings accomplished very little. As a result of the hearings two laws were eventually enacted—The Johnson Act controlling the interstate shipment of slot machines, and an anti-gambling statute that required gamblers to purchase a $50 tax stamp and pay ten percent of gross receipts. Since most bookmakers work on less than a five percent profit, this law would, in theory, put an end to illegal off-track betting. In 1968 the United States Supreme Court ruled the law unconstitutional, a violation of the Fifth Amendment guarantee against self-incrimination.

5.  For a journalistic account of the Cleveland syndicate, see Messick, 1967.

6.  Valachi agrees that Maranzano was killed on orders from Luciano, but maintains that the reason was Maranzano's plot to kill Luciano and his "underboss," Vito Genovese (Maas, 1969: 115–118).

7.  Nicholas Gage reported that membership in the five New York crime families had been closed since 1957: "The membership books were closed in 1957 to prevent gangsters who were informers for law enforcement agencies from gaining entry into the Mafia families." According to Gage the "books" were reopened on a limited basis in 1976. Quoting "a United States Justice Department official," Gage states: "There's no doubt they've opened the books again on a tightly controlled basis. They've been holding initiation ceremonies in New York for the past month" (1976: 40). Another reason for limiting membership, besides security, is to maintain the status quo with respect to the relative strength of each family. Otherwise, a family might be tempted to improve its strength relative to other families by significant increases in membership.

# FOUR

## The Business of Organized Crime:
### *Goods and Services*

---

*"We believe that organized crime by gangsters is in large measure based upon the law of supply and demand. We as a nation have failed in our attempt by legislation to make the physical man and the moral man identical. (Report of the Committee on Mercenary Crime, 1932).\**

Herbert Packer argues that when we consider translating morality into law, we should inquire whether there exists any significant body of dissent from the proposition that the conduct in question is indeed immoral. If a social group will be offended, "then prudence dictates caution in employing the criminal sanction" (1968: 264). Unfortunately, as Prohibition taught us, when it comes to questions of morality, *prudence* is not often the dictator. Packer, with a great deal of insight, concludes (1968: 279):

> Regardless of what we think we are trying to do, when we make it illegal to traffic in commodities for which there is an inelastic demand, the effect is to secure a kind of monopoly profit to the entrepreneur who is willing to break the law. In effect, we say to him: 'We will set up a barrier to entry into this line of commerce by making it illegal and, therefore, risky; if you are willing to take the risk, you will be sheltered from the competition of those unwilling to do so.

Thus, translating morality into a statute backed by the criminal sanction does not provide for greater morality; it merely widens the scope of the law and creates both temptation and opportunity for a particular set of social actors. Like any business, the better organized are usually the more successful, and organized crime is basically a business enterprise. Walter Lippman noted in 1931 that organized crime "performs a function based ultimately upon a public demand" (1962: 60).

The goods and services of organized crime must be understood in terms of structural inconsistencies. Gardiner states, for example, that "public attitudes are much more permissive toward gambling than the statutes which are common in the United States; gambling is either positively desired or else not regarded as particularly reprehensible by a substantial proportion of the population" (1967: 134). Usurious loans are, likewise, prohibited by statute, but

---

\* Source: MacDougal, 1933: 342.

they are often the only ones available to many people. We have already experienced the results of the "great experiment" called Prohibition, while we continue to prohibit the use of a variety of drugs in face of the great demand for these substances; and prostitution and pornography, while publicly condemned, are privately enjoyed. Thus, while the arrest and conviction of "conventional" criminals is applauded, the successful suppression of organized crime would make a large portion of the public quite unhappy. This writer can recall, as a youth in New York City, that the arrest of a local bookmaker upset many residents. There were discussions throughout the neighborhood about when he would be able to return to "business as usual." Today, New York has legalized off-track betting, in addition to an "instant lottery," bingo, and restricted casino gambling permitted in churches and synagogues.

We should note that as in more conventional business ventures, organized criminal activities are not always consistently lucrative. In a recorded conversation from the "de Cavalcante Tapes" Anthony Russo, an underboss in Long Branch, New Jersey, complained to Sam de Cavalcante that the *amici nostri* ("friends of ours": syndicate members) cannot even support themselves (Volz and Bridge, 1969: 98). In another incident, de Cavalcante arranged for the removal of a local union official who was also a syndicate member, because he was not providing legitimate employment to the *amici nostri* as construction laborers (1969: 66). Peter Reuter and Jonathan Rubinstein report "a high rate of bankruptcy among bookmakers" (1978a: 51). While there is ample evidence that important members of organized crime live quite well,[1] less prominent members must make out as best they can. In this chapter we will review the "goods and services" most closely associated with the business of organized crime.

## THE BUSINESS OF
## ORGANIZED CRIME: "SERVICES"

### Bookmaking

Bookmakers "book" bets on two types of events—horse (and sometimes dog) races and sporting events like football, basketball, and boxing. In earlier days "horse parlors" or "wire rooms," neighborhood outlets, were often set up in back of a legitimate business, where results were posted on a large chalkboard. Many bettors would wait for race results to come in over the wire service. Today, most bets are placed by telephone (see Fig. 4-1). To maintain security, some bookmakers change locations frequently, often monthly. Others may use a "call-back" system. The bettor calls an answering service or answering machine and leaves his number. The bookmaker returns the call, and the bet is placed. A more elaborate system is the "black-box" or "back-strap." The telephone company installs telephones in a vacant apartment rented by the bookmaker, who runs an extension wire to a second location where the wire-

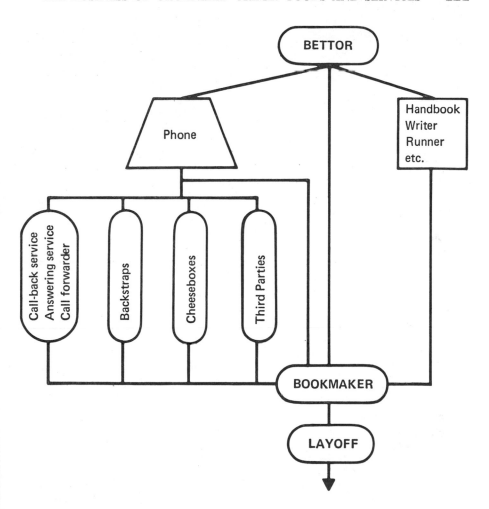

Fɪɢ. 4-1. The wagering process is shown with the bettor seeking to place his wager with a bookmaker. (Source: Kier T. Boyd, *Gambling Technology*, Washington, D.C.: United States Government Printing Office, 1977)

room is set up. A police raid on the telephone location will turn up only an empty apartment and several telephones. By the time the extension wire is traced and a new search warrant secured, the bookmaker has left to set up in a new location.

Bets are usually written down and may also be tape-recorded by a machine attached to the phone. This may avoid any discrepancies over what arrangements actually transpired over the phone. The bookmaker usually employs clerks and "sheetwriters" or "runners." The clerks handle the telephone, record the bets, and figure out the daily finances. The runners call the clerks and are given the day's totals for the bets they booked; based on this information, they either collect or pay off. The runners receive a portion of the winnings, usually half, and they must also share in the losses. Rubinstein and Reuter explain how (1977: 10):

> ... if his customers win in the first week a total of $1000, then the bookmaker will give the sheetwriter $1000 to pay them. This will give the sheetwriter a "red figure" of $1000. In the next week, let us assume that the sheetwriter's customers lose $400; then the red figure will be reduced by that amount, to $600. In the next week assume the customers lose $2000. The sheetwriter will pay the bookmaker the remaining $600 of the red figure plus half of the $1,400 which represents the net winnings, a total of $1300. His risks are the same as the bookmaker's but he invests no money.

## HORSE RACE WAGERING (Boyd, 1977)

Although the oldest of the major bookmaking activities, horse race wagering today ranks behind sports and numbers wagering in terms of illegal activity. The typical bettor is middle age or beyond and wagers amounts from two to ten dollars per selection.

Information as to the horses which are running on a given day may be obtained from a local newspaper, a "scratch sheet" (such as the "Armstrong Daily News Review," "Turf and Sports Mirror, or "Illinois· Sports Journal"), or the "Daily Racing Form." Voluminous data is available in the "Daily Racing Form" and the scratch sheets provide information on the time and nature of each race, the jockeys, the post positions, the weights carried, the probable odds, and the handicapper's estimate of the horses' finishing position. This data, especially that in the scratch sheet, is the basic information needed by the bookmaker in handling his wagers.

Payoffs at the track are, except where a bookmaker's limits are reached, the basis for the bookmaker's payoffs. His vigorish is obtained in this manner: before the track makes a payoff under the parimutuel system (in which the track acts as a broker to pay the winners from moneys it collects from the losers) it deducts for taxes and its operational expenses. The bookmaker, by keeping his wagers roughly equal to the track's, percentage-wise, realizes his profit from that portion which, at the track, goes to expenses and taxes. Since this deduction is generally from fifteen to twenty percent, there is comfortable room for maneuvering. When the bookmaker has too much money on a horse, vis-à-vis the track, he lays off the excess. This layoff process continues wherever lack of balance exists until it reaches the top layoff operations which have their agents stationed near major tracks. Upon being given their orders they make an ultimate layoff by placing large wagers at the track's parimutuel window. In the event that the wager is a winning one, money to assist in making payoffs comes from track winnings. Also, by placing large wagers at the track the track's potential payoff, and consequently the bookmaker's, is reduced.

The bookmaker cannot, of course, know precisely what percentage of money will be wagered on each horse at the track; however, information supplied by the scratch sheet or the "Daily Racing Form" is generally an acceptable guide and, in the event of a high track payment, the bookmaker invokes his limits (generally 15 to 1 or 20 to 1 for a "win" bet, 6 to 1 or

8 to 1 for a "place" bet, 3 to 1 or 4 to 1 for a "show" bet, and 50 to 1 for two-horse events such as the "daily double").

## WAGERS

Shown below are the common wagers together with ways in which they may be recorded by a bookmaker. The bookmaker will generally record the bettor's identity, the racetrack, the identity of the horse, the type of wager and the amount of the wager. The name of the track is almost always abbreviated (either by name or location). The identity of the horse may be written out fully or represented by its post position number or the handicapper's number as found on the scratch sheet.

Win—choose the horse which will finish first.

| | |
|---|---|
| 1 NY JOEY BOY 2/1 <br> 6 L #8 5-0-0 | (First race, New York (e.g., Aqueduct), $2 to win on Joey Boy) (Sixth race, Laurel horse with post position or handicap number 8, $5 to win) |

Place—choose the horse which will finish first or second.

| | |
|---|---|
| 4 GS MARY MARY X-10-X | (Fourth race, Gulfstream, $10 to place on Mary Mary) |

Show—choose the horse which will finish first, second, or third.

| | |
|---|---|
| 9 5/A   6 5/3 | (Ninth race, Santa Anita, horse #6, $5 to show) |

Combo (Across-the-Board)—a single bet encompassing equal amounts for win, place, and show.

| | |
|---|---|
| B 6 2   2-2-2 | (Sixth race, Bowie, horse #2, $2 to win, $2 to place, $2 to show) |

## SPORTS WAGERING

"From a gross dollar volume standpoint, sports wagering is the king of bookmaking" (Boyd, 1977: 13). Kier Boyd notes that as in other forms of bookmaking, the sports bookmaker acts as a broker, *not a gambler* (Ibid.). "In order to achieve an equality between teams, one which the bookmaker hopes will attract like sums of money on each contestant, a 'handicapping' process takes place" (Ibid.) through the use of a *line*. R. Phillip Harker explains (1977: 2):

The line theoretically functions as a handicap to balance the relative strengths of the opposing teams. It consists of points either added to the underdog teams' final scores or subtracted from the favorite teams' final scores. Then again, theoretically having balanced the relative strengths of the teams, wagers are accepted by bookmakers usually at 11–10 odds. Thus, for instance, if a bettor desires to bet $500 on the Washington Redskins at −6 (meaning Washington is favored by 6 points, and 6 points are subtracted from Washington's final score to determine the result of the wager), he would actually risk $550 to the bookmaker's $500.

As stated above, the line is only *theoretically* a balancing of the strengths of the teams. However, as a practical matter, the line is really a number of points, either added to the underdogs' scores or subtracted from the favorites' scores, which the bookmakers feel will tend to attract relatively even amounts of wagering on both sides of the contest. If the bookmaker achieves an even balance of wagering on a game and he has no gamble or risk, his profit is assured of being 10 percent, the "juice" or "vigorish" of the losing wagers.

Harker explains how the line is derived (Ibid.: 3–5):

To a great extent the line is developed in Las Vegas, Nev. Not only may the line be formulated legally there and posted publicly in legal bookmaking establishments, but Las Vegas is the recognized hub of wagering and the clearing house for much of the intelligence information used to develop the line. Persons there, who are instrumental in line development, have vast sources of information about the games, as well as knowledge of major trends or "moves" in game wagering, especially by the so-called "smart" or knowledgeable bettors. Each week in Las Vegas, the football line is developed, legally printed, and published. Thereafter, line information is disseminated almost instantaneously, usually via telephone, to various persons throughout the country.

Every bookmaker, by necessity, has a source for the Las Vegas line. The line may come directly from Nevada, from Nevada indirectly through one or more other cities, or from other local bookmakers who obtain it from sources ultimately obtaining it from Las Vegas. This accessibility is necessary for several reasons: First, as indicated above, the Las Vegas gambling community is considered extremely knowledgeable in all aspects of line development; and second, since other bookmakers and bettors are also aware of this line, the individual must start out using the Las Vegas line as his basis lest he become immediately out of balance, and hence, unable to lay off. For example, if the bookmaker felt the proper line on a game should be Team A favored by 4 points and used this line for taking bets, and if other bookmakers used the Las Vegas line of 12 points, our bookmaker would find immediately that no one would bet with him on the underdog getting only 4 points; whereas everyone would bet with him on the favorite giving up only 4 points rather than 12. Thus, he would experience a tremendous imbalance of betting on the favorite, which we have indicated is not a desirable situation. Moreover, he could not lay off with other bookmakers, since he must lay off with them at *their* line, which would be 12 rather than 4. And if he should lay off with the other bookmakers on the favorite giving up 12 points when his imbalance is at 4 points, and if the final score showed Team A winning by more than 4 points but less than 12 points, he would then lose not only his imbalance of bets on the favorite at 4 points, but his layoff bets at 12 points—a very dismal situation generally referred to as being "middled."

When the bookmaker obtains *the* line, he then often adjusts it to suit his needs or makes up *his* line. He may well know his usual bettors and be able to anticipate what volume on various games he can expect. If the line he receives is 4 and he knows that his bettors are likely to bet heavily on the underdog (the hometown favorite, perhaps), he might decide to use 3 or 3½ as his line. Then, as wagering progresses during the wagering period, such as often from Tuesday until Sunday on professional football games, he may vary his line upwards or downwards one-half point at a time to tend to attract betting, or conversely, to discourage betting on the other side, in order to balance the betting. The traditional thought is that the use of half points stems from the bookmakers' desires to eliminate "pushes" (or ties) when the bet is a draw. Although half points do have this effect, the real purpose is to facilitate varying the line by small increments. There is a tremendous difference between a line of 3 and 3½ points, but very little practical difference between 25 and 25½ points.

The bookmaker must know not only the Las Vegas opening line, but he must get frequent updates in the line. A change in the Las Vegas line does not mean that Las Vegas has changed its collective mind as to the anticipated final score (as if the line were a true power rating); it means that there has been an influx of wise money on the game. The bookmaker must be wary of the same influx. Also, the Las Vegas books may either "scratch" a game or "circle" it. To scratch a game means to eliminate further betting or to take it off the board. To circle it means literally to draw a circle around the game on the line sheet, resulting in a limitation of wagering on the game. Bookmakers may take no betting on a circled game or may accept only a limited amount of wagers on it, such as a maximum of $100. In either case, scratching or circling arises because of some unusual factors developing after the opening of betting. These factors include critical injuries, rumors of a fix in the game, or extremely unusual patterns of wagering. This type of information is of vital importance to every bookmaker because by the time he learns of the scratching or circling, he frequently will have been besieged with bets by bettors who have also been privy to the information.

It is worth noting that contrary to popular thought, a crucial injury occurring *after* the opening of betting cannot effectively be handicapped. Bookmakers cannot change the line enough to reflect the value of the loss of a good quarterback, such as possibly 6 or 7 points, or else the bookmaker would be in the position of possibly being "middled," as indicated above. All he can then do is stop further betting and hope for the best.

Likewise, other changes in factors, such as weather and internal disputes, cannot affect the line *after* its opening. These things only cause the game to be scratched or circled. The only factor affecting the line after opening is solely the volume of the wagering.

The question frequently arises as to why a bookmaker cannot use line information published fairly regularly in many newspapers. He cannot for two reasons. First, the bookmakers only trust money. If they could go to the newspapers and bet on the line appearing in it, then they could trust it.

However, as far as a bookie is concerned, a line is only a line if he can place bets on it. And second, whatever appears in the newspaper is not timely enough for the bookmaker; he must be able to learn of the changes in the line immediately and not the next day, at which time he may have already been inundated by smart money.

## BASEBALL

In football, basketball, and hockey, handicapping takes the form of points added to the underdog or subtracted from the favorite for wagering purposes. Except in rare cases, handicapping in baseball is done by varying the amount of money which a bettor must put up to obtain a wager of a stated denomination. Thus, if the Pittsburgh Pirates are favored over the St. Louis Cardinals the line might be quoted as "Pirates 6½–7½, Briles 135–145," or simply "Pirates 7½, Briles 145." The first quotation, 6½–7½, would be the "point" or "twenty-cent" line. Wager mechanics would be as follows:

Wager on Pirates:     Risk $7.50 to win $5.00
Wager on St. Louis:   Risk $5.00 to win $6.50

It will be seen that with a five dollar wager on each team the bookmaker will keep one dollar if the Cards win and break even if the Pirates win. This vigorish of one dollar (the difference between what he collects from the favorite and pays to the underdog) is the source of the bookmaker's profit.

Just as in sports handicapped by point spreads, there is an area where the baseball bookmaker can achieve balance (i.e., make a profit regardless of which team wins). However, this is not so easy a matter to determine since it depends upon the precise line quoted. For the line given above, Pirates 6½–7½, the balance limits would be determined as follows:

Maximum percentage of money on the Pirates

$$X + \frac{5.00}{7.50} X = 100$$

$$12.5 X = 750$$

$$X = 60\%$$

Maximum percentage of money on the Cards

$$Y + \frac{6.50}{5.00} Y = 100$$

$$11.5 Y = 500$$

$$Y = 43.478\%$$

It follows that as long as the bookmaker retains between 56½% and 60% of his wager money on the favorite, he is in balance (the ideal balance would be approximately 58% of the wager money on the Pirates, where the bookmaker would win close to $3.50 per $100 in wagers regardless of which team won).

The second line quoted above, Briles 135–145, is called the "pitching" or "ten-cent" line and will culminate in a wager only if the named pitchers are the starters. The wager mechanics are as follows:

> Wager on Briles:          Risk $145 to win $100
> Wager on other pitcher:   Risk $100 to win $135

On this line, the balance limits would be approximately 57½% and 59% on Briles.

Added to the considerations above is the fact that there is no standard method of quoting the baseball line. For some the base is $5, for others $10 or $100. Thereafter variations may arise as to whether or not either or both the lay and take figures start with the base and/or end with it. Some examples of regional variations on the basic line quoted are set forth:

Basic odds: 7 to 5 Pirates
1. 6½–7½ (explained above)
2. 135–145 (explained above)
3. 7–8 ($10 to win $7 on favorite, $8 to win $10 on underdog)
4. 2/3–13/10 ($15 to win $10 on favorite, $10 to win $13 on underdog)
5. 5–3;5–6 ($5 to win $3 on favorite, $5 to win $6 on underdog)

From the above it may be seen that layoff wagers from one section of the country to another frequently involve communication problems (what system is the other party using?) and conversion problems (what are the applicable equivalents and how nearly do they conform with my balance limits?). Use of a conversion chart is essential.

With a low margin of potential profit, narrow and complex balance limits, and convertibility problems when dealing with distant bookmakers, it is small wonder that baseball bookmaking is for the stout of heart.

Straight wagers may be written a number of ways. Some of the most common listed below:

PIRATES – 7½ 100

BRILES – 29°

BRILES – 145 – 100

FOSTER    200 – 270

CARDS  13/10  200

PIRATES  ⅔  150

Occasionally when a contest is so one-sided that a money line will not attract bettors, a point-spread type of line is used. Also in a very few areas (e.g., Honolulu) a point-spread type line is used exclusively.

Aside from straight wagers, the baseball bets may include over-and-under wagers and parlay wagers. Although baseball parlays may be computed, bookmakers almost always rely on a chart to determine the payoff amounts.

Just as in football, wager records of a baseball bookmaker may be distinguished from those of a mere bettor by the appearance of multiple wagers on the same team, self-defeating wagers (i.e., wagers on both sides of the contest where, when the line is reduced to a common base, the vigorish is on the bookmaker's side), and the presence of bettors' names or coded identities. (Boyd, 1977)

Because of the use of the point spread (line), when there are attempts to "fix" games, the approach is to have key players "shave points." That is, their play will reflect the need to keep the score within the point spread. The National Football League has been extremely outspoken in its opposition to the legalization of sports betting. Pete Rozelle, speaking for the NFL stated (quoted in Tuite, 1978: B21):

The league believes legalized gambling on professional sports will dramatically change the character of the fan interests in the sports. No longer will sports fans identify their interests with the success or failure of their favorite teams, but with the effect of their team's performance in the winning or losing of bets.

The NFL's real fear, of course, is that "legalized gambling will greatly multiply the security problems confronting all professional sports" (Ibid.).

The NFL sued the state of Delaware which experimented briefly with football betting in 1976. The NFL lost the suit, but the league's chief security officer, Jack Danahy, explains why the suit was brought: "We are not naive. We are not unaware of the fact that there is a great deal of gambling going on, but we don't think that the state or any governmental authority rightfully should come in and impose a gambling situation on our game" (Marshall, 1978: 21). Interestingly, Eliot Marshall reports that Delaware "gave it up after it found that state officials were less adept at setting odds than the underworld. Professional gamblers realized they could take advantage of Delaware's inexperience in bookmaking and collect a lot of easy money" (Ibid.). (For an inside look at the effect of gambling on college basketball, see Rosen, 1978.)

A sports betting line may appear in the daily press, such as Fig. 4-2, from the *Miami News* of July 24, 1979.

### ORGANIZED CRIME INVOLVEMENT IN BOOKMAKING

In an earlier period bookmaking was an important source of income for organized crime. The latter either ran the operation directly or "licensed" syndi-

| AMERICAN LEAGUE | | | ST. LOUIS | 8-9 | Atlanta |
|---|---|---|---|---|---|
| Favorite | Odds | Underdog | HOUSTON | + Even-6 | Chicago |
| BALT. | x 1½-2 | Seattle | SAN DIEGO | ++ Even-6 | Montreal |
| BOSTON | 2-2½ | Oakland | SAN FRAN. | 7½-8½ | New York |
| NEW YORK | 7-8 | California | LOS ANG. | 5½-6½ | Phila. |
| DETROIT | Pick 'em | Milwaukee | + Vs. Rick | Reuschel, | otherwise |
| CHICAGO | 5½-6½ | Kansas City | Astros 6½-7½ | | |
| MINN. | 6½-7½ | Cleveland | ++ Vs. Rogers, otherwise Padres | | |
| x Both games of doubleheader | | | 6½-7½ | | |
| NATIONAL LEAGUE | | | SOCCER (NASL) | | |
| Favorite | Odds | Underdog | Favorite | Odds | Underdog |
| PITT. | 6-7 | Cincin. | Tampa | 5½-6½ | ROCH. |
| | | | Home Team in CAPS | | |

## The Greek Line

**Jimmy Snyder's Odds**

AL — BALTIMORE (McGregor and Martinez) 11-5 over Seattle (Bannister and Jones) (both games); BOSTON (Eckersley) 3-1 over Oakland (Morgan); NEW YORK (Tiant) 7-5 over California (Aase); Milwaukee (Travers) 6-5 over DETROIT (Underwood); MINNESOTA (Koosman) 7-5 over Cleveland (Wise); Kansas City (Gale) 6-5 over CHICAGO (Kravec)

NL — PITTSBURGH (Kison) 7-5 over Cincinnati (Norman); ST. LOUIS (Vuckovich) 8-5 over Atlanta (Brizzolara); HOUSTON (Forsch) 6-5 over Chicago (Reuschel); SAN DIEGO (Perry) 6-5 over Montreal (Rogers); LOS ANGELES (Hooton) 6-5 over Philadelphia (Lerch); SAN FRANCISCO (Montefusco) 8-5 over New York (Kobel)

(CAPS indicate home team)

FIG. 4-2.

cate bookmakers. As we have seen in Chapter Three, the wire service was an important source of organized crime control over bookmaking. However, most wagering today involves sports, as opposed to horse racing, and uses the telephone; the quick results provided by the wire service are no longer vital. In addition, the almost exclusive use of the telephone provides greater security and has reduced the need for police protection, often another important syndicate service. Rubinstein and Reuter (1978a and 1978b) report that their research in New York City revealed very little syndicate involvement in bookmaking.

Bookmaking, without the need for a wire service and elaborate police payoffs, is a relatively easy entry enterprise. This easy entry has made it impossible to maintain monopolistic control. In addition, the profit margin ("vigorish") is only between 4.5 and 5 percent; only a large operation would be of financial interest to an organized crime syndicate. Independents, as long as they did not get too big or compete seriously with a syndicate operation, could continue unmolested. However, syndicate involvement in bookmaking is very much in evidence. The arrest of six members of the family headed by Tony Corallo in 1979 highlights this situation. The six were operating a $273 million-a-year bookmaking operation that did almost $750,000 worth of business on the May 15, 1979, hockey playoff game ("The Police Blotter," *NYT,* May 17, 1979: B4).

## Lotteries: Numbers, Policy, Sports Pools

Henry Chafetz notes that the "American colonies were floated on lotteries." In 1612, King James I authorized a lottery to promote the Colony of Virginia. The colonies themselves used lotteries, and such outstanding men as George Washington bought and sold lottery tickets (1960: 20–21). The lottery was used (unsuccessfully) to help finance the Revolutionary War (Ibid.: 25). Many of America's outstanding institutions of higher learning were supported through the use of lotteries—Brown (Rhode Island College), Columbia, Harvard, University of North Carolina, William and Mary, and Yale (Ibid.: 25).

During the nineteenth century lotteries under state license or control were found throughout the United States. Because of the negative publicity surrounding problems with the Louisiana Lottery, in 1890 the United States enacted legislation prohibiting lotteries from using the mails, and even denied newspapers that carried lottery advertisements from using the mails (Ibid.: 306–307).

During the 1960s and 1970s, the state-operated lottery reappeared, essentially for the same reason that it was used in earlier times, as a means of supplementing tax revenues. The extent to which the legalized lottery has impacted on illegal lotteries, "numbers," "policy," or "sports pools," has not yet been determined. As of this writing fourteen states operate their own lotteries, while thirty-one allow betting on horse racing, seven on dog racing, and four on jai alai games (Satchell, 1979: 8).

## Numbers/Policy

In numbers and policy a player selects one, two, or three digits from zero to nine, with the odds of winning thus running from ten to one, one hundred to one, and one thousand to one. For a single digit ("single action") play the payoff is six or seven to one; for two digits ("boledo" or "bolito") the payoff is between fifty and sixty-four to one; for three digits the payoff is between five hundred-fifty and six hundred to one. On certain popular numbers, e.g.,

711, the payoff may be reduced to five hundred to one or even lower. A player can also "box" his numbers—bet all the possible three-digit combinations. While this increases the chances of winning, it also reduces the payoff to about one hundred to one.

There are several schemes for determining the winning numbers. For example, the first digit is determined by adding what the horses coming in first, second, and third (win, place, show) paid on a two-dollar bet in the first race; the second digit is a repeat for the second race; and the third digit is determined using the third race, all at a particular racetrack.

|  | Win | Place | Show | TOTALS |
|---|---|---|---|---|
| First Race | 58.80 | 26.80 | 10.40 | 96.00 |
| Second Race | 11.00 | 5.40 | 2.80 | 19.20 |
| Third Race | 10.20 | 5.60 | 4.20 | 20.00 |

The final three numbers are determined by reading the first digit to the left of the decimal point from the top down: 6  9  0.

Another widely used system is the last three digits of the daily total gross receipts ("handle") of a designated racetrack, e.g., $2,534,940. The winning number is: 9  4  0. Other methods include the last three digits of the daily balance of the United States Treasury, stocks traded, or agricultural prices for eggs or other commodities, amounts generally reported in the daily press. When the numbers are determined by a drawing (lottery), the game is usually called *policy* and the places where the drawings conducted are referred to as *wheels,* after the container from which the lottery balls are drawn. However, policy and numbers are terms often used interchangeably as are wheels and numbers banks.

During the 1930s, an extremely popular form of gambling was the "Italian lottery," which was played throughout the United States, almost exclusively by persons of Italian birth or descent. Weekly income for the lottery in 1935 was estimated at two million dollars a week in the New York metropolitan area alone. The winning numbers were reportedly drawn from a wheel by a blind boy every Friday in eight different Italian towns and cities. One letter and five numbers, from one to one thousand, are drawn in each of the eight locations; thus:

| B | 7 | 41 | 17 | 86 | 48 |
|---|---|---|---|---|---|
| E | 78 | 22 | 9 | 38 | 6 |
| H | 16 | 39 | 28 | 63 | 81 |
| J | 96 | 7 | 18 | 53 | 59 |
| L | 2 | 78 | 61 | 24 | 8 |
| M | 12 | 71 | 3 | 46 | 89 |
| Q | 83 | 6 | 4 | 66 | 3 |
| V | 31 | 14 | 51 | 9 | 72 |

If a player has correctly guessed a letter with two of the numbers (out of five) next to it, there is a payoff of 250 to 1; if three numbers, the payoff is 5000 to

1; four numbers win 50,000 to 1. The winning letters and numbers are cabled from Italy and printed on Saturday in a variety of handouts and publications (*NYT,* March 4, 1935, "$2,000,000 Lottery Unmolested Here").

In an affadavit supporting a search warrant, an Asheville, North Carolina, police officer describes a version of the numbers game called *bolita:* *

> I am Sgt. L. Williams, having been employed by the Asheville Police Dept. for 29 years. It has been my responsibility to enforce gambling laws and, more recently, to initiate gambling investigations. This affadavit describes "Bolita," which is a numbers game and wagering system; Bolita employs strips of paper which are numbered 1 through 100 and sold by individuals on a daily basis. Each slip of paper or number which is sold has a value assigned by the seller, usually 25 cents, 50 cents, or $1.00. If $1.00 is invested on a winning number, the holder of that number would be paid $80.00. The winning number is determined on a daily basis at a designated time in the following manner; several subjects stand at various locations in close relation to one another, at this time a bag is passed around which contains small balls numbered 1 through 100. When this bag is passed to a designated person, he or she grasps one ball from the outside of the bag and it is tied off. The rest of the balls are then removed from the bag. The ball remaining in the grasp of the designated person represents the winning number (which is the number appearing on the ball). Having arrested or assisted in the arrests of more than 100 persons for possession of Bolita strips and interviewing many of them, I believe the above description is accurate in describing the gambling system known as "Bolita."

Fig. 4-3 shows a copy of a sheet of bets seized in a raid on a policy bank. Lasswell and McKenna explain the notations (1972: 87):

> The sheet contains three columns of numbers. Each column shows a three-digit number (the number bet upon separated by a hyphen from the number or numbers indicating the amount of the wager). Some amounts on the wager side of the column have the letter C before them which indicates the number was bet as a combination. A combination bet means that any of the six possible combinations of the original three-digit number was also being bet.
>
> The first series of numbers in the first column are 612–25 C 1.50 which mean 612 was bet individually for 25¢ and again as a combination for $1.50. Thus, if any combination of 612 (621, 126, 162, 216, 261, and 612) became the winning number, the bettor would collect on a 25¢ bet (1.50 divided six ways).
>
> Note on the lower part of the paper the designation "D.B.Q." This is the code name for the runner turning those bets. The sheet of bets represented by this page is usually turned into the bank in an envelope bearing the code designation for the controller for whom the runner is working.

## NUMBERS ORGANIZATIONAL STRUCTURE

At the bottom of the hierarchical totem pole is the person who accepts wagers directly from the bettors. These are known as writers, runners, sellers,

* I wish to thank Melvin Tucker, Chief of Police, Asheville, for his cooperation.

| | | |
|---|---|---|
| 612 - 25 (1.50 | 564 - 15 | 263 - 1.5 (.30 |
| 261 - 1.00 | 673 - 15 | 800 - 30 (.30 |
| 166 - 25 (.30 | 148 - 15 | 580 - 25 |
| 186 - 25 (.30 | 516 - 15 | 120 - 25 |
| 575 - 25 (.30 | 109 - 10 | 111 - 25 |
| 938 - 20 (.30 | 320 - 10 | 729 - 25 |
| 832 - 20 (.30 | 230 - 10 | 445 - 25 |
| 902 - 20 (.30 | 666 - 25 | 061 - 25 |
| 604 - 20 (.30 | 222 - 25 | 318 - 25 |
| 500 - 20 (.30 | 054 - 10 | 544 - 25 |
| 940 - 5 (.60 | 579 - 10 | 568 - 25 |
| 923 - 5 (.60 | 112 - 10 | 625 - 25 |
| 157 - 5 (.60 | 209 - 10 | 418 - 25 |
| 186 - 5 (.60 | 165 - 10 | 302 - 5 (.30 |
| 316 - 5 (.60 | 243 - 10 | 045 - 5 (.30 |
| 317 - 5 (.60 | 276 - 10 | 597 - 5 (.30 |
| 813 - 5 (.60 | 369 - 10 | 121 - 5 (.30 |
| 225 - 25 (.15 | 520 - 10 | 092 - 5 (.30 |
| 989 - 25 (.15 | 358 - 10 | 116 - 5 (.45 |
| | 942 - 10 | 823 - 25 |
| | | 427 - 15 |
| | | 526 - 15 |

Fig. 4-3.

etc., and generally are individuals with ready access to the public (e.g., elevator operators, shoeshine boys, newspaper vendors, bartenders, waitresses). Customarily they are paid a percentage of the wagers they write (unlike sports bookmaking, numbers wagering is done on a cash basis), usually from fifteen to thirty percent, and frequently they are given a ten percent tip from bettors receiving payment for hits. In only a very few places do writers furnish their customers with a written record of the wager.

The numbers writer is strictly a salesman and assumes no financial burden for the numbers he writes. It is essential, therefore, that his wagers reach trusted hands before the winning number or any part of it is known.

Sometimes this is done by telephone; other times the wager records (commonly known as work, action, business, etc.) are physically forwarded to a higher echelon by a pickup man (frequently a taxi driver, vending machine serviceman, etc.).

In a small operation the wagers may go directly to the central processing office (commonly called the bank, clearinghouse, countinghouse). More often, in large enterprises they are given to management's field representative (known as the field man, controller, etc.) who may be responsible for making a quick tally to determine the existence of any heavily played numbers which should be laid off. At such levels of operation one frequently finds charts consisting of 1,000 spaces numbered 000 to 999 where tallies can be made for all wagers or only for certain wagers meeting a minimum dollar value.

Near the top of the totem pole is the bank, the place where all transactions are handled. During the collection process the bank will be making decisions as to whether or not to layoff certain heavily played numbers. After the winning number is known the bank will meticulously process the paperwork to determine how much action has been written, how many hits are present and the controllers and/or writers involved. Provision will be made for the payment of hits. Frequently, if the hits are small the payment will be made directly by the writer and deducted from the amount he owes the bank. In other cases, particularly large hits, payment will first be made to the writer by the bank or the controller.

Numbers wagers produce a large volume of records, hence the bank will seldom keep the recorded wagers for much longer than a week. Some retention is necessary in case of claims arising by bettors or writers. Not infrequently a winning number may be missed by the bank's clerical personnel, resulting in a claim for an "overlook."

Behind the bank and at the top of the totem pole is the financial backer who may or may not be associated with the day-to-day operations. He will frequently provide the funds to furnish bond and legal counsel to employees who are arrested.

Settlement with the writers may be on a daily basis, but more frequently it is done on a weekly basis. The bank will prepare a "tape" (i.e., adding machine tape showing the gross action written, deductions for the writer's commission plus any payment for hits he has made from his own funds, and ending with the amount due from the writer to the bank) advising the writer how much to pay the collector, controller, or other person who represents the bank. (Boyd, 1977)

The paper used to record bets may be deliberately treated with chemicals so that it is quite flammable and thus easily destroyed in order to avoid arrest and prosecution. Records of bets may be made on metal strips which can be swallowed and later retrieved; in New York's Chinatown bets are recorded on rice paper which can be easily swallowed.

Numbers or policy games permit the player to select his or her desired numbers, as opposed to various state authorized lottery systems which use preprinted lottery tickets. The player in the illegal lottery has an opportunity to play "hunches," "lucky numbers," and to use "dream books." The dream book is an indispensable part of the game for many players. The book, which contains "lucky" numbers associated with the bettor's dreams, is sold (legally) on newsstands. One of the more popular publications is called the *Three Wise Men,* which is printed on Long Island, New York. The availability of dream books in any local is a tip-off that numbers gambling is occurring.

Groups of writers or runners transfer their bets to a controller who receives about 10 percent of the bets while the writer receives 25 to 30 percent. The controller transfers the bets to the bank, a central operating location. After the number is determined ("comes out"), the bank calculates the winnings to be paid out and this is returned to the writer through the controller. The writer is the only contact with the player, and he or she makes the payoff. If payments exceed collections, the writer may be in "debit," and thus not receive any commissions until his accounts are even. This situation is compensated, somewhat, by receiving the usual 10 percent of any "hits" as a tip from the winning player.

The *sports pool* has several versions, but the essentials are the same. A series of "tips" are placed on a "tip-board" or in some container. Each tip bears two three-digit numbers, with the last two digits of each number representing a major league baseball (or other) team. Players purchase a tip, which they select blindly; if this tip bears the two numbers representing the two teams which scored the most runs (points, goals, etc.) that day, they are winners. In a baseball pool there are 153 different combinations (tips) and the payoff is usually 120 times the amount wagered.

In this form of lottery the seller receives about 10 percent of the wagers he collects, while payoffs come from the bank through the seller. Between the bank and the seller is often a tip-board salesperson, someone who does not solicit bets, but who sells the tip-boards for the bank and receives a 10 percent commission.

Several aspects of lotteries help to enhance the game. Desmond Cartey points out that the writer often provides valuable information to the player on matters ranging from vacant apartments for rent to securing stolen merchandise at discount prices (1970: 35). William Whyte reported that in Boston the men who ran the numbers "are known as free spenders and liberal patrons of local enterprises. They spend money in local stores. They patronize the activities of the corner boys with purchases of blocks of tickets to dances and with other contributions" (1961: 142). Whyte points out that local storekeepers often depend on the money they receive from selling numbers, and, in addition, the people who are attracted by the availability of the numbers are also patrons for his or her primary business (1961: 143–144). Charles Silberman states that numbers profits make it possible for a small storekeeper to compete with supermarkets and chain stores (1978: 102). Whyte notes that numbers provide employment for many local men who are unskilled and who would not otherwise be able to secure gainful employment (1961: 145). Harold Lasswell and Jerimiah McKenna found that in Bedford-Stuyvesant the numbers business was the largest single private employer (1972).

Rubinstein and Reuter report on a number of changes in numbers operations in New York City. The most startling aspect of their findings is that *reduced* police activity with respect to numbers apparently dealt a damaging blow to organized crime (1977: 102):

> The dominance of Italian-American operators at least until the time of the Knapp Commission [investigating police corruption] is also quite striking. While they were never exclusive operators of the racket, and several large Numbers operations in the Bronx and Brooklyn are operated by members of other ethnic groups, it is not an exaggeration to say that the Numbers was an Italian-run racket until quite recently.

Now, they report, the number of independent operators is increasing and the men who run them are black and Hispanic. Rubinstein and Reuter also report the absence of any clear territoriality in the numbers—no one group has a monopoly (1977: 125–127). They speculate, based on their initial findings, on the reason for the increasing emergence of black and hispanic numbers operators (1977: 146–147):

> ... it is clear that corrupt policemen were important agents in the operations of Numbers banks prior to 1970 and are relatively unimportant now. Without implying that corrupt police discriminate in the acceptance of bribes, we might assume a strong preference on their part to take money from established operators, who can offer credible promises to keep the peace. Also, these established operators had the necessary connections to make arrangements with corrupt agents in the other criminal justice agencies which were necessary to assure their dominance. Certainly the police would have incentives to cooperate with the existing Numbers operators in disciplining their controllers who might be tempted to leave the bank. The elimination of routine, embedded corruption in the police, combined with a reduction in street-level enforcement seems sufficient to explain emerging autonomy of black and Hispanic racket operators.

## Casino Gambling, Card Games, Dice Games

Among the gambling services provided by organized crime is the "Las Vegas type" casino. As we noted earlier, Las Vegas was "founded" by Bugsy Siegel: "Before the advent of Benjamin 'Bugsy' Siegel, Las Vegas served principally as a comfort station for tourists fleeing across the desert heat ..." (Reid and Demaris, 1964: 12). The illegal casino, like its legitimate counterpart, requires a great deal of financial investment—equipment, personnel, treasury, not to mention political and police protection. A fully equipped casino operation will have available a variety of games of chance including roulette, card games, dice games, and the "slots" (one-armed bandits). In some places, New York City for example, there is a tradition of holding "Las Vegas Nites." These events are often run by organized crime elements using the legitimate front of a religious or charitable organization. The latter will share in some of the profits, while organized crime will provide the gambling devices, manpower, and financing.

Organized crime operatives may also organize or sponsor card or dice games. These may be in a permanent location, e.g., a social club, or for security reasons may float from place to place. The games may be held in private residences or in houses or apartments rented for that purpose. The games may be operated in the home of a person in debt to a loanshark as a form of paying off his loan. The operators of the game take a cut of the bets wagered in return for providing the services. Gambling activities not operated under syndicate protection run the risk of being raided by the police or being held up by independent or robbery teams authorized by the syndicate.

Vincent Siciliano, an armed robber whose father was a Prohibition gangster, reports: "The organization knows there is this game and when some friend in the police needs an arrest, to earn his keep as a protector of the people against the bad gamblers, the organization guy tells the police and off they go with sirens wailing" (1970: 50). During the raid, Siciliano notes, the police can also help themselves to much of the games proceeds (Ibid.: 50–51). Siciliano, who robbed independent ("outlaw") games and some syndicate operations, for which he got in serious trouble, points out: "There were some sure ones to stay away from though. If you so much as thought about robbing the games on Elizabeth Street or Grant Street [sic, probably Grand Street in downtown Manhattan], you would wind up dead." Even the dumbest stick-up man knew these were syndicate games, they "were as safe as Chase Manhattan [Bank]" (Ibid.: 56).

## Prostitution/Brothels

"A brothel is a place that is exclusively used for the business of prostitution and where the inmates almost invariably share their earnings with the operator." The name probably derived from the public baths which in Europe were used as places for assignation (Winick & Kinsie, 1971: 137). (For the history of prostitution see Bullough, 1965.) The brothel is sometimes referred to as a bordello.

During the 1920s and '30s madams arranged for opening a brothel, attracting prostitutes and customers, and securing protection from the police (Winick and Kinsie, 1971: 97). The madam also acted as a "house mother," preventing quarrels and providing advice; she was both a friend and an employer: "Her work made it almost inevitable that she would assume traditionally maternal functions" (Ibid.: 98). In Chicago and its suburbs, however, brothels were often owned and managed by men belonging to organized crime groups. There was an elaborate system for procuring and transporting girls between New York, Milwaukee, St. Louis, and Chicago (Landesco, 1929: 25). The constant transfer of girls provided "new faces" and was good for business. This type of interstate activity, and incidents of actual "white slavery," the use of force to recruit or maintain prostitutes, led to the passage of the White Slave

Traffic Act of 1910, called the Mann Act after its sponsor, Congressman James R. Mann of Illinois. "White slave" was actually something of a misnomer; many of the girls were orientals, particularly on the West coast, who were sold by their families in China and smuggled into the United States.

With the advent of the Depression, organized crime groups began looking for new areas of income. In many cities they organized independent brothels, and the madams paid syndicate middlemen for protection from the police and from violence. If the madam did not pay, the syndicate would resort to violence. Gangsters like David ("Little Davie") Betillo, a member of the crime family of Lucky Luciano, organized the heretofore independent brothels in New York City. In the case of the *State of New York v. Charles Luciana* [*Lucky Luciano*], *et al.,* Thomas E. Dewey claimed that the organization under Luciano's control had more than 200 brothels employing over 3000 prostitutes and grossed more than $12 million a year.

The brothel reached its peak in 1939 (Winick and Kinsie, 1971: 158). During the war, and more significantly after 1945, the importance of brothels as a source of income for organized crime has steadily declined. Charles Winick and Paul Kinsie report that today there are relatively few communities where prostitution is under organized crime control (1971: 237). This is in marked contrast to the number of "wide-open towns" throughout the United States—places such as New Orleans, Calumet City and Cicero in Illinois, San Antonio, Texas, Covington and Newport in northern Kentucky, and Phenix City in Alabama, a town where the governor declared martial law and sent in the National Guard. On June 19, 1954, Albert L. Patterson, a Phenix City reformer who had been nominated Alabama Attorney General, was murdered. It was his son, Governor Gordon Patterson, who sent in the guard and inspired the movie *The Phenix City Story* (Wright, 1979: 14).

In some American cities there are "massage parlors" and other types of establishments fronting for brothels, and some of these are either controlled or have been financed by organized crime groups. Prostitution, however, is for the most part unorganized, with pimps, usually black or Hispanic, having a "stable" of from three to eight girls working for them. These pimps often dress in a "uniform" of flashy, often outlandish, clothes and drive equally outlandish automobiles—custom pink Cadillacs and Lincolns with real leopard upholstery, for example. Ianni, however, sees the socializing between pimps and other illicit black and Hispanic entrepreneurs as providing the basis for a "Black Mafia" (1974: 25–71).

Only Nevada has legalized prostitution, on a county option basis; elsewhere in the United States it is a misdemeanor (although pandering can be a felony). In Nevada brothels prostitutes are fingerprinted and carry official identification cards. They are usually required to have periodic medical examinations and are prohibited from leaving the brothels to mingle with community residents.

Prostitution, like pornography, is apparently suffering from a great deal of "amateur" involvement. Pornography, which at one time was a business of organized crime, is widely available throughout the United States. With liberal court decisions virtually legalizing pornography, legitimate entrepreneurs have entered the market. This has resulted in a proliferation, and a substantial improvement in quality, of pornographic movies. In 1978, members of the New York City Police Department, acting officially, produced a pornographic film. The idea behind the production was to gather information and evidence about organized crime. The film, however, was of such poor quality that the undercover police officers were unable to find any buyers. As if to add insult to injury, when the story "leaked," the news media had a grand time at the expense of the embarrassed police. The Task Force on Organized Crime reports how organized crime became involved with the successful porn movie *Behind the Green Door* (1976: 227):

> Organized crime figures approached the producers concerning distribution rights, which the producers continuously refused to grant, despite threats of piracy. Within a short time, hundreds of pirate versions appeared all over the country. The producers lost several key markets—Las Vegas, Miami, and Dallas among them. Also, because the pirated versions were often of poor quality, the movie got a bad reputation, which further reduced its market.

An article in a popular magazine states that a "network of pornography that may gross $4 billion a year" is dominated by five men. Four of the men apparently have business connections with each other; the fifth is allegedly a *caporegime* in the Bonanno crime family. One of the four is also described as a member of organized crime, a soldier in the New Jersey crime family of Sam de Cavalcante. The article, based on "confidential reports from the FBI, Justice Department, and other agencies," states that the "pornography industry is infested by organized crime, particularly in wholesaling and distribution" (Michael Satchell, "The Big Business of Selling Smut," *Parade,* August 19, 1979: 4–5).

## THE BUSINESS OF ORGANIZED CRIME: "GOODS"

### Drugs

As we have noted, the sale of heroin and cocaine parallels the experience of Prohibition, despite important differences. Heroin and cocaine use are not socially accepted in the wider society that accepts at least the moderate use of alcohol. Thus, fewer people use these two drugs, a fact offset by the inflated prices that heroin and cocaine demand.

Opiates were legally available in the United States until five years before the Volstead Act and Prohibition. Edward Brecher refers to the United States during the nineteenth century as a "dope fiend's paradise." Opiates, including heroin, a derivative of morphine, were "as freely accessible as aspirin is today." Brecher notes that in addition to availability through physician's prescriptions, opiates were sold without prescription in drugstores and groceries, or they could be ordered by mail. Opiates were used in a host of patent medicines, and widely advertised in magazines as "pain-killers" and "cure-alls" [2] (1974: 3). He points out that while the use of opiates was frowned upon by some as immoral, it was not the subject of the sanctions, legal or social, that are experienced today. An employee was not fired for being an addict, and children were not taken from their addicted parents and placed in foster care (1974: 6). Indeed, there were prominent opium users in earlier days, one being Dr. William Stewart Halsted (1852–1922), one of America's greatest surgeons and one of the four founders of Johns Hopkins Medical School (1974: 33). Cocaine[3] was also quite popular in the United States through the early twentieth century. An effective stimulant, cocaine was often ingested with wine and was an ingredient in Coca-Cola until 1903.

In 1914, because of international pressure over the opium trade, the United States enacted the Harrison Act. Brecher stresses that the focus of this law was the international and not the domestic problems with opium; the Act also dealt with cocaine, which was mistakenly deemed a narcotic (1974: 48–49). The original intent of the Harrison Act was to license and thus control domestic drug traffic. However, as Edwin Schur notes, restrictive federal regulations and harassment from federal drug enforcement officials "effectively and severely limited the freedom of medical practitioners to treat addict-patients as they see fit—in particular, to provide addicts with drugs when that is believed medically advisable" (1965: 130). In 1922, the United States Supreme Court decided the case of the *United States v. Behrman* (258 U.S. 280), which involved an obvious abuse by a medical doctor who had given an addict a huge quantity of narcotics to use as he saw fit. The Federal Bureau of Narcotics interpreted this decision to mean that regardless of the medical intent, treatment of addicts involving the administration of narcotics was prohibited (Schur, 1965: 131). Federal agents moved to close down narcotic clinics and arrested thousands of doctors. Between 1914 and 1938 some 25,000 doctors were arrested for supplying opiates, and about forty heroin maintenance clinics were closed down (Epstein, 1977: 104). The outlawing of opiates and cocaine spawned a flourishing, albeit illegal, traffic in drugs.

OPIUM AND HEROIN

Opium is derived from the poppy which is grown in Turkey, India, Southeast Asia, and Latin America. In Turkey farmers grow the poppy legally and sell it to a government monopoly in order to export it for medical use. Turkish farmers can safely divert about three to five kilos of raw opium (a kilo is 2.2046 pounds) for the black market. Illegal opium dealers collect the raw opium from numerous farmers until they have accumulated about 1000 kilos, enough to produce about 100 kilos of heroin. The raw opium is moved across Turkish minefields into Syria, where it is converted into base morphine. From there it is shipped from Aleppo to Marseilles and sometimes Sicily, or through Beirut to Marseilles, by sea. Smugglers may also move the base morphine by land through Bulgaria or Yugoslavia into Marseilles. In Marseilles and Sicily it is converted into heroin in clandestine laboratories, and shipped to the United States, often through Canada or Mexico. In all, no fewer than eighteen links are involved in this operation (Lamour and Lamberti, 1974: 23–25). (See Fig. 4-4.)

Heroin, an extremely potent derivative of opium, is an analgesic that suppresses pain by reducing sensory sensitivity. It also reduces the appetite and lessens the sex drive. The euphoric response it produces in those addicted to heroin is called a "high," although physiologically it is actually a "low."

More than half of all the illegal heroin used throughout the world comes from the Golden Triangle where the borders of Burma, Laos, and Thailand meet (Ibid.: 36). There tribesmen, government officials, and private armies grow, cultivate, and smuggle opium and base morphine into Hong Kong or Marseilles. Most of the world's smuggling networks are dominated by Corsicans or overseas Chinese; they share close knit and protective family relationships that facilitate the international black market in heroin (Ibid.). Opium is also grown in Mexico; the brownish color of Mexican heroin distinguishes it from the white color of Eastern heroin. In addition, other countries in Latin America, Colombia, Nicaragua, Ecuador, are known to grow the opium poppy (Ibid.: 57), while Afghanistan is said to be a major supplier of heroin to the European market.

Importation is the highest level of operation in drugs; the actual smugglers ("mules") take much of the risk, while the organizers who arrange for the importation and wholesale distribution avoid physical possession. After importation the drugs are "stepped on," diluted, often several times. The wholesaler, basically a facilitator, arranges for the cutting (diluting) of the almost pure heroin. The actual physical work is often done by women brought together for the task. Between ten and twenty women cut anywhere from ten to fifty kilos in an apartment rented only for this purpose. Under guard, often working without any clothes on (as a precaution against stealing any of the precious powder), wearing surgical masks to avoid inhaling heroin dust, they mix the heroin with quinine, lactose, and dextrose. The mixture is usually four or five parts of the dilutant to each ounce of heroin. The women work through the night, receiving more than a thousand dollars each, making the risks and embarrassment worthwhile.

When the cutting is complete (see Fig. 4.5), jobbers, who have been waiting for a telephone call, arrive with the necessary cash, which they exchange for the cut heroin, now packaged in glassine envelopes of the kind used by stamp collectors. The jobbers move it to retail outlets where it is usually cut again. From there it moves to street wholesalers and eventually to addicts. (See Fig. 4-6.)

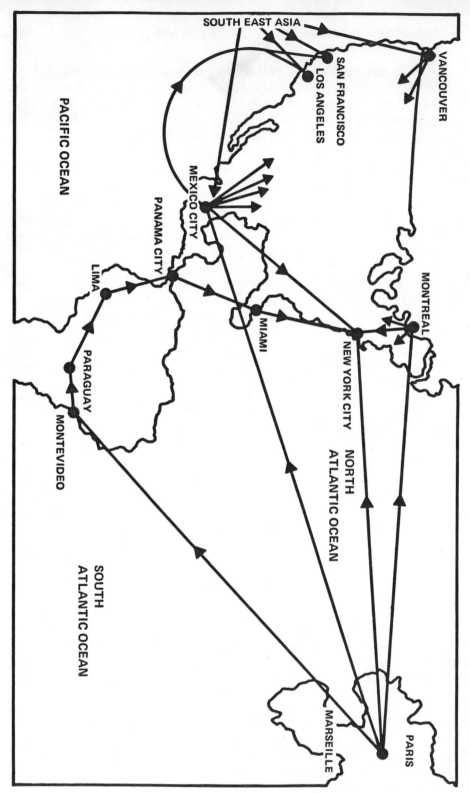

**Fig. 4-4.** Examples of narcotic routes from Asia and Europe into the United States.

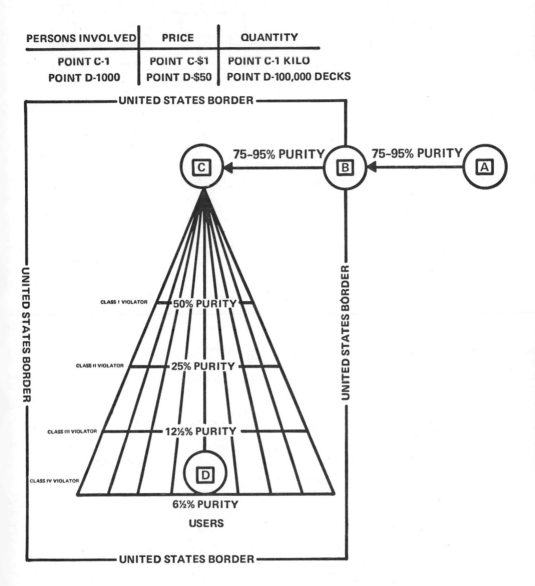

| PERSONS INVOLVED | PRICE | QUANTITY |
|---|---|---|
| POINT C-1 | POINT C-$1 | POINT C-1 KILO |
| POINT D-1000 | POINT D-$50 | POINT D-100,000 DECKS |

(Source: Hearings on Federal Drug Enforcement before the United States Senate Committee on Government Operations, Subcommittee on Investigations, 94th Congress, Part 1: June 9–11, 1975.)

FIG. 4-5.    Basic pattern of narcotic distribution in the United States.

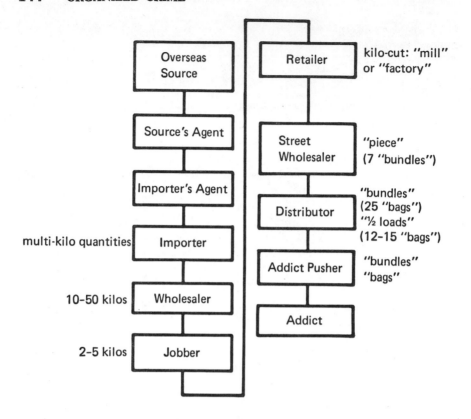

Fɪɢ. 4-6. Heroin distribution organization (adapted from Lasswell and McKenna, 1972: 94).

Cᴏᴄᴀɪɴᴇ ᴀɴᴅ Mᴀʀɪᴊᴜᴀɴᴀ *

Cocaine is a white, crystalline alkaloid derived from the leaf of the coca bush that thrives in the Andean highlands of Peru, Bolivia, and Ecuador, and harvested four times annually. Its use as a drug has been traced back to Inca ceremonies, and the Andean Indians continue to chew the leaves to ward off hunger, cold, and fatigue. The leaf is also nutritious, containing vitamin C and several B vitamins. Cocaine is useful as a local anesthetic and for toning the digestive tract. It is legally manufactured in the United States for pharmaceutical purposes.

Cocaine is a stimulant which is habituating but, unlike heroin, not addicting. It is the preferred drug among certain social sets, ranging from pimps to sports and entertainment luminaries who inhale ("snort") the substance. A great deal of myth and mystique surrounds the use of cocaine; users often claim that it enhances sexual performance. Prolonged use can cause the nasal tissues to wear away and the nose to collapse. Chronic use has reportedly led to psy-

* See Chapter Two for a discussion of Cuban and Colombian organizations that dominate the cocaine trade.

chosis, and overdoses can result in convulsions, heart and respiratory failure, and death.[3]

In the illicit trade in cocaine, jobbers purchase the leaves from Indians and distill them into a base, 150 pounds making a one-pound base worth more than $2000. The base is crystallized into a pound of pure cocaine worth more than $7000 to a smuggler ("The Colombian Connection," *Time,* Jan. 29, 1979: 24).

Marijuana, unlike cocaine and heroin, does not have to be imported since it can be, and often is, grown in several areas of the United States. The highest quality marijuana, however, is grown in Colombia. Smoking marijuana produces an alcohol-like reaction, and potential dangers (and uses—it apparently reduces eyeball pressure in glaucoma patients) are still a matter of some controversy.

## THE ECONOMICS OF DRUGS

The enormous profits available for those involved in wholesale drug trafficking is quite startling. A kilo of almost pure heroin (2.2046 pounds), purchased in Bangkok for about $12,000, when prepared for street sale, 3.5 percent purity, has a gross sale value of more than $2 million in the United States. Mexican heroin sells for about $45,000 a kilo, and also reaches a value of more than $2 million when cut for street sale. Cocaine, selling for about $2800 a pound in Colombia, brings anywhere from $900 to $1800 an ounce in th United States. Street level purity is about 12.5 percent. Marijuana selling for about $75 a pound in Colombia can be sold for more than $500 a pound in the United States.

A typical wholesaler with 20 kilos of heroin, after expenses, can net more than half-a-million dollars in cash for an operation that he sanctioned, financed, and organized, but in which he had no physical part.[4] The high profits in drugs also makes it a high-risk business. While trafficking in drugs is often well organized, at the lower distribution level it need not involve sophisticated or extensive organization. Various informal groups, friends, street gangs, and assorted individuals who may come together only to "deal drugs" are part of the business. Entry into drug trafficking is relatively easy and there are quick profits, if not wealth, for those willing to take the risks. In New York City one can find teenagers earning $500 a day running drugs; schoolyards and playgrounds are the scene of basketball games played for $1000 per game or contests for $100 per basket. The easy entry into drug trafficking was noted by a *NYT* story on the "Black Tuna Gang" in 1979. The leaders of this group, Robert J. Meinster and Robert E. Platshorn, were in 1974 a used car dealer and a gadget seller at fairs, respectively. Both were in their late thirties when they bought 2,500 pounds of Colombian marijuana. At the time of their indictment in 1979 they headed a group of forty men and women including pilots, boat captains, communications experts, and enforcers. By 1977 "Black Tuna" had "successfully imported its first million pounds of marijuana worth $250 million wholesale" (Volsky, 1979: 26).

There is, of course, a rather direct relationship between the risks involved in a particular enterprise and the profits that can be realized. Drugs represent the highest profits and thus the highest risks. These are from two sources— law enforcement and rival criminals. The danger from the latter source is reminiscent of the Prohibition era. In 1978, for example, in one three-week period four syndicate drug dealers were murdered in an apparent feud between two rival crime families in New York. One of those killed, Ralph Broccoli, age 35, was described as a key figure in the crime family of the late Carlo Gambino. Selwyn Raab describes his murder (1978: 39):

> Broccoli *** was sitting alone in the rear of Jay's Lounge, 2568 68th Street [Brooklyn], reportedly waiting for a companion. A man arrived with a shotgun, his face covered with a ski mask, burst into the cafe, and told the barmaid and four other customers not to move or talk. Simultaneously, two men, one with a shotgun and the other with a pistol, approached Mr. Broccoli from the rear entrance. He was killed by shotgun blasts and large caliber pistol bullets in the head and body.

A risky business indeed! This writer knew Ralph when he had just been released from state reformatory for his involvement in large-scale commercial burglaries. These burglaries were organized and directed by the Gallo brothers organization in Brooklyn, and Ralph was only a teenager at the time.

In 1978 there were fourteen drug-related murders in Jackson Heights ("The Colombian Connection," *Time,* Jan. 29, 1979, p. 28.). Some of these murders have been quite brutal. In 1975, one member of a cocaine smuggling ring in Jackson Heights, New York, found his five-year-old daughter stabbed in the thighs and abdomen and strangled to death. His ten-year-old son and their seventeen-year-old babysitter were also strangled; the latter had been raped (Schorr, 1978: 52).

The vicious nature of some of those involved in the drug trade is noted by Howard Blum and Leonard Buder who report that rival Puerto Rican drug dealers in the South Bronx section of New York City (called "Fort Apache" by the police) were found dismembered. They had been cut up with an electric saw while still alive: "A man present in the room who later became a police witness remembered that there was a loud click immediately followed by the rapid, whirring drone of an electric saw. The buzzing of the saw was lost in a fury of screams" (December 21, 1978: B8). In a series of articles in the *NYT,* Blum and Buder report on an extensive Puerto Rican run heroin and cocaine network moving drugs from Mexico to California, and finally into the South Bronx. The violence that erupted from a struggle to control this estimated $30 million-a-year operation led to twenty-seven deaths (Ibid.).

### Fencing of Stolen and Illicit Goods[5]

A fence provides a readily available outlet for marketing stolen ("hot") merchandise. He thus provides an incentive to thieves and may also organize, finance, and direct their operations (Walsh, 1977: 13). Marilyn Walsh found that about 13 percent of the fences she studied were involved in organized crime. "For these individuals fencing appeared to be just another enterprise in a varied and totally illegal business portfolio." Their other activities included loansharking and gambling, and some operated as "enforcers" (1977: 42). Walsh reports that the prices paid varies according to the thief—a "junkie" (drug addict) may only receive 10 percent of the retail price, while a "pro" (who steals as a livelihood) may get between 30 and 50 percent of the wholesale price. The fence may also vary his prices to guide the stealing behavior in accordance with the resale market (1977: 71). Walsh reports that fences may avoid competition by recognizing territory and refusing to do business in violation of this; coercion may be used to maintain this arrangement (1977: 74).

The fence is able to provide an outlet for stolen merchandise by selling it to (otherwise) legitimate businesses at discount prices. These businesses can then mix fenced goods with their legitimately purchased stock. The fence may also "retail" goods directly, out of a garage or warehouse, or through the use of a legitimate business front. Desmond Cartey reports that in one New York City neighborhood, the Bedford-Stuyvesant section of Brooklyn, a black ghetto, the selling of stolen goods is highly organized: "The goods are stolen only if there is an order and a market" (1970: 28). Stolen merchandise is sold in beauty parlors, shoeshine shops, poolrooms, and after-hours clubs (unlicensed bars), the same establishments where numbers are also sold (Ibid.: 30–31). The key to a successful operation, Cartey points out, is police corruption, which includes not only cash payoffs, but sharing in the stolen merchandise (Ibid.). Charles E. Silberman, apparently finding a need to justify lower-class participation in buying stolen property, argues: "From a lower-class perspective, buying a name-brand item at 50 percent or more below list price is a means of correcting a social imbalance, of redressing the maldistribution of income from which they suffer" (1978: 94). However, since all but the "rich" can suffer from relative deprivation, this justification can be used for the middle as well as the lower class. This writer has not experienced a reluctance among middle-class persons toward purchasing a "bargain" whose origin is not questioned. That such activity is more prevalent among the lower class is probably due to a greater amount of opportunity and a lesser degree of hypocrisy.

Besides stolen goods, other items can be marketed, one of the more important being cigarettes. Cigarettes can be purchased in North Carolina, where the per-pack tax is two cents, and sold in New York City where the per-pack tax is 23 cents. Federal officials estimate that 400 million dollars a year is lost in tax revenue, while the estimated gross for organized crime is 1.5 billion dollars. Racketeers avoid paying the cigarette tax by stealing or counterfeiting state tax stamps (information from officials of the Federal Bureau of Alcohol, Tobacco and Firearms).

As a result of increased pressure from high tax states, in 1979 a new federal statute became effective in an effort to combat cigarette smuggling. Under the law, buying, selling, and transporting contraband cigarettes became an offense punishable by a $100,000 fine or five years in prison. Contraband is defined as a quantity of 60,000 cigarettes (or 300 cartons) bearing no evidence of the payment of state cigarette taxes in the state in which they are found. The law also provides a reward of up to 50 cents per carton (varies with the destination of the cigarettes) for information leading to the seizure of contraband cigarettes.

Another illicit operation associated with organized crime, which has the appropriate outlets, involves the manufacture of counterfeit tapes or records. A master recording is illegally cut from a popular tape or record, and this master is used to manufacture thousands of duplicates. This scheme also requires the use of counterfeited labels and album covers. The counterfeited tapes and records are marketed through legitimate record shops or to nonmusic outlets such as automobile service stations.

In her research on fences, Walsh discovered a rather unique position in organized crime which she calls the "hood," a person with "a floating illegitimate status" (1977: 110). The hood is an older member "whose operating days are about over, but who maintains an important illegitimate status, somewhat analogous to that of a pensioner in the legitimate employment world." She reports that "he is granted a sort of license to establish a new and less active set of criminal endeavors as an entrepreneur rather than as an operative." Often, this means fencing or acting as an intermediary in fencing operations where the right "connections" are essential (Ibid.).

## Loansharking

Between 1880 and 1915 a practice known as "salary lending" thrived in the United States. This quasi-legal business provided loans to salaried workers at usurious rates. The collection of debts was ensured by having the borrower sign a variety of complicated legal documents that subjected him to the real possibility of being sued and losing his employment. Through the efforts of the Russell Sage Foundation, states began enacting small loan acts to combat this practice. The first state was Massachusetts in 1911. These laws, which licensed small lenders and set ceilings on interest, eventually led to an end of salary lending, and credit unions, savings banks, and similar institutions began to offer small loans. However, it also led to the wholesale entry of organized crime into the illicit credit business (Goldstock and Coenen, 1978: 16–20).

Prohibition permitted criminals to accumulate huge amounts of liquid assets, and the advent of the Depression gave them a new source of continued income in the form of loansharking. Charging interest in excess of the legal limit is referred to as loansharking or shylocking. There are two basic types of usurious loan, the "knockdown" and the "vig." Jonathan Rubinstein and Peter Reuter report that the knockdown requires a specified schedule of repayment including both principal and interest: e.g., $1000 might be repaid in thirteen weekly installments of $100 (1978b; Appendix, 2). The vig is is a "six for five" loan: for every five dollars borrowed on Monday, six dollars is due on the following Monday. The one-dollar interest is called "juice." If total repayment of the vig loan, principal plus interest, is not forthcoming on the date due, the interest is compounded for the following week. Thus, a loan of $100 requires repayment of $120 seven days later. The debt will increase at the following rate on the original $100:

at the end of
one week—$120
2nd week— 144
3rd week— 172.80
4th week— 207.36

The insidious nature of the vig loan is that the borrower must keep paying interest until the principal plus the accumulated interest is repaid at one time. It is quite easy for the original loan to be repaid many times without actually decreasing the principal owed on the loan; the loanshark is primarily interested in a steady income of interest and is quite willing to let the principal remain in debt for an indefinite period. Donald Cressey reports that one Cosa Nostra boss divided a half-million dollars in cash among five of his lieutenants —each was to repay him $150,000 within the year. This was considered a benevolent gesture since in the usurious loan market the $100,000 would more than double itself within the year (1969: 82). When loans are outstanding, a loanshark will refer to this as having "money out on the street" or "money working for me."

Rubinstein and Reuter, based on their research in New York, made four *tentative* conclusions about loansharks (1978b: Appendix, 3–5):

First, there is strong evidence for specialization by loansharks. Some deal with legitimate businessmen only, some with illegal entrepreneurs. One medium level loanshark specialized in fur dealers, though he might make loans to other small businessmen. Some specialize in lending to gambling operators.

They report that loansharks "frequently provide capital for a bookmaker who is in financial difficulty" (1978b: 53). Individual gamblers may also borrow from a loanshark. The latter may stay around card and dice games or accept "referrals" from a bookmaker. In one case familiar to this writer, a young gambler borrowed from a loanshark to pay his bookmaker. He continued to gamble and borrow, and eventually was unable to repay his loanshark. As a result, he embarked on a series of illegal activities that eventually led to a prison term. Among his activities were running high-stakes poker games, at which his wife played hostess, and securing fraudulent loans from numerous banks. On one occasion, he decided to use some of this money to continue gambling and missed his loanshark payment. A severe beating in a parking lot ensued, leaving him with two black eyes and a broken nose. For collecting debts, the loanshark obviously has means not usually used by other lending institutions and is thus more willing to lend money to otherwise "poor risks." The threat of violence or the reputation of the loanshark may make the actual use of violence unnecessary. Indeed, syndicate criminals find the newspapers, books, and movies that portray loansharks the best form of "public relations."

> Second, those [loansharks] that we have looked at are not predatory in the sense usually claimed. They lend money to customers whom they expect will pay off and eventually return as customers again. The loanshark is not attempting to gain control of the customer's business. That is not to say that predatory loansharks are unknown or that the ones we have learned about have never acted in a predatory fashion. (Rubinstein and Reuter, 1978b: 3–4)

Joseph Valachi worked as a loanshark and reported that most of his customers were themselves involved in illegal activities, such as numbers and bookmaking (Maas, 1968: 167). However, Valachi recalled that he lent money to a legitimate businessman, the owner of a dress and negligee company, and became a partner when the loan could not be repaid. With Valachi's financial backing, and his ability to keep the union from organizing the factory, the business actually prospered (Ibid.: 174–77).

> Third, collection very rarely involves violence, or even the threat of violence. Loansharks are interested in making credit assessments in the manner of legitimate lenders. Often they secure collateral for the loan, though it may be of an illiquid form. Sometimes a borrower will have to produce a guarantor. In many cases the loan is very short term, less than a month, and collection is simply not an issue. Repeat business is the backbone of those operations we have studied. A good faith effort to make payments will probably guarantee the borrower against harassment particularly if he has made substantial payment of interest before he starts to have repayment problems.
>     Finally, there is little to suggest that entry into the loansharking business is controlled by any dominant group. (Rubinstein and Reuter, 1978b: 4)

Ianni (1974: 39) reports that "Irwin," the owner of a dry cleaning store in Harlem, is also a loanshark:

> If a borrower defaults on a loan, Irwin has little choice but to shrug it off. He is not an enforcer and has no associates who are enforcers. He has never sought any connection with any of the mobs that operate in Harlem— black or Italian—and has never had any connection forced upon him. But Irwin doesn't worry much about defaults. He knows that most people will pay him back, no matter how slowly, because some day they will need cash again, and where else can they go? Banks don't lend money to welfare recipients or to the sometimes-employed.

One loansharking operation with which the writer is familiar, however, made the threat of violence an explicit part of the loan procedure. The lender, an important organized crime figure in New Jersey, would tell a potential borrower, in a calm, business-like manner, "If payments are not made according to our agreement, you will have your legs broken." This threat was not an idle one since the loanshark had a reputation for violence.

## THE BUSINESS OF ORGANIZED CRIME: MISCELLANEOUS ACTIVITIES *

### Racketeering

The origin of the term *racket* is uncertain, although racketeering clearly refers to illegal transactions. A "beer racket" was a term used to indicate a type of social event highlighted by a large supply of beer and usually including music and dancing. Various types of groups, ranging from street gangs to college fraternities, sponsored "rackets." At some point in history the racket was used for extortion: tickets to rackets would be sold to storekeepers, often with an implied or explicit threat of violence; often the ticket that was sold did not in fact represent an actual social event, but was merely used as a ruse for an outright shakedown.

There are many forms of racketeering, some of which will be reviewed in this section. The employer association involves organizing firms into an association controlled by racketeers; employers "faced with the constant threat of cutthroat competition are subject to easy temptation to pay gangsters for protection against competitors" (Lippmann, 1962: 61). Walter Lippman also noted in 1931 that "racketeering in many of its most important forms tends to develop where an industry is subject to excessively competitive conditions" (Ibid.). As we have already seen, Chicago was noted for business racketeering, much of which consisted of outright extortion in the form of a "protection racket." Another form of racketeering resulted in sixty million dollars in arson losses sustained by the Great Atlantic and Pacific Tea Company (A & P), while two of its store managers were murdered, two committed suicide, and others were beaten (Demma and Renner, 1973: 303–304). Best Sales, operated by Eugene Catena, a syndicate member from New Jersey, attempted to sell a detergent, Ecolo-G, to the A & P in 1964. When the A & P tested the product, it proved inferior and was rejected. A campaign of terror followed (Demma and Renner, 1973).

#### LABOR RACKETEERING

The origins of labor racketeering in the United States can be traced to the "walking delegate." In its early days organized labor needed an agent whom

---

* There are activities of organized crime that do not fit, or at least fit clearly, into "goods" or "services." Labor racketeering, for example, does at times provide a "service," but it also is often outright extortion or embezzlement.

an employer could not fire or intimidate. They employed the "walking delegate" or business agent, who was often empowered to call a strike without any
formal ratification. This power was seen as instrumental in allowing the union
to strike quickly and at the most opportune time. The men chosen for this
position were usually tough, and it was this quality, rather than intelligence
or integrity, that abounded in business agents (Seidman, 1938: 5–6). It was
not long before these agents began abusing their power, calling needless strikes,
and engaging in extortionate practices (Ibid.: 8). Unions also collaborated
with employers to establish monopolies. Picket lines and strikes would be used
to drive out competition, while protected businesses were free to raise prices
while paying higher wages. Such business-labor collaboration eventually
opened the door to organized crime (Ibid.: 43), which has proven adept at
acting as an intermediary between business and labor.

Another entry for organized crime was the use of private detective agencies,
often employing street gangs, by employers seeking to combat unions (Jeffreys-
Jones, 1978: 91). Harold Seidman points out that until 1909 unions did their
own slugging. However, in that year, for the first time, a large number of
women in the garment trades participated in strikes, and they required protection. "Dopey Benny" Fein, who was everything but dopey, became the chief
supplier of sluggers for the International Ladies Garment Workers Union. Fein
formed alliances with such New York City street gangs as the Hudson Dusters,
assigning territories and working out business-like agreements and patterns of
operation. He also assisted the union in keeping its members in line. It would
soon become clear, however, that it was easier to hire gangsters than it was to
fire them (Ibid.: 45–49). As we noted in Chapter Three, gangsters such as
Lepke Buchalter, Gurrah Shapiro, and Dutch Schultz soon began to dominate
some unions.

The "de Cavalcante Tapes" are laced with various forms of labor racketeering. Sam de Cavalcante, in collusion with union officials who were syndicate
members, was able to arrange for nonunion, and thus cheaper, labor on construction sites. For this service de Cavalcante received kickbacks or was
awarded the plumbing contract (Zeiger, 1970: 94–95, 99–100, 122, 129).
A similar, although more involved scheme, was used by Anthony ("Tony
Pro") Provenzano who, Steven Brill reports, "ran his New Jersey Teamsters
union as an arm of organized crime" (1978: 10). Brill states that for a fee,
Provenzano permitted certain companies to avoid paying union scale by allowing them to contract with "labor-leasing" companies that hired nonunion drivers (1978: 53).

A more direct approach was used in Michigan where Teamster representatives would solicit cash from retailers to guarantee that they would not suffer
unionization. In one incident Frank Kierdorf, a Teamster official, set himself
on fire in 1958 while attempting put a Flint dry cleaners to the torch. The
Latrielle Cleaners had refused a Teamster offer of "protection" (Brill, 1978:
66–67). Frank Kierdorf, until his fiery end, was a close associate of James
Hoffa, who before his imprisonment in 1967 was president of the International

Brotherhood of Teamsters, the largest union in the world (Kennedy, 1960: 86–87).

Another form of labor racketeering uses "labor consultants" as a conduit between employers seeking "sweetheart contracts" and dishonest union officials. Robert Kennedy, who had been chief counsel to the McClellen Committee,[6] describes an incident that occurred in 1949. Laundry drivers of Teamsters Local 285 were working a six-day week, and negotiations for a new contract were underway (the union was demanding a five-day week). This would be very costly to the laundry owners, represented by the Detroit Institute of Laundering (DIL), but so would a strike. The DIL contacted Moe Dalitz of the Cleveland syndicate, who was in the laundry business. He referred them to the labor consulting firm of Jack Bushkin and Joe Holtzman, who requested $25,000 in cash to guarantee a satisfactory contract with a six-day week. This was negotiated down to $17,500, and the money was raised by assessing each laundry owner according to the number of trucks he owned. Kennedy describes the final bargaining session between Isaac Litwak of Local 285 and DIL representatives headed by Charles Meissner (1960: 96–100):

> Late in the last session the door opened and in came Jimmy Hoffa [then Detroit Teamster boss]. Mr. Hoffa told the group there would be no strike. He wanted the contract signed on the owner's terms and signed immediately or he would step in himself. Mr. Litwak was stunned and angry—Meissner described him as "furious"—but he had no choice. He surrendered. The contract was signed without a five-day-week provision.

Kennedy points out that of the fifty-eight men identified as part of the famous Apalachin crime conference in 1957, twenty-two were involved in labor or labor relations (1960: 228). One of the participants, who was also caught in the state police raid, was Carlo Gambino, who for ten years was a partner in SGS Associates, Inc., a labor relations firm that Paul Meskil notes "attracted large business and industrial companies as clients" (1973: 60). Meskil named some of the SGS clients (Ibid.: 61):

William Levitt: builder of Levittown, N.Y., etc.

Concord Hotel: major recreation center in upstate N.Y.

Howard Clothes: chain store corporation now out of business

Flower and Fifth Avenue Hospital

Bond Clothes

SGS went out of business in 1965 as a result of pressure from federal investigators. Meskil reports: "Several clients agreed that a contract with SGS was a virtual guarantee of labor peace" (Ibid.).

In 1971, the Mobil Oil Company engaged the Sular Company as "labor consultants" to deal with fuel oil truck drivers, members of the International Brotherhood of Teamsters, who were going on strike. Sular, since it was run by several members of the crime family headed by Joseph Colombo, was uniquely qualified. The Teamsters, however, fought back and prevented strike-breakers from making deliveries. Sular responded by having five of its men in a car accompany each truck to guarantee delivery. The union settled. While the scheme came to the attention of the FBI, no prosecution resulted (Villano, 1977: 181–185).

Walter Sheridan, an investigator for the McClellen Committee, reports that one firm, Labor Relations Associates, headed by Nathan Shefferman, purported to be a consultant to employers in personnel matters. However, he notes, the firm "was a creation of the Sears, Roebuck and Company and was engaged in widespread, subtle and sinister union-busting activities on behalf of Sears, its subsidiaries and suppliers, and a variety of other clients" (1972: 33). Shefferman was a friend of Dave Beck, then president of the International Brotherhood of Teamsters (he was later imprisoned). If Shefferman's other techniques, e.g., using strike-breakers, did not work, he would arrange "sweetheart contracts" with "friendly" unions (Ibid.: 50). Sheridan also points to a number of trucking companies in New York who signed contracts with an honest union local even though they knew they would receive a better contract with a racketeer-dominated one. These responsible employers decided that they would be better off dealing with tough, but honest, union officials (Ibid.: 25).

### "Paper Locals" and the Teamsters

"Paper locals" are a device for extorting money from employers by providing a barrier against legitimate unionization. The paper local was used by Jimmy Hoffa in his successful bid to dominate the Teamsters Union.

In 1956, elections were scheduled to choose officers of the International Brotherhood of Teamsters (IBT) Joint Council 16 in New York City. If Hoffa could effect the outcome of the Joint Council 16 elections, he could pave the way for winning control of the IBT presidency. In 1955 Hoffa had seven new Teamster charters issued to a union friend of John ("Johnny Dio") Dioguardi[7] who along with Anthony ("Tony Ducks") Corallo[8] filled the locals with a variety of gangsters who could then vote in the 1956 election. Five of the seven locals did not have a single member; they were paper locals (Sheridan, 1972: 26). Corallo had already gained control of five Teamster locals, although he held office in only one, Local 239, whose president, Sam Goldstein, took orders from Corallo. Walter Sheridan reports that Dioguardi and Corallo brought into the newly chartered locals some forty men "with an aggregate record of 178 arrests and 77 convictions" (Ibid.: 27).

While Hoffa was interested in winning over the locals and their votes, Dioguardi and Corallo were interested in financial rewards. The newly "elected" officers of the paper locals would approach various nonunion employers with *an offer they couldn't refuse:* "pay the union fees and membership dues for your employees, who often did not even know they were union members, and you keep your business free of all labor problems including demands by legitimate unions: fail to pay and labor problems, and worse, will result." By the time Hoffa gained control of the Teamsters in New York, twenty-five of these men had been convicted on new charges including bribery, extortion, perjury, and forgery (Ibid.: 27–28). Those convicted included Sam Goldstein and Harry Davidoff.

The latter is deserving of special mention because of the power that he has exerted over Kennedy International Airport in New York. For many years Davidoff was Secretary-Treasurer of Teamster Local 295, which represented many key airport employees. In 1971 he was convicted of extortion, but that conviction was later overturned on a technicality. He has since been barred from holding office in Local 295, although he is still the business agent for Local 851, a clerical employee sister union of Local 295. When Davidoff was forced out of Local 295, his son Mark took over. He has since resigned, but is still described as the Local's advisor and the Secretary-Treasurer of Local 851, a job that reportedly pays $1100 a week (Maitland, 1979: B2). Although Mark Davidoff has no record of criminal convictions (Kwitny, 1979: 272) as of this writing, he is about to stand trial for charges stemming from an airport labor battle. The *NYT* quotes him as boasting that he could "close the airport" if he wanted to (Maitland, 1979: B2). The *NYT* also reports that federal officials are looking into Davidoff's connection with other syndicate criminals who are apparently expanding their influence over the airfreight industry in the eastern United States (Ibid.: B1).

Steven Brill provides some of the history of the Teamsters' involvement with organized crime. He reports that in the early 1950s, Jimmy Hoffa made a deal with Paul ("Red") Dorfman, a Chicago gangster. With Dorfman's help, Hoffa was able to tie in with syndicate figures throughout the country, and they helped him gain control of the International Brotherhood of Teamsters (IBT) (1978: 13–14). The result was the use of the IBT to extort money from various companies, provide sweetheart contracts, and the "rape" of the union's Central States Pension Fund which in twenty-two states is the primary IBT pension fund. Loans were made from the fund to organized crime members or those who fronted for them—loans that were often never repaid (1978: 204). For example, a group headed by Moe Dalitz received loans totaling ninety-seven million dollars (1978: 239). In 1974 the Fund had about one billion dollars in outstanding loans in real estate alone (1978: 204). This will result in a curtailment in benefits to retired union members in twenty-two states.

Interestingly, some of the money from the fund was loaned to William Loeb, the publisher of the politically influential *Union Leader,* a Manchester, New Hampshire, newspaper noted for its conservative viewpoint. Before the two million dollar loan Loeb had been a severe critic of the Teamsters. After the loan, this changed, and Loeb was a leader in the effort to get Hoffa paroled after his 1967 imprisonment (1978: 200). Hoffa was eventually released from prison on December 21, 1971, after President Nixon approved a clemency application. By 1975, Hoffa was actively seeking the IBT presidency, and Brill maintains that this is what led to his disappearance in July of that year. Hoffa's body has never been found, and Brill argues that Anthony Provenzano was responsible for his murder. Provenzano was convicted in 1978 of the murder of another IBT official.

Jonathan Kwitny reports that racketeers in collusion with bank officials use union pension funds to enrich themselves. A small bank is approached with an offer to deposit hundreds of thousands of dollars in union funds at a very profitable rate of interest. To secure the deposits, however, certain unsecured loans must be approved, and sometimes the banker receives a kickback on each loan as an added incentive (1979: 202). In one New Jersey case, five union officials of a Teamster local were convicted in 1979 of arranging for loans totaling $800,000 from nine banks. Many of the loans were never repaid. One of the principals in the scheme was a former law partner of New Jersey Governor Brendan Byrne, who acted as an intermediary between the banks and the union and arranged for loans and payoffs ("5 Jersey Teamster Officers Guilty of a Kickback Plot With 9 Banks," *NYT,* May 6, 1979: 57).

### Scam

The scam is a bankruptcy fraud that victimizes wholesale providers of various goods. The business used as the basis for the scam may be set up with the scheme in mind, or it may be an established business that has fallen into syndicate control as a result of gambling or loanshark debts. Edward De Franco notes that scam operations are popular in industries with merchandise having a high turnover potential, readily transportable, and difficult to trace.

The following are the most common types of scam operations (1973: 5–7):

- *Three-Step Scam:*
  1. A new corporation is formed, managed by a front man or "pencil" who has no prior criminal or bankruptcy record.
  2. An initial large bank deposit, known as the "nut," is made to establish credit. This money, plus all other money subsequently deposited, is later withdrawn.
  3. A large store is rented and orders for merchandise placed with as many companies as possible. The size of these orders appears to indicate a successful operation to the suppliers.
  4. Smaller orders are placed during the first month, and such orders are almost always completely paid in full.
  5. During the second month, larger orders are placed and about a quarter of the balance due on such orders is paid.
  6. During the third month, using the credit established as a result of payments made for the previous orders, very large orders are placed. Items easily converted into cash, such as jewelry and appliances, usually constitute a large proportion of these orders.
  7. Thereafter, merchandise is converted into cash through a fence or a surplus property operator, normally one with a sufficiently large

legitimate inventory to easily intermix the scam merchandise into his normal inventory. The company is then forced into bankruptcy by its creditors, since according to plan, all cash has been appropriated by the scam operator.

- *One-Step Scam*—Since the Three-Step Scam requires several months for completion, the more rapid One-Step Scam is now more frequently used. This involves the following:
  1. A successful business with a good credit reference is purchased.
  2. No notice of the change in management is provided to Dun and Bradstreet or other credit agencies, thus trading on the previous owner's good credit reputation.
  3. Manufacturers are approached in person or at trade shows to arrange for the purchase of merchandise.
     (a) Since the orders placed are usually of a large quantity, suppliers who did not sell the company previously are very politely informed by the scam operator that if he does not sell him, some other company will be glad to do so. This technique is known as the "sketch."
  4. Large orders are then placed, including orders for many items not previously purchased by the company.
  5. After the orders have been received, the merchandise is sold, as with the Three-Step Scam; the money is milked from the business; and the company is forced into bankruptcy, just as the scam operator had planned.
- *Same Name Scam*—This technique, which is a variation of the One-Step Scam, operates as follows:
  1. A company is organized with a name deceptively similar, and often almost identical, to that of a successful company in the same area.
  2. Large orders are placed with suppliers, who assuming legitimacy of the company based on the similarity in firm names, fill the orders.
  3. The merchandise is then sold in the same fashion as for other types of scam operators, the money is milked from the business and as with other type scams, the company files for bankruptcy.
- *Scam by an Established Company*—This technique, which is a variation of other scam operations, operates as follows:
  An individually owned business or a company which has operated legitimately for many years decides to make a quick killing. They then use the One-Step Scam techniques to rapidly withdraw money from the company and force it into planned bankruptcy. In such situations, the operators of the company usually blame gambling losses or below-cost sales for the bankruptcy into which they have deliberately placed themselves.

A popular time for the scam operator is just before a seasonal increase in the popularity of a particular merchandise when rush deliveries are commonplace and thorough credit checks often overlooked.

De Franco also provides a summary of a scam that occurred in New York during 1960 and 1961 as the result of a loansharking debt (1973: 8–12).

The facts disclose that Murray Packing Company, owned and operated by the Weinberg family and David Newman, a supplier of meat, poultry, and eggs to wholesalers and markets, was infiltrated by the underworld late in 1960 when it began to encounter financial problems.

In 1960, the owners of Murray, short of working capital, borrowed $8,500 at an interest rate of 1% per week. This loan was arranged by Joseph Pagano, a salesman for Murray, and was advanced by the Jo-Ran Trading Corporation owned by Peter Castellana. As the debt increased, the legitimate owners accommodated Castellana's demand that Pagano be promoted and made an executive with the company with broad financial power.

Upon becoming president, Joseph Pagano with the assistance of David Newman as well as Joseph and Stanley Weinberg and others manipulated Murray Packing into a series of business transactions with Pride Wholesale Meat and Poultry Corporation, which was also controlled by Peter Castellana. During January and February, 1961, Murray Packing made a substantial number of relatively small purchases throughout the United States of meat and poultry and paid for these purchases within its normal credit terms of one week. Most of this merchandise was in turn sold to Castellana who paid Murray promptly during this same period.

In March, 1961, there was a marked change in events. Purchases increased enormously, eventually exceeding one million dollars with most of the merchandise going from Murray to Castellana who paid almost simultaneously, but who arbitrarily paid Murray below cost or slightly above cost in most instances. Murray, however, stalled on its payments to its creditors. During the period March 20 to March 29, 1961, Pagano, as President of Murray, cashed Murray checks totalling $745,000. These funds were never recovered. Approximately $170,000 worth of merchandise was sold by Murray to Gondolfo Sciandra, an associate of Castellana. Murray never received payment from Sciandra.

In April, 1961, three creditors of Murray filed an involuntary petition in bankruptcy in the United States District Court for the Southern District of New York under Section 70e of the Federal Bankruptcy Act of 1898 (Title 18, U.S. Code).

In May, 1961, Murray Packing Company was adjudged bankrupt, owing some eighty-five creditors approximately $1,300,000. Total Murray assets were $1,060,422.15, consisting of $745,000 in promissory notes from Joseph Pagano and $268,692.15 accounts receivable. The remainder of its assets totalled less than $50,000.

In May, 1963, Joseph Pagano, Peter Castellana, David Newman, Gondolfo Sciandra, Joseph Weinberg, and Stanley Weinberg were indicted (63 CR 454) and charged with the crime of conspiracy to violate the Bankruptcy Laws, under Section 152 of Title 18 U. S. Code (fraudulently transferring property of a corporation that was in contemplation of bankruptcy) and on one count of violating 18 U. S. C. Section 371 (1964). The substantive count charged the fraudulent transfer of $1,300,000 of Murray's assets. The conspiracy count charged agreements to defraud creditors of Murray and to commit acts which would cause Murray to transfer to various conspirators substantially all of Murray's property and assets. In December, 1964, all defendants were found guilty on all eight counts of the indictment. In July, 1965, Pagano's conviction was affirmed on appeal. *United States* vs.

*Castellana,* et al., 349 F. 2d. 264 (2d CIR. 1965). Subsequent petitions to the Supreme Court of the United States for a writ of *certiorari* and then for a hearing were denied in February, and April, 1966, respectively, 383 U. S. 928 (1966).

According to the United States Attorney, Robert M. Morgenthau, Jr., this case was the "biggest, boldest, most audacious bankruptcy fraud" ever perpetuated in the Southern District of New York involving the takeover of a legitimate business by criminal elements.

The criminal prosecution of Joseph Pagano, Peter Castellana, Joseph Weinberg, Stanley Weinberg, David Newman, and Gondolfo Sciandra delayed civil judgment. The Trustee in Bankruptcy sought to impose civil liability upon them for their fraudulent acts seeking damages in excess of $1,000,000.

In October, 1968, after conclusion of the bankruptcy proceedings, Judge Walter R. Mansfield, United States District Court, signed three orders directing the entry of a monetary judgment in favor of the Trustee as follows: against Castellana, Pride and Jo-Ran, $10,000; against Stanley Weinberg, $500; against Joseph Pagano, Gondolfo Sciandra, Joseph and Gussie Weinberg, and David and Terry Newman, $1,038,999.47. The Trustee was successful in recovering some $83,244.30 from the various participants in the fraudulent scheme, and both Jo-Ran Realty Trading Co. and Pride Wholesale Meat and Poultry Corp. went out of business.

On February 10, 1970, the Honorable Asa S. Herzog, Referee in Bankruptcy, signed an order authorizing the Trustee to accept an offer of settlement by Pagano for the sum of $75,000. Almost nine years had elapsed since it all began.

In 1977, Joseph Pagano was reportedly involved in extorting money from "Medicaid Mills" in the Bronx, New York. A medicaid mill is a health facility shared by physicians in low-income neighborhoods where residents depend on the Department of Welfare to pay for their health care—Medicaid. Pagano, reputedly representing the crime family of the late Vito Genovese, threatened the owners of the facilities with beatings or fires if they withheld payments, and offered protection from competition if they complied. The syndicate would guarantee that no other Medicaid facility would be permitted to open within a twenty-block area (Raab, 1977: 1, B4). The investigation and prosecution of Pagano ended suddenly when a potential witness, a medical doctor, was shot in the head (Kwitny, 1979: 308).

### Robbery, Theft, and Frauds

Predatory crimes are not frequently engaged in by criminals once they become part of organized crime. However, a great deal of organized crime may be involved in this activity nevertheless. Syndicate members often provide the financing and sometimes the expertise necessary to carry out such predatory crimes as payroll robberies, large-scale commercial burglaries, hijackings, thefts of stocks, bonds, and securities; they will finance frauds, swindles, and any conventional crime that can bring in a profit substantial enough to make the effort worthwhile. They will help to market stolen merchandise such as stocks, bonds, securities, checks, and credit cards. Organized crime members are in a unique position to provide these "services." Their widespread connections to legitimate and illegitimate outlets provide a link between more conventional criminals and the business world.

A thief, robber, or swindler knows he can usually trust a member of the syndicate. On the other hand, the syndicate member can be assured that his investment is secure, that he will not be "ripped off." As one informant told this writer: "When I invest in a job—payroll heist—if the job goes down all right, I get a percentage of the take plus my investment back. If the job is blown, I don't want to hear about it—I get my investment back no matter what!" The "no matter what" means that if his money is not returned, violence will result.

In 1972 the federal government estimated "that thefts representing 15 to 20 percent of the value of all stolen cargo are committed by organized crime" (Dept. of Justice and Dept. of Transportation, 1972: 26). (See Fig. 4-7.) It has been estimated that about 40 percent of the securities thefts in New York City is connected to organized crime, while "associates and members of criminal syndicates are still in control of the major fencing outlets" for these stolen items (Yeager, 1973: 57).

In a fine article on the relationship between organized crime and stolen securities, Matthew Yeager points out the conditions that facilitated organized crime's entry into this lucrative field. He suggests that syndicate involvement in white collar crime "may be a rational response to changing conditions in the economic marketplace" (Ibid.: 54). In the latter half of the 1960s the volume of stock and securities transactions overwhelmed accounting procedures, "and many firms lost control over the whereabouts of the securities they handled" (Ibid.: 55). Important syndicate figures like Carmine Lombardozzi controlled employees of these firms by their gambling indebtedness. In addition, independent thieves also dealt with syndicate figures, who arranged for the fencing of stolen securities (Ibid.: 57).

Two major methods are used to convert stolen securities into cash:

1.  They are used as collateral for bank loans. An operative presents the stolen securities at a bank to secure a loan, which is defaulted. Often the victim of the theft, the brokerage firm, is not even aware of the theft until months after the securities are stolen. Sometimes the operative will deal with a "cooperative" bank official—cooperation having been purchased.
2.  The stolen securities are taken outside the United States to banks in Switzerland or the Bahamas whose bank secrecy laws protect such transactions. The stolen securities are deposited in the banks which issue letters of credit. These letters of credit are used to secure loans or to purchase legitimate securities which are then resold for cash.

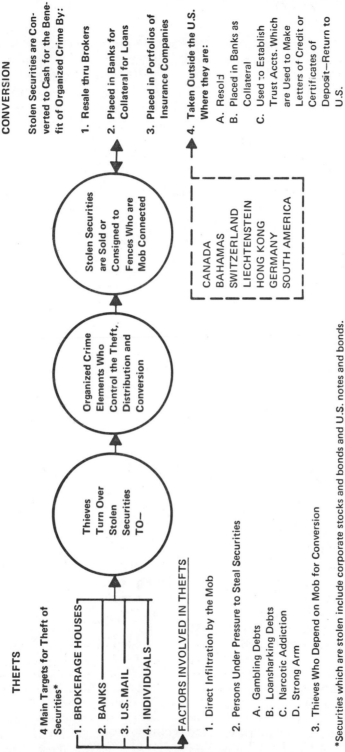

## THEFTS

4 Main Targets for Theft of Securities*

1. BROKERAGE HOUSES
2. BANKS
3. U.S. MAIL
4. INDIVIDUALS

### FACTORS INVOLVED IN THEFTS

1. Direct Infiltration by the Mob

2. Persons Under Pressure to Steal Securities

   A. Gambling Debts
   B. Loansharking Debts
   C. Narcotic Addiction
   D. Strong Arm

3. Thieves Who Depend on Mob for Conversion

*Securities which are stolen include corporate stocks and bonds and U.S. notes and bonds. These securities are either in "street name", bearer instruments or in name of companies or individuals.

Source: "Organized Crime-Stolen Securities", Part I—1971. Permanent Subcommittee on Investigations of the Committee on Government Operations, U.S. Senate, June 1971.

Thieves Turn Over Stolen Securities TO—

Organized Crime Elements Who Control the Theft, Distribution and Conversion

Stolen Securities are Sold or Consigned to Fences Who are Mob Connected

CANADA
BAHAMAS
SWITZERLAND
LIECHTENSTEIN
HONG KONG
GERMANY
SOUTH AMERICA

## CONVERSION

Stolen Securities are Converted to Cash for the Benefit of Organized Crime By:

1. Resale thru Brokers

2. Placed in Banks for Collateral for Loans

3. Placed in Portfolios of Insurance Companies

4. Taken Outside the U.S. Where they are:

   A. Resold
   B. Placed in Banks as Collateral
   C. Used to Establish Trust Accts. Which are Used to Make Letters of Credit or Certificates of Deposit—Return to U.S.

Fig. 4-7. Conversion of stolen securities.

Yeager stresses that there does not appear to be organized crime infiltration into the legitimate securities business, but simply "organized thieving and organized fencing of stolen securities" (Ibid.: 64). However, a scheme used by the late John ("Johnny Dio") Dioguardi would seem to belie this contention. Dioguardi had stock brokers fronting for him. He would have them acquire the stock of a failing company for relatively no money. They would then report fictitious sales to the National Daily Quotation Service, which would artificially inflate the price of the stock. The inflated stock would be sold at a great profit (Kwitny, 1979: 307–308).

Stolen or counterfeit securities may also be "rented" to a businessman in trouble. For a fee of 5 percent a businessman is able to rent millions in "dirty paper" and then "adds the bad paper to the legitimate assets of his company's financial statement. He then shows the new statement to a bank and secures the financing needed to save his company" (Clarke and Tigue, 1975: 205).

Thurston Clarke and John Tigue report that organized crime is dependent on "papermen" since they themselves are usually without sophistication in this area. As one of their informants notes: "They could get hold of plenty of securities by stealing or buying them from someone who stole them. But they couldn't tell you what the security meant in terms of conversion to cash," and "didn't have the faintest notion of how to convert them to cash or use them in financial dealings" (Ibid.: 190). Thus, in the 1960s, a new organized crime task specialty became part of various crime family operations, the *paperman*. (This was not a new criminal occupation; "paper-hangers" are discussed in Sutherland's book first printed in 1937).

## ENDNOTES

1. Anthony Accardo of the Capone organization, for example, reported to the Internal Revenue Service (IRS) that he earned more than 1.5 million dollars from 1940 until 1955. The IRS did not find his report satisfactory (Peterson, 1963: 33).
2. It is of some historical interest to note that William ("Big Bill") Rockefeller, great grandfather of Nelson, peddled these patent medicines. Their sale enabled him to provide his son John Davidson with the financing needed to get into the oil business which became the basis for the Rockefeller fortune (Epstein, 1977: 34–35).
3. For a thorough medical analysis of cocaine, see Freud, 1974; for a comprehensive review see Grinspoon & Bakalar, 1976.
4. Durk points out that "the key figures in the Italian heroin establishment never touched heroin. Guys who were in the business for twenty years and had made millions off of it had never seen it" (Durk and Silverman, 1976: 49).
5. For an in-depth look at the operations of a fence, see Klockars, 1974.
6. The United States Senate Select Committee on Improper Activities in the Labor or Management Field. Senator John L. McClellen of Arkansas was Chairman.

7. John Dioguardi died on January 14, 1979. At the time he was serving a federal prison sentence for stock fraud in a car-leasing company case. His obituary reported that Dioguardi was born on the Lower East Side of Manhattan on April 29, 1914, and was the nephew of Jimmy Doyle (real name James Plumeri), an important organized crime figure. His first conviction was in 1937 for extorting money from the trucking industry. In 1956 he was indicted for the acid-throwing attack that blinded labor columnist Victor Riesel. The charges were dropped when witnesses refused to testify. In 1967 he received a five-year sentence for bankruptcy fraud (scam), and when he finished that term in 1973, he was convicted in the stock fraud case (Kihss, 1979: B6).

8. Anthony Corallo received his nickname because of his ability to escape ("duck") assassinations or convictions. During the 1960s, this "ability" apparently faded. In 1961 he tried to bribe J. Vincent Keogh, a New York State Supreme Court Judge, and Elliott Kahaner, Chief Assistant United States Attorney for the Eastern District of New York. The three received two-year terms. In 1969 he was convicted of conspiracy and bribery in cases that involved James Marcus, New York City Commissioner of the Department of Water Supply, Gas, and Electricity, and eventually Carmine De Sapio, who had been the most powerful Democratic leader in New York State and boss of Tammany Hall. As of this writing, Corallo is reportedly the head of the Lucchese crime family.

# FIVE

# Organized Crime and Corruption

Stuart Hills (1969: 26) points out that "it is doubtful that organized crime could thrive so successfully in America without the cooperation and outright connivance of a portion of our political and law enforcement machinery." He notes that the history of "bribes, delivery of votes, fixes, payoffs, and public officials beholden to the syndicate continues ad nauseam, allowing organized crime in many large and small cities to operate in comparative immunity. At various times, organized crime has been the dominant political force in Chicago, New York, Miami, and New Orleans, although few large metropolitan centers have been immune to such corrupting influences" (1969: 26).

Much of this corruption is rooted in the urban politics of an earlier period, the era of the "machine." John Buenker (1973: 22) states: "The traditional view of the political machine stressed the notion of unscrupulous politicians manipulating masses of unthinking voters and reaping great bundles of graft and corruption." He argues that while this picture "contained a goodly measure of truth," critics and opponents of the machine were often tinged with nativist prejudice and "held up standards of political morality that probably never prevailed anywhere in the real world." These critics "demanded a level of voter performance that could have only been the product of education, experience, and economic security that the urban masses had no way of acquiring" (1973: 22). Indeed, the situation in which immigrants found themselves was quite wretched (Ibid.: 3):

> The new arrivals were forced into substandard housing in sections of the city seemingly reserved for their own ethnic group. Higher education and advancement into the white-collar world was extremely difficult because of the need for youthful employment and the social discrimination exercised by professional and business elites. The urban immigrant also found his customs and religious beliefs subjected to stringent attack from many quarters of the native population, ranging from those who wished to ostracize him completely from polite society to those who sought to remake him in the image of English Protestantism.
>
> Beset by hostility and discrimination on virtually all sides, the immigrant gradually found that he possessed at least one commodity that some native Americans coveted: his vote.

The urban political organization, the "machine," harnessed the immigrant vote by providing the only readily available assistance in pre-social welfare

America. The cost of this assistance was achieved by the ability of the machine to control such important aspects of government as police services (Rubinstein, 1973: 372):

> Many police captains were actually little more than gambling and liquor commissioners whose primary responsibility was to enforce the illegal licenses which the political machines granted to favored operators. The police did not organize protection but carried out the orders established by the elected leaders of their city or state. Policemen were frequently employed as steerers, bouncers, and doormen for gambling houses and speakeasies.

## POLICE

As we have seen, organized crime in the United States dates back more than a century, while organized police forces are only a little older. American police development was fostered by the British experience, particularly the reforms of Sir Robert Peel in 1829, from whom the London "Bobbies" get their name. However, the American experience differed from the British. Police in New York, as well as Chicago and elsewhere, depended on political appointments for their jobs and promotions, and they had to be residents of the wards to which they were appointed and served (Richardson, 1975: 20). James Richardson highlights problems in the New York system: "The group tensions and antagonisms which required an improved police system for New York made the creation of such a system more difficult" (Ibid.). There was disagreement over what laws should be enforced, how they were to be enforced, and who would enforce them. "Those who provided such sought-after but illegal services as gambling, prostitution, and saloons that opened on Sunday wished to limit police activities in these areas. Those who were morally opposed to such services pressed the police to be as energetic as possible in suppressing them" (Ibid.).

Herbert Packer states that the police must be sure of their role—that what they are doing reflects the "common consensus" (1968: 262). He suggests: "The way to keep these processes recurring at peak efficiency is to ensure that those who operate them are convinced that what they are doing is right" (Ibid.). He argues, "If the criminal sanction is widely used to deal with morally neutral behavior, law enforcement officials are likely to be at least subconsciously defensive about their work, and the public will find the criminal law a confusing guide to moral, or even acceptable behavior" (Ibid.). This is highlighted by a statement from Patrick Murphy, former New York City Police Commissioner and as of this writing president of the Police Foundation: "I am unable to regard gambling as a mortal sin; I also felt, somewhat intuitively, that gambling enforcement is demeaning and quite possibly beneath the dignity of the police. And, as a practical matter, the law against gambling was utterly impossible to enforce, even by the most professional, assiduous police action" (1977: 44).

Edwin Schur points to a serious functional problem involved in enforcing statutes concerning activities most closely associated with organized crime—the absence of a complainant. He argues that the lack of a complainant-victim lies at the heart of the unenforceability of statutes outlawing so-called "victimless crimes" (1969: 196). The lack of a complainant-victim leads to engaging informants, often persons who are themselves involved in criminal activities. The informant is provided with a form of "license" to continue in crime as a reward for his assistance to law enforcement. Edward Jay Epstein reports that in 1975 the chief narcotics officer in Baltimore claimed "that there were 800 active *criminal* narcotics informers working with the police in Baltimore, and most of these informers were in fact dealers who had a de facto franchise from the police department which they preserved by turning in 'competitors' not on the police payrolls" (1977: 106). In one case familiar to this writer, a bookmaker in Brooklyn was given a certain amount of immunity in return for the information he provided on drug activities. This immunity only provided protection from the police, however, and he was eventually executed.

Law enforcement personnel who deal with organized crime activities and who operate in the field (as opposed to the office), must, more or less frequently, maintain personal contact with criminals, either as undercover operatives or by dealing with informants. This contact is a potentially corrupting influence. It is often only a small step from using drug traffickers as informants to entering into business with them. Epstein notes that in 1968 it was discovered "that a number of federal agents in the New York office [of the Bureau of Narcotics] were in the business of selling heroin or protecting drug dealers and that the bureau itself had been a major source of supply and protection in the United States" (1977: 105). This problem may account for the reluctance of the Federal Bureau of Investigation, under J. Edgar Hoover, to become involved in combatting organized crime. Murphy states that "organized crime could not have reached the proportions it has without the neglect of the Federal Bureau of Investigation" (1977: 86). The first FBI agent ever convicted of a felony accepted a $10,000 bribe from a syndicate bookmaker (Cook, 1979: 38).

The Task Force on Organized Crime stated in 1967: "All available data indicate that organized crime flourishes only where it has corrupted local officials" (1967: 6). Anthony Simpson refers to the Task Force statement and notes: "This point should be well-taken as support for it is generated throughout the literature" (1977: 88). However, there is a difficulty with viewing the problem as simply *organized crime corrupts officials;* we have already noted in previous chapters that the line between organized crime and corrupt officials is often unclear, at times nonexistent. In Chapter Three we saw that at times the *officials were organized crime.* In both Chicago and New York those who ran organized criminal activities, gambling and prostitution, were political figures and often elected officials. In other instances, for example the case of Harry Gross, it was actually the police who organized the handbooks into a syndicate. Gross was a smalltime handbook—i.e., a bookmaker with no fixed business location—in Brooklyn when he met James E. Reardon, a New York City plainclothes police officer. Reardon not only protected the Gross operation but acted as "muscle" by arresting or physically threatening competitors: "Rival bookies were given the choice of going out of business or joining the Gross combine" (Mockridge and Prall, 1954: 33–34). Reardon was kicked out of plainclothes and placed back into uniform because of his activities. He quit the force and went to work for Gross—a more accurate portrayal would probably be that he became Gross's partner or even his boss. Gross began to gamble, betting with the Frank Erikson bookmaking syndicate, and he lost heavily. Fearing Erikson, who he owed a great deal of money (Erikson was a partner of Frank Costello), Gross fled to California, leaving the business to Reardon. Reardon kept the business together; he went to other police officers who were able to secure more than $100,000 through Joe Adonis (Ibid.: 36–37). This enabled Gross to return from California and head up the police–organized syndicate. By the time he was arrested on September 15, 1950, Gross and his syndicate were paying about $1 million annually for police protection (Ibid.: 38).

During the 1970s, federal authorities conducted a six-year investigation of police corruption in Chicago. What they found was a distribution of payoffs within the police structure that was hierarchical, having "many of the features similar to the handling of money within organized crime" (Beigel and Beigel, 1977: 271). The corruption originated in saloons whose owners paid for police "protection," i.e., for the freedom to operate without interference (Ibid.: 10). As the payoffs became organized, district commanders began to use the vice coordinators to collect money from tavern owners engaged in illegal activities. The vice coordinator might also designate an assistant who would actually make the collections when the vice coordinator was not on duty. The collector, known as the "bagman," split the payoffs with the district commander, giving a percentage of his own take to his assistant. A bookmaking tavern owner divided his own profits with the syndicate after making the payoffs. As a result of the federal investigation of police-originated corruption, more than sixty police officers were sentenced to imprisonment, and many others were given immunity from prosecution in return for their testimony (Ibid.: 267).

James Q. Wilson offers a conceptual framework for explaining corruption in drug law enforcement. Narcotic officers/agents "know with reasonable confidence that one or more persons has committed or is about to commit a crime; their task is to observe its commission, usually by creating under controlled conditions a suitable opportunity." Wilson refers to such agents as "instigators" (not meant in a derogatory sense) as opposed to the conventional "investigator" who acts after being informed of a crime, i.e., after receiving a complaint (1978: 57). He points out that both investigators and instigators "are exposed to opportunities for corruption, but the latter far more than the former" (Ibid.: 59):

> The detective [investigator], were he to accept money or favors to act other than as his duty required, would have to conceal or alter information about a crime already known to his organization. The instigator can easily agree to

overlook offenses known to him but to no one else or to participate in illegal transactions (buying and selling drugs) for his own rather than for the organization's advantage.

Shaw and McKay (1972) provide us with another dimension for explaining the persistence of police corruption, now seemingly divorced from its roots in the urban political machine—"cultural transmission." Police departments train new officers, rookies, at least in part, by teaming them up with more experienced officers, veterans. Police departments usually promote police officers to higher positions from within their own ranks. Both of these factors insure the continuity of unofficial mores and customs that are taught to and eventually shared by the new officers. Thus, despite recurring scandal and periodic personnel shake-ups, patterns of corruption can be passed down through generations of police officers.

Several years ago, John Mingo (a pseudonym), a friend of this writer, became a police officer. After a relatively short period of time, based on his ethnic background and proven undercover ability, John was assigned to a plainclothes gambling enforcement unit. This is usually considered a choice assignment since "plainclothes" often serves as a training period before promotion to the position of detective. After completing the official training program, John was teamed up with a veteran plainclothes officer—"unofficial" training. He and his partner were soon approached by their commanding officer, and the lieutenant asked for his "envelope." After seeing his partner hand the lieutenant a ten-dollar bill, John did the same. After the commanding officer left, John waited some time for an explanation, but none was forthcoming. Naively thinking that the money was for some type of "sunshine fund" (used to buy gifts in cases of births, marriages, or deaths), John asked about the "occasion." The reply was direct and informative: "That was for the C.O. [commanding officer]. Now we can go out and make it back while 'scoring' [graft] for ourselves. But, the C.O., he don't care, as long as he gets his up front."

Whoever can act as an intermediary between corrupt officials and illegitimate business operations is in a position to control the organized criminal activities in a given locality. Harry King (Chambliss, 1972: Chapter 4) reports that in Portland, Oregon, the bordellos and gambling establishments were owned or "licensed" by one operator, James Elkins, who with a small number of employees, including four "enforcers," made large payoffs to the police and was permitted to operate without serious interference. On two occasions, King reports, syndicate operators from outside Portland attempted to move in and take over the Elkins operation. On the first attempt, the Minneapolis syndicate agent could not secure police cooperation and was forced to leave. The second attempt by the Teamsters Union was reported by Robert Kennedy, who noted that Elkins was one of the best witnesses who appeared before the McClellen Committee (Senate Select Committee on Improper Activities in the Labor or Management Field.) In 1954, Kennedy reported, two Seattle racketeers, who were also Teamster officials, tried to move in on Elkins

(1960: 245–246). Kennedy notes that at first Elkins cooperated, but eventually broke with the Teamsters over the issue of prostitution. According to Kennedy, Elkins refused to have anything to do with prostitution (Ibid.: 247). This naive conclusion conflicts with Harry King, who worked for Elkins and collected the "protection" money from the bordellos. The Teamster officials were eventually able to take over gambling and prostitution in Portland because they succeeded in securing the cooperation of the political officials who controlled the police.

In 1961, as part of a reform effort in Newport, Kentucky, and the rest of Cambell County (just across the river from Cincinnati), George Ratterman, a former professional football player, agreed to run for sheriff of Cambell County. In a rather famous incident, Ratterman was drugged, and with the cooperation of the Newport police was arrested with a striptease dancer and taken to police headquarters wearing a bedspread. The ploy failed, and Ratterman was elected * (Messick, 1967: 283–284).

David Durk, a New York City police officer who worked with Frank Serpico, reports on corruption that made it difficult to determine *who* actually made up organized crime (1976: 36):

By 1969, there were two major marketing operations of heroin in New York City. One operated out of Pleasant Avenue; the other operated out of the fourth floor of the First Precinct station house in lower Manhattan—the headquarters of the Special Investigations Unit of the police department's Narcotics Division.

Durk states that the police acted as enforcers for the larger drug dealers by arresting their competition (1976: 33). They also kept the dealers "in line": a narcotics dealer "who wasn't 'cooperating' might be locked in a car trunk, and left there for several hours. When a dealer 'really had to be taught a lesson,' a snake was put in the car trunk with him" (Ibid.: 38). (For an interesting account of the corruption in the New York City Police Department, and the Special Investigations Unit (SIU) in particular, see Daley, 1978. Daley takes a more benign view of the SIU than Durk. See also Grosso and Rosenberg, 1978).

*Stating that organized crime corrupts public officials obscures more than it explains.*

* Eighteen years after the "clean-up" this writer visited Newport for a first-hand look at what had been a "wide-open town." Newport, a city of only 1.5 miles and a population of about 25,000, is still touted on a Cincinnati tourist map as "sin" city, a reason to hold conventions just across the bridge in Cincinnati. However, except for a couple of X-rated movie houses and a few bawdy shows, like those found in many urban areas of the United States, Newport is hardly filled with sin. It is, however, filled with poverty and abandoned buildings; some had served as luxury gambling houses. The Flamingo still has its large neon sign in front, unused for eighteen years. People who depended on gambling, directly or indirectly, for their livelihood were left behind when the Cleveland syndicate pulled out. Many of these persons drifted into conventional criminal activity and became known to the police in Cincinnati.

## Knapp Commission

When plotted on a graph, the regularity of the *corruption-scandal-investigation* syndrome in New York City will actually appear as a horizontal line; the years being:

1894 (Lexow)
1912 (Rosenthal)
1932 (Seabury)
1950 (Gross)
1970 (Knapp)

Each of these major episodes resulted in the same findings: systematic police corruption from vice activities, prostitution, gambling, bootlegging, narcotics. The last episode resulted from the failure of responsible city officials to take effective action on the complaints presented by plainclothes patrolman Frank Serpico and Sergeant David Durk in 1966 and 1967. In 1970, the officers presented their information to David Burnham, a reporter for the *NYT*. As a direct result of Burnham's (1970) disclosures, Mayor John Lindsay issued Executive Order No. 11 on May 21, 1970, creating *A Commission to Investigate Allegations of Police Corruption and the City's Anti-Corruption Procedures*. The Commission was composed of five distinguished New Yorkers and is usually referred to by the name of the chairman, Whitman Knapp. The Knapp Commission submitted its final report to the mayor on December 26, 1972. A summary of the Commission's findings follows:

## SUMMARY

### THE EXTENT OF POLICE CORRUPTION

We found corruption to be widespread. It took various forms depending upon the activity involved, appearing at its most sophisticated among plainclothesmen assigned to enforcing gambling laws. In the five plainclothes divisions where our investigations were concentrated we found a strikingly standardized pattern of corruption. Plainclothesmen, participating in what is known in police parlance as a "pad," collected regular bi-weekly or monthly payments amounting to as much as $3,500 from each of the gambling establishments in the area under their jurisdiction, and divided the take in equal shares. The monthly share per man (called the "nut") ranged from $300 and $400 in midtown Manhattan to $1,500 in Harlem. When supervisors were involved they received a share and a half. A newly assigned plainclothesman was not entitled to his share for about two months, while he was checked out for reliability, but the earnings lost by the delay were made up to him in the form of two months' severance pay when he left the division.

Evidence before us led us to the conclusion that the same pattern existed in the remaining divisions which we did not investigate in depth. This conclusion was confirmed by events occurring before and after the period of our investigation. Prior to the Commission's existence, exposures by former plainclothesman Frank Serpico had led to indictments or departmental charges against nineteen plainclothesmen in a Bronx division for involvement in a pad where the nut was $800. After our public hearings had been completed, an investigation conducted by the Kings County District Attorney and the Department's Internal Affairs Division—which investigation neither the Commission nor its staff had even known about—resulted in indictments and charges against thirty-seven Brooklyn plainclothesmen who had participated in a pad with a nut of $1,200. The manner of operation of the pad involved in each of these situations was in every detail identical to that described at the Commission hearings, and in each almost every plainclothesman in the division, including supervisory lieutenants, was implicated.

Corruption in narcotics enforcement lacked the organization of the gambling pads, but individual payments—known as "scores"—were commonly received and could be staggering in amount. Our investigation, a concurrent probe by the State Investigation Commission and prosecutions by Federal and local authorities all revealed a pattern whereby corrupt officers customarily collected scores in substantial amounts from narcotics violators. These scores were either kept by the individual officer or shared with a partner and, perhaps, a superior officer. They ranged from minor shakedowns to payments of many thousands of dollars, the largest narcotics payoff uncovered in our investigation having been $80,000. According to information developed by the S.I.C. and in recent Federal investigations, the size of this score was by no means unique.

Corruption among detectives assigned to general investigative duties also took the form of shakedowns of individual targets of opportunity. Although these scores were not in the huge amounts found in narcotics, they not infrequently came to several thousand dollars.

Uniformed patrolmen assigned to street duties were not found to receive money on nearly so grand or organized a scale, but the large number of small payments they received present an equally serious if less dramatic problem. Uniformed patrolmen, particularly those assigned to radio patrol cars, participated in gambling pads more modest in size than those received by plainclothes units and received regular payments from construction sites, grocery stores and other business establishments. These payments were usually made on a regular basis to sector car patrolmen and on a haphazard basis to others. While individual payments to uniformed men were small, mostly under $20, they were often so numerous as to add substantially to a patrolman's income. Other less regular payments to uniformed patrolmen included those made by after-hours bars, bottle clubs, tow trucks, motorists, cab drivers, parking lots, prostitutes and defendants wanting to fix their cases in court. Another practice found to be widespread was the payment of gratuities by policemen to other policemen to expedite normal police procedures or to gain favorable assignments.

Sergeants and lieutenants who were so inclined participated in the same kind of corruption as the men they supervised. In addition, some sergeants had their own pads from which patrolmen were excluded.

Although the Commission was unable to develop hard evidence establishing that officers above the rank of lieutenant received payoffs, considerable circumstantial evidence and some testimony so indicated. Most often when a superior officer is corrupt, he uses a patrolman as his "bagman" who collects for him and keeps a percentage of the take. Because the bagman may keep the money for himself, although he claims to be collecting for his superior, it is extremely difficult to determine with any accuracy when the superior actually is involved.

Of course, not all policemen are corrupt. If we are to exclude such petty infractions as free meals, an appreciable number do not engage in any corrupt activities. Yet, with extremely rare exceptions, even those who themselves engage in no corrupt activities are involved in corruption in the sense that they take no steps to prevent what they know or suspect to be going on about them.

It must be made clear that—in a little over a year with a staff having as few as two and never more than twelve field investigators—we did not examine every precinct in the Department. Our conclusion that corruption is widespread throughout the Department is based on the fact that information supplied to us by hundreds of sources within and without the Department was consistently borne out by specific observations made in areas we were able to investigate in detail.

## Patterns of Corruption in
## Narcotics Law Enforcement in New York*

The most common form of narcotics-related police corruption is not the systematic pad common in other areas such as gambling, but the individual score of money, narcotics, or both, seized at the scene of a raid or arrest.

### EXTORTION AND BRIBE-TAKING

In many cases police officers actively extort money and/or drugs from suspected narcotics law violators. Recently, for example, the motel room of a "dealer" (actually a federal undercover agent who was recording the conversation) was raided by two detectives and one patrolman. They found $12,000 in cash on the premises and demanded that the "dealer" surrender $10,000 to avoid arrest. The "dealer" was finally able to persuade them to leave him $4,000 as getaway money. The detectives later paid a $1,000 finder's fee to another detective who had alerted them to the "dealer's" presence in town.

In June, 1972, a dismissed plainclothesman who had been assigned to the Narcotics Division was convicted in New York County and sentenced to up to four years in prison for his part in an extortion scheme which involved six members of the Narcotics Division. According to testimony at the trial, he and two other police officers contacted a restaurant owner and demanded $6,000, threatening to arrest his daughter-in-law on a narcotics charge un-

* Source: Knapp Commission Report, pages 94–103.

less he paid them. They further threatened to send the woman's two children to a foundling home in the event of her arrest. The restaurant owner paid them what they asked.

Within a few months, the same policeman, along with some other members of the unit, again approached the man and demanded an additional $12,000. The man told them to return in a few days, and in the interim he arranged for police surveillance of the next transaction. The plainclothesman was arrested when he accepted a down payment in marked money.

Two of the Commission's informants in the narcotics area were hardcore heroin addicts who, as registered police informants, were able to witness and sometimes record many instances of police profiteering on the street level. While these informants' credibility is necessarily suspect, there is ample evidence from other sources that the extortion practices they described were common occurrences in the Narcotics Division at the time of the Commission's investigation.

They told of participation in police shakedowns of narcotics "cribs" and said that it was standard practice for an informant to find a location where drugs were being sold in large quantities, and by attempting to make a buy with a large denomination bill, to induce the seller to reveal the hiding place of his cash supply. (Sellers in stationary locations try to keep as little money as possible on their person in order to minimize losses in case of an arrest or shakedown.) On leaving, the informant would arrange to return later to make another buy. On his next visit, as the seller opened the door, the police would crash in behind the informant. If the police felt they could score without risk, they would take whatever money and narcotics were available and let the seller go. If the amount of money was small, they would usually arrest the seller but still keep most of the narcotics, turning in only the amount necessary to charge a felony or misdemeanor as the case might be.

The informants stated that three out of every four times they went out on a raid with plainclothesmen from the Narcotics Division, no arrests were made and scores ranged from a few hundred dollars to as much as $20,000 on one occasion, with the informants getting some money and quantities of drugs as compensation.

The Commission found that, even without prompting from the police, it was quite common for an apprehended suspect to offer to pay his captors for his release and for the right to keep part of his narcotics and cash. This was especially true at higher levels of distribution where the profits to be made and the penalties risked by a dealer were very high. One such case was that of a suspended Narcotics Division detective who was recently indicted in Queens County and charged with taking bribes to overlook narcotics offenses. The indictment alleged that this officer accepted $1,500 on one occasion for not arresting a suspected drug pusher who was apprehended while in possession of $15,000 worth of heroin. There is evidence that on another occasion this detective was paid $4,000 by a different narcotics pusher for agreeing not to confiscate $150,000 worth of heroin. The detective has pleaded guilty to attempting to receive a bribe, and his sentence is pending.

Even after arrest, a suspect would sometimes try to pay the arresting officer to leave him enough money for his legal expenses, or to downgrade the arrest by holding back a large part of the seized narcotics, or to make sure that his case would be a "throw-out" in court. Police officers have accomplished this favor by writing up an ambiguous complaint which did not explicitly link the evidence seized in the arrest to the defendant. For example, an officer's affidavit could aver that narcotics had been discovered not on the defendant's person, but on the ground near his feet. In such a case, of course, the evidence would be inadmissible against the defendant and the case would be thrown out.

The opportunity for an arresting officer to score does not end at the scene of an arrest. As suspended patrolman William Phillips told the Commission in the course of his testimony about similar fixed arrest affidavits in gambling cases, "It's never too late to do business." That is, a police officer who is skillful or experienced enough can write an affidavit which appears to be very strong, but is still open-ended enough to work in favor of a defendant when coupled with appropriate testimony from the arresting officer. For example, an officer could state in his complaint that the suspect threw the evidence to the ground at the approach of the police. Should that officer later testify that he lost sight of the evidence as it fell, the evidence and the case could well be dismissed. The Commission learned that it was not uncommon for defense attorneys in narcotics cases to pay policemen for such favors as lying under oath and procuring confidential police and judicial records concerning their clients' cases.

It was, of course, beyond the scope of this Commission to seek out evidence of narcotics-related crime among agencies and officials outside the Police Department. However, the temptation of a police officer to profit illegally from a narcotics arrest could not be examined completely apart from his awareness or suspicion of corruption among those charged with the prosecution and adjudication of cases he has made. Evidence uncovered by the United States Attorney's Office in Manhattan in a current investigation of bribery by heroin dealers confirms the fact that corruption in narcotics law enforcement goes beyond the Police Department and involves prosecutors, attorneys, bondsmen, and allegedly even certain judges. While this fact does not excuse the illegal conduct of policemen who accept bribes, it does serve to illustrate the demoralizing environment in which police are expected to enforce narcotics laws.

The experience of one Narcotics Division detective who worked as an undercover agent for the U.S. Attorney's Office illustrates the pressures many police officers face after making a legitimate narcotics arrest. In a secretly recorded conversation, an attorney for a defendant in a narcotics case offered the detective various amounts ranging from $15,000 to $30,000 to give false testimony on behalf of his defendant. In an earlier recorded conversation, a co-defendant who had won a dismissal of charges told the detective that he had paid the attorney $20,000 to fix the case.

The belief that an officer's efforts to enforce narcotics law have been or may be nullified by dealings higher up in the legal system has in some instances caused members of the Department to rebel against such corruption. Unfortunately, it seems to be much more common for policemen exposed to such high-level corruption to try to get in on the profits. Such was the case of one Tactical Patrol Force officer who was apparently so confident of the acceptability of bribery that he attempted to arrange for a significant narcotics violator to bribe an assistant district attorney. He later pleaded guilty to bribery and resigned from the force after having served in the Department for eighteen years.

## ILLEGAL USE OF WIRETAPS

An extortion attempt by police officers is sometimes the end product of careful surveillance of a target, often by means of wiretaps. The wiretap is an essential tool in the Police Department's efforts to make cases against narcotics law violators. One state official with extensive experience in the enforcement of narcotics laws told the Commission that he didn't know of a single significant narcotics case prosecuted in the New York State courts without evidence or leads obtained through wiretapping, legal or illegal.

Theoretically, police may not secretly tap a suspect's telephone without a warrant. However, since strict constitutional safeguards and a certain amount of red tape surround the procedure for obtaining a warrant, it was not uncommon for Narcotics Division detectives to monitor and record the conversations of suspects without the required court order.

Since the Police Department has no official record of a wiretap installed without a warrant, no arrest is officially expected. Thus, information obtained by means of illegal taps can be used as easily to extort money and drugs from suspects who have been overheard as to make cases against them. Two Narcotics Division detectives were recently observed by a federal undercover agent as they engineered just such a score. The detectives illegally tapped the telephone conversations of a suspect in order to determine the extent of his dealings in narcotics. They then confronted the suspect with the evidence they had against him and threatened to arrest him unless he paid them $50,000. The suspect acceded to their demand and was given his freedom. The undercover agent, a former member of the Narcotics Division, told the Commission that in his experience the case is not unique.

## STEALING MONEY AND NARCOTICS

A score in the narcotics area is by no means dependent upon a suspect's offer or agreement to pay off the police. Most often a police officer seeking to score simply keeps for himself all or part of the money and drugs confiscated during a raid or arrest. One former member of the Narcotics Division recently assigned to other duties told the Commission that in his experience eighty to ninety percent of the members of the Narcotics Division participated in at least this type of score. While it was not possible for the Commission to verify this estimate, Commission investigators did ascertain that the holding back of money or narcotics contraband is very common and not limited to the Narcotics Division or other special squads.

The Commission learned of several sizable scores made by policemen during narcotics arrests. One such score was described by a plainclothesman in a secretly recorded conversation with Patrolman William Phillips. He told Phillips of an arrest he had made where $137,000 was turned in to the Department while three policemen split an additional $80,000.

Captain Daniel McGowan, then assigned to the Department's Public Morals Administrative Division, testified before the Commission about one matter he had investigated involving the arrest of several people and the confiscation of $150,000. Of this amount, McGowan stated, only $50,000 was turned in, the arresting officers keeping $100,000 for themselves.

Dismissed Patrolman Waverly Logan testified before the Commission about similar stealing, albeit on a lesser scale, by members of the elite Preventive Enforcement Patrol (PEP) Squad. Logan told the Commission that in his experience it was very common for arresting officers to keep confiscated money and drugs for themselves, and he gave many examples of the practice. After one narcotics arrest, for example, Logan and two other patrolmen vouchered $200 and held back $300 to divide among themselves. Later, Logan said, he discovered that one of the arresting officers had pocketed still another $500 which he had seized during the arrest. After another arrest during which Logan had scored $200, he watched from the precinct house window as another patrolman and a sergeant from his squad searched the suspect's car. The sergeant took a black fur coat from the trunk of the car and hid it in his own, while the patrolman walked away with a stereo tape device and several tape cassettes. Other situations described by Logan indicate that theft by police of furnishings and other personal property from premises where a narcotics raid had taken place were not uncommon.

Logan testified that his PEP Squad sergeant taught him the various techniques of scoring, and that such scoring was standard police procedure among his fellow officers. Logan told of one arrest he made where he did turn in all the money and contraband that he had seized. At the precinct station house where he vouchered the evidence, no one would believe that he was turning in the full amount of money confiscated. No matter how much money an arresting officer vouchered, Logan testified, other officers always assumed that he had kept back some for himself. As a result, in Logan's words:

"When you're new, you turn in all the money. But when you're working on the job awhile, you turn in no money. That's been my experience, that you don't voucher no money, or you voucher very little of what you made when a boss is there, and the boss is straight."

At the Commission hearings, Waverly Logan also described the attitude of some members of the Department that even if narcotics bribes are "dirty money," thefts from arrested drug dealers are "clean":

"[T]he general feeling was that the man was going to jail, was going to get what was coming to him, so why should you give him back his money and let him bail himself out. In a way we felt that he was a narcotics pusher, we knew he was a narcotics pusher, we kind of felt he didn't deserve no rights since he was selling narcotics."

This rationalization, certainly a departure from the unwritten rule that not even a "bad cop" would make money in narcotics, was repeated in various terms by other police officers. One former detective in the Narcotics Division told the Commission that money taken from a narcotics dealer or pusher is considered to be "clean" by police officers because no innocent person is directly injured by such a score. Former Detective Frank Serpico testified about the same attitude in hearings before the SCI. "Something that is accepted in narcotics," Serpico said, "is the fact that . . . if you were to make an arrest and there were large sums of money, that the money would be confiscated and not vouchered and the rationale there is the City is going to get it anyway and why shouldn't they." Serpico said that policemen who take money in this way do not worry that the arrested person will complain, because a narcotics team usually consists of four men, and "[t]he feeling is that it is his word against theirs."

Waverly Logan, on the other hand, apparently was bothered by the fact that arrested suspects might complain about having their money stolen by the police. Although he continued to make scores, Logan testified that he began to let suspects go after he had taken their money, so that they would be less likely to complain. This practice was in keeping with the philosophy of scoring taught to Logan by his sergeant: "[W]hen you are scoring a guy, try to leave him happy. If you leave a guy happy, he won't beef, won't make a complaint against you." Logan explained in his testimony that this could be accomplished even after a large amount of money was taken from a suspect by releasing him with enough of his narcotics to get him back into business.

It is clear from evidence assembled by this Commission and by other investigatory agencies that Waverly Logan's experiences and attitude with respect to holding back money and drugs are not unique in the Department. During the SCI public hearings on police corruption in narcotics law enforcement, a former Narcotics Division patrolman who had been convicted for supplying a heroin addict with narcotics to sell on the streets for him was asked to reveal the source of his heroin supply. He testified that one of the ways in which he obtained narcotics was to take it from dope addicts in the street, without making an arrest.

"Q. Was this a common thing in the Narcotics Division?
"A. That's where I learned it from.
"Q. You learned it from other members of the Narcotics Division?
"A. Yes.
                    *    *    *
"Q. Would you say this practice was generally known not only to the patrolmen and detectives, but by superiors?
"A. I would.
"Q. And on what basis do you make that statement?
"A. Being an ex-officer and knowing the routine of the office. It was pretty general knowledge what went on in the streets.
                    *    *    *
"Q. In addition to obtaining narcotics in the fashion you just described, were there ever occasions where you would make an arrest but hold back the amount seized?
"A. That is true.
"Q. Was that practice also common with the Narcotics Division?
"A. It was."

Another detective, assigned to a squad in Queens, had been a full partner in a narcotics wholesale enterprise, and testified at the same hearings that when he decided to join the partnership, he discussed with fellow officers the fact that at least part of his heroin supply would come from holding back large quantities of heroin from important narcotics arrests.

In addition to sale at a profit, either directly or through addict-pushers, drugs seized and retained by police officers were put to a variety of illegal uses by police, including payment of finder's fees to police informants and payment to addicts for merchandise stolen to order for policemen. Narcotics retained from prior arrests are also used for "padding," that is, for adding to the quantity of narcotics found on a subsequently arrested person, thus enabling the arresting officer to upgrade the charge to a felony. It is also common to use illegally retained narcotics to "flake" a narcotics suspect, that is, to plant evidence on a person in order to make a narcotics arrest.

Rubinstein and Reuter are critical of the Knapp Commission which, although it succeeded in focusing public attention on police corruption, "did not in fact document its case very well." They state that virtually all of the examples of corruption involved the cooperation of plainclothes policeman William Phillips, whom they regard as unreliable (1977: 61–62), and who is currently serving a sentence for murder. Documenting police corruption in New York City, however, has been perennial. In 1938, for example, a Depression year when the salaried position of policeman was highly prized, Governor Herbert Lehman had to convene a Grand Jury in Brooklyn (Kings County) to investigate charges of police corruption. The Grand Jury sat in extraordinary session until 1942 when it submitted its final report, which concluded (Supreme Court of the State of New York, 1942: 5):

> This Grand Jury received evidence that during the period covered by the investigation bookmaking and policy flourished openly in the County of Kings.

Among the activities documented by the Grand Jury were (Ibid.: 5–6):

> (a) a tendency to make unfounded arrests in order to create a record of apparent efficient enforcement and (b) a practice of presenting the evidence in such a manner that a conviction cannot possibly result. Many cases have been found in which the defendant was charged with violation of the gambling laws upon a police officer's affidavit containing a statement of sufficient facts to warrant conviction, and in which at the hearing before the Magistrate the police officer refrained from testifying to essential facts or contradicted his own affidavit as to essential facts.
>
> Examination of the plainclothesmen who were assigned to gambling cases in Kings County during the period covered by this investigation revealed that in all except a few cases the assignment to plainclothes work on gambling violations was accompanied by a distinct change in financial status. The vast majority of plainclothesmen examined were found to be in possession of financial means substantially in excess of any which could be attributed to their salaries, such means consisting variously of cash, at home or in safe deposit boxes, real estate, and securities, acquired subsequent to their assignment to plainclothes work. In addition, many of them were found

to have purchased new automobiles at frequent intervals, fur coats for their wives, and to have taken periodical vacations in Florida and elsewhere in winter and summer while retaining assignments in plainclothes to gambling work.

The Grand Jury noted, "During the course of the investigation by this Grand Jury of charges of neglect and corruption on the part of police officers in the enforcement of gambling laws, numerous police officers, who had either been mentioned in the testimony of others or who had themselves been examined before the Grand Jury, filed their applications for and/or were retired from the Police Department." These included one deputy chief inspector, two inspectors, and one deputy inspector (Ibid.: 153).

Rubinstein and Reuter note a dramatic reduction in police corruption in New York since the Commission made its findings public. This they view as the result of the sharp reduction in the amount of police manpower deployed in New York City for gambling enforcement—from about 700 in 1971 to less than 265 by 1975 (1977: 68–70). After the Knapp Commission the police stopped "street harrassment" and concentrated their efforts on specific targets, the large numbers banks: "The result has been in the last four years more large banks have been seized than at any time in the last thirty years" (1977: 78–79). However, in certain parts of the city "spots opened where gambling is conducted not only publicly but flagrantly," and "uniformed officers have been prohibited from making gambling arrests" (1977: 79).

The authors approve of the New York "strategy," which, they argue, has effectively reduced the importance of organized crime in numbers operations. They recommend: "The aid of enforcement can, and should, be limited to restraining the power of the organizations. Every effort should be made to ensure that entry into the market is not controlled and that banks have disincentives to growing large" (1977: 150). This can be accomplished by repeated enforcement against targeted banks, and not just a few of its outlets, and will cause the controllers to set up operations on their own or find new banks (1977: 151).

Their recommendation would appear to be in accord with information contained in the *Task Force Report: Organized Crime* (1967), but which appeared only as a footnote without any narrative or follow-up (fn. 9, p. 30; emphasis added):

Charles R. Thom, Commissioner of Police of Suffolk County, Long Island, New York:

It is somewhat startling to learn that the syndicates are particularly happy with the consolidation of the nine police departments into the Suffolk County Police Department, as they feel that protection is easier to arrange through one agency than through many. *The intensive campaign against gamblers instituted by this Department commencing January 1 [1960] had the astounding side effect in solving the recruitment problem of the syndicate, as our drive successfully stampeded the independents into the arms of the syndicate for protection, and the syndicate can now pick and choose which operators they wish to admit.*

William Chambliss argues that "the people who run the organizations which supply the vices in American cities are members of the business, political, and law enforcement communities—not simply members of a criminal society" (1976: 182). In his study of "Rainfall West" (apparently a pseudonym for Seattle, Washington), Chambliss found that the syndicate (he calls it a *cabal*) "that manages the vices is composed of important businessmen, law enforcement officers, political leaders, and a member of a major trade union" (1976: 163).

A similar situation was found by John Gardiner in his study of Wincantan (a pseudonym for Reading, Pennsylvania), where the syndicate boss even arranged for the appointment of the police chief—the latter paid the boss for this service. Gardiner reports on the extent of corruption: "The range of officials went from a weekly salary for the mayor to liquor and a Christmas turkey for many patrolmen." In between, receiving a share commensurate with their positions, were the police chief and other city and county officials (1973: 167).

Chambliss points out that the business and professional community is divided in its attitude toward vice (gambling, prostitution, and pornography): "The law enforcement system is thus placed squarely in the middle of two essentially conflicting demands. On the one hand, their job obligates them to enforce the law, albeit with discretion; at the same time, considerable disagreement rages over whether or not some acts should be subject to legal sanction. This conflict is highlighted by the fact that some influential persons in the community insist that all laws be rigorously enforced while others demand that some laws not be enforced, at least not against themselves" (1976: 165). The result is selective enforcement, containing vice activity in certain ecological (lower class) areas and reaping financial rewards (bribes) by "licensing" the activity.

William Whyte makes a similar observation: "There are prevalent in society two general conceptions of the duties of the police officer. Middle-class people feel that he should enforce the law without fear or favor. Cornerville [pseudonym for a Boston ghetto] people and many of the officers themselves believe that the policeman should have the confidence of the people in his area so that he can settle many difficulties in a personal manner without making arrests" (1961: 136). Whyte points out (1961: 138):

On one side are the "good people" of Eastern city, who have written their moral judgments into the law and demand through their newspapers that the law be enforced. On the other side are the people of Cornerville, who have different standards and have built up an organization whose perpetration depends upon freedom to violate the law. Socially, the local officer has more in common with Cornerville people than with those who demand law enforcement, and the financial incentives offered by racketeers have an influence which is of obvious importance.

# SIX

# Combatting Organized Crime

---

Strategies for dealing with organized crime are often reduced to sterile law enforcement techniques; they fail to consider the *latent functions* (Merton, 1967) performed by organized criminal activities. We noted earlier, for example, that in some neighborhoods the numbers business is the largest single private employer. Moreover, syndicate activities often employ young men who, because of their limited skills and education, would not otherwise find gainful employment. These unemployed persons represent a significant risk to the community if, as is easy to imagine, they move into more conventional criminal activities such as robbery and burglary. We have seen that the cutting of heroin requires large numbers of women who are able to secure an income that exceeds all other available employment, and then often saves them from destitution.

Law enforcement efforts have been largely devoted to "head hunting," the targeting of specific organized crime figures with the goal of successful prosecution of management-level members. This technique has had little impact on organized crime; indeed, since it creates management-level vacancies, "head hunting" may actually be good for the morale of ambitious lower-level members. Certainly the successful dislodging of any organized crime figure, no matter how high, does not reduce the market for "goods and services." In an effort to increase the risks while decreasing the profits related to these goods and services, Congress enacted the Racketeer Influenced and Corrupt Organizations section of the Organized Crime Control Act of 1970. (Sections of this law appear in the index.) John M. Dowd, United States Attorney-in-Charge of Strike Force* 18, provides the highlights of this statute (John M. Dowd, "Manifestations of Organized Crime: Infiltration of Legitimate Business,"

---

* Strike Force: Federal enforcement efforts against organized crime have traditionally been hampered by interagency rivalry. In an effort to deal with this problem the United States Department of Justice assembled twenty-six units across the country to handle the investigation and prosecution of organized crime and corruption cases on a coordinated basis, beginning in 1967 with the first Strike Force in Buffalo, New York. Each Strike Force has seven to fifteen Assistant United States Attorneys on a full-time basis as well as investigators from such diverse agencies as the Secret Service, Drug Enforcement Administration, Postal Inspection Service, Bureau of Alcohol, Tobacco and Firearms, Internal Revenue Service, FBI, Department of Labor, Department of Agriculture, Customs, Immigration and Naturalization Service, and sometimes personnel from the United States Marshal's Service and the Securities and Exchange Commission. State and local investigative personnel may also be part of a Strike Force.

pages 37–39 of U.S. Dept. of Justice, *Report of the National Conference on Organized Crime*. Wash., D.C.: U.S. Gov't. Printing Office, 1975):

In the simplest terms it is the business of organized crime to acquire power and profit. Until very recently those of us in law enforcement have sought to impede, frustrate and halt the activities of the organized professional criminal by pursuing specific violations against individuals in positions of leadership and influence in the criminal community. In many respects, this effort has been successful, but has not stopped the growth and development of the criminal organizations which continue to infiltrate and corrupt this nation's economy.

Organized crime has successfully infected the economic and financial system of the United States. Through illegal gambling, loansharking, fencing, fraud and outright theft, the professional criminal has produced sufficient revenues to invest in legitimate economic and financial institutions throughout the United States. In addition to acquiring an economic foothold by investment, they have illegally acquired legitimate businesses and have continued their patterns of criminal activity in order to maintain, expand and use these economic enterprises in furtherance of their criminal activity. The effect of this sophisticated and professional criminal effort has been to weaken the stability of the nation's economy, bringing untold damage to innocent employees, investors and competing organizations.

Up until 1970, one of the impediments to attacking this criminal-economic organization was the nature and interpretation of the criminal law. Historically, the criminal law was narrowly drawn and narrowly interpreted to reach specific types of individual conduct. The criminal law was not designed to outlaw and eradicate criminal organizations engaged in economic activity or patterns of criminal activity. Since the criminal law required a specific and narrow approach, investigations of criminal activity were conducted in a similar manner. Thus, it is no surprise when one reflects on past investigations and prosecutions to take note that courts and juries very seldom were permitted to view or hear proof of a criminal organization engaged in a variety of illicit economic activities. For example, if the funds generated by a policy operation were used to buy an interest in a restaurant, the investigators and prosecutors spent their time investigating, developing and proving the elements of a crime outlawing the illegal gambling operation. If a legitimate business were acquired through fraud or extortion, we concentrated on gathering the proof as to the elements of fraud or extortion. We did not direct our attention to the acquisition of the business itself or taking remedial action to restore the economic enterprise to its rightful owners. If a legitimate enterprise were used as a front for a fencing operation, our normal approach would be to indict and convict the fence for receiving and selling stolen goods. The difficulty with this approach is that it did not stop the criminal organization from replacing the fence and continuing the fencing operation. Thus, the illegal economic enterprise was permitted to continue and flourish.

Simply put, we have failed to hit organized and professional crime in the pocketbook. Due to the narrow approach required by our criminal laws, we have never had the tool to attack the organization, the enterprise or the pat-

tern of criminal activity which is at the core of the effort of org
to acquire power and profit.

I have been requested to come here today to tell you about an ...
nary statutory weapon which was enacted by the United States Congre...
part of the Organized Crime Control Act of 1970. You may ask, why do we
tell you about a new federal statute when you have your hands full enforcing
your own state and local criminal laws? The answer is easy. We need your
help and cooperation. I'm going to tell you today about some cases which
have been developed and successfully concluded against organized and professional criminals which could not have been accomplished without the
cooperative effort of local, state and federal investigative agencies. This new
statute does not lighten the investigative or prosecutive burdens which we
carry every day. This statute requires greater effort, imagination, and
cooperation.

This statute is entitled "Racketeer Influenced and Corrupt Organizations." It is by definition and legislative purpose a broad and remedial
statute. It is designed to effectively halt patterns of criminal activity. It is
designed to strike at the acquisition of power and profit by organized crime.
It is designed to reach the criminal economic organization. It is designed to
stop the infiltration and infection of legitimate economic enterprises.

The patterns of criminal activity can consist of major felonies which are
outlawed by the states. The pattern of criminal activity can consist of the
major anti-racketeering statutes, anti-fraud statutes, labor statutes and narcotics laws of the United States. The pattern of criminal activity can consist
of both federal and state violations. This is true because the heart of this
statute is what we call the "enterprise." An enterprise, as defined by the
statute, can be an individual, a partnership, a corporation, an association, a
union, or any legal entity capable of holding a property interest. More significantly, an enterprise can be a group of individuals associated in fact. This
novel concept permits us to attack the criminal enterprise as long as the
enterprise has some affect on interstate commerce.

This new statute creates four new crimes:

It outlaws the investment of proceeds derived from illegal activity in any
enterprise. It outlaws the acquisition of any interest in an enterprise by a
pattern of criminal activity and the maintenance of any interest in any
enterprise through a pattern of criminal activity. The statute outlaws the use
of any enterprise to commit a pattern of criminal activity. Finally, the
statute outlaws a conspiracy to violate any of the three substantive crimes.
As can be readily seen, an enterprise can be legitimate or illegitimate. The
purpose of the statute is to reach the fruits of the crime as well as the vehicle
used to commit the crime with criminal sanctions as well as substantial
remedies to bring a halt to the actual economic activity.

The statute is designed to attack the loanshark, the fencing operation,
the drug laboratory, the stolen securities ring, the corruption of police and
public officials, the labor kickback scheme, the shakedown of a business, the
bust out operations, the large schemes to defraud and the day-to-day economic and financial operations of professional and organized criminals.

The statute permits the prosecutor to allege and prove the entire history
of the criminal enterprise or the history of the pattern of criminal activity
even beyond the normal statute of limitations. We have combined state vio-

lations of arson and kidnapping to form a pattern of activity in a case against professional torches in Connecticut. We have combined nine counts of Hobbs Act extortion to attack a takeover of the canteen food business in New York. We have combined multiple counts of state bribery violations to stop a large cigarette smuggling operation in Philadelphia and wholesale corruption of an entire police detective squad in Macon, Georgia. We have combined several counts of the interstate transportation of money and persons involving a fraudulent scheme to take over a nine million dollar hotel and casino in the Dutch West Indies. We have stopped a multi-jurisdiction prostitution ring which involved the kidnapping of children to coerce young women to engage in prostitution. We have utilized numerous Taft-Hartley violations to halt the invasion of union pension funds and to stop the illegal kickback schemes of labor officials. We have combined the state extortion, federal extortion and a new anti-loansharking provision to halt an in-house shakedown of bookmakers, loansharks and pornographic bookstores by the top organized crime figures in central California. We have combined a variety of the anti-fraud statutes to stop one of the largest multi-jurisdiction bust out schemes of small retail clothing operations in the United States.

We are utilizing this statute to challenge some of the largest bookmaking, sports action and policy operations in our major cities. We are using this statute against the wholesale looting of banks using loans collateralized by stolen or fictitious securities, the wholesale defrauding of governmental agencies, large scale loanshark operations which financed large securities promotions.

Let me take a few moments to describe to you the provisions of this statute, what is outlawed, the methods of establishing a violation and the remedies available to the government to halt the activity.

Congress outlawed the investment of illgotten gains into any economic enterprise. For example, if you are able to trace the proceeds of a numbers operation into a financial institution where the money is converted to stock in an enterprise, then you have a potential violation of 1962(a). The acquisition of the stock is in all respects legal. The gravamen or basis of the crime is the source of the funds—that is, whether the funds were derived from a pattern of racketeering activity or the collection of an unlawful debt.

Congress further outlawed the acquisition of any interest—directly or indirectly—in any enterprise through a pattern of racketeering activity or the collection of an unlawful debt—we tried a case in New York—which required investigation with the assistance of local, state and federal agents in five jurisdictions in the United States, Canada, and the Dutch Antilles in the Caribbean. A gambling junket operator named Parness perpetrated a scheme to defraud upon the owner of a hotel-casino on the island of St. Martin. Parness, a loanshark and an associate of Gyp de Carlo of New Jersey, caused the junket customers to gamble on credit in the casino, thus requiring the payment of the gambling markers in New York. After a few months, Parness had the treasury of the casino in a small bank in New Jersey. When the owner needed to pay a corporate debt secured by all of his stock, Parness told him collections were slow. When action was commenced to foreclose on the stock, the owner went to Parness for funds. Parness told the owner he would borrow the funds and take the stock as security. Parness, unknown to the owner, loaned him the collections from the gambling debts. When the owner was unable to pay off the loan, Parness took the stock and the ownership of the casino. Parness received 10 years in prison and $55,000 in fines.

This statute also outlaws the maintenance of any interest—directly or indirectly—in any enterprise through a pattern of racketeering activity or the collection of an unlawful debt.

An example of the maintenance through a pattern of criminal activity of an economic enterprise can arise in a situation where organized crime engages in a pattern of bribery and obstruction of justice to prevent the proper investigation of the affairs of the enterprise. Another example occurred when the owners of an automobile dealership engaged in a fraudulent double financing scheme to further their business interests. In effect, the automobiles would be sold twice to obtain loan proceeds from a bank. Another example is the case of the owner of a construction company who financed a large scale loanshark operation in several locations throughout a large metropolitan area. The proceeds from the loanshark operation were used to purchase more equipment and capital for the construction company. Thus, through the collection of unlawful debts and extortionate credit transactions, the owner was able to maintain and expand his construction company. This activity could also constitute a violation covering the investment of illgotten gains.

The third new crime outlawed by this statute is the use of any enterprise to commit a pattern of criminal activity. This section permits us to directly attack the criminal economic enterprise. In a classic example, the combined efforts of local, state and federal law enforcement brought the top leaders of the Licata organized crime family of Los Angeles, California, to the bar of justice and eventually to prison for conducting a massive shakedown of their own kind. At the suggestion of two soldiers in the family, the leadership approved and ordered executed a plan to shakedown the bookmakers, the loansharks and the pornographic bookstores in Los Angeles. Over a period of several months the defendants carried out the plan by extortion, force and violence to collect the protection payments. In the case of one bookmaker who was required to pay $10,000 up front and 1,000 per week—he offered to give the extortionists an easy mark to relieve the pressure. One of his best customers was a wealthy Idaho potato farmer who was anxious to go into the bookmaking business. They set him up in a business of handling sports action. In a period of a few months, they fleeced the potato farmer of $164,000 in an elaborate scheme to defraud. The "enterprise" in this instance was a group of individuals associated in fact for the purpose of engaging in extortion, shakedowns, collection of unlawful debts and fraudulent schemes.

What this case teaches is that you must look at criminal activity from the economic and financial vantage point of the criminals. They are in business for power and profit as so graphically demonstrated by this case.

In another case a local bookmaking investigation led to the discovery that the perpetrators had a veritable supermarket of crime under way which was reaping large profits. In addition to taking bets on sports, horses, and numbers, the subjects were using extortion to collect the gambling debts, loaning money at usurious interest rates, bribing public and police officials to prevent interference with their enterprise; deploying their agents to steal clothing and fence the goods; hijacking truck loads of beef; taking over a local health club by arson and muscle and engaging in multi-jurisdiction transactions to move and sell cocaine. What is this operation? It is a criminal business enterprise which can be effectively dealt with by this statute. Again, it is a group of individuals associated in fact for the purpose of bookmaking, loansharking, hijacking, arson, extortion, theft, and the sale of narcotics. This case was developed by state and federal agents who had the patience, skill and fortitude to inquire as to the total criminal activity undertaken by the defendants.

Cases developed under this statute are of high quality and impact in the criminal community. This statute has and is changing the view we take of organized and professional crime. It has also caused an enormous cooperative effort among the many federal investigative agencies and between local, state and federal agencies. This is true because of the increased burden of developing cases against the professional organization. Another reason is the heavy punitive and remedial sanctions which are imposed following conviction.

This statute carries a 20-year sentence, a $25,000 fine and a mandatory criminal forfeiture of any property interest acquired, maintained or used as a source of influence in violation of the statute. The statute provides for temporary remedies at the time of indictment to freeze the particular property interest which has been used, acquired or maintained in violation of the statute.

In addition to the criminal sanctions, there are substantial civil remedies designed to restore the legitimate economic enterprise to its original healthy state. The victim or victims of any violation of this statute is entitled to sue for treble damages. The cost of the lawsuit and reasonable attorneys fees are provided in the statute.

The impact of the RICO statute varies according to whom one speaks. Members of the FBI, from special agents up to the director, express a great deal of enthusiasm for the statute. In one very imaginative case the FBI was able to use RICO for the successful prosecution of a high-ranking member of organized crime.

Joseph Gambino, cousin of Carlo Gambino and a high-ranking member of his crime family, took over Terminal Sanitation, a private garbage carting concern, as a result of usurious loans. Using this firm as a base, Gambino organized private carters in the Bronx, and they in turn paid him a monthly fee. This fee protected the carters from undue competition as well as from incidents of violence—perpetrated by the Gambino organization.

In February 1976 a new firm, American Automated Refuse, opened in the Bronx. It was operated by several FBI agents using some old military sanitation trucks. However, the service that they provided was so poor that they soon ran into trouble with the New York City Consumer Protection Agency. Responding to this experience, the FBI purchased four well-conditioned trucks and business began to improve. (One is tempted to say business "picked up.") Several months later, Joseph Gambino and an aide, Carlo Conti, came into the office of American Automated Refuse, which was equipped with video and sound recording devices. Gambino was friendly and outgoing, and during the course of his conversation he mentioned the need for a monthly payment based on the number of accounts ("stops") the firm serviced. Several more Gambino visits were recorded, and each time the agent in the office stalled on the issue of the payments. After the firm had been in operation five months, the agent was threatened and ordered to pay a fee of $200 a month.

During his last visit to American Automated Refuse, Gambino suddenly walked outside and Conti began to administer a severe beating to the FBI agent who declined to draw his weapon or identify himself—quite a brave effort to further the case against Gambino. Two months later Gambino and Conti were indicted under the RICO statute and both were convicted. Gambino was sentenced to a term of forty years and a fine of $50,000 and was ordered deported upon completion of the sentence.* As of this writing he is free on bail, awaiting the results of his appeal. As a condition of bail he is required to report daily to the New York City office of the FBI. This case was reported by Special Agent Lance Emory.

It should be noted that other federal (non-FBI) law enforcement officials are less enthusiastic about the RICO statute. They point out that making a case under RICO is quite complex, and they maintain that the statute is not much of an improvement over already existing federal statutes. The remainder of this chapter will be concerned with other law enforcement efforts and programmatic responses to organized crime.

## ANTI-LOANSHARKING LEGISLATION

In 1968 the federal government enacted the Consumer Credit Protection Act to deal with "extortionate credit transactions." "Extortionate credit transactions are characterized by the use, or the express or implicit threat of the use, of violence or other criminal means to cause harm to person, reputation, or property as a means of enforcing repayment." To overcome the usual difficulties involved in securing witnesses to testify, the act provides for prima facie evidence if four conditions can be established (Malcom and Curtin, 1968: 773–774):

1.  The repayment of the extension of credit, or the performance of any promise given in consideration thereof, would be unenforceable, through civil judicial processes against the debtor
    A.  in the jurisdiction within which the debtor, if a natural person, resided, or
    B.  in every jurisdiction within which the debtor, if other than a

---

* Gambino, who entered the United States illegally in 1957, has been under a deportation order since 1967. Years of legal maneuvers have succeeded in keeping him in the United States (Barrett and Tompkins, 1977: 41).

    natural person, was incorporated or qualified to do business at the time the extension of credit was made.

2. The extension of credit was made at a rate of interest in excess of an annual rate of 45 percent. . . .

3. At the time the extension of credit was made, the debtor reasonably believed that either

    A. one or more extensions of credit by the creditor had been collected or attempted to be collected by extortionate means, or the nonrepayment thereof had been punished by extortionate means or

    B. the creditor had a reputation for the use of extortionate means to collect extensions of credit or to punish the nonrepayment thereof.

4. Upon the making of the extension of credit, the total of the extensions of credit by the creditor to the debtor then outstanding, including any unpaid interest or similar charges, exceeded $100.

The act also provides a means for reaching management levels in organized crime by stating that "whoever wilfully advances or supplies money or property to any person with reasonable grounds to believe that the person will use the money to make extortionate extensions of credit is guilty of a federal crime . . ." (Ibid.: 775). The penalty for violating this statute is twenty years imprisonment and a fine of $10,000.

## STATEWIDE PROSECUTOR

The National Advisory Commission on Criminal Justice Standards and Goals notes that there is always some degree of partisan political commitment on the part of the law enforcement agency (1975: 224):

> Complete independence from political influence is rare in the case of a law enforcement unit; pressure may be felt directly through election or appointment, or indirectly through budget control. The political histories of local jurisdictions within a given State, therefore, are also important for analysis. Such factors as whether local prosecuting attorneys are elected or appointed, whether electoral districts are highly competitive or areas of one-party control, whether prosecuting attorneys who have been in office for a number of years have kept their offices free from political influence and favoritism, and what trends in priorities operate in such jurisdictions—all contribute to the development of an environment that is favorable or unfavorable to successful prosecution of corruption cases. The courageous prosecutor who wants to attack the corruption problem in his jurisdiction must know the forces he will confront.

The Commission argues (Ibid.: 224–225):

> Corruption involving local-level functionaries may be handled effectively by the local prosecutor without extraordinary tools at his disposal. This may

be true even if the problem is within police ranks, but here absence of
prosecutor initiative is a greater risk. The interdependency of police and
prosecutor is enormous. It would be easy merely to decry the social and
professional relationships that make prosecutions of police corruption difficult. Where this is the case, the Commission does condemn the nullification
of law enforcement that results. But for the prosecutor who is anything less
than courageous in bringing corruption cases against the police or other
agencies within the criminal justice system, there must be found some prosecutorial mechanism that is insulated from or independent of the agencies or
officials accused. The standards that follow this discussion suggest such
remedies.

When the nature or level of government service comprised has made it
politically difficult for corruption cases to be prosecuted vigorously, either
within or outside the criminal justice system, other remedies must be developed. In many cases, the most serious or most important corruption cases
fall into this category.

The Commission points to the dilemma inherent in the office of the prosecutor
(Ibid.: 224–226):

> The political pressures a local prosecutor faces when he decides whether
> or not to bring a corruption case require critical analysis. On the one hand,
> it is good politics to make a name for oneself by successful prosecutions of
> officials corruption cases. The crusading D.A. is one who is respected and
> feared in a community. On the other hand, many people fail to realize that
> there are tremendous political risks involved in bringing such cases, with
> the reward coming only at the time of conviction. A district attorney can
> find no better way to destroy his effectiveness than by earning a reputation
> for witch hunting. Nor is it unlikely that a prosecutor's charges of corruption
> will be labeled as political maneuvers and met by rebuttals from those
> charged. Allegations concerning a prosecutor's political motivations some-
> times have credence with the American public.
>
> The interdependence of members of the criminal justice system often
> makes it unlikely that even the most blatant corruption within the system
> will surface. Local prosecutors, though otherwise honest and competent, are
> often loathe to deal with the problem aggressively.
>
> Their dilemma, for example, extends into the area of investigating police
> corruption. In many cities, the police are the sole investigative arm of the
> prosecutor's office. Virtually every case brought to the district attorney's
> office each year is dependent in some part on police testimony. A cooperative
> relationship thus inevitably develops between the prosecuting attorney and
> the police department. The district attorney can abrogate his responsibility
> to eradicate corruption among police, if he rationalizes that the police de-
> partment is best equipped, by staff and experience, to keep its affairs in
> order.
>
> The police department, then, is permitted through its internal affairs
> division to handle inhouse virtually all corruption matters. To preserve his
> relationship with the police department, a prosecutor may react only to spe-
> cific complaints charging wrongdoing by a named officer. Even if there are
> reports of widespread corruption in a particular division (e.g., narcotics or
> gambling enforcement), the prosecutor may maintain an attitude of caution,
> avoiding sweeping investigations of systematic corruption.
>
> Other partnership relationships develop within the criminal justice system
> that also tend to obscure corruption. In communities where the prosecutor,

police, public defender, courts, and judges are thought of as one unit, operating in an atmosphere of cooperation and mutual support, the whole adversary process can break down. In many such instances, corruption, even within a single agency, has low visibility.

The Commission provides recommendations for maintaining integrity in the prosecutor's office (Ibid.: 226–228):

Standard 14.1: Maintaining Integrity in the Local Prosecutor's Office

1.  States should redefine their law enforcement districts so as to combine smaller jurisdictions into districts having sufficient workload to support at least one full-time district attorney.
2.  States should devise training standards for prosecution service, and should provide prosecutors' salaries that will attract the best-qualified personnel.
3.  All local prosecutors and their staff attorneys should be prohibited from engaging in partisan political activity. Local prosecutors who are elected should be elected in nonpartisan elections.
4.  All local prosecutors should be required to publish and make available annual reports detailing the deployment of personnel and resources during the preceding reporting period. Such reports should disclose the number of cases pending, hours spent in court and before the grand jury, and other details cataloging the number and kinds of cases handled by the prosecutor and their status at the time of reporting. Reports should be available for public inspection.

Standard 14.2: Statewide Capability to Prosecute Corruption
States having a history of concern regarding the existence of public corruption and organized crime, both within and outside the criminal justice system, should establish an ongoing statewide capability for investigation and prosecution of corruption.

1.  The office charged with this responsibility should have clear authority to perform the following functions:
    a.  Initiate investigations concerning: the proper conduct and performance of duties by all public officials and employees in the State, and the faithful execution and effective enforcement of the laws of the State with particular reference but not limited to organized crime and racketeering;
    b.  Prosecute those cases that are within the statutory purview and that the State unit determines it could most effectively prosecute by itself, referring all other evidence and cases to the appropriate State or local law enforcement authority;
    c.  Provide management assistance to State and local government units, commissions, and authorities, with special emphasis on suggesting means by which to eliminate corruption and conditions that invite corruption;

    d.  Participate in and coordinate the development of a statewide intelligence network on the incidence, growth, sources, and patterns of corruption within the State; and

    e.  Make recommendations to the Governor or State legislature concerning: removal of public officials, government reorganization that would eliminate or reduce corruption and encourage more efficient and effective performance of duties and changes in or additions to provisions of the State statutes needed for more effective law enforcement.

2.  The office should have the following minimum characteristics and powers:

    a.  Statewide jurisdiction;

    b.  Constant capability to obtain and preserve evidence prior to the filing of formal complaints;

    c.  Power to compel testimony for purposes of investigation and prosecution; authority to subpoena witnesses, administer oaths, obtain grants of immunity, and have access to the sanction of contempt; ability to hold private and public hearings; and power to prosecute cases in court;

    d.  Adequate budget, protected from retaliative reduction;

    e.  Specialized staff: investigators, accountants, and trial attorneys, with access to others as needed;

    f.  Consulting services available to all units of State and local government, commissions, and public corporations for counsel on means of maximizing the utilization of available staff and resources to meet workload demands, with special priority for service to licensing, regulatory, and law enforcement agencies; and

    g.  Annual disclosure of financial interests to the State Ethics Board by all persons performing regular duties in fulfillment of the above. Legislation should be enacted to authorize these and other powers as needed.

The Commission notes the advantages of a statewide prosecutor's office (Ibid.: 228):

> Aside from the immediate benefits of developing new evidence and new cases to prosecute, the agency would encourage local prosecutors and others charged with responsibility in this area to give a higher priority to official corruption cases. The agency would in no way detract from the existing jurisdiction of local prosecutors. In fact, pressures created by the successes of the State agency would encourage the local prosecutor to be more aggressive in his jurisdiction.
>
> Reform also will come from within city, county, and State agencies, as well as from within the criminal justice system itself, when the anticorruption unit brings integrity problems to the attention of these agencies and the public. Likewise, the State unit will provide the public with an unimpeachable, sympathetic forum to which complaints of official misconduct might be brought with confidence. The accompanying restoration of the public's faith in city and State government would be no small benefit.

The Commission reports that most (if not all) state investigation commissions lack the power to prosecute cases that they develop (Ibid.):

> The power to prosecute in court is the singularly absent criterion in all existing State investigation commissions. The same political forces that make the creation of the State agency essential often make it impossible for corruption cases to be brought at the local or State level, even if the cases are referred by the anticorruption agency.

The Commission stresses that the power to prosecute is vital in combatting organized crime and attendant corruption of public officials. The office of a statewide prosecutor must be provided with the assistance of a variety of specialists including accountants, management systems experts, and tax experts. The Commission also notes the need for a degree of budgetary independence (Ibid.: 229):

> Experience has shown that effective performance of these duties has caused public officers and citizens to react with anger. It is reasonable to expect retaliation by legislators in the form of attempts to slash the budget. One means of budget protection is to require a two-thirds vote of the legislature to reduce the appropriation below the level of the previous fiscal year. Another way might be to offer the protection within the State's constitution, even specifying a fixed percentage of the State's general fund as an absolute floor to the annual funding of the office. . . .

## PROSECUTOR'S RACKET BUREAU

One of the most important methods for combatting organized crime on a local level is the "racket bureau" of a prosecutor's office. While most specialized units (homicide, robbery, sex crime) are *reactive,* that is they respond "after the fact," a racket bureau is basically *proactive.* A proactive response requires looking for crime, often before it actually occurs. In their study Blakely, Goldstock, and Rogovin provide a look at the racket bureau in the most famous prosecutor's office in the United States.

### III. THE NEW YORK COUNTY DISTRICT ATTORNEY'S RACKETS BUREAU *

#### A. GENERAL INFORMATION AND JURISDICTION

Most American cities are located within counties; New York City contains five counties and as a result has five independent D.A.'s. Among these, and nationally as well, the New York County (Manhattan) D.A. has traditionally been a leader. Like other D.A.'s in the state, he is an elected, constitutional officer, responsible only to his constituents and the Governor.

* Source: Blakely, G. Robert, Ronald Goldstock, and Charles H. Rogovin, 1978, *Rackets Bureaus: Investigation and Prosecution of Organized Crime.* Wash., D.C.: U.S. Govt. Printing Office.

His office employs about two hundred assistant district attorneys who serve in a trial division, appeals unit, and three investigative bureaus. Narcotics prosecutions are handled by the Special City wide Narcotics Prosecutor. Specialized programs exist from time to time in response, not surprisingly, to the ever-changing menu of LEAA grants.

New York County D.A.'s have historically been commanding figures; consider Thomas E. Dewey and Frank Hogan. Hogan set standards not only for his own successors, but to a large extent for offices across the country. Several features have distinguished the Manhattan D.A.'s office. It insists on nonpolitical criteria for hiring and promotion. A.D.A.'s may not engage in politics (except campaigning on their own time for candidates of their choice, where such campaigning is essentially behind the scenes and not public in character) or in outside law practice or other business (except teaching or writing, again on their own time). The public has traditionally considered the office honest, efficient and dedicated.

The current D.A., Robert Morgenthau, is a former U.S. Attorney for the Southern District of New York, which includes Manhattan. Morgenthau, who regards anti-racketeering efforts as critically important, is the first D.A. in years who is not a product of the office itself.

A gathering of all agencies which deal with organized crime and official corruption in the city would make a considerable crowd. The four other D.A.'s, the U.S. Attorneys for the Southern and Eastern Districts, the Federal Strike Forces in each district, the New York State Organized Crime Task Force, the Special Citywide Anti-Narcotics Prosecutor, the Special Prosecutor for Criminal Justice System Corruption in New York City—all these conduct activities similar to those of Morgenthau's office. Although there is more than enough business to go around, coordination is difficult, and interagency jealousy hardly unknown.

The office has no strict definition of organized crime, although its refers frequently to concentration of economic power and conspiratorial activity.

B.   STRUCTURE AND STAFF
     OF THE RACKETS BUREAU

Considering the strong supervisory role of the Rackets Bureau chief, it can be fairly said that organized crime is present when he and one of his assistants see it the same way. The bureau chief has complete discretion to accept, reject, or refer to other bureaus or outside agencies any investigation.

Under the former chief, A.D.A.'s developed specialties; the waterfront, gambling and loan sharking, securities, airline ticket and credit card operations, infiltration of businesses (including bars, hotels, private garbage collection services); hijacking, fencing, and the garment center. Each assistant was charged with gathering information from appropriate agencies, developing resource files, and filling speaking engagements about his specialty. The current chief uses this system less extensively.

The bureau chief has ten years' experience in the office; his deputy five. In contrast to the situation in the Hogan-era, eight of the bureau's nine other assistants have less than five years' experience; three have only six months.

The chief makes $32,000 per year; his deputy $25,000. A.D.A.'s hired right from law school make $11,500 before admission to the bar, $13,000 after.[1] Those with relevant prior experience start at somewhat higher salaries. Considering that large New York law firms offer high-ranking law school graduates $25,000, office salaries are far from competitive. Yet such is the prestige of the office that it receives more than a thousand applications —many from first-rate graduates of first-rate schools—each year. On the other hand, the financial sacrifice, and the tiny likelihood of significant raises from a financially strapped city, lowers morale considerably.

The bureau chief believes that his assistants should have prior trial experience, so he and nearly all rackets assistants have had experience in one of the "junior" bureaus, though not the long apprenticeships of the Hogan years. (The belief is not universally held. Some argue that most misdemeanor trial work—because of the volume of cases—does not lead to the development of the unique skills and habits essential for complex rackets trial work.) Advancement to the bureau is informal. When bureau members notice a promising A.D.A., the chief interviews him and consults his superiors. Final decisions rest with Morgenthau.

When an A.D.A. with little trial experience joins the bureau, his main training consists of work with an experienced prosecutor on a major felony trial. There is little formal in-house training aside from the mandatory reading of the Rackets Bureau Manual. The manual, informative, concise, and well written, emphasizes the necessary balance between aggressive investigation and concern about overreaching. Assistants who know it thoroughly avoid many serious mistakes.

Each of the city's D.A.'s has a police unit drawn from the New York City Police Department. Morgenthau's squad, commanded by a deputy inspector, has sixty-five officers, including a lieutenant and five sergeants; the rest are detectives or plainclothes officers. The squad commander, who has eighteen years' police experience and is a graduate of the Senior Command Course at the British Police College, Bramshill, selects—subject to the Police Commissioner's approval—squad members. Politics seems to play no part in the selection.

Detectives need not fill out financial forms or submit to routine polygraph examinations. All employees do, however, fill out complete employment questionnaires. The squad conducts thorough background checks, including local and FBI name and fingerprint searches, of new personnel.

The squad is formally available to all bureaus; in practice, it works mainly with the Rackets and Frauds Bureaus. The squad commander and his colleagues are shrewd, tough professionals with all the qualities of the best of New York's "First Grades": street "smarts"; a wide streak of skepticism of humanity; a willingness to work long, often boring hours; and, a somewhat messianic zeal about putting "bad guys" away.

The squad commander reports to the D.A. and to the chief of detectives, unlike commanders in the other D.A.'s squads who report to their respective borough detective commanders.

The office has no funds for training detectives. They do, however, participate in some of the Police Department's programs.

In addition to the police officers assigned to the District Attorney, there

---

[1] As of September 1976, the salary was $15,725.

is a group of civilian agents known as D.A.'s investigators. According to office legend this unit was primarily responsible for investigations of police corruption. Because of the establishment of a special prosecutor in New York, the retirement of the chief investigator and as a result of a stagnating rigidity in the unit, the bureau was broken up and members of this group were assigned to each of the office's bureau chiefs. The man assigned to the Rackets Bureau maintained wiretap or other electronic surveillance orders and tapes. In addition, he served as a liaison with outside investigative agencies and police units, and aided in the coordination of the bureau's work. He was also charged with maintaining the bureau's intelligence files, and served as an intelligence analyst. (A position which surprisingly had never existed in the past). Within the last year, however, Morgenthau has attempted to revitalize the investigators as a bureau by recruiting a former Alcohol, Tobacco, Firearms Agent as a new supervisor for this group. What, if any, impact this move will have is unknown, but presently the Rackets Bureau rarely relies upon these agents for investigative work.

### C.  METHODS OF INVESTIGATION

The bureau uses undercover officers—frequently equipped with concealed recorders or transmitters—to infiltrate certain criminal groups and to carry out physical surveillance of selected targets of investigation. Manpower shortages preclude routine, or even intermittent, physical surveillance of known criminal figures for general intelligence.

Consensual surveillance is especially important in view of New York law's legal requirement of corroboration of accomplice testimony. The bureau chief claims that, "The major case, especially in the area of official corruption is often made by informants [who are willing to testify] wearing concealed recorders."

The bureau relies greatly on electronic surveillance, as the considerable space the manual devotes to it suggests. New York was among the first states to authorize court-ordered surveillance. The manual treats in great detail application and custody procedures and other matters.

Much of the bureau's electronic equipment is obsolete. The Hogan tradition required avoidance of entangling alliances, hence a reluctance to seek Federal funds. Since Morgenthau has no such reluctance, the bureau will soon use LEAA funds to bring its electronic equipment up to date. The detective squad contains officers trained in its use, and in photographic work.

Morgenthau himself brought to the office a group of informants developed during his time as U.S. Attorney. According to the bureau chief, who has another group developed by the Bureau, these often provide valuable information. The D.A. also brought from his Federal work—where no corroboration of accomplice testimony was required—a relaxed attitude toward "dirty" witnesses, a departure from the Hogan tradition.

Nevertheless, the bureau is greatly concerned about informant control. The chief prefers to give informants a specific assignment rather than to use them as general information collectors. Where disclosure requirements do not mandate otherwise, they are equipped with recorders, which produce permanent records of conversations and inhibit the tendency to embellish them.

The bureau has a reputation, which it strives to protect, for protecting its sources of information. The manual warns, under the heading "Investigative Rules," of the dangers of discussing investigations with non-bureau people and of leaving warrants in unsecured places. That no informant or witness be interviewed by an assistant alone is a bureau rule; an investigator (normally the detective working on the particular case) must be present.

Very likely, no anti-racketeering unit—Federal, state, or local—uses investigative grand juries better than the Manhattan Rackets Bureau does. New York law provides for both regular and extraordinary investigative grand juries. The law now provides only for transactional immunity; attempts to obtain a use immunity statute have failed, but the years ahead will bring new efforts. The law of contempt—civil and criminal—and of perjury is well developed. The bureau has been a pioneer in the use of evasive contempt.

Bureau members read the law to require that a review of grand jury minutes—always likely to be requested by defense counsel—disclose, from the beginning, an arguable criminal basis for the investigation. Assistants must always keep in mind the prospect of such review.

### D. STRATEGY AND GOALS

No one really knows how to measure the effectiveness of anti-racketeering work. The standard measure, conviction and imprisonment of organized crime figures, appears inadequate. The bureau chief (who employs several financial analysts) suggests focusing on illegal concentrations of economic power, yet no one knows how to assess objectively the results of investigations and prosecutions on such concentrations. Lack of resources is one reason; no prosecutor has the resources to do even most of what he would like. Inertia is another reason; lawyers are not notorious for innovation. Even so obvious a technique as determining the best allocation of resources by cost-effectiveness studies has not been used.

While the bureau has been of necessity generally reactive, it has made some proactive efforts, like its extensive probes of labor racketeering. Under the previous chief it undertook studies of the evolution of black and Chinese organized crime groups.

The major strategy used by the bureau in investigating organized criminal activity is exemplified by the *Fraulein* investigation reported by the National Wiretap Commission. Put most simply, the strategy involves the identification of an individual, known as a "mover," who, while partially insulated, must operate to some degree in the open. The "mover" is generally the individual trusted by the bosses to act in their behalf, to enter into pacts and hold negotiations, and to supervise the execution of the criminal venture. Since he is not the person carrying the contraband, hijacking the truck, or sporting the big name, he is often overlooked as the potential target of surveillance. Yet by keying on him and subjecting him to physical and electronic surveillance, where authorized, it is frequently possible to piece together the nature and scope of the entire operation. Apparently ambiguous evidence obtained with respect to the bosses, when analyzed in conjunction with the comprehensive information gleaned from investigating the "mover," is often sufficiently meaningful and unambiguous to secure convictions of those top men.

The bureau chief speaks with enthusiasm about a reformulation of the prevailing conceptual approach to organized crime and public corruption prosecution, but acknowledges that his program continues to be essentially a matter of targeting upon individuals suspected of illegal conduct. He disputes, and labels as fallacious, proceeding on a hypothesis grounded upon some rigid "Mob" structure. Rather, he suggests, resources should be focused and committed upon situations where economic analysis indicate illegal concentrations of power; such as the entertainment field, liquor industry, etc. The theory is excellent, but in the absence of any internal, economic analytical expertise or substantial outside work in this area, strategic guides of this type will apparently remain on the prosecutorial "wish list."

The bureau has no systematic intelligence-gathering program and no trained intelligence analysts. Matters of potential interest come from several sources: the D.A. directly, other bureaus, Federal agencies, "walk-ins" or letters (people contacting the bureau directly), and outside police units. The bureau assigns such a matter to an A.D.A. as a "potential inquiry." The assistant explores it and reports his findings within two weeks to the bureau chief who decides whether to proceed further. A matter the chief wishes investigated further is called a "preliminary investigation" and given a code name. An investigative report form summarizes the information available and gives the investigative plan, devised by the assigned A.D.A., the investigative supervisor, or both. Thereafter case reports are filed monthly until indictments are obtained or the case dropped as unproductive. Rackets assistants on occasion, but rarely, handle their own appellate matters.

The D.A. receives monthly reports on all "major investigations." These are investigations which (1) are likely to be long and active, (2) involve high ranking or important public officials, (3) involve notable crime figures, (4) involve labor racketeering, or (5) involve police corruption.

In spite of the intriguing discussion of reconsidering approaches to organized crime, "the steady kid on the block," as one assistant called the office, plays the game essentially as it always has, with dedication and competence, but only rarely with innovation. It seeks to react swiftly and skillfully and to hang as many scalps from the lodgepole as possible.

## APPENDIX C
### RACKETS BUREAU INVESTIGATIVE PLAN *

What follows is a hypothetical investigation and investigative plan:

PART I.

At the inception of every investigation the assistant assigned to the matter should complete an *INVESTIGATIVE REPORT*.

* Source: Blakely, G. Robert, Ronald Goldstock, and Charles H. Rogovin, 1978, *Rackets Bureaus: Investigation and Prosecution of Organized Crime*. Wash., D.C.: U.S. Govt. Printing Office.

The *Synopsis* should be a clear and concise precise of the facts upon which the investigation is based. It need not be exhaustive, including every bit of information known. Its value is in allowing the reader to immediately understand the nature of the matter under investigation.

The *Investigative Plan* should articulate a thoroughly and carefully thought-out plan for accomplishing the objectives of the investigation. Generally, alternative approaches should be suggested accompanied by an evaluation of the relative merits of each.

Potential *Legal Issues* should be noted as they are perceived and should be researched and analyzed in the context of the various investigative alternatives.

Under *Police Command* and *Officers,* the assistant should enter the name of the superior officers, and one or two knowledgeable detectives or police officers who could be contacted for information about the case. The *Criminal Activity* category can contain either a list of the statutory crimes being investigated (e.g. forgery, conspiracy) or preferably a more general and informative description (e.g. counterfeiting of gas rationing coupons). Finally the known *Subjects* of the investigation should be identified by name and/or alias.

### Part II.  Sample Investigative Plan

The sample investigative plan, set forth below, is based on the following hypothetical fact pattern:

During the execution of a search warrent on a bookmaking establishment on May 25, the police observed one Joseph Black, who was ultimately charged with illegal gambling activity, flushing some pieces of paper down the toilet. By the time they reached him, they were only able to retrieve a single piece, information from which is reproduced below. In addition 83 slips of paper bearing wagers were seized from a table.

| May | | | 2 | 9 | 16 | 23 | 30 |
|---|---|---|---|---|---|---|---|
| Dom | 500 | 2 | v | v | v | v | |
| Nick | 1000 | 3 | v | | | | |
| Yo Yo | 1000 | 2 | v | v | v | v | |

A search of Black's person disclosed a small telephone book containing approximately 150 entries, most of which corresponded to names on the seized bookmaking records. Included in the book were numbers for "Dom," "Nick," and "Yo Yo," which, according to the telephone company, were assigned to Dominick Mossi, Nicholas Poulas, and Frank Connell respectively.

The police department's loansharking expert has examined the records and concluded the number next to the name represented the outstanding principal as of May 1, the number to the right was the interest charged in % per week, "v" represented a vigorish payment, and a number next to the v, a principal payment. The expert has heard of Black and doubts that he personally could put a large amount of money on the street.

Mossi, Poulas, and Connell were interviewed with the following results:

Mossi stated he never heard of Joe Black, never borrowed any money from a loanshark, and thinks it's nobody's business whether or not he gambles.

Connell refused to answer any questions.

Poulas bet with a bookmaking operation through an answering service. He received the number from his runner—Art Tisdale. He lost $1,500, had only $500 and asked Tisdale for a loan. Tisdale set up a meeting between Black and Poulas and Poulas borrowed $1,000 at 3%/week. He paid $30/week for 5 months but missed a payment on May 23. Black slapped him around and warned that it better not happen again. Poulas is scared and will not testify under any circumstances. He does not have the money to keep paying Black.

He has Tisdale's number, but has not been given the new number for the bookmaking office. He meets Black every week at the Hemlock Cigar Store where Black hangs out between 2:30 and 4:30. On numerous occasions Black has used the telephone in the store. (On the 23rd, Black pointed to the phone and said that "All I have to do is call, and have you taken care of"). Poulas thinks that the cigar store is involved, because on two occasions when he payed the vig by check, it had been deposited in the Hemlock account.

PART III.   RACKETS BUREAU—INVESTIGATIVE PLAN

CRIMINAL ACTIVITY: Gambling                    ASSISTANTS:
                   Usury
                   Extortion
SUBJECTS:          Joseph Black                 POLICE OFFICERS:
                   Arthur Tisdale
                   Hemlock Cigar Store  DATE:

SYNOPSIS: The investigation was initiated after a search of bookmaking wireroom, disclosed the clerk, JOSEPH BLACK, in possession of loansharking records. A borrower, NICHOLAS POULAS, introduced to BLACK by a runner ARTHUR TISDALE, borrowed $1,000 from BLACK at 3 points in January to pay off a gambling debt. POULAS missed an interest payment in May and was threatened by BLACK. On two occasions, POULAS paid BLACK by check, both of which were deposited in the account of the HEMLOCK CIGAR STORE, the location where POULAS makes the payments and frequented by BLACK. POULAS will not testify because of fear, but has no money to continue paying BLACK. BLACK is most likely lending money for an UNKNOWN INDIVIDUAL and may have access to an ENFORCER. Two other probable borrowers have refused to cooperate.

INVESTIGATIVE PLAN: To determine if BLACK has a "MONEY MAN" and "ENFORCER" and if so, to identify and obtain evidence sufficient to convict those individuals.

There is sufficient evidence to indict and convict BLACK for bookmaking and possible possession of usurious loan records. It is not likely, however, that, even with the threat of a prison sentence, he would disclose the identity of his accomplice(s).

Nevertheless, it does appear that BLACK must carry some notations of the identity of his borrowers, the amount of the outstanding principal, and the interest rate, if he is to continue his collections. Since the list seized was incomplete, a second search might be beneficial in identifying additional borrowers. The search could be made pursuant to a warrant (surveillance and additional information from Poulas would likely produce probable cause) or as incident to an arrest of BLACK on possession of usurious records charges. Once the list is obtained, the borrower could be identified from the previously seized telephone book. Even if the borrowers chose to cooperate they would unlikely, however, be able to implicate BLACK's higher-up(s).

The examination of the books and records and bank account of the HEMLOCK CIGAR STORE should be undertaken. But to do it now, before additional investigation, would tip off the targets to the extent of our knowledge.

The use of an undercover officer may be indicated. Since POULAS needs money to pay BLACK, he may be willing to introduce an undercover as a "friend" or "relative" willing to assume the obligation. BLACK is likely to agree since the $1000 principal is still outstanding. After the undercover makes a number of payments, he can ask to bet with BLACK. He then has the option of: (1) asking for a large loan for a short period of time for "his business" (which could be set up on paper) in the hopes that BLACK could not handle it, and the money man be brought in, or (2) in defaulting and producing the enforcer, or both.

It may be necessary to use electronic surveillance with the above plan or instead of it, in the event that course of action is unsuccessful. Given the use of the store and its telephone by BLACK and BLACK's statement to POULAS regarding calling "to have him taken care," it seems possible that the additional physical surveillance might produce probable cause for the crimes of usury, extortion, and assault.

LEGAL ISSUES: 1) Would a search of BLACK for loan records as incident to the execution of an arrest warrant be considered a "subtrafuge search?"

2) Would the federal RICO statute apply to the HEMLOCK CIGAR STORE if that business were being used to "launder" loanshark payments?

# GRANT OF IMMUNITY

In Chapter Three we noted that Abe Reles of Murder, Inc. had agreed to cooperate in the prosecution of his associates, and that Sam Giancana of Chicago had refused to testify, under a grant of immunity. The grant of immunity is often used in efforts against organized crime.

The Fifth Amendment to the United States Constitution provides that no person "shall be compelled in any criminal case to be a witness against himself," thus prohibiting compulsory self-incrimination. In an effort to secure information or evidence without violating Constitutional guarantees, prosecutors (and various legislative and administrative bodies) can secure a grant of immunity for witnesses. An individual who, after being granted immunity, refuses to answer questions can be imprisoned for *contempt*. In cases of contempt of a grand jury, the person can be imprisoned until he or she agrees to answer the grand jury's questions or the term of the grand jury has expired. The term of a grand jury is usually eighteen months. In 1969, Vito Genovese died while serving time for a narcotics conviction. Gerardo Catena of New Jersey became (at least) the acting head of the Genovese crime family. In 1970, as a result of his refusal to testify before an investigating committee, after being given a grant of immunity, Catena was imprisoned. Despite numerous court appeals, Catena served more than five years because of his refusal to testify.

There are two basic types of immunity (Committee on the Office of Attorney General, 1978: 3):

1. *Transactional* immunity means that once a witness has been compelled to testify about an offense he may never be prosecuted for that offense, no matter how much independent evidence may come to light.
2. *Use* immunity means that no testimony compelled to be given and no evidence derived from or obtained because of the compelled testimony may be used if the person were subsequently prosecuted on independent evidence for the offense.

For example, a witness compelled to testify before a grand jury investigating a murder might be compelled to also testify about his involvement in the incident. If that witness had been given transactional immunity, he could not be prosecuted for any crime, including the murder, about which he was compelled to testify before the grand jury, even though his testimony revealed criminal activity on his part. If the immunity granted was "use" rather than transactional, then the witness could still be prosecuted for any crime revealed in his testimony, as long as the evidence used against him was obtained completely independently of the testimony he gave before the grand jury (Ibid.).

In 1972 the United States Supreme Court dealt with this issue in *Kastigar v. United States* (406 U.S. 441, 92 S.Ct. 1653). The persons who petitioned the Court had been subpoenaed to appear before a federal grand jury in California in 1971. The Assistant United States Attorney, believing that the petitioners were likely to assert their Fifth Amendment privilege, secured from the Federal District Court an order directing them to answer all questions and produce evidence before the grand jury under a grant of immunity. The persons involved refused to answer questions, arguing that "the scope of the immunity provided by the statute was not coextensive with the scope of the privilege against self-incrimination, and therefore was not sufficient to supplant the privilege and compel their testimony." The Supreme Court, in upholding the order, quoted from the federal immunity statute:

... the witness may not refuse to comply with the order on the basis of his privilege against self-incrimination; but no testimony or other information compelled under the order (or any information directly or indirectly derived from such testimony or other information) may be used against the witness in any criminal case, except a prosecution for perjury, giving a false statement, or otherwise failing to comply with the order.

The Supreme Court concluded that since the statute prohibits the prosecutorial authorities from using the compelled testimony in *any* respect, it therefore insures that the testimony cannot lead to the infliction of criminal penalties on the witness. A dissenting opinion, Justice Thurgood Marshall, pointed to the possibility of using the testimonial information as investigative leads designed to secure evidence against the witness. The majority of the Court agreed that the statute barred such use of testimony.

Rufus King raises some additional issues (1963: 651):

... the immunity bargain is a somewhat unsavory device per se, inaccurate and potentially very unfair; it should be used only sparingly and where it is absolutely required. Immunity grants are always exchanges, a pardon for crimes that would otherwise be punishable, given in return for testimony that could otherwise be withheld. In every case the interrogating authority must enter into a special "deal" with a wrongdoer to buy his testimony at the price of exoneration for something he would otherwise deserve punishment.

King points out (Ibid.):

Such bargains are always somewhat blind. Ordinarily the witness will be hostile, so that his examiners cannot be sure in advance exactly what value the withheld testimony will have. And at the same time, especially in broad legislative or administrative inquiries, it is impossible to tell beforehand just what crimes are likely to be exonerated. Conceivably, the witness may have a surprise ready for his questioners at every turn of the proceedings.

Because, as King has noted, the decision to grant immunity is so full of potentially undesirable repercussions, some prosecutors have developed guidelines for consideration when making an immunity decision. The following are from the New Jersey Division of Criminal Justice (quoted in Committee on the Office of Attorney General, 1978: 27):

1. Can the information be obtained from any source other than a witness who wants to negotiate immunity?
2. How useful is the information for purposes of criminal prosecution?
3. What is the likelihood that the witness can successfully be prosecuted?
4. What is the relative significance of the witness as a potential defendant?
5. What is the relative significance of the potential defendant against whom the witness offers to testify?

6.  What is the value of the testimony of the witness to the case (is it the core evidence upon which the prosecution is based)?
7.  What impact will immunity have on the credibility of the witness at trial? Are the terms of the immunity agreement so favorable to the witness that the jury will not accept the testimony?
8.  What impact will immunity have on the prosecutor's personal credibility and that of his office?

It should be noted that a person who testifies under a grant of immunity, while saved from criminal sanctions, can suffer other consequences: loss of employment or social status; and most important, revenge from associates who are often not adverse to murder.

## Investigative Grand Jury

The power to compel testimony under a grant of immunity, as well as quite broad investigative and subpoena authority * makes the investigative grand jury an important tool for dealing with organized crime. "Any subpoena issued by a grand jury is presumed to be valid, and when it is properly served it must be obeyed to the full extent of its terms. There is no redress in the courts for persons who have been subpoenaed, nor is a grand jury liable for the subpoenas it issues" (Lewis, et al., 1978: 187). A grand juror cannot be punished or sued for his actions as a juror, and the proceedings of the grand jury are secret. Testimony is given under oath and recorded; false testimony is subject to statutes against perjury.

In states that have laws providing for an investigative or "special" grand jury, the authority to convene the grand jury rests with the prosecutor or a judge of a trial court of general (superior) jurisdiction; many states also permit the attorney general and/or the governor to convene a special grand jury. In a few instances there have been "run-away" grand juries which, as is in their power, defy the leadership of the prosecutor and conduct their own investigation. One such grand jury in New York City resulted in the appointment of Thomas Dewey as a special prosecutor. Some areas may have a full-time investigative grand jury that meets each week or as needed. A few states, seven as of 1978, have statutes authorizing statewide grand juries (Committee of the Office of Attorney General, 1977: 16):

A local grand jury is restricted to the investigation of criminal offenses committed or triable within the county in which the panel is sitting or within

---

* In *United States v. Dionisio* 410 U.S. 1, 93 S.Ct. 764 (1973), the United States Supreme Court held, "A grand jury has broad investigative powers to determine whether a crime has been committed and who has committed it. The jurors may act on tips, rumors, evidence offered by the prosecutor, or their own personal knowledge." In *United States v. Calandra* 414 U.S. 338 (1974), the Supreme Court ruled that even illegally obtained evidence may be used as a basis for questioning witnesses subpoenaed to appear before a grand jury.

the jurisdiction of the court to which it is attached. It has no authority to indict for offenses committed outside its jurisdiction. Since large-scale and organized criminal activity is frequently not limited to any one locality, investigation of such activity is more efficiently conducted by a body of statewide jurisdiction. A state grand jury can avoid the needless repetition of testimony and the inefficient use of resources required by successive grand jury investigations of multi-county crimes.

A statewide grand jury also has the advantage of statewide investigative resources and develops expertise as a result of its ability to concentrate on certain kinds of cases, e.g., organized crime (Ibid.).

In addition to the power to indict, a grand jury can issue a report of its findings which often contains a recommendation for public action. While such reports are merely advisory, they usually generate a great deal of news media coverage and public support.

In the federal system an investigative grand jury can be convened by a District Court judge at the request of the United States Attorney. The 1970 Organized Crime Control Act provides for the impanelment of special grand juries. "These grand juries are impaneled automatically on a regular basis and cannot be discharged by the court in its uncontrolled discretion, as is the case with regular federal grand juries" (Ibid.: 7).

> Special grand juries are established in judicial districts having a population of over four million and in other districts where the Attorney General or his designee certifies to the chief judge that such a jury is necessary 'because of criminal activity in the district.' In such districts title 1 requires that a special grand jury be summoned at least once each 18 months unless another special grand jury is serving. It can serve until the majority of its members determine that its business has been completed, but not for more than 18 months unless the court orders a six-month extension. No jury is to serve more than 36 months, unless the grand jury is taking testimony concerning noncriminal misconduct of a public official on direction of a court (Ibid.).

# CONSPIRACY STATUTES *

Conspiracy may be defined as an agreement by two or more persons to commit an act, which if committed would be in violation of some criminal statute. Thus, it is the agreement itself which becomes the corpus of the crime, and the crime is committed even though the object crime of the conspiratorial undertaking is not committed.

* Unless otherwise cited, information in this section comes from Robert W. Johannesen, Jr., special agent of the Drug Enforcement Administration, who specializes in conspiracy cases.

Substantive criminal violations in organized crime matters are often, if not always, rooted in some conspiratorial undertaking. Thus where the evidence permits, prosecution may be undertaken for both the substantive and conspiracy violations. Both are separate and distinct crimes.

Following are some legal aspects of conspiracy and conspirators.

1.  During the development of a conspiracy, statements by one of the co-conspirators in furtherance of the conspiracy is binding on the other members of the conspiracy.
2.  A co-conspirator *need not* have joined the conspiracy at its *inception*. Upon joining the conspiracy *each* co-conspirator is therefore *bound by* the prior acts and statements of his/her co-conspirators which were made in furtherance of the conspiracy.
3.  To be *guilty* of a conspiracy violation, a defendant must be proven to have had *knowledge* of the conspiracy and its essential *objective*. It is not sufficient merely to show that he furthered the conspiracy, even through commission of unlawful acts, or that he associated himself with other members of the conspiracy.
4.  Statute of Limitations (five years) does not begin to run until the commission of the *last* overt act.
5.  Regarding withdrawal, a defendant who claims to have withdrawn from the conspiracy prior to the indictable period, *has* the burden of presenting affirmation proof that he did, in fact, actually withdraw. This means some affirmation action, *not* just inactivity.
6.  *Venue* in a conspiracy prosecution generally lies in *any* judicial district (or jurisdiction) in which the agreement was made or in which one of the overt act(s) has been committed, including where a telephone call is made between two jurisdictions, district or state, assuming such a call can be said to have been an overt act in furtherance of the conspiracy.
7.  Generally, a *party* to a conspiracy is responsible for any substantive offense committed by a co-conspirator in furtherance of the conspiracy even though he did not participate in such substantive offense and even though he had no actual knowledge of it.
8.  Usually conspiracies are so secretive and complex that direct evidence of the agreement is not available. As a result, the U.S. Supreme Court has held that the existence of the conspiracy can be established or inferred from circumstantial evidence. Circumstantial evidence can be defined as something to support what a reasonable person deduces to be true. An example: a bright sun-drenched courtroom at 10:00 a.m. The judge orders the drapes drawn. At 3:30 p.m. a witness walks into courtroom wearing a raincoat, rubbers, carrying an umbrella and appearing *all* wet. This is circumstantial evidence.
9.  It is not necessary that *each party* to the conspiracy *know* the number or identity of all of his co-conspirators.
10. Acquittal, or dismissal, of one or more defendants will not impair conviction of co-defendants.

11. Crime of conspiracy necessarily involves at least *two* parties. They may be husband and wife, a corporation and its officers and employees, etc.
12. Acquittal of all but one of the co-conspirators, absent evidence of involvement by others, is acquittal of *all.*
13. Because of the plurality requirement, there can be no conviction of an individual for conspiracy where the only other party thereto is a government agent.
14. There can be no conspiracy unless at least one overt act is committed by one of the co-conspirators in furtherance of the conspiracy.
15. The overt act need not be criminal in nature.
16. Prosecution need not prove all of the overt acts charged. Proof of one is sufficient.

Earl Johnson points out, "The fundamental essence of a conspiracy obviates the necessity of establishing that the organization leader committed a physical act amounting to a crime or that he even committed an overt act in furtherance of the object of the conspiracy. It is sufficient if he can be shown to have been a party to the conspiratorial agreement" (1963: 2). Johnson notes that once the management-level member of organized crime "is shown to be a member of the conspiracy, all out-of-court statements of his co-conspirators which are made in furtherance of the conspiracy are admissible against an organization leader. Accordingly, statements of other organization members to third parties can be used to convict its leading figure" (Ibid.).

There are three limitations to using conspiracy statutes for prosecuting organized crime figures. One is minor; two are serious:

1. In most jurisdictions the penalty exacted for conspiracy cannot be greater than that for which an individual committing the substantive act could receive (Ibid.). Since gambling usually carries minimum penalties, invoking conspiracy statutes in gambling investigations is often not productive;
2. Conspiracy cases are quite complex and require a great deal of time and skill to prepare in a manner that will not confuse a jury; in many conspiracy cases there can be tens of defendants—sometimes more than one hundred;
3. Evidence in conspiracy cases usually requires direct testimony of "eye witnesses"; this often means a participant in the conspiracy who agrees to testify ("flips") against his co-conspirators in exchange for leniency or immunity from prosecution.

In Chapter Four we reviewed the activities of Frank Matthews, an important black narcotics operator. His indictment provides an example of the usefulness of the conspiracy charge. The indictment shows how a sound conspiracy violation is put together by a painstaking investigation and collection of detail.

UNITED STATES DISTRICT COURT
EASTERN DISTRICT OF NEW YORK

. . . . . . . . . . . . . . . . . . . . . . . . . . . . . . . . . x

UNITED STATES OF AMERICA

- against -

FRANK MATTHEWS, a/k/a "Pee Wee,"
  "Big Book," "Frank McNeil,"
  "Mark IV Frank,"
BARBARA HINTON, a/k/a "Barbara
  Matthews,"
GATTIS HINTON, a/k/a "Bud," "Slim,"
  "Joseph Jackson,"
WILLIAM BECKWITH, a/k/a "Mickey,"
  "McGill," "Miguel,"
DONALD CONNER,
ROBERT CURRINGTON, a/k/a "Pedro,"
CHARLES WILLIAM CAMERON, a/k/a
  "Swayzie,"
JAMES WESLEY CARTER, a/k/a "Brother
  Carter," "Big Head Brother," "Big B,"
JOHN DARBY, a/k/a "Pop," "John Smith,"
THELMA DARBY, a/k/a "Flossie,"
  "Thelma Reese,"
DAVID CLEMENT BATES, a/k/a "Rev,"
WALTER ROSENBAUM,
ERNEST ROBINSON, a/k/a "Ernie,"
JAMES E. MARTINEZ,
SCARVEY MC CARGO,
FRED BROWN,
LUCY MATHEWS,
MARZELLA STEELE WEBB,

Crim. No. _____
(T.21, U.S.C., §§173,174,812
841(a)(1), 843(b),846
952(a),960(a)(1),963)

           Defendants.

. . . . . . . . . . . . . . . . . . . . . . . . . . . . . . . . . x

THE GRAND JURY CHARGES:

## COUNT ONE

From on or about September, 1968, and continuously thereafter up to and including the date of the filing of this indictment, within the Eastern District of New York and elsewhere, the defendants FRANK MATTHEWS, a/k/a "Pee Wee," "Big Book," "Frank McNeil," "Mark IV Frank," BARBARA HINTON, a/k/a "Barbara Matthews," GATTIS HINTON, a/k/a "Bud," "Slim," "Joseph Jackson," WILLIAM BECKWITH, a/k/a "Mickey," "McGill," "Miguel," DONALD CONNER, ROBERT CURRINGTON, a/k/a "Pedro," CHARLES WILLIAM CAMERON, a/k/a "Swayzie," JAMES WESLEY CARTER, a/k/a "Brother Carter," "Big Head Brother," "Big B," JOHN DARBY, a/k/a "Pop," "John Smith," THELMA DARBY, a/k/a "Flossie," "Thelma Reese,"

DAVID CLEMENT BATES, a/k/a "Rev," WALTER ROSENBAUM, ERNEST ROB-INSON, a/k/a "Ernie," JAMES E. MARTINEZ, SCARVEY MC CARGO, FRED BROWN, LUCY MATHEWS, and MARZELLA STEELE WEBB together with Emerson Dorsey, Nathaniel Elder, a/k/a "Nat," Donald James, John Edward Jones, a/k/a "Liddy Jones," George Mosley, Ana Ramos, Jorge Ramos, James Aubrey Scott, and John Thorp, a/k/a "Pete," named herein as co-conspirators but not as defendants, and others known and unknown to the Grand Jury, wilfully, knowingly and unlawfully did combine, conspire, confederate, and agree to violate prior to May 1, 1971, Sections 173 and 174 of Title 21, United States Code, and to violate on and after May 1, 1971, Sections 812, 841(a)(1), 952(a), and 960(a)(1) of Title 21, United States Code.

1.   It was part of said conspiracy that prior to May 1, 1971, the defendants and co-conspirators fraudulently and knowingly would import and bring into the United States large quantities of heroin and cocaine, narcotic drugs, contrary to law.

2.   It was further a part of said conspiracy that prior to May 1, 1971, the defendants and co-conspirators wilfully, knowingly, and unlawfully would receive, conceal, buy, sell, and facilitate the transportation, concealment, and sale of large quantities of heroin and cocaine, narcotic drugs, after the narcotic drugs had been imported and brought into the United States knowing the same to have been imported and brought into the United States contrary to law.

3.   It was further a part of said conspiracy that on and after May 1, 1971, the defendants and co-conspirators knowingly and intentionally would import large quantities of heroin and cocaine, Schedule I and Schedule II narcotic drug controlled substances, into the United States from places outside thereof.

4.   It was further a part of said conspiracy that on and after May 1, 1971, the defendants and co-conspirators knowingly and intentionally would distribute and possess with intent to distribute large quantities of heroin and cocaine, Schedule I and Schedule II narcotic drug controlled substances.

5.   It was further a part of said conspiracy that the defendants and co-conspirators would obtain large quantities of mannitol, quinine, glassine envelopes, and other paraphernalia in order to enable defendants and co-conspirators to adulterate, dilute, process, and package the narcotic drugs for unlawful distribution.

6.   It was further a part of said conspiracy that the defendants and co-conspirators would conceal the existence of the conspiracy and would take steps designed to prevent disclosure of their activities.

In furtherance of the conspiracy and to effect the objects thereof, the following overt acts, among others, were committed within the Eastern District of New York and elsewhere:

## OVERT ACTS

1.   In or about the middle of 1969 the defendant CHARLES WILLIAM CAMERON and others met in Brooklyn, New York.

2.   In or about Summer, 1971, the defendant WILLIAM BECKWITH met with co-conspirator John Thorp and others in Brooklyn, New York.

3.   On or about January 31, 1972, the defendants FRANK MATTHEWS, SCARVEY MC CARGO, JAMES E. MARTINEZ, and co-conspirator Nathaniel Elder met in Brooklyn, New York.

4.   On or about June 5, 1972, the defendant JAMES WESLEY CARTER made a telephone call to the defendant FRANK MATTHEWS.

5.   On or about June 22, 1972, the defendant WALTER ROSENBAUM caused to be transported from Genoa, Italy, to Philadelphia, Pennsylvania, a quantity of mannite.

6.   In or about June, 1972, the defendant GATTIS HINTON received 11 kilograms of cocaine from co-conspirator Jorge Ramos in New York, New York.

7.   On or about July 8, 1972, the defendants FRANK MATTHEWS and DAVID CLEMENT BATES had a telephone conversation.

8.   On or about August 1, 1972, the defendant FRANK MATTHEWS received six (6) kilograms of cocaine from co-conspirator Jorge Ramos in New York, New York.

9.   On or about September 5, 1972, the defendants FRANK MATTHEWS, WILLIAM BECKWITH, and JOHN DARBY had a telephone conversation.

10.   On or about September 16, 1972, the defendants BARBARA HINTON and THELMA DARBY had a telephone conversation.

11.   On or about January 16, 1974, the defendants DONALD CONNER, JOHN DARBY, and ERNEST ROBINSON met in Brooklyn, New York.

12.   On or about March 1, 1974, the defendants FRED BROWN and LUCY MATHEWS had a conversation in Newark, New Jersey. (Title 21, United States Code, Sections 173,174,846 and 963.)

### COUNT TWO
On or about the 8th day of July 1972, within the Eastern District of New York and elsewhere, the defendants FRANK MATTHEWS, a/k/a "Pee Wee," "Big Book," "Frank McNeil," "Mark IV Frank," and DAVID CLEMENT BATES, a/k/a "Rev," knowingly, intentionally, and unlawfully did use a communication facility, to wit, the telephone, in committing and in causing and facilitating the commission of the conspiracy set forth in Count One of this indictment. (Title 21, United States Code, Section 843(b)).

### COUNT THREE
On or about the 8th day of July 1972, within the Eastern District of New York and elsewhere, the defendants FRANK MATTHEWS, a/k/a "Pee Wee," "Big Book," "Frank McNeil," "Mark IV Frank," and DAVID CLEMENT BATES, a/k/a "Rev," knowingly, intentionally, and unlawfully did use a communication facility, to wit, the telephone, in committing and in causing and facilitating the commission of the conspiracy set forth in Count One of this indictment. (Title 21, United States Code, Section 843(b)).

### COUNT FOUR
On or about the 1st day of September 1972, within the Eastern District of New York and elsewhere, the defendants JOHN DARBY, a/k/a "Pop," "John Smith," and BARBARA HINTON, a/k/a "Barbara Matthews," know-

ingly, intentionally, and unlawfully did use a communication facility, to wit, the telephone, in committing and in causing and facilitating the commission of the conspiracy set forth in Count One of this indictment. (Title 21, United States Code, Section 843(b)).

### COUNT FIVE

On or about the 5th day of September 1972, within the Eastern District of New York, the defendants FRANK MATTHEWS, a/k/a "Pee Wee," "Big Book," "Frank McNeil," "Mark IV Frank," and JOHN DARBY, a/k/a "Pop," "John Smith," knowingly, intentionally, and unlawfully did use a communication facility, to wit, the telephone, in committing and in causing and facilitating the commission of the conspiracy set forth in Count One of this indictment. (Title 21, United States Code, Section 843(b)).

### COUNT SIX

On or about the 6th day of September 1972, within the Eastern District of New York, the defendants FRANK MATTHEWS, a/k/a "Pee Wee," "Big Book," "Frank McNeil," "Mark IV Frank," WILLIAM BECKWITH, a/k/a "Mickey," "McGill," "Miguel," and JOHN DARBY, a/k/a "Pop," "John Smith," knowingly, intentionally, and unlawfully did use a communication facility, to wit, the telephone, in committing and in causing and facilitating the commission of the conspiracy set forth in Count One of this indictment. (Title 21, United States Code, Section 843(b)).

### COUNT SEVEN

On or about the 7th day of September 1972, within the Eastern District of New York and elsewhere, the defendants FRANK MATTHEWS, a/k/a "Pee Wee," "Big Book," "Frank McNeil," "Mark IV Frank," and JOHN DARBY, a/k/a "Pop," "John Smith," knowingly, intentionally, and unlawfully did use a communication facility, to wit, the telephone, in committing and in causing and facilitating the commission of the conspiracy set forth in Count One of this indictment. (Title 21, United States Code, Section 843(b)).

### COUNT EIGHT

On or about the 11th day of September 1972, within the Eastern District of New York and elsewhere, the defendants FRANK MATTHEWS, a/k/a "Pee Wee," "Big Book," "Frank McNeil," "Mark IV Frank," and JOHN DARBY, a/k/a "Pop," "John Smith," knowingly, intentionally, and unlawfully did use a communication facility, to wit, the telephone, in committing and in causing and facilitating the commission of the conspiracy set forth in Count One of this indictment. (Title 21, United States Code, Section 843(b)).

### COUNT NINE

On or about the 16th day of September 1972, within the Eastern District of New York and elsewhere, the defendants BARBARA HINTON, a/k/a "Barbara Matthews," and THELMA DARBY, a/k/a "Flossie," "Thelma Reese," knowingly, intentionally, and unlawfully did use a communication facility, to wit, the telephone, in committing and in causing and facilitating the commission of the conspiracy set forth in Count One of this indictment. (Title 21, United States Code, Section 843(b)).

A TRUE BILL.

_____

Foreman.

_____

UNITED STATES ATTORNEY

## WITNESS PROTECTION PROGRAM *

One of the more controversial programs that the federal government originated was provided for in the Organized Crime Control Act of 1970 (18 U.S.C. 1961):

The organized Crime Control Act of 1970 went into effect October 15, 1970. Title V., sections 501-504 pertained to the protection of witnesses. Those sections provided:

SEC. 501. The Attorney General of the United States is authorized to provide for the security of Government witnesses, potential Government witnesses, and the families of Government witnesses and potential witnesses in legal proceedings against any person alleged to have participated in an organized criminal activity.

SEC. 502. The Attorney General of the United States is authorized to rent, purchase, modify or remodel protected housing facilities and to otherwise offer to provide for the health, safety, and welfare of witnesses and persons intended to be called as Government witnesses, and the families of witnesses and persons intended to be called as Government witnesses in legal proceedings instituted against any person alleged to have participated in an organized criminal activity whenever, in his judgment testimony from, or a willingness to testify by, such a witness would place his life or person, or the life or person of a member of his family or household in jeopardy. Any person availing himself of such an offer by the Attorney General to use such facilities may continue to use such facilities for as long as the Attorney General determines the jeopardy to his life or person continues.

SEC. 503. As used in this title, "Government" means the United States, any State, the District of Columbia, the Commonwealth of Puerto Rico, any territory or possession of the United States, any political subdivision, or any department agency, or instrumentality thereof. The offer of facilities to witnesses may be conditioned by the Attorney General upon reimbursement in whole or in part to the United States by any State or any political subdivision or any department, agency, or instrumentality thereof the cost of maintaining and protecting such witnesses.

SEC. 504. There is hereby authorized to be appropriated from time to time such funds as are necessary to carry out the provisions of this title.

* See also Appendix D.

This very broad *enabling* legislation was amended in 1977 with the passage of the Criminal Code Reform Act:

"§ 3121. Witness Relocation and Protection

"(a) *Relocation*—The Attorney General may provide for the relocation of a government witness or a potential government witness in an official proceeding involving racketeering activity, an offense similar in nature, or an offense the investigation or prosecution of which appears likely under the circumstances to cause the commission of an offense described in section 1323 (Tampering with a Witness or an Informant) or 1324 (Retaliating against a Witness or an Informant) The Attorney General may also provide for the relocation of the immediate family of, or a person otherwise closely associated with, such witness or potential witness if the family or person may also be endangered.

"(b) *Related protective measures.*—In connection with the relocation of a witness, a potential witness, or an immediate family member or close associate of a witness or potential witness, the Attorney General may take any action he determines to be necessary to protect such person from bodily injury, and otherwise to assure his health, safety, and welfare, for as long as, in the judgment of the Attorney General, such danger exists. The Attorney General may:

"(1) Provide suitable official documents to enable the person relocated to establish a new identity:

"(2) Provide housing for the person relocated;

"(3) Provide for the transportation of household furniture and other personal property to the new residence of the person relocated;

"(4) Provide a tax free subsistence payment, in a sum established in regulations issued by the Attorney General, for such time as the Attorney General determines to be warranted;

"(5) Assist the person relocated in obtaining employment; and

"(6) Refuse to disclose the identity or location of the person relocated, or any other matter concerning the person or the relocation program, after weighing the danger such a disclosure would pose to the person relocated, the detriment it would cause to the general effectiveness of the relocation program, and the benefit it would afford to the public or to the person seeking the disclosure.

"(c) *Civil action against a relocated person.*—Notwithstanding the provisions of subsection (b) (6), if a person relocated under this section is named as a defendant in a civil cause of action, arising prior to the person's relocation, for damages resulting from bodily injury, property damage, or injury to business, process in the civil proceeding may be served upon the Attorney General. The Attorney General shall make reasonable efforts to serve a copy of the process upon the person relocated at his last known address. If a judgment in such an action is entered against the person relocated, the Attorney General shall determine whether the person has made reasonable efforts to comply with the provisions of that judgment. The Attorney General shall take affirmative steps to urge the person located to comply with any judgment rendered. If the Attorney General determines that the person has not made reasonable efforts to comply with the provisions of the judgment, he may, in his discretion, after weighing the danger to the person relocated, disclose the identity and location of that person to the plaintiff entitled to recovery pursuant to the judgment. Any such disclosure shall be made upon the express condition that further disclosure by the plaintiff of such identity or location may be made only if essential to the plaintiff's efforts to recover under the judgment, and only to such additional persons as is necessary to effect the recovery. Any such disclosure or nondisclosure by the Attorney General shall not subject the government to liability in any action based upon the consequences thereof.

§ 3122. Reimbursement* of Expenses.

"The offer provision of facilities transportation, housing, subsistence, or other assistance to a person under section 3121 may be conditioned by the Attorney General upon reimbursement of expenses in whole or in part to the United States by a state or local government.

The United States Senate Subcommittee on Administrative Practice and Procedure (1978) provides the purpose and evolution of the program:

### Evolution of Witness Protection

Prosecutors and law enforcement agents have long recognized that witnesses who testify against certain individuals do so at serious risk to themselves and their families. The Kefauver Committee found in the 1950s that a major organized crime syndicate:

... will eliminate anyone who stands in the way of its success and destroy anyone who betrays its secrets and will use any means available, including intimidation to defeat any attempt by law enforcement to interfere with its operation.

Law enforcement officials also have come to agree that the single most effective tool for prosecuting persons involved in organized crime is the testimony of insiders who decide, for whatever reason, to give information against their former associates.

Before the existence of a formal witness protection program, police officers, investigative agents, and prosecutors periodically aided witnesses whose cooperation with the Government placed them in jeopardy. The assistance varied from arranging for relocation to a new residence, to assisting in establishing a new identity or in obtaining employment. Often, the assistance was little more than a bus ticket to some distant location.

In 1967, the Task Force on Organized Crime of the President's Commission on Law Enforcement and Administration of Justice reported that no jurisdiction had made adequate provisions for protecting witnesses from reprisal in organized crime cases. To resolve the problem, the Task Force recommended that:

The Federal Government should establish residential facilities for the protection of witnesses desiring such assistance during the pendency of organized crime litigation.

Congress responded to the Task Force recommendations in the Organized Crime Control Act of 1970, which provided for the funding of witness protection activities.

* For witness protection.

The language of the statute clearly indicates that the Congress anticipated that the first security method would be to protect witnesses in secured facilities, known as "safehouses," during the period when they were in danger. However, the statute did not limit the Attorney General to the safehouse approach. It provided expressly that he was authorized "to otherwise ... provide for the health, safety and welfare of witnesses" and their families.

Safehouses often had been used by the intelligence community to debrief defectors and agents; and its application to the concept of witness protection seemed logical. In the late 1960s the U.S. Marshals Service employed safehouses to protect witnesses, most of whom were prisoners and had been moved from regular prison facilities. The effort to apply this approach to witnesses who were not prisoners proved to be unreasonably expensive, inefficient, and not particularly effective from a security perspective. The locations of the safehouses were highly *publicized and round-the-clock guards were needed.* Furthermore, the safehouse model had obvious drawbacks for witnesses with families, especially those with children. The safehouse environment precluded normal family life.

As the limited value of safehouses for protecting witnesses who were not prisoners became increasingly apparent, the Department began to rely upon the relocation of witnesses as its principal security tool. It was simply more efficient and more beneficial to relocate a witness secretly than to provide round-the-clock protection at a known location.

*Initially, the Criminal Division had primary responsibility for administering the Program.* The necessary witness services, including job assistance and financial assistance, were performed by the Criminal Division staff, with the U.S. Marshals Service limited to supplying guards when a need for protection arose.

As the Witness Security Program developed, that division of responsibility between the Criminal Division and the U.S. Marshals Service had to be reevaluated. Questions were raised about the possible impropriety—or at least the appearance of impropriety—of prosecuting attorneys securing money for witnesses. Furthermore, program administration was becoming a considerable burden for the Criminal Division.

## WITNESS SECURITY PROGRAM
### ESTIMATED TOTAL COSTS 1971–1977

| Fiscal Year | Direct Costs | Indirect Support Costs | 1971–1977 Total |
|---|---|---|---|
| 1971 | $    428,075 | $ 2,300,870 | $ 2,728,945 |
| 1972 | 744,852 | 3,511,470 | 4,256,322 |
| 1973 | 1,252,264 | 4,722,480 | 5,974,744 |
| 1974 | 2,274,000 | 6,012,580 | 8,286,580 |
| 1975 | 2,762,415 | 5,555,130 | 8,317,545 |
| 1976 | 4,030,000 | 5,633,790 | 9,663,790 |
| 1977 | 5,950,000 | 5,725,150 | 11,675,150 |
| | $17,441,606 | $33,461,470 | $50,903,076 |

It was therefore decided that the U.S. Marshals Service should be charged with the primary responsibility for the Program and given the authority to make expenditures for subsistence. The legal divisions of the Department retained the authority to place witnesses in the Program. However, once a witness had entered, security and maintenance were the responsibility of the U.S. Marshals Service. Although there have been difficulties associated with the allocation of functions, the Program continues to operate under this arrangement.

### CONTINUED NEED FOR PROGRAM

There is almost universal agreement as to the need for some form of witness protection, especially in organized crime and narcotics cases. A recent Criminal Division report, *Violence in Organized Crime,* concludes:

Because discouraging witnesses with the use of violence is such an effective tool for neutralizing law enforcement, the most cruel and inhuman torture before death is not uncommon. Those suspected of cooperating with law enforcement officials have been beaten, burned, blown up, shot, drowned, and/or garrotted. The hits are typically well planned and executed by professionals who leave few traces, and on the rare occasion where there are witnesses, as soon as the word goes out that it was a mob hit, the witnesses become very reticent. Hence, effective programs for protecting and relocating witnesses are essential if the criminal justice system is to work.

The same report notes an increase in violence associated with organized crime, and quotes the concluding remarks of a protected witness before a Federal grand jury in Kansas City:

"You people just don't realize—you go home and you walk the streets and you see a beautiful city, which it is . . . , and you don't realize how bad these people are. You just have no idea. Not only my family (has · been) ruined, they have ruined 50 families. I'm the first one that has even had enough guts to stand up like I'm doing now, and I don't know if I'll make it or not, but at least if they get me, I'm going to take some of them with me."

Another Criminal Division report that tabulates murders related to organized crime in the United States indicates that the victims in almost 10 percent of all such murders in the last four years were prosecution witnesses who were not included in any protection program.

The following are typical recent cases involving murder of witnesses, none of whom were in the Witness Security Program:

*Bompensiero, Frank:* Murdered February 22, 1977, while scheduled to appear before a Federal grand jury in Los Angeles concerning extortion in the pornography business.

*Bowen, Harold:* Murdered February 22, 1977. It is believed that Bowen upset the organized crime community when he testified before a Federal grand jury on a theft charge which involved a member of a criminal organization.

*Delia, Ellen:* Shot to death February 17, 1977, in Sacramento, California, where she had gone to give testimony concerning fraud and misuse of Federal and state funds in the operation of East Los Angeles Community Projects.

*Delman, Gerald:* Shot by an unknown assailant two days after being subpoenaed and two weeks prior to scheduled testimony in a gambling case in Las Vegas, Nevada.

*Ota, Stanley:* Shot to death November 17, 1976, in a public housing project. Two months earlier, Ota had been arrested for the sale of one pound of heroin to undercover Federal agents. Shortly after his arrest, there were widespread rumors that the crime syndicate had ordered his death because of the possibility of his cooperation with government authorities.

*Getch, Anthony:* Gunned down February 14, 1975. He had turned state's evidence in a gangland killing of Louis Mariani in 1963.

*Giancana, Samuel:* Murdered in his Oak Park, Illinois, home on June 19, 1975, prior to a federal grand jury hearing.

*Rand, Tamara:* Shot in the head November 9, 1975. Rand was a San Diego realtor. After being cheated in several potentially lucrative real estate transactions, Rand began compiling evidence for a judicial retaliation.

*Wellman, Alan E. and his wife Renate:* Murdered December 15, 1975, in their Sherman Oaks, California, home. Alan Wellman was scheduled to testify in a Federal court in Philadelphia in January 1976.

*Dubeck, John and wife:* Murdered in courtyard of their Las Vegas apartment complex March 19, 1974. Dubeck was scheduled to testify the following week against several organized crime figures.

*Fucillo, Joseph:* Shot and killed October 17, 1974. Fucillo had testified against two major organized crime figures.


Other reports examined by the Review Committee showed a clear and distinct pattern of violence directed at informers and unprotected witnesses. One report, covering fifty narcotics-related prosecutions, showed forty-five murders, nine attempted murders, nine threats of murder, and an assortment of other physical attacks.

Although the number of witnesses actually killed each year is not large, the Review Committee found convincing evidence that the danger to witnesses is real and serious. The Review Committee found no evidence that the risk to actual or potential state and federal witnesses had declined over the years, and there is some indication that such risks are increasing.

Consequently, the Review Committee concludes that there is no realistic and fair alternative to continued protection for witnesses. The choice is either to provide a Witness Security Program or to abandon efforts to prosecute the most dangerous criminals.

The Witness Protection Program has been subjected to a great deal of criticism. Fred Graham states that the legislation authorizing the program was "sneaked" through Congress: "Thus, there was never any debate on legal and moral problems that might arise as the government undertook to wash away the past lives of hundreds of people—many of them hoodlums—and infiltrate them back into society under false pretenses" (1977: 45). One of the legal questions relates to the offering of inducements in order to secure testimony —an area of dubious legality. Is the program an illegal inducement? Graham reports that this issue has not yet been resolved (1977: 39). Another issue relates to the federal agency responsible for the program; the United States Marshals' Service is primarily a unit that transports prisoners and serves legal papers. Graham questions its ability to operate the program, and relates one incident that occurred during the guarding of New Jersey syndicate associate-turned-informer, Gerald Zelmanowitz. On the first night after the marshals had placed him and his family in a motel, someone stole all of the marshals' shotguns, ammunition, and walkie-talkies (1977: 57). This writer was told of an incident during which the witness informed his two marshal bodyguards that the car they were in was being followed. The marshal made an effort to speed away from the pursuers, but the government car did not have the horsepower of the late model Lincoln that was following. The writer asked what type of firearms were available in the marshals' car; each marshal had a .38 revolver, hardly equal to gunmen who often use shotguns and magnum handguns. The writer asked if there was a two-way radio in the car; yes, but it was after six p.m. and the base-station was not operative. The marshals escaped their pursuers through some rather daredevil driving and not an insignificant amount of luck.

Some protected witnesses and their families have expressed displeasure over the program: poor documentation for their new identities; hostile attitudes on the part of the marshals. One witness told this writer that the program only provided him with a social security card, and he was left to create a new identity of his own. An arrest and fingerprinting for a minor charge revealed his real identity, and the fact that he was a "protected witness" soon appeared in the newspapers. A recent *60 Minutes* program (CBS-TV) revealed the poor treatment provided to a female witness, treatment that caused her and her family to leave the program. Most disheartening was the fact that she was not a criminal seeking leniency, but a responsible citizen who provided important information.

Perhaps the most controversial aspect of the program is the nature of some of the individuals who have received assistance. The case of Ira Pecznick highlights the problem. A half-Jewish, Polish immigrant, Pecznick was already a street criminal when he became part of the Campisi operation in Newark, New Jersey. The Campisi family was involved in gambling, mostly numbers and dice games, loansharking, narcotics, and armed robbery. Pecznick's involvement included even more—he participated in several murders and, while some victims were also criminals, some victims were quite innocent persons. In exchange for his testimony against the Campisi family, Pecznick was given a full pardon. This very dangerous person is now at large in our society with a new identity, courtesy of the Witness Protection Program.

## INCOME TAX AND
## ORGANIZED CRIME

In 1927 the United States Supreme Court decided the case of *United States v. Sullivan,* 274 U.S. 259, which denied the claim of self-incrimination as an excuse for failure to file income tax on illegally gained earnings. This decision enabled the federal government to successfully prosecute Al Capone and members of his organization.

As taxpayers management-level organized crime figures can be prosecuted for several acts:

1.  For failing to make required returns or maintain required business records;
2.  For filing a false return or making a false statement about taxes;
3.  For willful failure to pay federal income tax or concealment of assets with intent to defraud; and
4.  For assisting others to evade income taxes.

Earl Johnson points out, "Acts which do not comprise a violation or attempt to violate any of these substantive sections may be punishable as part of a conspiracy 'to impair, defeat, and obstruct the functions of the Commissioner of Internal Revenue' by concealing matters relevant to collection of federal taxes" (1963: 17). An employer can be prosecuted for not complying with social security withholding requirements relative to employees. Thus, the manager of an illegal enterprise, a gambling operation for example, can be prosecuted for such evasions (Ibid.).

> In the Internal Revenue Service there is a national office, seven regional offices, and fifty-eight district offices. The Intelligence Division [now called Criminal Investigation Division] has approximately 2,600 Special Agents who investigate and report criminal violations of the Internal Revenue Code to the Department of Justice.
>
> Additional income for criminal tax purposes is established by both direct and indirect methods. The direct method consists of the identification of specific items of unreported taxable receipts, overstated costs and expenses (such as personal expenses charged to business, diversion of corporate income to office-stockholders, allocation of income or expense to incorrect year in order to lower tax, etc.), and improper claims for credit or exemption. The advantage of using this method is that the proof involved is easier for jurors and others to understand. (Committee on the Office of Attorney General, 1974: 49–50)

Organized crime figures have devised methods for successful evasion of taxes—dealing in cash, keeping minimal records, setting up fronts. This is countered by the indirect method known as the *net worth theory:* "The government establishes a taxpayer's net worth at the commencement of the taxing period [requires substantial accuracy], deducts that from his net worth at the end of the period, and proves that the net gain in net worth exceeds the income reported by the taxpayer" (Johnson, 1963: 17–18).

In effect, the Internal Revenue Service reconstructs the total expenditures by examining the standard of living and comparing it with reported income (see Table 6-1). The government can then maintain that the taxpayer did not report his entire income; the government does not have to show a probable source of the excess unreported gain in net worth (Ibid.: 18). Earl Johnson points out that the Capone case taught many criminals a lesson: management-level members of organized crime have scrupulously reported their income—at least the part of it that they spend (Ibid.).

The Internal Revenue Service explains the net worth theory as follows (Office of the Attorney General, 1974):

The net worth method is an indirect method of computing income during a year by determining net worth increases and other outlays. Any change in net worth is adjusted to allow for non-taxable receipts and for reported income—the balance being unreported income. The formula here is: assets minus liabilities equals net worth; ending net worth minus beginning net worth equals net worth increase; net worth increase plus other expenditures plus (or minus) tax adjustments equals adjusted gross income; adjusted gross income minus deductions and exemptions equals corrected taxable income; and corrected taxable income minus reported taxable income equals additional taxable income.

Another indirect method is the expenditures method—related to net worth, but expressed differently. Funds are measured by their flow during the year, rather than by observing changes in net worth from the beginning to the end of the year. The formula here is: non-deductible applications of funds minus non-taxable sources equals adjusted gross income; from there, the formula is the same as for the net worth method. Note that the starting point for the beginning of the first year must be established in order to eliminate reasonable doubt that subsequent expenditures did not come from conversion of existing assets.

Another indirect method is the bank deposits method. This one is unlike the net worth and expenditures methods, which measure income at the point of its outflow—here, income is measured at the time of receipt. In this method, the three immediate dispositions of receipts for the year are determined: how much was deposited into banks; how much was spent without going through banks (cash expenditures); and how much was stored in other places (increases in cash on hand). The formula is: total deposits, plus cash expenditures, minus non-income items, equals gross receipts.

The stages in an IRS investigation are as follows: Information is received

TABLE 6-1.
NET WORTH STATEMENT *
JOHN AND MARY ROE
DAYTON, OHIO

| Assets | 12–31–65 | 12–31–66 | 12–31–67 |
|---|---|---|---|
| 1. Cash—First National Bank | $ 4,500.00 | $ 150.00 | $ 2,500.00 |
| 2. Cash on hand | 25.00 | 25.00 | 25.00 |
| 3. Inventory, Liquor Store | 4,800.00 | 13,000.00 | 29,000.00 |
| 4. U.S. Savings Bonds | –0– | 3,750.00 | –0– |
| 5. Note Receivable, Frank Roe | –0– | –0– | 300.00 |
| 6. Note Receivable, Roger Jones | –0– | –0– | 16,000.00 |
| 7. Accounts Receivable, Doc's Market | –0– | 1,600.00 | –0– |
| 8. Lot on Dayton Road | 1,000.00 | 1,000.00 | 1,000.00 |
| 9. Ohio Tourist Camp | 12,000.00 | 12,000.00 | 12,000.00 |
| 10. Residence, 1100 Vine Street | 2,800.00 | 2,800.00 | –0– |
| 11. 30 Acre Farm, East Dayton | –0– | 7,400.00 | 7,400.00 |
| 12. 150 Acre Farm, North Dayton | –0– | –0– | 7,000.00 |
| 13. Equipment—Liquor Store | 800.00 | 800.00 | 800.00 |
| 14. Buick Automobile | 2,800.00 | 2,800.00 | 2,800.00 |
| 15. Farm Truck | –0– | –0– | 800.00 |
| 16. Farm Equipment | –0– | 1,250.00 | 2,250.00 |
| 17. Livestock on Farm | –0– | 900.00 | 1,300.00 |
| Total Assets | $28,725.00 | $47,475.00 | $83,175.00 |

| Liabilities | | | |
|---|---|---|---|
| 18. First Federal Savings & Loan Assn | $ 2,400.00 | $ 1,800.00 | $ –0– |
| 19. First National Bank | 2,900.00 | 2,700.00 | –0– |
| 20. Depreciation Reserve | 2,500.00 | 3,200.00 | 4,300.00 |
| Total Liabilities | $ 7,800.00 | $ 7,700.00 | $ 4,300.00 |
| NET WORTH | $20,925.00 | $39,775.00 | $78,875.00 |
| Less: Net Worth of Prior Year | | 20,925.00 | 39,775.00 |
| Increase in Net Worth | | $18,850.00 | $39,100.00 |

| Adjustments | | | |
|---|---|---|---|
| Add: | | | |
| 21. Living Expenses | | $ 2,500.00 | $ 2,500.00 |
| 22. Life Insurance Premium | | 300.00 | 500.00 |
| 23. Federal Income Taxes Paid | | 750.00 | 900.00 |
| Less: | | | |
| 24. Long-Term Capital Gain on Sale of Residence (50%) | | –0– | (500.00) |
| 25. Inheritance | | –0– | (10,000.00) |
| Adjusted Gross Income | | $22,400.00 | $32,500.00 |
| Less: Standard Deduction | | 1,000.00 | 1,000.00 |
| Balance | | $21,400.00 | $31,500.00 |
| Less: Exemptions (4) | | 2,400.00 | 2,400.00 |
| Taxable Income | | $19,000.00 | $29,100.00 |
| Less: Taxable Income Reported | | 6,100.00 | 6,400.00 |
| Taxable Income Not Reported | | $12,900.00 | $22,700.00 |

* Source: Internal Revenue Service Agent's Manual.

by the Intelligence Division relating to an allegation of violation. Each information item is evaluated by the Chief of the Intelligence Division of the district involved, or by his designated representative, to determine whether it indicates a criminal violation. If criminal potential is apparent, the allegation may be assigned to a special agent for an investigation.

Steps taken by the special agent in a tax evasion case are outlined below. Whether or not any of the following steps are taken, and the order in which they occur in an investigation, vary according to the facts of the particular case involved. The special agent scrutinizes the tax returns for the years under investigation. A certificate of assessments and payments for the years involved in the investigation, and for prior years, if pertinent, is obtained. If returns were prepared by someone other than the principal, the person who prepared the return is interviewed concerning the circumstances surrounding the preparation of the returns. The books and records are reconciled with the returns and differences are noted. Documents (invoices, canceled checks, receipted bills, etc.) supporting amounts shown on records and returns are examined, if available. The principal is questioned regarding his assets, liabilities, and personal expenditures. This information is of the utmost importance in a case where there are no books and records or where the records are incomplete or inadequate.

Where a corporation is involved, the agents may also analyze the officers' personal accounts to determine the source and disposition of funds credited or charged thereto. If a partnership is involved the agents will examine the capital accounts and the personal drawing accounts of the partners to determine the source and disposition of funds. For the same purpose, the personal and proprietorship accounts of a sole proprietorship are also examined.

If the taxpayer has not maintained adequate books and records, the agents may list and analyze all the canceled checks and classify them into business expenses, capital expenditures, personal items, and non-deductible expenditures. The agents may examine records of deposits to bank accounts.

During the course of the investigation information may be obtained from: banks; customers of the principal; other persons who have had business transactions with the principal; records of the principal; public records; and newspapers, etc., regarding sources of the principal's income. The agents may interview, and obtain records from, persons who have had, or have knowledge of, transactions with the principal to determine what payments the principal received and the purposes thereof. Transactions involving purchases or sales of property may be examined. Information relative to those matters may be obtained from the purchaser or seller, from real estate agencies, and from public records. Information regarding the principal's personal and financial history is obtained from the principal, from those who know him, and from documents. This includes determining whether or not the principal has a record of prior violation of federal, state or local laws.

If the case is based on a net worth computation, evidence must be obtained to support the value of each item appearing in the net worth statement. The principal will be questioned regarding whether all assets and liabilities are included, especially in the beginning and ending computations of net worth. He also may be questioned about inheritances and gifts both during the period under investigation and in prior years. Further questions will be asked about the taxpayer's assets and liabilities at the beginning and end of each year which is included in the investigation and of any prior year pertinent to the case. The principal will be given an opportunity to explain the alleged discrepancies, and his explanations will be verified to whatever extent is possible. In the examination of records and during interviews with witnesses, the special agent is constantly alert for any facts or circumstances that cast light on the principal's intent, that is, any conduct the likely effect of which would be to mislead or to conceal.

Where a violation involves a failure to file a return, the agent obtains from the District Director or Service Center a certificate stating that a search of the files failed to disclose a return in the name of the principal. The special agent also will question the principal concerning whether or not he filed a return and the reasons for his failure. If the principal alleges that he has filed a return, evidence is obtained to prove or disprove his statement. In other respects the investigation of a failure to file a return proceeds in much the same manner as that of a case involving a willful attempt to evade or defeat income tax.

In many instances other methods of determining income may be used to corroborate the method on which the case is primarily based. For example, in a case based on proof of specific items of omitted income, a net worth computation may be used as corroborative proof; to show that the additional income was used to increase the financial position of the principal rather than to pay deductible expenses which were not claimed on the return but which the principal now alleges were incurred. At the conclusion of the investigation, the special agent writes a report setting forth the history of the principal, the evidence of additional income and willful intent, the principal's explanation and defense, and any evidence obtained to prove or disprove the defense. The special agent also sets forth in the report his conclusions regarding specific portions of evidence and concerning the case as a whole, together with his recommendations regarding criminal prosecution and the assertion of the appropriate civil penalties.

The district group manager is responsible for the initial technical review of all prosecution case reports prepared by special agents under his supervision. The purpose of the review is to determine whether the special agent's report is complete, logically presented, clear, concise, accurate, and that statements made in the report are supported by the facts and evidence. The Chief, or his designated representative, also reviews all prosecution case reports. The Chief must forward to the Regional Counsel for review all cases in which a recommendation for prosecution has been made by the special agent and approved by the Chief, except for certain type cases which may be sent directly to the United States Attorney. If the Chief does not concur in the recommendation of the special agent that a completed investigation of the special agent be forwarded for prosecution or closed as a non-prosecution case, he will request a written opinion and recommendation from the Assistant Regional Commissioner (Intelligence) (ARC-I). After receipt of the opinion and recommendations from the ARC-I, the Chief, as the representative of the District Director, will make the final decision as to the disposition of the case.

In regional level case processing, the ARC-I is responsible for providing technical assistance to districts within his region. The Chief will notify the ARC-I in writing when he desires technical assistance. In rendering technical assistance, the ARC-I, through his representative, will assure objectivity and region-wide uniformity in the application of Service policies. The regional representative will examine evidentiary material to the extent necessary to make an evaluation of prosecution potential. He may suggest alternative or additional investigative steps and make recommendations concerning the special agent's final report.

The Regional Counsel performs a legal review of the case. If the Regional Counsel concurs in the recommendation for prosecution, he forwards the case to the Department of Justice. If the Regional Counsel does not concur with the recommendations for prosecution in a case, he will confer with the Chief, Intelligence, in an effort to resolve the difference of opinion.

If the Department of Justice approves the recommendation for prosecution, the case is forwarded by the Department to the United States Attorney for the district in which the case is to be tried. If the Department of Justice does not approve the recommendation for prosecution, the case is returned to the Internal Revenue Service for disposition as a civil case. Procedure by the U.S. Attorney in criminal tax cases is the same as that for any other criminal case, namely, presentation to a grand jury or the filing of a criminal information (statement of charges). Appeals may be taken to the Circuit Courts of Appeals and to the Supreme Court.

Informants furnish information regarding alleged violations for a variety of reasons. Treasury Decision 6421, adopted October 23, 1959, provides for the payment of rewards for information relating to violations of the internal revenue laws. The amount of the reward depends upon the value of the information furnished in relation to the facts developed by the investigation. Informant's communications are forwarded to the Intelligence Division for evaluation and appropriate action. Information that indicates a violation of the internal revenue laws, discovered by officers of other federal, state, and local law enforcement agencies during their investigations, is forwarded to the Intelligence Division for evaluation and appropriate action.

The sections of the Code under which taxpayers are most frequently prosecuted in connection with violations of income tax laws are Section 7203 of Title 26, U.S.C., relating to the willful failure to file, and Section 7201 of Title 26, U.S.C., relating to willful attempts to evade or defeat any taxes. Section 7201 of the Internal Revenue Code of 1954 provides as follows: "Any person who willfully attempts in any manner to evade or defeat any tax imposed by this title or the payment thereof shall, in addition to other penalties provided by law, be guilty of a felony and upon conviction thereof, shall be fined not more than $10,000, or imprisoned not more than 5 years, or both, together with the cost of prosecution."

It is the question of what is the willful attempt in any manner to evade taxes that is the primary concern in determining whether or not there is proof of fraud. Willfulness is one of the crucial elements of the offense of attempted evasion and involves a specific intent, "the tax evasion motive." The attempt to defraud the government must be made intentionally. The phrase "willfully attempt in any manner" as provided in this section of the Code has been the subject of many court decisions. These decisions have established certain acts and circumstances as indicia of fraud. The most frequently quoted Supreme Court decision on the subject of willful attempts to evade or defeat is that of *Spies v. U.S.* in which the Court states as follows:

> Congress did not define or limit the methods by which a willful attempt to defeat and evade might be accomplished, and perhaps did not define lest its effort to do so result in some unexpected limitation. Nor would we by definition constrict the scope of the Congressional provision that it may be accomplished in any manner. By the way of illustration and not by way of limitation, we would think affirmative willful attempt may be inferred from conduct such as keeping a double set of books, making false entries or alterations, or false invoices or documents, destruction of books or records, concealment of assets or covering up sources of income, handling of one's affairs to avoid making the records usual in transactions of the kind, and any conduct, the likely effect of which would be to mislead or conceal. If the tax evasion motive plays any part in such conduct, the offense may be made out even though the conduct may also serve other purposes such as concealment of other crime.

This decision has briefly enumerated some of the taxpayer's actions which in the court's opinion would be indicative of fraud.

It is also apparent from this quotation that neither Congress nor the Supreme Court has attempted to in any way limit the circumstances or conduct of the taxpayer which may be interpreted as indicative of an attempt to evade tax.

It is important to distinguish between tax evasion and tax avoidance. Tax avoidance, as distinguished from tax evasion, implies that the taxpayer has only availed himself of all legal means of reducing his tax liability without the intent to evade or without the practice of intentional deception.

As a consequence of the Tax Reform Act of 1976, the Internal Revenue Service has been severely restricted with respect to the information that it can disclose even to law enforcement agencies that have a bona fide need to know. The IRS cannot even disclose if the person actually filed his income tax as required by law. Information from IRS can only be secured with a federal court order.

Under federal statutes (see Appendix F) all persons operating a gambling business must purchase an occupational tax stamp. This Special Income Wagering Tax Stamp costs $500, and the business is liable for an excise tax of 2 percent on the gross income.

### INTERNAL REVENUE SERVICE
### CRIMINAL INVESTIGATION DIVISION

I.  Criminal Sanctions:

    A.  Title 26 United States Code

| *Code Section* | *Maximum Sentences/Fines* |
|---|---|
| 7201—Evasion | 5  years/$10,000 |

| 7203—Failure to File | 1 year/$10,000 |
| 7206(1)—Signing a False Return | 3 years/$5,000 |
| 7206(2)—Preparation of False Return | 3 years/$5,000 |
| 7207—False Returns Altered Documents | 1 year/$1,000 |

B. Title 18 United States Code

| Code Section | Maximum Sentences/Fines |
|---|---|
| 287—False Claims | 5 years/$10,000 |
| 1001—False Statements | 5 years/$10,000 |
| 1621—Perjury | 5 years/$2,000 |
| 2—Aiding & Abetting | Same as substantive violation |
| 371—Conspiracy | 5 years/$10,000 |

II. Civil Sanctions:

    A. 50% fraud penalty (i.e., if taxpayer liability is determined to be $100,000 he would owe $150,000).

    B. Seizure of real (land, buildings) and personal (auto, boat, bank accounts, cash, etc.) property.

    C. Jeopardy or termination assessments used in on-going Examination or Criminal Investigation Division investigations, when at least one of the following conditions are present:

        1. Taxpayer is, or appears to be, designing to quickly depart from the United States or to conceal himself/herself.

        2. The taxpayer is, or appears to be designing to quickly place his/her/its property beyond the reach of the government either by removing from the United States, or by concealing it, or by transferring it to other persons, or by dissipating it.

        3. Taxpayer's financial solvency is or appears to be imperiled. (This does not include cases where the taxpayer becomes insolvent of virtue of the accrual of the proposed assessment of tax and penalty, if any.)

## Laundering "Dirty Money"

To avoid prosecution for evasion of taxes on illegally earned income, organized crime (as well as non-organized criminals) has devised schemes to "launder" its "dirty money." This laundering is usually a three-step operation (Clarke and Tigue: 91):

1. Smuggling dirty money to a Swiss or Caribbean bank;
2. Altering its nature and/or origin; and
3. Returning the now laundered money to the United States.

The dirty money is smuggled out of the United States by couriers (who also transfer stolen and counterfeit bonds and securities). Clarke and Tigue report that some organized crime families have regular couriers: "They are usually well-trained and sophisticated people who know how to open foreign bank accounts and understand European customs procedures. They must be familiar with the intricacies of European banking and speak the appropriate foreign languages" (Ibid.: 92). The Bank Secrecy Act requires that all persons shipping money from the United States to a foreign country, and vice-versa, in excess of $5000, file a declaration with customs. Failure to do so can result in arrest and confiscation of the money (Ibid.: 99–100).

A second step in the operation requires the setting up of a "paper company," often in Liechtenstein where the annual tax is only $100 and the names of the real owners do not have to be registered; only the name of the company and the Liechtenstein lawyer who manages it must be listed with the government. The real owners remain secret (Ibid.: 116–117).

The criminal courier instructs his Liechtenstein lawyer to open a Swiss bank account in the name of the paper company. In Switzerland, bank accounts are protected by strict bank secrecy laws that protect criminals engaged in this laundering process. If American authorities are able to penetrate Swiss bank secrecy and obtain bank records, all these records will indicate that the Swiss account is owned by a company in Liechtenstein (Ibid.: 118).

The final step of the operation is often accomplished by the "loan-back." In this scheme, the now laundered money is returned to the United States in the form of a loan from the Liechtenstein company through a lawyer or company in the United States on behalf of the criminal operator. This also enables organized crime figures to invest in legitimate businesses using a dummy company as a front (Ibid.: 131–132).

Clarke and Tigue note that organized crime prefers legitimate businesses that do a great deal of cash business—bars and lounges, motels, vending machines, and car washes. A cash business allows the successful criminal to launder his money domestically. He merely over-reports his income on the legitimate business, pays the required taxes, and is thus free to spend his actual income from criminal sources (Ibid.: 134).

## INTELLIGENCE

A basic tool used by law enforcement agencies to combat organized crime is *intelligence,* a process that refers "to the handling of individual items of information and their conversion into material useful for law enforcement purposes" (Godfrey and Harris, 1971: 2). The process includes (Ibid.):

1. Collection of data;
2. Collation and storage of data;
3. Evaluation and analysis of the collated and stored data; and
4. Dissemination of the analyzed and evaluated material.

There are two basic categories of intelligence, and at times they may overlap (Ibid.: 2–3:

1. *Tactical Intelligence:* "that which contributes directly to the success of an immediate law enforcement objective."
2. *Strategic Intelligence:* that which contributes to producing an informed judgment with respect to long-range law enforcement objectives and goals. This information is collected over time and "put together by an analyst to indicate a new (or newly discovered) pattern of activity by organized criminals" (Ibid.: 12). The information may be unsubstantiated ("raw") and require further investigation for confirmation.

The collection of intelligence can be *overt* or *covert*. Overt collection can involve investigators assigned to an intelligence unit, or information received from other law enforcement officers as a result of encounters during their particular activities.* Overt collection also includes monitoring the newspapers and maintaining news files on appropriate subjects. Covert collection involves the "acquisition of information from a subject who is unaware he is being observed or overheard" (Ibid.: 19). Since covert collection is usually quite expensive in terms of required manpower, it is usually tied directly to the goal of securing evidence that can be used in prosecution; that is, its use is more tactical than strategic.

## Analysis

Drexel Godfrey and Don Harris refer to analysis as the "heart" of the intelligence system (Ibid.: 24). An analyst uses the methods of social science research, and central to this process is the hypothesis. The analyst develops an hypothesis, i.e., makes an "educated guess" about the relevance of the information that has already been collected and collated. Investigators will now be given direction, they will seek data that will permit "hypothesis testing." If the hypothesis does not withstand an adequate test, alternative hypotheses must be developed and also tested.

An hypothesis that has been supported by the data after rigorous testing becomes the basis for an intelligence report. This report will serve for guiding tactical and/or strategic law enforcement efforts. In many departments, the intelligence function has been greatly improved by the use of computers and information-retrieval equipment.

Abuses in the collection, maintenance, and dissemination of (non-organized crime) intelligence information has resulted in a distrust of the intelligence function in general. The use of the intelligence function to compile data on political opponents or "dissidents" has brought disfavor to an activity that, when used properly, is vital for combatting organized crime:

---

* A basic error in regard to the intelligence function committed by (usually smaller) police agencies is to combine the intelligence function with internal affairs; the latter involves investigating improprieties committed by policemen. When investigations of police officers are handled by the intelligence unit sources of important information— police officers from other units—will dry up.

A basic principle in collecting information for a criminal intelligence file is that such information should be restricted to what an agency needs to know in order to fulfill its responsibility to detect and combat organized crime in its jurisdiction. The ethnic origin or the political or religious beliefs of any individual, group, or organization should never be the reason for collecting information on them. Criminal activities or associations must be the key factors. If associations are found to be not criminal in nature, the data collected on them should be dropped from the files. (Task Force on Organized Crime, 1976: 122)

The Task Force on Organized Crime (1976: 127) notes that "organized crime figures today enjoy a high degree of mobility." The Task Force reports that "some criminal organizations have headquarters in many states and members travel constantly between these cities to conduct their business and avoid detection" (Ibid.). Thus, the Task Force recommends the forming of regional organized crime intelligence networks to facilitate the sharing of information (Ibid.). In 1956, the nationwide Law Enforcement Intelligence Unit (LEIU) was formed "to provide the means of organizing law enforcement officials to exchange information on certain criminals and criminal organizations" (Bishop, 1971: 30).

LEIU began with twenty-six departments and now has a membership of several hundred agencies throughout the United States. An agency must apply for membership (LEIU is a private, non-governmental organization) and meet the standards for integrity and information security set by LEIU. In 1978, a member agency in Nevada compromised intelligence information and was expelled from LEIU. LEIU does not maintain intelligence files on organized crime, but acts as a clearing house for member agencies to access each other's intelligence information.

On an international level is the International Criminal Police Organization headquartered in a Paris suburb, and usually referred to as *Interpol*. The organization's charter restricts activities to strictly criminal matters, and it is forbidden "to undertake any intervention or activities of a political, military, religious, or racial character" (Fooner, 1973: 28). Like LEIU, Interpol acts as a clearing house and promotes international cooperation in law enforcement. The United States is represented through the Treasury Department.

## EXAMPLE: STRATEGIC
## INTELLIGENCE REPORTING *

BOOTLEGGED CIGARETTES
In April 1971, the tax on cigarettes in the Commonwealth of Massachusetts was increased by $0.04 to $0.16 per pack. This increase brought Massachusetts level with Connecticut on the per-pack tax for cigarettes. The increase in Massachusetts was part of the Governor's tax program and was

* Source: New England Organized Crime Intelligence System. Reprinted in Godfrey and Harris, 1971: 137.

expected to raise an additional $24 million in tax revenue. Connecticut and Massachusetts are now tied for third highest cigarette tax in the country. The actual per-pack tax rates for cigarettes in New England are:

| | | | |
|---|---|---|---|
| Connecticut | $0.16 | New Hampshire: | |
| Maine | .12 | Regular and king | $0.085 |
| Massachusetts | .16 | 100 mm. | .09 |
| Rhode Island | .13 | Vermont | .12 |

*NEOCIS comments:* The tax increases in Massachusetts and Connecticut with the concomitant increases in the total price per pack of cigarettes leads *to the projection that organized crime in New England will be attracted to the business of smuggling and distributing bootlegged cigarettes.* The tax on cigarettes in all six New England States greatly exceeds that of the two large tobacco producing States of Virginia ($0.025 per pack) and North Carolina ($0.02 per pack). Organized crime has both the funds and expertise to conduct large-scale operations in bootlegging cigarettes in New England as they have done in other States. As a result, the expected tax revenue from the increase may not be as great as projected as more and more untaxed cigarettes are brought north and sold through organized crime controlled distributors, vending machines, and stores.

A front page article in the May 9, 1971, issue of the New York Times reported that New York State Tax Department officers recently estimated the total tax loss (city and State) due to bootlegged cigarettes at $6.9 million a year. Joseph Carter, assistant director of the Special Investigations Bureau, said he thought a figure of between $20 and $30 million annually would be more realistic, while a cigarette wholesalers group estimated a 5-year loss to all States to total $441 million. The Times article further reported that in New York, a flourishing market, Governor Rockefeller has called for a thorough examination of contraband cigarette traffic. It is noted that the $0.12 per-pack tax of New York is equalled or exceeded by five of the six New England States.

## Local Gambling Law Enforcement

Based on their sample of sixteen* cities with populations of a quarter-million or more persons, Fowler, Mangione, and Pratter provide a summary description of local gambling law enforcement and some recommendations for improvement (1978: 44–56):

* Atlanta, Birmingham, Boston, Buffalo, Cleveland, Detroit, El Paso, Los Angeles, Newark, New York City, Phoenix, Portland, San Jose, St. Louis, Tampa, Toledo. They report that "there were seven cities where local police thought they had clear evidence that gambling was directly tied to multi-service regionally organized crime operations" (1978: 29–30). The authors state that "the best predictor of the likelihood of a police problem [corruption] in connection with gambling law enforcement is the direct involvement of multi-service regional criminal organizations in gambling" (Ibid.). They speculate that this is because it usually requires "a very large-scale illegal business operation to support system-wide police corruption and make it worthwhile" (1978: 30).

# POLICE DEPARTMENTS

## SPECIALIZATION

Most gambling enforcement in larger cities is carried out by vice officers. Overall, very few arrests are made by patrol officers, particularly arrests requiring extended investigation and warrants. There were only four departments in the sample which gave enforcement responsibilities to general detectives at the district level and only in two of them did detectives make a significant number of arrests.

There were several degrees of specialization within vice enforcement units. Several departments had either separate gambling units apart from the vice squad or officers in the vice unit who specialized in gambling. In the remaining departments gambling was one of several responsibilities for all vice officers.

The more specialized an officer's assignment with respect to gambling, the more important he thought gambling law enforcement was, the more serious he felt gambling was, and the more satisfied he was with gambling enforcement as an assignment. We found that vice officers felt this way more than patrol officers or detectives, and that gambling specialists felt this way more than vice officers.

We believe that gambling enforcement will be better if it is carried out by specialists. One basis for this belief has to do with expertise. Officers who are going to make arrests that are more complicated than on-view arrests have to be skilled and knowledgeable about laws and procedures. In fact, the general impression of the study team is that the gambling specialists in police departments were consistently more knowledgeable about gambling laws than anyone in the criminal justice system.

A more important reason for recommending gambling specialization, however, has to do with priorities. Across the span of responsibilities that police departments have, gambling is relatively low in priority. However, that does not mean it is not important or that enforcement should be ignored. If an individual officer has responsibility for gambling enforcement in addition to the enforcement of laws against other kinds of offenses, including violent and property crimes, gambling is likely to receive little of his attention. If he is a general vice officer, gambling is still competing for priority with prostitution, other sex offenses and after-hours liquor violations. In that context, gambling may well receive its fair share of attention. However, gambling specialists looked on gambling enforcement even more positively than general vice officers. As a general management principle, it seems to us that the job will be done best if it is being done by someone who thinks that the work is important, serious and worthwhile. Thus, given a choice between having a ten-person vice squad, all spending a third of their time on gambling, and assigning three persons to work almost full-time on gambling within the vice squad, it seems to us that the latter strategy is preferable.

The extreme of specialization is to have a special "gambling squad." The size of the resource commitment to gambling enforcement in many departments would not justify having a specialized gambling unit. Moreover, having gambling specialists within a vice unit provides the potential for additional manpower for special operations. Which method is best for a department would depend on the local situation.

To a large extent, as we have indicated, police departments in major cities have put gambling law enforcement in the hands of specialists.

## COORDINATION

Police efforts in gambling enforcement would be improved if coordination were better between gambling enforcement units and others in the police department as well as with others in the criminal justice system. This is not a remarkable conclusion, but it was surprising to find few serious attempts at coordination.

WITHIN THE POLICE DEPARTMENT.    In many departments there are several units with formal gambling enforcement responsibility but which do not work closely together. The relationship among gambling enforcement, other investigative and patrol units is one that depends primarily on information flow. In particular, vice officers report receiving very little information from patrol officers. Although there are limits to the role that patrol officers can play in gambling law enforcement, in many cities they probably could be a good source of information if the kind of information that would be helpful were made clear to them.

One department was actively taking steps to encourage a transfer of information. This department sent vice officers to district roll calls to brief patrol officers on enforcement efforts, targets and problems. They also reported back on the outcome of cases that had been referred to vice by patrol officers in that district. This type of effort clearly reinforces officers' willingness to communicate to vice, and the vice officers felt they received more help from patrol officers than was the case in most cities.

WITH PROSECUTORS.    Police officers' perceptions of lack of support from prosecutors correlated highly with their expression of frustration in gambling enforcement. Improved coordination between police and prosecutors, including agreement on priorities, would be an important step both toward relieving police discontent and achieving a set of goals.

We found only a few cities where there were obvious discrepancies between police and prosecutor definitions of a "good" case, such as the one department which had 98 percent of its cases refused by the prosecutor's office. However, there were many places where police and prosecutors did not agree on the appropriate penalty for those bookmakers or numbers operators who could not be definitely tied to a major criminal organization. Moreover, there were only two cities in which police and prosecutors worked together closely on all gambling cases. A few more cities had close coordination on cases involving organized crime. For the rest of the cities there was little evidence of joint efforts or even close coordination.

This need is particularly important because prosecutors have a great impact on the outcome of a gambling case. Individual prosecutors have a great deal of latitude in deciding whether to dismiss a case, what charge to file, whether to plea bargain, the terms of the bargain, and what penalty to recommend. By close coordination with prosecutors, the police can improve the effectiveness of their efforts. If nothing else, if they can accurately anticipate how a case will be disposed, they can take that into account in setting their own priorities.

## ACCOUNTABILITY SYSTEMS

We found that departments had three major but interrelated reasons for having accountability systems in gambling law enforcement:

1. To ensure that vice enforcement strategies and priorities were carried out in ways that were consistent with departmental priorities and goals;
2. As a management tool, to ensure that citizen complaints were followed up effectively; and
3. To minimize opportunities for corruption or the appearance of corruption.

We found that the number of men devoted to gambling enforcement varied considerably from department to department. Elaborate accountability systems may be more feasible and more necessary in large departments than in small ones. However, some departments were using more complete accountability systems than others, and it seems likely that all departments in cities over 250,000 population could improve their enforcement efforts by implementing these types of procedures, if they have not already done so.

Some departments have established certain procedures to ensure that gambling enforcement activities coincide with departmental priorities and goals. One such procedure, which is both modest and useful, is to have a monthly briefing of the chief, or some senior administrator officer designated by the chief, on vice enforcement activities. We found that in a significant number of departments, as many as half, there was no one outside of the vice squad itself who had good knowledge of vice enforcement activity. There is nothing wrong with autonomy, but there should be accountability in the form of an information flow to ensure a correspondence between vice squad activities and departmental goals.

Another simple procedure is for vice enforcement goals and priorities to be put in writing. We found this was the case in only two departments in the study sample. Writing down policies and priorities is not simply a matter of creating paper. It is a way of being explicit about trade-offs that otherwise might go unnoticed, and permitting explicit discussion and review of the desirability of those trade-offs.

Every department said it wanted to be responsive to citizen complaints. When a department receives a citizen complaint, it is important that it be followed up adequately. One of the primary reasons citizens were dissatisfied with enforcement efforts was their perception that police would not act on a citizen complaint. Also citizens were much less likely to call in a complaint if they felt police would not act.

One way to help ensure adequate responses to citizen complaints is to have a multi-copy standard complaint form filled out when the complaint arrives. It is difficult to monitor follow-ups to complaints if they are not in writing. The key step, however, is to have a copy that goes in a file maintained by an officer outside the vice or gambling unit, who reviews the department's response to the complaint. Such procedures do not necessarily ensure full follow-up, but they would appear to be an important first step.

There is another aspect of complaint management which could be very useful and applies to complaints of all kinds. In every department, we asked about the number and types of gambling-related complaints received. Only one department routinely keypunched and tabulated this information. This provides an excellent, relatively low-cost procedure by which to evaluate the correspondence between citizen concerns and the activities of the department. Although citizen complaints are only one source of data about citizen concerns, they are a ready source of such information. It would seem that such tabulations would serve a variety of useful managerial purposes within police departments.

One final administrative procedure which could greatly aid departments striving to achieve effective accountability would be the creation of a separate unit that is independent of the vice enforcement unit to review the investigative work for a sample of all cases. In addition to going over the paperwork associated with cases, this review unit would also actually carry out its own investigations on a sample of citizen complaints and investigations initiated by vice officers. Smaller departments could use such a procedure for all vice cases, rather than simply gambling cases. A procedure such as this, which was actually being done in two of the sample departments, would be a major addition to the quality control efforts of most police departments.

### PRIORITIES

Perhaps the most important management-related finding of this project was the need for police departments to clarify their policies and priorities with respect to gambling law enforcement. Three-fourths of all sample officers felt departmental policies were not clear and two-thirds agreed that the responsibilities of patrol officers were not clear. In addition to the lack of clarity being undesirable in itself, it also contributes to a sense of frustration and ineffectiveness in gambling law enforcement.

One source of ambiguity lies in the assignment of responsibility. In most departments, almost all gambling law enforcement is done by vice or gambling specialists. Formal policies continue to imply that all officers have a role to play, but the nature of that role is unclear. Few departments have routine procedures set up to encourage and reinforce reporting possible gambling violations to specialists, nor clear guidelines for what is, or is not, a circumstance that should be reported. Moreover, it was generally conceded, and reinforced by the police questionnaire responses, that non-specialists lack the expertise to be much help even in identifying possible illegal gambling operations. Thus, non-specialists have a responsibility, but lack a clear definition of what it means and lack the expertise to fulfill what they think it might mean.

A second source of ambiguity occurs at a departmental level. About half the sample departments appeared to have established some priorities (usually unwritten) within the wide range of concerns they might have about illegal gambling. Three were clearly very aggressive against street-level gambling. Two were distinctly aggressive against commercial gambling. Three were most concerned with corruption control. The balance of the departments had a more general approach to gambling law enforcement, basically trying to cover all their possible concerns as well as they could, given the available resources.

Analysis showed that the departments where priorities could be identified by the study team gained some additional benefits. Not only did officers consider policies and responsibilities to be clearer in those departments, they also considered police efforts in gambling law enforcement to be more effective than did the officers in departments with a more general approach to gambling. It appears, therefore, that there is real merit in a department deciding what it can do and wants to do and emphasizing some aspects of gambling law enforcement over others.

The above data do not suggest that any one emphasis is better than another. Among the alternative goals observed, it is clear that most departments with a publicly exposed corruption problem would emphasize control of that over everything else. Given a choice between aggressive street-level enforcement and emphasis on commercial gambling, however, the choice may be more difficult.

Public confidence is a potential problem for police. The data are fairly clear that non-enforcement, rather than strict enforcement, is most likely to undermine citizen respect for police. The sample departments that have set clearer priorities have (with one exception) either emphasized public gambling and numbers, and neglected bookmaking, or emphasized bookmaking and numbers, dealing with public social gambling only when necessary for other reasons (such as a complaint or public disturbance).

As with most choices, there are pros and cons to an emphasis on either street-level or commercial gambling. Aggressive street-level enforcement produces a large number of relatively non-serious arrests for public gambling. It does not require much support from prosecutors, as the arrest itself accomplishes the goal of breaking up the game and communicating a police presence.

Emphasizing commercial gambling will lead to the arrest of what are considered to be more serious offenders. Because such cases are time consuming, fewer arrests will result and enforcement may be less comprehensive. Moreover, to be effective in controlling commercial gambling, appropriate sentences are probably needed for convicted gambling operators, which requires a coordination with prosecutors that is relatively rare.

An important aspect of commercial gambling is its link to multi-service criminal organizations. This potential or perceived link helps to transform commercial gambling from a non-serious to a serious crime. Police officials may need to be careful about the way they present the role of organized crime in gambling law enforcement. In cities where multi-service organizations were said to be directly involved in gambling, local police usually were not particularly effective in dealing directly with these organizations. Their main role would seem to be to stop illegal commercial activities, such as gambling, that may finance the organizations. For police in these cities, a main problem seems to be to communicate to prosecutors and courts their

COMBATTING ORGANIZED CRIME **235**

conviction that all or most commercial gambling offenses are serious, even if they cannot be directly tied to criminal organizations.

In cities in which organized crime is less present, the rationale that commercial gambling law enforcement helps to keep out organized crime may be even harder to sell to prosecutors. It would seem that reflecting the wishes of the public and communicating an effective law enforcement system to the citizens may be a more convincing rationale for commercial gambling law enforcement than citing a tenuous link between gambling and organized crime. Police need to remember that citizens generally want laws enforced; that commercial gambling violations are certainly more serious to citizens (and more likely associated with corruption) than public social gambling; and that responding to the public is probably the most concrete and stable basis on which to establish priorities.

In the end, we cannot definitely recommend one set of priorities over another on the basis of our data. However, we do believe that addressing the issues discussed above squarely, communicating the answers clearly, and translating the answers into clear policies that recognize the choices that police officers need to make can only be beneficial to police departments.

## PROSECUTORS

After an arrest is made, the prosecutor becomes the most important element in the criminal justice system in determining what will happen to the case. There were only three cities in which police prosecuted their own cases with little or no involvement of the prosecutor.

It turns out that very few gambling cases actually result in a trial of fact. Therefore, the prosecutor is the central figure in all the remaining decision points of a case. The prosecutor decides whether to accept the case or not; he decides what charge to file, particularly whether to file for a misdemeanor or felony-level charge; he decides whether to plea bargain or not (and in the vast majority of cases the decision is to bargain); he decides what bargain to make; and he decides what penalty to recommend to the courts.

Given the extreme importance of the prosecutor's role, it was startling to discover that there is little specialization, only casual expertise in gambling law, no written policies about criteria for plea bargaining, few close working relationships with police, and little accountability for bargains made.

There was only one city in which the prosecutor's office had designated a team of attorneys to specialize in gambling and organized crime cases. In this city, prosecutors had to demonstrate knowledge and expertise in gambling trials before they were formally qualified as gambling specialists. This team worked closely with police at all phases of the investigation. Only one other city had designated a prosecutor who worked closely with police on all gambling cases after the arrests had been made. In the latter city, the level of support from prosecutors perceived by police was higher than average. However, it was only in the first city, where there was extensive specialization, that a majority of the police considered that prosecutors took gambling cases seriously.

In a few other cities, if and when an organized crime figure was involved, there was closer coordination with police. For the remaining cities, in the vast majority of cases, prosecutors took over the case after the arrest and had relatively little interaction with police. Furthermore, with the exceptions noted above, gambling cases were spread among prosecutors, and hence they did not have the opportunity to develop expertise in gambling prosecution.

There was no district attorneys' office which had specified criteria as to the circumstances under which bargains should be made, or about what penalties should be recommended. There was no system of accountability to assess whether or not the decisions were the right ones. There was no information routinely kept on conviction rates, size of penalties recommended, and circumstances in which pleas were made. Not only were we unable to gather the data, but, more importantly, no one within the cities themselves could review what was happening in order to determine whether the prosecutors were making decisions consistent with the demands of the local situation.

Based on our findings we feel that the following are implications for the prosecution of gambling cases:

1.  Within a prosecutor's office, there should be at least one individual who is identified as a gambling specialist. In those places where one person would not be kept busy full-time working on gambling cases, we would suggest having a specialist on all vice-related crimes. We think that an individual who is given more responsibility and has more involvement in gambling prosecution is likely to be more expert in gambling prosecution, more knowledgeable about the different kinds of gambling laws and possible charges, better able to discriminate serious violators from those who are less serious, and will treat the prosecution of gambling cases more seriously.

    Furthermore, if only one or a few prosecutors handle gambling cases, it will be much easier to formulate and implement prosecutorial policies, to review these policies when appropriate, and to coordinate prosecution with police department activities.

2.  The arresting officer probably should play a more significant role in the prosecution of gambling cases. In many cities, we found that police gambling specialists were the most knowledgeable people about local illegal gambling organizations and best able to make distinctions among various kinds of gamblers. Moreover, these men were most likely to feel that gambling offenses were serious.

3.  There should be written criteria for plea bargaining which spell out in considerable detail the kinds of penalties that are deemed appropriate for various kinds of defendants. Having written guidelines would serve two obvious functions: it would improve the consistency of prosecutorial bargaining, and it would make it possible for prosecutorial policies (which are now largely unstated) to be reviewed within the district attorneys' offices and coordinated with police and judges.

4.  Information systems should be developed which keep track of convictions, plea bargains, penalties recommended, and reasons for dis-

missals. Only by having this type of information available can anyone effectively review the decisions being made by prosecutors.

We want to emphasize that we are not necessarily saying anything about the current content of the decisions made by prosecutors—whether they are too tough or too lenient with gambling offenders. There is a clear discrepancy in many cities between police and prosecutors about the seriousness of a commercial gambling offense that cannot be tied to a criminal organization; but it is difficult to tell which position is more just. All of the above imply only three criteria for prosecution: that it be expert, that it be consistent, and that it be reviewable, by having written policies and documentation of decisions.


## COURTS

As noted above, very few gambling cases result in a trial of fact. Either the defendant pleads guilty or the case is dismissed. Therefore, judges play a relatively passive role in the enforcement of gambling laws. For many of the cases the defendant pleads guilty, the prosecutor recommends the penalty arrived at as part of the bargain for a guilty plea, and the judge simply imposes the sentence.

Although disposition data were not available in many cities, the information we could gather suggested that a relatively low fine, under $200, was the most common penalty. There were indications in some cities that for felony convictions about 20 per cent of the defendants were given jail sentences.

The severity of the penalty seemed to be the largest concern of police with respect to courts; 86 per cent of the officers responding to the police questionnaire felt that fines and sentences given to convicted gamblers were not severe enough.

As noted before, the problem seems to be most acute with cases that are of a medium level of severity (i.e., street-level commercial gambling). Police, prosecutors, and judges were most confident that higher ups in criminal organizations would receive stiff penalties and/or jail terms if convicted, and were also in agreement that a low fine was the appropriate penalty for card and dice violations.

The system does not seem to be discriminating very well on cases that are somewhere in between these two extremes. Some of the improvements discussed above as part of police and prosecutor efforts may help in this regard. However, another aspect of the problem is that there was no specialization among judges with respect to gambling cases (with one notable exception). Judges saw relatively few cases in which a trial of fact was necessary. The cases which did go to trial were spread among all judges. This discouraged the development and implementation of a systematic set of criteria for penalties. It probably also contributed to judges playing a relatively passive role in setting sentences.

One city had a special sentencing judge who imposed penalties in all gambling cases in the county. In this city, police were much more satisfied with the penalties imposed by the courts, since this administrative procedure provided a mechanism for policy to be developed and consistently applied.

A single judge deciding on penalties appears to us to be much more likely to implement consistent policies and appropriate level penalties. In a city where there are not enough gambling cases to keep one judge busy, the role could be expanded to sentencing all offenders convicted of vice-related crimes.

The important change, however, is to have a specific judge responsible for imposing penalties. This would facilitate coordination of criteria and policies between police, prosecutors, and the courts.

## Electronic Surveillance and Wiretapping

Probably that area of organized crime law enforcement that can generate the hottest debate is electronic surveillance and wiretapping. The first wiretap case confronted the United States Supreme Court in 1928. In *Olmstead v. United States* (277 U.S. 438 S.Ct. 564), telephone wiretaps were used to prosecute persons involved in large-scale Prohibition violations. The interception of Olmstead's telephone line was accomplished without trespass. Chief Justice William Howard Taft, writing for the majority, determined that since telephone conversations are not tangible items, they cannot be the subject of an illegal seizure, and thus wiretapping is not prohibited by the Fourth Amendment. Shortly after the *Olmstead* decision, Congress prohibited interception without authorization of telephonic communications.

The first electronic surveillance ("bugging") case to reach the Supreme Court was *Goldman v. United States* (316 U.S. 129, 62 S.Ct. 993) in 1942. The court, consistent with *Olmstead,* ruled that a detectaphone placed against an office wall did not violate the Fourth Amendment since there was no trespass. In *Silverman v. United States,* 365 U.S. 505, 81 S.Ct. 679 (1961), a foot-long spike with a microphone attached was inserted under a faceboard into a wall until it made contact with a heating duct that ran through Silverman's house. The court found this activity unconstitutional, not because of trespass but upon actual intrusion into "a constitutionally protected area." This set the precedent for the case of *Katz v. United States,* 389 U.S. 347, 88 S.Ct. 507 (1967). Katz regularly used a public telephone in a booth to transmit wagering information interstate in violation of federal law. Evidence used against Katz included tapped information secured from an electronic device attached to the outside of the phone booth. In ruling the evidence secured as unconstitutional the court stated that the Fourth Amendment protects *people,* not just places, from unlawful intrusions.

In 1968, in order to bring some uniformity into the use of electronic surveillance and wiretapping, Congress enacted Title III of the Omnibus Crime Control and Safe Streets Act. This law provides for federal officials and officials in states that conform to the federal statute to petition for court authorization to intercept wire or oral communications provided that:

1.  There is probable cause for belief that an individual is committing, has committed, or is about to commit a particular offense that is enumerated in this chapter;
2.  There is probable cause for belief that particular communications concerning that offense will be obtained through such interception;
3.  Normal investigative procedures have been tried and have failed or reasonably appear to be unlikely to succeed if tried or to be too dangerous; and
4.  There is probable cause for belief that the facilities from which, or the place where, the wire or oral communications are to be intercepted are being used, or are about to be used, in connection with the commission of such offense, or are leased to, listed in the name of, or commonly used by such person.

Such a court order terminates in thirty days or less, unless extended by the judge. A most interesting aspect of Title III is that it requires that the target(s) of the court order be notified of the order within ninety days after its termination. Although Title III regulates the interception of wire and oral communications, Congress did not explicitly provide authority for the surreptitious placement of a listening device ("bug") to intercept oral communication. The federal courts remained in conflict over the issue until 1979. In *Dalia v. United States* the United States Supreme Court held that Congress had implicitly given the federal and state courts the power to authorize "covert entries" in order to plant a bug pursuant to Title III. In the *Dalia* case, FBI agents had pried open a window in the New Jersey office of Lawrence Dalia in order to install a bug in his ceiling. As a result of the intercepted communications, Dalia was convicted of receiving stolen property from an interstate shipment.

Title III has been criticized by law enforcement officials because of the extensive investigation and documentation necessary to secure a court order. In addition, when the bug or wire has been effected, numerous cautions must be exercised. The device must be monitored at all times, in addition to being recorded. Certain communications are privileged for example those between doctor and patient, lawyer and client, clergyman and congregant. If the monitoring agent should hear a privileged conversation, he must discontinue the interception. Agents usually wear earphones and these must be taken off and placed where the conversation cannot be overheard. Personal conversation unrelated to the investigative order, between husband and wife, for example, cannot be intercepted. Each time such a conversation comes across the wire the agent is permitted to listen only briefly, long enough to establish that the nature of the conversation is outside the scope of the court order. A duplicate of each tape and the log pertaining to it is filed with the court that issued the order. A monitoring agent who fell asleep and caused a privileged conversation to be recorded could jeopardize the results of the investigation.

The extensive documentation and monitoring makes electronic surveillance rather costly. In 1970 the cost was estimated as $1000 per day; today it has probably doubled. (Information from Special Agent-in-Charge William J. Williamson, United States Secret Service.)

Any wire or oral communication may be intercepted legally without a court order if one of the parties to the communication gives prior consent. Thus, law enforcement officers and informants may be "wired" to secure incriminating conversation without a court order. In 1979, the United States Supreme Court (by a 5–3 vote) ruled that the police do not need a search warrant to record the numbers dialed from a particular telephone. In *Smith v. Maryland* (78-5374), the Court affirmed the robbery conviction of a man linked to the crime by a pen register which, when installed at a telephone company switching office, can record the numbers dialed from a particular telephone.

### DEBATE OVER THE ISSUE

The President's Commission on Law Enforcement and Administration of Justice stated (1968: 468):

> The great majority of law enforcement officials believe that the evidence necessary to bring criminals to bear consistently on the higher echelons of organized crime will not be obtained without the aid of electronic surveillance techniques. They maintain these techniques are indispensable to develop adequate strategic intelligence concerning organized crime, to set up specific investigations, to develop witnesses, to corroborate their testimony, and to serve as substitutes for them—each a necessary step in the evidence-gathering process in organized crime investigations and prosecutions.

The Task Force on Organized Crime stated (1976: 148):

> Because of their organization and methods of operation, organized crime activities require sophisticated means of evidence gathering. Often witnesses will not come forward; and members of some organizations are bound either by an oath of silence or threats of violence. Often the use of informants is of limited value, and many organizations are difficult, if not impossible, for undercover agents to penetrate to the point where they can obtain useful evidence.
>
> One way to break through these conspiratorial safeguards is to enact a State statute permitting non-consensual wiretap and microphonic surveillance. States should recognize the conflicting needs of effective law enforcement and individual rights and provide for adequate protection of such rights by statute consistent with the problem of organized crime within their own jurisdictions.

The Task Force noted the 1976 report of the National Wiretap Commission,[1] which revealed that wiretapping has been particularly effective in gambling, fencing, and drug investigations.

Herbert J. Stern, the young United States Attorney in New Jersey, logged an enviable record in successfully prosecuting organized crime figures and corrupt public officials: in less than four years he convicted eight mayors, two secretaries of state, two state treasurers, two county leaders, a Congressman, and more than sixty other public officials. Stern reports: "My office has never applied for a wiretap. None of the cases that we've discussed involved any wiretapping." He adds, however, that "where it is indispensable, is in the gambling operations. Unless you just want to be satisfied with picking up street runners, the lesser likes who are just collecting, who tend to be poor and insignificant in terms of criminal activity, while letting the higher-ups go free, you have to use eavesdropping" (Hoffman, 1973: 238).

Ramsey Clark, former United States Attorney General, has been a constant critic of electronic surveillance and wiretapping. He argues that in cities where wiretapping has been used extensively, if not promiscuously (e.g., New York), organized crime is still flourishing. He states that wiretapping is slow, costly, and ineffective (1970: 288), and reports that the FBI used electronic surveillance against organized crime from the late 1950s until July 1965. "Hundreds of man-years of agent time were wasted. As many as twenty bugs were used in a single city. So far as is known not one conviction resulted from any of the bugs" (1970: 290). Clark's real fear, however, is the potential for abuse, and he cites several cases, including the bugging of Martin Luther King by the FBI. Clark argues (1970: 287):

> Privacy is the basis of individuality. To be alone and be let alone, to be with chosen company, to say what you think, or don't think, but to say what you will, is to be yourself.
> Few conversations would be what they are if the speakers thought others were listening. Silly, secret, thoughtless and thoughtful statements would all be affected. . . . To penetrate the last refuge of the individual, the precious little privacy that remains, the basis of individual dignity, can have meaning to the quality of our lives that we cannot forsee.

Herman Schwartz, representing the American Civil Liberties Union, argues (1968: 161):

> To permit law enforcement authorities to wiretap, even under limited circumstances, would seriously impair this privacy so necessary to a free society. Awareness by the public of the power to wiretap is alone sufficient to reduce drastically the sense of security and privacy so vital to a democratic society. The mere thought that someone may be eavesdropping on a conversation with one's wife or lawyer or business associate will discourage full and open discourse.

Despite the fears of Clark and Schwartz, the 1968 statute certainly seems adequate to ensure the continuation of the personal freedom to express ideas and opinions. Indeed, the restrictive nature of Title III has placed a substantial burden on law enforcement efforts against organized crime, as most federal agents are quick to point out.

## ENDNOTE

1. National Commission for the Review of Federal and State Laws Relating to Wiretapping and Electronic Surveillance, *Commission Studies.* (Washington, D.C.: United States Government Printing Office, 1976.)

# SEVEN

# Organized Crime:
# Policy Considerations

The keen interest in organized crime is obvious from films ranging from *Public Enemy* to *The Godfather,* books presenting both fictional and allegedly truthful accounts, and newspaper and periodical stories on organized crime and its luminaries. A symbiotic relationship exists between media representations, public reaction, and government activity: one (or more) can trigger activity by the other(s). Whether it is the government (by providing "anonymous" sources or "leaking" information) that influences the media or vice-versa, with the public playing some type of intervening role, depends on the scenario. Government acted as the independent variable when it provided the disclosures of Joseph Valachi. The media reaction was extensive: newspapers, magazines, televised hearings, a best-selling book,* and a movie. The public was properly primed for further governmental action, the Organized Crime Control Act of 1970.

In large part, the problem with information on organized crime is its source —criminal informants, always low-level operatives with limited knowledge and understanding of the entity that is organized crime, and who turn non-events into "history"; government officials who provide erroneous or misleading information for their own ends; journalists who must meet deadlines and generate interesting copy.

## CONSTRUCTING ORGANIZED CRIME

One question that is important to the study of organized crime is the amount of influence that the media have exerted on the phenomenon, particularly the degree to which criminals reflect or even act out roles that are inspired by movies or books. Earlier we noted that Joey Gallo copied George Raft and

---

* Peter Maas (1968) in his book provides an author's note that is quite revealing: *"The Valachi Papers* could not have in fact been written without the help and encouragement of a number of concerned individuals, particularly in the Department of Justice and the Federal Bureau of Investigation." Maas reports that he discovered that Valachi was writing for the Justice Department and "unofficially, I obtained a copy of his manuscript to judge its potential" (1968: 2).

later Richard Widmark when he "played" the gangster. Carl Klockars, in his study of a fence, Vincent Swaggi (a pseudonym), notes that Swaggi believes that film characters strongly influence the style if not the techniques of criminals (1974: 95). Criminals also read, and they appear to like books about crime. Ianni reports that one member of the Lupollo family began to refer to the family patriarch as the "Godfather" soon after Mario Puzo's book came out (1972: 112–113). Rubinstein and Reuter report that all of their informants ("alas") read *The Valachi Papers* or saw *The Godfather* (1978a: 63). This writer was with an organized crime figure when he pointed to Gay Talese's book *Honor Thy Father* in the writer's library and began discussing its central character, Joseph Bonanno. Renée Buse reports that when John Ormento was arrested for violating narcotics laws, federal agents found in his Lido Beach, New York, home a copy of *Brotherhood of Evil* by Frederic Sondern: "It had obviously been read carefully, as dog-eared pages and underlined passages marked the text which dealt with Ormento" (1965: 206).

That criminal organization can reflect media influence is highlighted by Ianni. He reports that Bro Squires, a pseudonym for a prominent black narcotics operator in Newark, New Jersey, decided upon a paramilitary organization: "He got the idea from the movie *The Battle of Algiers*." Ianni states that the Squires' organization was patterned after the movie—"and it worked" (1974: 95).

One can only speculate about how much of the information Joseph Valachi provided came from his own experiences and recollections, and how much came from information-based queries posed by his interrogators. Salerno states that Valachi did not provide new information; he only "*confirmed* and added depth and dimension to the knowledge or fragments of information the police already had" (Salerno and Tompkins, 1969: 310–311; emphasis added). Nevertheless, Salerno argues, "The Valachi confessions are ranked next to Apalachin as the greatest single blow ever delivered to organized crime in the United States" (Ibid.: 312). If Salerno is correct, this merely highlights the poverty of our response to organized crime, since, as in the case of Apalachin, nobody went to prison as the result of Valachi's revelations. Indeed, Salerno admits that Valachi "protected a few friends and acquaintances from the past by refusing to identify them or implicate them in specific crimes" (Ibid.: 310). Salerno maintains that the effort to impugn Valachi or downgrade his revelations was a *plot* instigated by the syndicate (*sic*) (Ibid.: 311). This raises another interesting question—how much of the information about organized crime had been deliberately "leaked" by members for their own ends? The *plot* thickens.

The Valachi revelations, however, did serve many important purposes. In 1963 the Federal Bureau of Narcotics had only 225 special agents. Now called the Drug Enforcement Administration, it has 1800.* The FBI, under

---

* James Q. Wilson presents the federal drug enforcement agency as a follower of public opinion, a benign view that discounts the agency's role in helping to shape this opinion (1979: 214–215).

prodding from Robert Kennedy, was able to justify "pulling out all stops" to fight this new menace, "La Cosa Nostra." * Since it had very little in the way of intelligence information about organized crime, the FBI played the game of "catch up"; it "bugged the United States." This illegal electronic eavesdropping brought it up to date quite quickly, but the agency is still suffering as a result of the public disclosures of its abuses. In 1963, illegal eavesdropping by the FBI actually destroyed three years of undercover work by the Internal Revenue Service in Las Vegas (Skolnick, 1978: 129).

Hank Messick argues that the revelations of Valachi relieved the FBI of its obvious neglect of organized crime: "La Cosa Nostra was created as a public image. This simple device of giving the Mafia a new name worked wonders. Hoover was taken off the limb where he had perched so long, and citizens had a new menace to talk about with tales of blood oaths, contracts for murder, secret societies," a picture thirty years out of date (1973: 8). In a more recent work, Messick alleges that Valachi was given an "unpublished manuscript" written by Nicola Gentile, an important Italian organized crime figure who returned to Sicily in 1936 after jumping bail in the United States. "This manuscript was given to Valachi to study, and he became an instant expert" (1979: 15). The Gentile manuscript had actually been published in Italian (*Vita di Capomafia.* Roma: Editori Ruiniti, 1963).

## RESEARCHING ORGANIZED CRIME

The social scientist or other scholar† who intends to research organized crime has, as noted throughout this book, a problem finding an adequate data base. To date, one must avail oneself of two basic (often supplemented by other "non-basic") sources. The first is official government documents that have not been compiled for research purposes, and interviews with government officials. The most notable work using these data is by Cressey (1969), who compiled his information while he was a member of the Federal Task Force on Organized Crime. His position as a government employee and the fact that his work reflected the official federal government position on organized crime have made his work suspect to other scholars.‡

A more recent work by Anderson (1979) also used official sources to study a particular crime family she calls "Benguerra"; the author does not, unfortunately, reveal the actual group or even the city, except to say that it is not New York. Anderson's conclusions, however, contrast with those of Cressey:

---

* FBI personnel refer to organized crime cases as "LCN."
† I use this term to refer to persons operating within a discipline that requires adherence to scientific enterprise, i.e., a commitment to discovery using rigorous methods of testing and analysis that can be verified by an impartial observer.
‡ Cressey reveals that he shifted his allegience from science to "propaganda" and argues that a social scientist "who is given access to information ordinarily inaccessible must be prepared to shift his role ..." (1967b: 106).

"If the activities of the Benguerra family are representative of the activities of other organized criminal groups in the United States, it is questionable whether the current level of resources devoted to fighting organized crime is warranted, and it is especially doubtful that fears of organized crime should be used to justify legislation involving incursions into privacy and the potential for abuse . . ." (1979: 141). Anderson recommends further systematic efforts at researching organized crime groups in different cities, using official sources, to determine "whether the current emphasis on the problem of organized crime is appropriate, and how resources to combat it ought to be allocated among different cities" (Ibid.: 142).

Ianni used two methods for compiling data on organized crime: participant observation (1972) and field research (1974), both of which comprise the second basic data source. His first work, based on three years with an Italian organized crime family in New York, provides an inside view not offered by other scholarly sources. (Using participant observation, Talese (1971) provides an interesting journalistic account of the Bonanno family.) Using his own ethnic background to good advantage, Ianni set out to gain an understanding of the code or rules by which an Italian organized crime family lives and operates, and he was able to test some of Cressey's observations, which he found wanting. However, we learn very little about the illegal operations of the "Lupollos"; for example, who provides the "muscle" or fills the enforcer role for the family's extensive loansharking business. In Ianni's second major work on organized crime, he engaged field assistants, "native informants"; eight black and Puerto Rican ex-convicts "who had been involved in organized crime activities—running numbers, pushing dope, or hijacking goods—prior to their imprisonment" (1974: 17). These assistants had to be convinced that the research was not part of a law enforcement effort, and were trained in the skills necessary to gather and report field information.

Research by Rubinstein and Reuter (1977, 1978a, 1978b) combines two of the above techniques. The researchers examined the financial records of gambling operations raided by the police, as well as other local (the FBI would not cooperate) gambling-related documents. They also used "informants who are participants in gambling and other criminal activities." Unfortunately, we are not given the details concerning these informants—recruitment, salary, verification of data, etc. It is usually a difficult strategy to work in the law enforcement world and the criminal world at the same time, since credibility in one can preclude acceptance in the other. (Researchers may also find themselves in the untenable position of being used as intermediaries between criminals and the police and vice-versa.) In a similar effort, Lasswell and McKenna (1972) were able to document the substantial economic impact of organized crime in one Brooklyn community.

An important deficiency in the scholarly literature on organized crime is the failure to produce a biographical work such as Sutherland's first-person account of *The Professional Thief* (1937). Two popular works, Maas (1968) and Teresa (1973), provide exciting journalistic accounts of two organized crime figures. One can only speculate on how this material would have been handled by a social scientist (probably better analyzed and documented; perhaps dull).

## ORGANIZED CRIME IN PERSPECTIVE

One of the popular activities of government officials, who often provide the grist for journalistic mills, has been to decry the infiltration of organized crime into legitimate business. Michael Maltz, however, points out that "the alternative to penetration of legitimate business is the reinvestment of the ill-gotten gains into the same criminal enterprises, which may cause greater social harm" (1975: 83). Annelise Anderson points out, however, that funds from illegal business enterprises cannot easily "be profitably reinvested in illegal market enterprises without aggressive expansion of the territory controlled by the group" (1979: 77). Thus, members of organized crime may be in the position of having an "oversupply" of illegal funds which they cannot profitably use to expand illegal activities (1979: 77). She also reports the various reasons for organized criminal involvement in legitimate business (Chapter 6):

1.  Establishment of a tax cover;
2.  Support for illegal market enterprises (providing a legitimate front for an illegal business);
3.  Providing services to members (e.g., jobs for members and their families without risk of arrest);
4.  Diversification to reduce the risks related to illegal business ventures; and
5.  Profit.

Anderson notes that one of the important reasons that organized crime members become involved in legitimate business appears to be the security of income that permits the transfer of assets to dependents (Ibid.). Maltz concludes that the penetration of organized crime into legitimate business can be viewed as the equivalent to the legitimation of family fortunes by the "robber barons" of an earlier era (1975: 83).

The writer's interest in this organized crime "penetration" led him to review a 1970 report by the New York State Commission of Investigation titled *Racketeer Infiltration Into Legitimate Business*. The "lead-off" case in the report concerned the New York Grinders Association, a trade group engaged in the cutlery grinding business; they supply knives and other commercial cutting equipment, freshly sharpened on a regular basis, to various customers, e.g., butchers and restaurants. The cutlery is owned by the grinder, whose fee for sharpening also includes a rental charge. In 1960 a new firm began taking business away from members of the association. The Commission reports that the new firm's work was inferior, and that its prices were about the same as association members. So why was the new firm successful? The first answer the Commission provides is that the firm is run by Salvatore Gugliemini and Paul Gambino. Both are described as members of the Carlo Gambino crime family, Paul being Carlo's brother, and Gugliemini his cousin. Despite the sinister implications, no evidence of criminal activity is posited. (Indeed, it appears that the grinder's association was involved in activities that can be viewed as "restraint of trade.") In an attempt to overcome the lack of evidence, innuendo is heightened; the Commission reports that Paul Gambino is connected to selling meat "at very good prices." Then the Commission notes that he was once "*arrested* for possession of a caseload of stolen canned hams" (emphasis added). Note, *arrested,* not convicted, and for *one* caseload of stolen canned hams. Hardly the "stuff" that will create boundless wealth for the syndicate.

The Commission then introduces New York City Police Inspector Robert McGowan, the commanding officer of the Central Investigations Bureau which specializes in organized crime. Inspector McGowan testifies that the hijacking of meat has grown to 170,000 pounds in 1966. The Commission adds that the sale and distribution of this amount of stolen meat requires "organization," hence, organized crime. The implications are clear: Paul Gambino sold stolen meat at discount prices to businesses that had previously been serviced by members of the Grinders Association. While the Commission does not explicitly say this, the implications are that the reason for the success of Gambino's firm was his ability to provide "bargain" meat.

One case in the report is particularly ironic; the owner of a large night club was provided with a loan of $70,000 from "organized crime sources." After six months the night club filed for bankruptcy. The owner had not paid back any of the loan. "I want my $70,000," the "syndicate's" representative demands—not an unreasonable request. Note that he had the money for six months with no interest, and the "mob," "racketeers," "organized crime," is only asking for the principal back. If only this author could arrange for such a "dream loan" from legitimate sources.

On the basis of the type of "hard evidence" provided in its report, the Commission concludes: "The evidence which was disclosed at this public hearing [the basis for the report] convincingly shows that racketeer infiltration of legitimate business is a very serious problem" (1970: 116). In its conclusion, the Commission quotes Inspector McGowan who recommended "that the federal and state statutes be amended to make court authorized wiretaps more easily available to law enforcement officials who so urgently need this important weapon against organized crime" (1970: 117). The Commission closed its report with the following message:

> It is hoped that the disclosures made at this hearing will not only alert the public to the invisible forces of organized crime but will stimulate meaningful counter-offenses to halt this dangerous menace to society.

In a more recent work, Jonathan Kwitny (1979) repeats some of the Commission's cases as well as some of the oft-reported activities of Teamster Union racketeers. His work bears the dramatic subtitle "The Mafia in the Market-place," and indeed "they" are there. In his most extensively reported case (over 150 pages) Kwitny describes the machinations of "racketeer-extraordi-nary" Moe Steinman, who dominated the wholesale meat industry in New York City. Because of his connections with such important syndicate figures as John Dioguardi and Paul Castellano, Steinman was able to deal with racketeer-controlled unions and thus effect labor relations in the meat indus-try. This ability secured for him a position as a supermarket chain executive who led industry-wide labor negotiations with meat industry unions. In this strategic position he effected under-the-table payments to the union leaders, and he could determine from whom the supermarkets bought their meat. Supermarket officials would buy from firms recommended by Steinman, over-paying for their beef, and receive "kick-backs." Steinman, in addition, would be paid handsome commission fees from the beef companies for these sales.

Steinman's greatest achievement was Currier J. Holman, founder of Iowa Beef, the largest meat processing firm in the world. The midwestern patrician business executive and the hard-drinking, inarticulate, New York racketeer had something in common—greed. (Important business figures involving them-selves in "organized crime" is obviously in the tradition established a century earlier and reviewed in Chapter Two.) In return for opening up New York markets for Iowa Beef and assisting them with "labor relations," Iowa Beef gave millions of dollars to Steinman and members of his family.

As we have briefly noted, organized crime involvement in "legitimate" busi-ness is indeed a reality. However, its importance has been exaggerated out of proportion by isolating organized crime from white-collar crime in general: "The semantic confusion is emphasized because 'organized crime in business is usually referred to as white-collar crime, except when committed by rack-eteers who enter into business, in which case it is called organized crime, even though the criminal acts may be identical'" (Yeager, 1973: 65). When cor-porations, in violation of antitrust statutes, fix prices or otherwise agree to avoid or reduce competitive activities, we have (by Sutherland's (1973) defi-nition) *white-collar crime*.[1] When a group of sanitation firms, under the guid-ing hand of a man whose name ends in a vowel, assigns territories and refrains from underbidding contracts for hauling garbage, we have *organized crime*.

The case of Moe Steinman shows how costly organized crime involvement in "legitimate" business can be. Let us look at the case of Dr. Currie. This former employee of the Hughes Aircraft Company, a military subcontractor, was until 1976 the Director of Defense Research and Engineering for the United States Department of Defense, in charge of a $10 billion-a-year budget. Like Steinman, Currie has been able to accomplish an intermediary position between the Defense Department and the Hughes Company, to which he returned after 1976. In this unique position (not unique because it is un-usual, it is quite usual), Currie was able to promote a missile contract between Defense and Hughes, much as Steinman was able to negotiate new market opportunities for Iowa Beef (Reisman, 1979: 60–61). Kwitny decries the lenient sentence handed out to Steinman, one year of imprisonment and a

$1000 fine (1979: 363). When Currie admitted to a conflict-of-interest indiscretion, he was fined a month's salary by the Secretary of Defense (Reisman, 1979: 60–61). W. Michael Reisman helps to put this all into perspective by citing a *New Yorker* cartoon by Lorenz (1975: 95):

> Warrington Trently, this court has found you guilty of price-fixing, bribing a government official, and conspiring to act in restraint of trade. I sentence you to six months in jail, suspended. You will now step forward for the ceremonial tapping of the wrist.

As if to underscore this cartoon in real life, the New York State Appellate Division handed down the *Dolkert decision* in 1976. Joel Dolkert, general counsel for Gulf and Western Industries and a prominent attorney, pleaded guilty to one of the eighty-nine counts alleging that he stole $2.5 million from the company. Overriding the sentencing judge, the Appellate Court resentenced Dolkert to probation (Hoffman, 1979: 54). In 1979, the *Miami Herald* reported that Charles Kraft, former treasurer of the Anaconda Company, was fined $12,000 and placed on probation for three years by a United States District Court Judge. Kraft had fraudulently obtained $35 million from six banks. (*Miami Herald*: "Former Anaconda Executive on Probation," July 25, 1979: C-1).

Probably the best example of what we are trying to show in this section is the "Great Electrical Industry Case," which began some time before World War II and climaxed in 1961. In that year forty-five persons representing twenty-nine corporations, including General Electric and Westinghouse, were indicted. The charge was conspiracy: price fixing by rigging bids and dividing the available market through a secret cartel that dealt with electrical equipment worth $1.75 billion annually. To effect the conspiracy, the defendants used secret codes and clandestine meetings in a variety of hotel rooms. The defendants pleaded guilty and received as punishment twenty-four suspended sentences, while the other twenty-one received imprisonment as high as thirty days (Lundberg, 1968: 121–122).

In Chapter Four we reviewed, under labor racketeering, how corrupt union officials would arrange for unsecured loans with corrupt bank officials. At this writing, the Associated Press reports that Bert Lance, President Carter's close friend and adviser, and the former federal budget director, has been indicted on charges of bank fraud, conspiracy, and misapplying bank funds. Lance, two bank officials, and one stockholder are accused of involvement in a conspiracy involving more than $20 million in loans, which allegedly caused losses of more than $500,000 to a number of banks (May 23, 1979). Judith Miller reports that Lance's attorneys are expected to argue that the overt acts cited by the government are common practice in small-town banks (1979: E4).

This discussion can easily lead us back to Chapter One and the definition of organized crime. However, the writer believes it more productive to maintain our operating definition of organized crime offered in the first chapter and then place the phenomenon in the proper perspective. Organized crime does not cost in revenue the amount lost in such white-collar offenses as masquerading low-grade lumber for high-grade lumber, using excessive fats in processed meat, placing Chevrolet engines in Oldsmobiles, and other similiar activities. United States Senator Philip Hart compiled a list of needless consumer spending, e.g., on auto repairs not needed or improperly handled, and it came to a grand estimate of from $174–$231 billion a year (reported in Wasserstein and Green, 1970: 214). The padding and "cost overruns" in military contracts can make organized crime revenue pale by comparison.*

In his review of corporate crime, Ferdinand Lundberg concludes that the crimes committed by well-established entrepreneurs "make Mafias and Crime Syndicates look like pushcart operations" (1968: 131). Of course organized (as well as nonorganized) criminals kill people, but so do coal mines and automobiles ("unsafe at any speed") which account for about 50,000 deaths annually. There is a need to recognize that organized crime is one of many social problems that are often interrelated. This must be appreciated in order to avoid intensifying already existing, or creating new, social problems.

## RESPONDING TO ORGANIZED CRIME

We can classify three basic alternatives with respect to responding to organized crime:

1. Maintain the current response;
2. Increase sanctions; and
3. Reduce opportunity.

The *first alternative* is a recognition of the fact that organized crime is an integral part of our social structure, that it cannot be effectively destroyed without drastic structural changes.[2] Furthermore, we have noted that organized crime has provided an opportunity for certain groups to move into the wider legitimate society on a level that would otherwise not be available. There are, of course, ethical and moral objections to "blasting" or "thieving" into the middle or upper strata, but this has been a feature of our history from earliest days. We must also note that very few management-level members of organized crime have been able to escape either assassination or significant prison terms (significant meaning actually serving a sentence of more than two years). Indeed, one can be impressed with law enforcement efforts, constrained as they are by the requirements of a democratic system which provides a great deal of legal protection even to its criminal citizens.

---

* A. Ernest Fitzgerald reviews the cost of some of these "overruns" in *The High Priests of Waste* (New York: W. W. Norton, 1972). He notes the "cozy" relationship between government and contractors that permits corporations to earn greater profits by producing inferior products. In the case of the ill-fated F-111 fighter plane, the electronic package was originally contracted for $750,000 and escalated to $4.1 million per plane. The F-111 proved too dangerous to fly.

The *second alternative* requires that we "up the cost of doing business" for organized crime. There are two thrusts. The first is legislative. Penalties, fines, and imprisonment, for the types of activities most closely associated with organized crime are significantly increased. State and federal penalties for possession or sale of large amounts of controlled substances are already quite substantial, and federal statutes for gambling, usury, and racketeering are likewise quite impressive, e.g., twenty years on each count. An increase in state penalties is the only real option, especially fines for gambling violations. It should be noted that increasing sanctions against gambling law violations can result in minor or nonorganized gamblers receiving harsh fines and/or imprisonment. It is often difficult to separate social gambling from commercial gambling; doing so requires a great deal of law enforcement discretion with the attendant risk of corruption. When the Organized Crime Control Act of 1970 went into effect, the federal government swept down on gamblers and made hundreds of arrests (1,532 in 1972, for example). However, only half of the defendants were convicted, and of these only 20 percent were sentenced to imprisonment. The courts were apparently unwilling to invoke the harsh penalties against minor operators or persons only tangentially involved in organized gambling (Rubinstein and Reuter, 1978b: 90).

Statutes can also be enacted that provide for a statewide prosecutor, investigative grand juries, and electronic surveillance by those states who do not have such authority. Rules of evidence can be modified in appropriate jurisdictions so that the prosecution of organized crime can be made easier, e.g., discarding the need for corroboration for the testimony of a co-conspirator.

The second thrust of alternative two requires increasing the level of funding that is used to deal with organized crime. More well-educated persons with the special skills needed to use the tools necessary to deal with organized crime, e.g., conspiracy statutes, would have to be hired and trained. It would be most dangerous to increase potential sanctions without a corresponding increase in effective manpower—the potential for corruption would be quite high.

The *third alternative* is one which this writer finds most attractive—reducing opportunity. There are two thrusts. The first is to break the monopoly over certain goods and services enjoyed by illicit entrepreneurs. This can be accomplished by legalizing these activities under government regulation. Many observers will state that we are already on the way to legalizing various forms of gambling. However, it should be noted that the reason for this is financial— an attempt to generate revenue—and only secondarily as a means of reducing profit opportunities for organized crime (if this were ever seriously considered at all). As a result, legalization in the United States has been accompanied by an increase in the number of people who gamble. In the United States, under the *Nevada Model*,[3] gambling is actively promoted by, or with the approval of, government. The writer has experienced this in New York where the Off-Track Betting Corporation (OTB), under city ownership, gained regular customers who had never bet on a horse before. The writer has been rather dismayed by the amount of attractive advertising the New York State Lottery and the New York City OTB Corporation have used to attract customers—i.e., to encourage people to gamble. Whatever else may be said about illegal gambling, its operatives did not advertise on radio, television, subway trains and buses, and in newspapers and magazines.

An alternative model is offered by England. Although legal, gambling in England is viewed as a social problem; it is tolerated, not to secure revenue, but because the alternative appears even more socially harmful. (Skolnick, 1978: 337–339). A serious attempt to deal with organized crime should follow the *English Model*.

England also provides a model for moving drugs out of criminal justice. Removing drugs as a law enforcement problem would reduce illegal profits and make whatever black market remains a low-profit business—not something attractive to organized crime. The impact in the United States that the ready availability of heretofore illegal substances would have, both on current abusers and potential abusers, is not known. It could conceivably reduce the plight of current victim-abusers while having the potential to increase the drug-abusing population. It should be noted, however, that there is often no cause and effect relationship between narcotics and criminal behavior. Studies indicate that most heroin abusers had an established pattern of delinquent/criminal behavior before the onset of addiction.

An alternative to legalization is a reduction in the current level of drug law enforcement. Reduced law enforcement would reduce risks and facilitate entry into the drug trade, thus increasing the availability of drugs. Any "street person," or street gang, can deal drugs. Lowered enforcement would have the effect of dramatically increasing competition and lowering profits, a situation that could deal a severe blow to organized crime.

By reducing profits in gambling and drugs, we can expect to experience organized crime efforts to secure new avenues of profit. The energy crisis may offer such an opportunity. The FBI reports that during the gasoline crisis in 1973, oil trucks were hijacked for the first time. If gas rationing is instituted, other opportunities will present themselves. Ralph Salerno recalled that he once asked Joseph Valachi what was the most profitable enterprise he was ever involved in. Without any hesitation, Salerno reported, Valachi said, "Ration stamps during W.W. II" (remarks delivered at the North Carolina Justice Academy, May 7, 1979). In a speech before the Annual Meeting of the Academy of Criminal Justice Sciences, March 14, 1979, William H. Webster, director of the FBI, stated that arson has already become a major source of profit for organized crime. Thus, by reducing opportunity in gambling and drugs, we could expect a shift toward other areas of profit, a return to the "protection" racket of yesteryear, for example.[4]

Reducing opportunity can have other serious consequences. As was noted in Chapter Three, Prohibition helped convert "street thugs" into "crime czars." Without Prohibition, however, these persons would probably have remained criminals of a more conventional, but often more dangerous, type. There is no reason to believe that by merely reducing the opportunity for involvement in organized crime, we will reduce criminality. The reduction of opportunity, if it is to be meaningful in terms of making society safer, must include changes that will substantially widen legitimate opportunity for those who will otherwise *innovate*. Thus, the second thrust to alternative three is a significant increase in the employment opportunity for those persons who represent an "at risk" population (e.g., adolescents from minority groups) with respect to significant involvement in organized crime. For many it is already too late. Ghetto youngsters in the drug centers of California and New York have already tasted *la dulce vida*—their role models and way of life have been established. Indeed, it is somewhat ironic that the changes suggested in alternative three would probably have its most serious effect on the "black mafia" and ethnic succession in organized crime.

Organized crime is one stage along a continuum dating back to the earliest days of our republic. Each of these stages, however, has been just that—a stage with a beginning, a middle, and an end. *Innovative* activity, in the illegitimate sense, is tied to the social structure of the era to which it belongs. Organized crime thus has its limitations in terms of time and place. If the "goods and services" upon which organized crime thrives, gambling and narcotics, for example, become increasingly available through legitimate channels, or if competition runs unabated, traditional ways of profit-making will be significantly diminished. For younger innovators, often more prone to violence than their more conservative elders, a reduction in market potential will act as a catalyst for increased competitive violence, and an end to what we currently refer to as organized crime.

## ENDNOTES

1. For a brief review of such activities, see Reisman, 1979: 41–42.
2. These changes include a drastic redistribution of wealth and power, a "leveling" process, and/or the setting aside of a great many civil liberties that have been a theoretical cornerstone of our democracy.
3. Nevada leads the nation in personal bankruptcies, suicides, and deaths from cirrhosis of the liver (Satchell, 1979: 9).
4. This may already be happening in the Chicago area. The Chicago Crime Commission reports that Albert Caesar Tocco, a syndicate power in the southern end of Cook County, receives a substantial portion of his income from the collection of tribute from the independent owners of auto salvage firms, called "chop shops." The Commission reports "that the assessments are determined by the gangster's assessment of what an operator can be made to pay. His failure to pay an assessment creates a debt that is then treated like a juice loan, complete with extortionate interest rates and the mob's unique collection methods." The Commission also notes: "In 1978 Chicago and Cook County recorded more than 42,000 auto thefts. A substantial portion of these cars have gone into the chop shops" (*Searchlight,* quarterly newsletter of the Chicago Crime Commission, May 1979: 4–5).

# APPENDICES

# APPENDIX A

## Police Guide On Organized Crime: Symptoms of Organized Crime for the Patrol Officer*

Specifically, what are some of the visible signs or symptoms of organized crime that the police officer may see or hear about while on patrol?

Though by no means an all-inclusive list, the following examples should help you to develop a healthly and effective curiosity about events you might normally attach little, if any, significance to as far as organized crime is concerned. Undoubtedly, you will be able to add your own examples to this list—especially as you gain experience in this area of investigation. Each item on this list was suggested by one or more of those who rank among the top law enforcement officials in the nation. A brief description of what you may see or hear while on patrol is followed by an indication (in italics) of how these occurences might be linked to organized crime:

1. A candy store, grocery store, drug store, or other retail establishment seems to be doing a brisk business—many customers coming and going. But the customers do not remain in the store very long and do not leave with packages or other evidence that purchases were made. The store may have a meager selection of merchandise, which raises the question of how it can attract so many customers day after day. *This could indicate the presence of a policy operation at the writer level or the place of business of a bookmaker's commissionman.*

2. At about the same time each day, a package is delivered to a newstand, bar, or other location. Later the package is picked up by another individual. *The newstand or whatever could be a policy drop—the place to which a policy writer sends his slips and/or day's receipts.*

3. A number is chalked on a street lamp pole. The same number is observed in other locations. *It might be the winning number for the day's policy play.*

4. You are called to investigate a beating in a bar or at a location near a factory or other place of employment. The incident may occur on a payday or within a couple of days thereafter. *The beating may have resulted from the impatience of a loan shark who has not been paid on schedule.*

5. A parked car—often double parked—is observed daily at the same location and at the same time. The driver remains in the vehicle while a number of "friends" come up to say hello. *Such a situation may indicate bet-taking activity.*

6. A well-dressed individual is often seen driving an expensive late model car in the area. No one seems to know what his occupation is. One patrolman pursued observations similar to this and found out that *the individual was a policy operator*—and had been for 21 years—without so much as an arrest. On the basis of this information and further investigation, a special squad of detectives made a case against the operator and his employers.

7. A shopkeeper complains about poor business and notes that as a result he had to borrow money recently. A few comments by the patrolman about the high interest rates and the shopkeeper might disclose the imposition of an interest rate above the legal maximum. *If so, the shopkeeper may have been dealing with a loan shark.* If the shop-

---

* Source: *Police Guide on Organized Crime.* 1976 (no author) Wash., D.C.: U.S. Gov't. Printing Office.

keeper advises that he cannot keep up with the payments, the officer might find an opportune time to ask for the identity of the shark. Depending on the desperation and temperament of the victim, the suggestion to cooperate may bring positive results.

8. After arriving at the scene of an assault, a patrolman learns that the victim is a union official. This information should be noted because if there have been other similar assaults in the city, the overall total, when analyzed by an organized crime intelligence unit, may strongly indicate an *attempt by racketeers to gain control over a union local.*

9. Merchants complain about another price rise by the cartage company that removes their garbage or trash. They also mention that there is either no competitor to deal with or if there is one, it will not accept their business. *Not infrequently, this is an indication that an organized crime group is trying to monopolize the cartage business or limit competition through territorial agreements.*

10. During a routine check of a restaurant, a patrolman recognizes several organized crime figures at a table, or many double-parked cars are spotted in front of a bar that is either known or suspected as a meeting place for racketeers. The patrolman should jot down the license plate numbers and phone in his observations immediately, so that investigators can be dispatched to the scene. *Such signs indicate that underworld figures are meeting for one reason or another. However, they also may be indicia of hidden ownership of the bar or restaurant by organized crime.* In some instances, bars can be closed down if they are frequented by criminals.

11. A new set of vendors begins to service a business—a restaurant, for example. The linen supplier is new, as are the meat provisioner, fuel oil company, and cartage firm. Perhaps new vending machines or jukeboxes are observed being installed. Some of these suppliers are recognized as enterprises run by organized crime. *These are fairly solid indicators that organized crime figures have purchased, or have otherwise secured a degree of control in the business being serviced.*

12. A rash of vandalism strikes a number of establishments engaged in the same type of business—such as dry cleaning. *Racketeers may be trying to coerce reluctant owners into joining an association or into doing business with mob-controlled vendors.*

13. Appliances are seen being loaded into the storeroom of a sporting goods store. *Scams or bankruptcy frauds frequently involve the ordering of goods (on credit, of course) unrelated to the customary line of the business.*

14. Determining who the bettors are in your area can be as important as knowing who the bookmakers are—indeed, many times the identification of a bettor leads to the identification of a bookie. Patrolmen have identified bettors through conversations with those on their posts—sometimes even by observing who buys racing forms. In some instances, you may even get close enough to a bettor to observe the number dialed when a bet is placed. *Observations such as these could trigger an investigation leading to the prosecution of the upper echelon of organized crime's gambling hierarchy.*

15. Just as identification of the bettor is important, so also is identification of addicts and loan shark customers. In two separate incidents, an arrested burglar revealed, under questioning by a patrolman, that he was stealing to finance his heroin purchases; while another arrested thief said he had to raise money to keep up with his loan shark payments. *This information led to the arrest of a pusher in one case and the loan shark in the other.*

16. Make a habit of checking out new businesses that set up shop in the area. If the enterprise is one that requires a license—such as a bar—ask to see it if for no other reason than to observe who the owners are, ascertain the identity of the company which distributes or services the jukeboxes, et cetera. *If, for example, the distributor of the jukeboxes or vending machines is a company controlled by the organized underworld, so also might be the bar in which they are located.*

17. You note pickets outside one or two stores in the same line of business. The

picketing may be a perfectly legitimate tactic, *or it may represent an attempt by organized crime to coerce employers into doing business with an underworld firm, to extort payments in return for labor peace, to convince employers to join an "association" and pay substantial dues, or to demonstrate the advisability of hiring a "labor consultant" who is able to resolve such troublesome activities as picketing.*

18. A cheap hotel appears to be doing a reasonably brisk business. Its patrons travel light—many do not carry luggage. A bar has a reputation for being a clip joint; charges of watered-down liquor are frequent. *These signs indicate a possible call-girl operation at the hotel and B-girl activity at the bar.*

19. A truck is loaded at a location other than a depot or shipping dock. Goods are transferred from a truck of a well-known company to an unmarked truck or vehicle. A warehouse that is almost always empty is now full. Unusual activity at an unusual time occurs in a warehouse area. Merchandise is transferred from a truck to the garage of a residence. *Any of these activities could point to a hijacking.* License numbers, locations, times and other facts should be noted.

20. A group begins to congregate at a certain street location at certain times during each day. *The group could be composed of addicts waiting for a pusher to make his rounds.*

21. A business establishment suspected of being mob-controlled burns to the ground.

*One possibility is that arson was committed to collect the insurance.*

22. Certain individuals always seem to frequent a certain bar although none of them live in the neighborhood. *Perhaps they use the bar as a bet-taking center.*

23. A club shuts down at irregular times—sometimes early in the afternoon, other times at mid-evening. Do these times coincide with the completion of racing or when the results of other sporting events become available? *If so, the club may be a base for gambling operations.*

24. A known racketeer frequently meets with certain unidentified individuals. If possible, note the license plate numbers of the vehicles of these individuals as well as the time and location of the conversations. *Racketeers, like most everyone else, are victims of habit and associate with each other.*

25. Many cars pull up and park in front of the suburban home of a suspected racketeer, who is ostensibly throwing a party for friends. Jot down license plate numbers and call in the information promptly. The party may be bona fide or *the real purpose of the gathering may be to conduct underworld business,* as was the case at the famed Apalachin meeting, where an alert officer noted unusual activity at a country estate and blew the whistle on what turned out to be a nationwide assembly of high-ranking members of the organized underworld. Knowledge of who associates with whom is highly important—whether the occasion is a bona fide social activity or otherwise.

# APPENDIX B

# Investigating Fencing: Identification of Questionable Transactions by Accounting Techniques*

Fencing is frequently a series of recurring transactions carried on within the framework of an otherwise legitimate business. An examination of financial records will often disclose a pattern of transactions documented in accordance with customary business practices.

The financial records that should be examined in order to detect suspect transactions are:

1. the bank statements, canceled checks and deposit tickets for a stated period of time,
2. cash disbursement books for the same period,† and
3. purchase invoices for the same period.‡

These three basic sources are generally all that are needed to determine whether a transaction is suspect.

In a legitimate transaction, the purchaser usually receives a purchase invoice, consisting of a printed form with the seller's name, address and telephone number printed at the top. The purchaser then draws a check made payable to the seller. An examination of the canceled check will disclose that the seller (whose name appears in the letterhead of the invoice) also endorsed and deposited the check. The check is usually recorded in the cash disbursement book. Payment for merchandise is generally made sometime after the invoice date—i.e., ten to thirty days subsequent thereto, depending on sales terms and discounts available for early payment. This, in brief, is the usual manner by which a business records purchases.

The Commission, in the course of its investigation, has determined from an examination of various concerns' financial records that a putatively legitimate

* Source: Thomas, Judy M., et al., 1978 A *Report on Fencing*. State of New York Commission of Investigation.

† The cash disbursement book usually provides the following information for each disbursement: the date of the disbursement, the check number, the amount of the disbursement, the purpose of the disbursement and the name of the payee.

‡ The purchase invoice should contain the name and address of the buyer and the seller written on the seller's letterhead, the date of the transaction, the terms, the quantities, a description of the goods and the price. The seller usually gives an invoice to a buyer at about the time the goods are delivered. From the viewpoint of the seller, the invoice is a sales invoice; to the buyer, it is a purchase invoice.

business engaged in fencing attempts to imitate the foregoing procedure in the acquisition of stolen merchandise. This is done in order to give a facade of legitimacy to questionable transactions. A record of the purchase and resale furnishes the fence with appropriate inventory controls and provides him with a method of documenting income tax deductions. In addition, the existence of appropriate documentation will tend to support a fence's claim that he acquired property without knowledge that it was stolen.

When it is suspected that a concern is engaged in occasional fencing, a review of the firm's canceled checks has been found to be most fruitful. All checks of significant amount payable to cash or to a named payee and then cashed, should be segregated. These checks should be compared with the related entries in the cash disbursement book. For all cashed checks that have been recorded in the cash disbursement records as purchases, the invoice covering the purchases should be reviewed.* The Commission's experience has been that invoices relating to stolen property are makeshift documents, with the seller's name either handwritten or rubber stamped. The distinctions between the legitimate purchase and the suspect purchase are:

1. The nature of the payment (i.e., a check payable to cash or to a named payee who cashes the check), and
2. An invoice covering the purchase which indicates that the merchandise was not acquired from an established source.

* The date of each check should be compared with the date on the related invoice. If a review of the firm's practices indicates that it pays its purchase invoices within 30 days, checks dated the same day as the invoice will frequently be found to have been cashed and supported by makeshift invoices.

# APPENDIX C

# Sample Debrief Form and List of Selected Specific Questions*

---

**INTELLIGENCE REPORT—DEBRIEF**

Name of debriefer _____ Date and time _____

Name of officer or other person debriefed _____

Reason for debriefing _____

General questions to be answered:

    Where did the event occur? _____

    When did the event occur? Date _____ Time _____

    Weather Conditions (if important) _____

    What was apparent cause of the event? _____

    Who was involved in the event? _____

    Were there any unusual circumstances connected with the event? _____

---

**Specific Questions To Be Answered**

The questions asked relating to the specifics of the event, for example the modus operandi if it were a hijacking or loan sharking, should be directed to gaining all knowledge the person debriefed perceived at the time of the event (or knows about from other experiences). The debriefer should prepare a list of questions to this end before he meets with the person to be debriefed. An intelligence unit can develop a series of standardized questions relating to specific crimes, adding to them as events and successive debriefing indicate.

Attached are a series of questions that indicate how the above suggested standard lists of questions might be started. They are drawn from a list prepared by Vincent Piersante, Michigan State Police.

**SUGGESTED SPECIFIC QUESTIONS BY CRIMINAL ACTIVITY**

*Corruption*

1. Are you aware of the acceptance or the offering of any gratuities or bribes for illegal or improper services rendered by:
    *a.* Law enforcement officers
    *b.* Attorneys
    *c.* Other public officials

---

* Source: Godfrey, E. Drexel, Jr. and Don R. Harris, 1971, *Basic Elements of Intelligence: A Manual of Theory, Structure and Procedures for Use by Law Enforcement Agencies Against Organized Crime.* Wash., D.C.: U.S. Gov't. Printing Office.

**262**

2. Do you know of any prosecutions being "fixed" or dropped due to illegal agreements or activities by involved officials?

3. Have you ever observed a public official in the company of a known racketeer?

4. Do you know of any places that are hangouts for known racketeers which are regularly frequented by public officials or police officers?

5. Do you know any payoff men?

6. Who handles payoffs for:

   *a.* Gambling
   *b.* Prostitution
   *c.* Narcotics
   *d.* Court Fixes

7. Do you know any hoodlums or racketeers who contribute to political campaigns?

   *a.* Who, when and how much

*Firearms violations*

1. Do you have any information regarding racketeers or hoodums who are known to travel with a gun on their person or in their luggage?

2. Do you have any information regarding the collection of guns by hoodlums and racketeers—any machine guns?

3. Do you have any information regarding any racketeers traveling out of State to purchase guns?

4. Do you know of any racketeers traveling on hunting or vacation trips where they are armed? If so, who, when, where and so forth.

5. Do you know anyone who keeps or stores weapons for the organization or its members?

*Gambling*

1. Do you know of anyone engaging in:

   *a.* Off-track betting (bookmaking)
   *b.* Numbers or policy
   *c.* Sporting events gambling
   *d.* In-house games of chance (this is intended for information and refers to barbuti, dice or poker games that are being cut by the operator for profit)

2. Do you know where one can:

   *a.* Place a bet
   *b.* Buy a number
   *c.* Buy a gambling ticket on a sporting event

3. Do you know the location of any bookmaking operation?

4. The names of those people operating the book.

5. Do you know of any persons engaging in or the methods used to transfer monies to a bank or drop point?

6. Do you know the location of the bank (be specific including a description of the physical layout, lookouts if any, and methods of entry)?

7. Do you know the number or types of vehicles used in these operations?

8. Do you participate in any type of gambling?

9. Could you introduce an undercover agent?

10. Do you have any knowledge relating to the transportation of gambling paraphernalia? (as bet pads, tip sheets, almanacs)

11. Do you know how the paraphernalia is shipped and from where?

12. Do you know of any wagering business which makes use of a wire communication facility including telephones? If so, were any of these communications interstate in nature?

13. Do you know any layoff men or set ups?

*Hijacking*

1. Do you have any information about any hijacking operation?

2. Do you know of any thefts from intrastate or interstate shipments?

3. If so:

   *a.* When did these thefts occur?
   *b.* From where was the merchandise taken (Acquire the name of the terminal, warehouse or platform where the theft may have occurred)
   *c.* Who are the persons responsible for the theft? (Complete description and vehicles driven)
   *d.* From what type of vehicle are thefts occurring?
      (1) Trains
      (2) Trucks
      (3) Aircraft

4. Where is stolen merchandise being stored? (Get as complete a description of the physical layout as possible)

5. How is the merchandise sold or disposed of?

   *a.* Through a fence
   *b.* Direct to friends and associates
   *c.* Shipped out for disposal elsewhere

6. Do you know the location of any stolen goods either being stored or already sold?

*Labor*

The following are areas to be explored which may develop information of the violations of the Taft-Hartley Act, the Labor-Management Disclosure Act, the Welfare and Pension Plan Act, as well as the Hobbs Act:

1. Employer or employer-representative payments to union officials;
2. Withholding dues from pay or employees and remittance to a union without written authorization from employees concerned;
3. Employer payment of dues from his own assets, that is, dues not checked off from employee's wages subject to written authorization;
4. Union officials with direct or hidden interests in companies employing members of that union or in companies which do business with the union;
5. Employers making purchases from union officials of articles and commodities at inflated prices;
6. Union officials failing to enforce contract terms with some employers;
7. Failure of union officials to process grievances of their members against certain employers;
8. Failure of unions to pursue organizational efforts relative to some employers in an industry that is generally organized;
9. Union officials permitting certain employers to pay less than union scale;
10. Union officials permitting certain employers to use less than the required working force on the job;
11. Union officials permitting employers to work employees in other than their own craft jurisdiction;
12. Known association of union officials with suspect individuals;
13. Direct or indirect control of unions by target or suspect person;
14. Shakedown of union member by union officials for job placement;
15. Cash collection of dues, initiation fees or service fees by union representatives from transient workers who may not be members of the union or only temporarily associated with the union;
16. Existence of fictitious employees on employer's payroll;

17. Nonworking and "no-show" union personnel on employer's payroll;
18. Union control of contract awards to companies, suggestive of collusive bidding arrangements;
19. Inducing employers to make political contributions;
20. Union contributions to candidates for Federal office;
21. Questionable loans made by union welfare and pension trusts to suspect initiates;
22. Evidence of kickbacks on loan arrangements from union welfare and pension plans;
23. Improper diversion or embezzlement of union funds;
24. Application of force or violence or the threat of such, against union members to deprive them of any of their rights as members;
25. Use of violence or threats against employers or firms being organized to gain a contract or to enforce improper terms;
26. Evidence of falsified information regarding financial reports required to be submitted by unions and welfare and pension plans;
27. Frequent changing of carriers of insurance in connection with pensions or welfare plans, suggestive of kickback arrangements on initial premiums.

*Legitimate business*

1. Do you have any knowledge of any hoodlum or racketeer in a legitimate business either:

   *a.* Owning the business directly
   *b.* Owning the business through a "front" man
   *c.* In partnership—openly or hidden
   *d.* Managing the business
   *e.* Operating the business

2. What specific business or businesses?
3. What are the locations of these businesses?
4. Are any of these businesses fronts for some form of illegal activity?
5. Approximately how many employees in each of the businesses?
6. Are any of the employees hoodlums or racketeers?
7. Do you know of any hoodlums or racketeers that are on the payrolls who do not work in the specific business?
8. Do you know of any tax violations occurring within a particular business:

a. Not declaring all income
b. Failure to pay proper revenues for employees
c. Writing off personal expenditures as business expenses

9. Do you know of any falsification of other required reports to Federal, State, or local governments:

a. Annual reports
b. Corporation reports

10. Do you know of anyone who has effected or tried to effect the operation of any business through the use of force, violence, robbery or extortion or threatened use thereof?

11. Do you know of any business establishments requiring a liquor license being operated by a front man and owned by a racketeer?

12. Do you know of any mob-connected taverns which acquire their liquor supplies from other than State licensed outlets?

13. Do you know of any business being operated by a hoodlum or racketeer that was acquired through loan shark payments?

14. Do you know the source of supplies and services for racketeer owned or operated businesses?

*Loan sharking*

1. Do you know of anyone involved in loan sharking, either as a lender or a victim?
2. If so, obtain:

a. Who is the loan shark
b. Who does he work for?
c. Who is the victim?
d. Who makes collections? (when, where and how)
e. What is the amount of the loan?
f. What is the rate of interest?
g. Have there been any threats of force used or implied, by whom?
h. Obtain the background of suspects, their vehicles, and so forth.
i. Do you know of any musclemen or collectors for loan sharks?

*Mafia-Cosa Nostra syndicate*

1. Are you familiar with an organization known as the *Mafia* or the *Cosa Nostra* or the *Syndicate*?
2. Do you know anyone who you believe is a member?

3. What makes you believe that this individual is a member?
4. Identify:

a. Occupation
b. Residence
c. Businesses
d. Criminal specialities
e. Familial connections
f. Criminal associates
g. Police and public official connections

5. Describe his organizational activities.
6. Does he have an in-State or an out-of-State residence?

a. How often does he use it?
b. What means of travel does he ordinarily use?
(1) In-town
(2) In-State and out-of-State
(3) Does he use a travel agency
(4) Does he visit Canada (give details)

7. Does he own an airplane or a boat?
8. Does he have connections with out-of-State or out-of-country members of the organization or any other criminals?

*Murder*

1. Do you have any knowledge about any murders being investigated?
2. Do you know of any deaths that appear accidental or natural, but were not?
3. Do you have any information about missing persons who may be dead?
4. Who are the musclemen?
5. Who are the enforcers or hit men?
6. Who do they work for?

*Narcotics*

1. Are you aware of any information relating to heroin, cocaine, marihuana, barbituates, amphetamines, or hallucigens?
2. Does the subject sell, use, or both?
3. What quantity is sold: Kilos, nickel or dime bags, or the number of pills:
4. What is the price charged per unit?
5. Have you ever purchased from the subject:
6. Could you introduce an undercover agent to the subject?
7. With whom is the subject associated?
8. What is the subject's answer of sale and delivery?

a. Hand to hand
b. Use of a front man
c. Use of the telephone in the transaction
d. Subject acts as a middleman

9. What out-of-town associates does the subject have?

10. Who is the subject's source of supply?

11. Does subject have any prior arrests?

12. Where does subject keep his supply of narcotics?

13. Obtain from the source any information relative to subject's description, vehicle, residence, telephone number, etc.

14. Are you aware of any members the medical profession, doctors or druggists, involved in the distribution of narcotics or drugs?

*Pornography*

1. Do you have any information about the manufacture, distribution, or sale of any pornographic material:

a. Motion picture films
b. Photographs
c. Books, pamphlets, or other printed material

2. Where is this material kept or stored?

3. What form of distribution is used:

a. Through fronts (as retail outlets)
b. The U.S. mail
c. Street men

4. Who are the people who handle sale and distribution of pornographic material?

5. Do you know the prices of the various types of pornographic material?

6. Where is the pornographic material manufactured?

7. What is the location of the studios in the case of films?

a. A professional studio during off hours
b. Someone's home
c. Other types of buildings
d. Locations for outdoor shooting

8. At what time of the day or night does the photographing take place?

9. What are the types of cameras or other equipment used?

10. Who are the models who pose for pornographic films? (get specifics as to description, age, address, and vehicles used)

11. Do you know of any regular customers of pornographic material?

12. Could you make a purchase of pornographic material or acquire samples as if for future sales?

*Prostitution*

1. Do you know the location of any houses of prostitution?

a. Who is the madame?
b. How many girls are in the house?
c. What is the cost?

2. Do you know any pimps?

3. Have you ever acquired the services of prostitutes for business purposes?

# APPENDIX D

# Memorandum of Understanding
# Sensitive Investigative Material*

---

WITNESS SECURITY PROGRAM
UNITED STATES MARSHALS SERVICE

## MEMORANDUM OF UNDERSTANDING

INTRODUCTION—Under Title V of Public Law 91-452, the purpose of the Witness Protection Program is to provide for the security of Government witnesses and potential Government witnesses, and members of their families whose life or person is placed in danger by virtue of being a witness or intended witness in legal proceedings against any person alleged to have participated in an organized criminal activity. Protection and maintenance are not provided in return for testimony. This memorandum is not a contract or an agreement to provide protection or maintenance in return for testimony. This is not a contract for employment between the witness and the Government, nor a contract to secure employment. Participation in the Witness Protection Program is purely voluntary and a witness may terminate participation in the Program at any time. Moreover, since it is within the Attorney General's discretion to approve participation in the Program, the witness may be terminated from the Program when the Attorney General determines that the life or person of the witness is no longer in danger, or for other reasons deemed appropriate by the Attorney General or his representative.

This memorandum sets out the assistance which will be provided by the United States Marshals Service under the Witness Protection Program as well as the obligations of the protected witness. This memorandum and its appendices, encompass all of the assistance which will be provided. Assistance not specifically contained herein, will not be provided by the United States Marshals Service, except as may be amended in writing. Investigative agents and government attorneys are not authorized to make representations concerning assistance which will be provided in effecting protection and relocation. Any representations made by such investigative agents or attorneys, which are outside those expressly prescribed herein, are made without authority and will

---

* Source: Hearings on Oversight of the Witness Protection Program before Senate Subcommittee on Administrative Practice and Procedure. March 20, 23, April 14, 1978. Washington, D.C.: U.S. Government Printing Office.

not be honored by the United States Marshals Service. State all promises or agreements which have been made by investigative agents or Government attorneys, concerning the Witness Protection Program.

_____

_____

_____

_____

Initials of Adult Family Members

_____

_____

_____

Once designated by the Attorney General or his representative, protection of a government witness becomes the responsibility of the United States Marshals Service.

The security of each witness depends on the witness' cooperation as well as the cooperation of family members. Willful acts on the part of the witness or family members, which jeopardizes the witness' security, WILL BE GROUNDS FOR TERMINATION from the Witness Security Program since the Marshals Service will be unable to provide adequate protection. Such actions as returning to the danger area without United States Marshals Service protection or against instructions of United States Marshals Service personnel, and involvement in criminal activity will result in IMMEDIATE TERMINATION from the Witness Protection Program. Likewise, the United States Marshals Service WILL NOT SHIELD witnesses from civil or criminal litigation initiated prior to or subsequent to entry into the Program.

Government protected witnessess WILL NOT act as undercover informants or in other witness roles without the prior approval of the Assistant Attorney General who authorized their admission into the Witness Protection Program. If authorization is not received then the witness will be terminated.

When assistance has been provided to the extent that the witness' life or person is no longer in danger subsistence may be discontinued. It is, therefore, imperative that witnesses begin vigorously seeking employment as soon as possible. Security assistance is continuing in nature and future security problems should be brought to the attention of the United States Marshals Service for evaluation.

The attached documents must be read and completed.

## A.    Security Assistance

1.  The United States Marshals Service is authorized to make all decisions concerning security assistance. Unless deemed appropriate by the Marshals Service, a witness will not be protected at his/her pick-up location and the witness must be willing to relocate immedi-

ately. The relocation is necessary since the danger at the pick-up location may present serious security risks.

2.  When deemed necessary by the Marshals Service, personal security will be furnished to the witness on a 24-hour basis when it is necessary for him or her to return to the place of danger to testify in court or converse with government attorneys in connection with preparation for trial, or at any other time when deemed necessary by the United States Marshals Service. Security will begin upon the witness' arrival in danger area.

3.  The Bureau of Prisons will normally determine where prisoner-witnesses will be housed.

## B. Documentation Assistance

1.  ONLY new documentation which is in the opinion of the United States Marshals Service, ESSENTIAL FOR THE WITNESS' SECURITY, will be provided. Fictitious or false records will not be provided and documentation will reflect only factual information. Bank references or credit histories WILL NOT BE PROVIDED. Certain verified information which is in the possession of the United States Marshals Service, may be provided, after security considerations have been made. Special documentation needs must be brought immediately to the attention of the United States Marshals Service for their consideration.

2.  The United States Marshals Service, by providing any documentation which reflects a new identity, has done so only for the witness' protection and security.

3.  This documentation WILL NOT be used for fraudulent purposes and any obligations which may be incurred by utilizing this documentation are liabilities of the witness and not those of the U.S. Government.

## C. Relocation Assistance

1.  After authorization has been received, a witness will be relocated immediately from the danger area to an area determined by the United States Marshals Service. Normally, a witness is located to a temporary site for a short period of time, and may then be relocated to a second temporary site until the trial has ended. If permanent relocation is necessary, only one permanent relocation will be made at gov-

Initials of Adult Family Members

_____

_____

_____

ernment expense. Subsequent permanent relocations will be at the witness' expense, unless the United States Marshals Service determines that the relocation is necessary for security reasons.

2. The relocation of household goods will be made by commercial moving establishments selected by the United States Marshals Service. It should be noted that our prior experience indicates that commercial movers frequently damage furniture. It should be noted that the United States Marshals Service assumes no responsibility for damage or loss which may occur through the movement of household goods by commercial movers. Any claims for such loss or damage must be made by the witness with the commercial mover. The United States Marshals Service will provide assistance in forwarding the claim to the commercial mover in order to protect the witness' identity and location to the extent consistent with maintaining the witness' identity and location secret. The United States Marshals Service will pay for the movement of household goods.

3. Jewelry, monies (gold, silver, or currency), coin or stamp collections are not covered for insurance purposes by commercial movers. The witness must carry these items to the area of relocation. Consideration should also be given to carrying other items of extraordinary value.

4. Relocation of the witness (and family members, if applicable), will be by a mode selected by the United States Marshals Service.

5. Family members of prisoner-witnesses will not be relocated unless deemed necessary by the Assistant Attorney General. Such relocation may not necessarily be to the area where the prisoner-witness may be located.

## D.    Subsistence Assistance

1. The United States Marshals Service has sole authority to arrange for the maintenance of protected witnesses and their family and/or household members.

2. The subsistence to be provided is determined by family size and geographic area, and is based on Bureau of Labor Statistics tables. Witnesses who are determined by the United States Marshals Service to be able to support themselves and their families, WILL NOT be furnished subsistence. Witnesses must immediately notify the United States Marshals Service of income received by them, household members, or held for their account. Witnesses may not receive both

Initials of Adult Family Members

_____

_____

_____

subsistence under the Witness Protection Program and statutory witness fees.

3. The United States Marshals Service will assist relocated witnesses in obtaining housing in the new area. Rents shall be paid from subsistence allocated in Paragraph 2, above. Rents will be consistent with funds available based on Bureau of Labor Statistics tables. The housing may be in the form of detached homes, apartments, motel or hotel rooms, and may be located on government installations.

4. The United States Marshals Service will not purchase houses or other real property for witnesses nor will it act as a surety or guarantor for the purchase of such property.

5. The witness (and family, if applicable) will be eligible for emergency or major medical treatment at Public Health Service facilities during the time they receive subsistence. Arrangements for normal or routine medical treatment will be arranged by the local United States Marshal through private facilities. No cosmetic medical treatment is authorized.

6. Family members of prisoner-witnesses who are not relocated WILL NOT normally receive subsistence, since their ability to work is in no way restricted.

## E.  Debts and Related Legal Matters

1. Attachment V. reflects all debts incurred by the witness or member of the witness' household. Arrangements must be made with creditors immediately, to settle all debts. Failure to do so will jeopardize participation in the Witness Protection Program since the United States Marshals Service WILL NOT SHIELD witnesses from legitimate creditors. Failure to settle debts may result in the disclosure of location to creditors. Additionally, creditors may resort to private investigators whose activities will seriously jeopardize the witness' security. In addition to debts, witnesses must list all property, personal or real, on which there is presently a lien, and the name of the person or entity holding such lien.

2. Witnesses may appoint private counsel to settle debts in their behalf. Payment of private counsel is the sole responsibility of the witness, and the United States Marshals Service assumes no responsibility for payment of private counsel. Witnesses may appoint private counsel to receive service of process in their behalf. If private counsel is not appointed, the witness hereby designates the General Counsel, United States Marshals Service, to receive and forward all process to the witness. The witness must then take those steps necessary to respond

Initials of Adult Family Members

_____

_____

_____

to said process. The United States Marshals Service will neither represent nor pay for private counsel to represent a witness' interest in such matters. No agency relationship of any kind is created by this Memorandum between the witness, members of his/her family, or any officer or employee of the United States Marshals Service. Under no circumstances will the General Counsel, United States Marshals Service, act as an agent for service of process for a witness or any member of his/her family. It is the responsibility of the witness to arrange for an agent to conclude ALL BUSINESS ARRANGEMENTS, such as the sale of a residence or business, prior to entering the Witness Protection Program. The United States Marshals Service assumes no responsibility for expenses incurred in concluding these arrangements.

3. All court orders which are directed to the witness must be immediately brought to the attention of the United States Marshals Service. Court orders which grant custody of minor children to persons other than a witness who is being relocated, will be honored and said minor children WILL NOT be relocated in violation of the court order. It is the responsibility of the witness to comply with or have amended or vacated, orders directing the payment of child support or alimony. Otherwise the United States Marshals Service may be compelled to pay these amounts from the witness' subsistence.

4. Should there be a dissolution of the witness' family structure, no element of the family will be provided subsistence above that described herein.

## F. Employment and Termination From Subsistence

1. Acquisition of gainful employment is the responsibility of the protected witness. EACH WITNESS IS EXPECTED TO ACQUIRE EMPLOYMENT WITHIN SIXTY (60) DAYS FOLLOWING HIS OR HER PERMANENT RELOCATION. The United States Marshals Service will assist the witness in attempting to locate one job opportunity. The United States Marshals Service can give no assurance that a job opportunity which may be located, will be equal to the witness' last job in either type, prestige, or pay. If a job opportunity is secured, however, the witness is expected to accept the job. If the witness fails to accept this job opportunity, he or she will be terminated from subsistence.

2. Immediately after permanent relocation, the witness must begin actively seeking employment. While resumes or background histories

Initials of Adult Family Members

_____
_____
_____

will not be prepared by the United States Marshals Service, witnesses who need their employment background verified must contact the United States Marshals Service, who will advise the employer of the witness' background and criminal record, if any. The witness WILL NOT represent that he or she is an employee or consultant of the United States Marshals Service or any other government agency. False information will not be provided to potential employers. 18 U.S. Code, Section 912, provides for a fine of not more than $1,000 or imprisonment for not more than three (3) years, or both, for anyone who assumes or pretends to be an officer or employee of the United States and demands or obtains money or any other thing of value.

3.  Family members of prisoner/witness who are not relocated will not normally receive subsistence, since their ability to work is in no way restricted. Relocated family members of witnesses who receive jail sentences and are incarcerated will be terminated from subsistence sixty (60) days after the witness goes to jail and the provision of (1) above will apply.

## G.    Mail Forwarding Services

A.    The witness acknowledges that the United States Marshals Service will only provide mail forwarding services for a period not to exceed one year after his/her last trial appearance.

B.    The witness agrees to complete a "Change of Address Order" changing his/her mailing address to a Post Office Box Number used by the United States Marshals Service. The witness acknowledges that forwarding service will only be provided for letters or other written material contained in an envelope.

C.    The witness acknowledges the necessity to terminate correspondence, where possible, with persons known prior to entry into the Witness Security Program for reasons of security.

D.    The witness agrees to present all mail addressed to correspondents having knowledge of his/her identity prior to entry into the Witness Security Program to the United States Marshals Service for forwarding to insure confidentiality of his/her new identity and address.

## I.    Movement of Household Goods

A.    The witness acknowledges that his or her household goods will be relocated only one time at government expense, unless otherwise determined to be

Initials of Adult Family Members

_____

_____

_____

necessary by the United States Marshals Service. Household goods will be relocated:

From_____

If the final relocation site is unknown, then household goods will be placed in temporary storage. If the witness desires to assume responsibility for placing household goods in long-term storage, then the cost of movement to permanent relocation site will be borne by the witness. The United States Marshals Service will handle security arrangements only.

B.    The witness acknowledges that the move will be made by a commercial moving establishment and the United States Marshals Service assumes no responsibility for the handling and care given those goods by the moving establishment.

C.    The witness acknowledges that any and all claims for loss or damage to household goods must be made with the moving establishment. These claims will be submitted through the U.S. Marshals Service in order to protect the witness' identity and location.

D.    The witness acknowledges that jewelry, monies (gold, silver or currency), coin or stamp collections are not covered for insurance purposes and SHOULD NOT, therefore, be shipped with household goods. Likewise, the witness understands the risks involved in shipping other items of extraordinary value with household goods.

E.    The witness acknowledges that household goods placed in storage by the United States Marshals Service and remaining in storage at the time the witness is terminated from allowances by the United States Marshals Service will cease to be the responsibility of the United States Marshals Service sixty (60) days following date of termination. The witness shall provide an address for delivery of household goods within sixty (60) days, or assume responsibility for payment of storage and subsequent delivery costs thereafter.

By:_____        _____
       U.S. Marshals Service                                      Witness Signature

Date:_____        _____
                                                                      Signature of adult family member(s)

                                                                      Date:_____

## II.    Movement of Witness
## and/or Family Member

A.    The witness acknowledges that he or she and family members will relocate by the following means, as determined by the U.S. Marshals Service.

_____

(LIST MEANS USED SUCH AS COMMON CARRIER OR PRIVATELY OWNED VEHICLE)

Number of family members being relocated _____.

B.    The witness acknowledges that the U.S. Marshals Service will pay the cost of common carrier transportation if used, or pay ——— cents per mile if movement is by privately owned vehicle. Motor vehicles with outstanding liens WILL NOT be moved out of state.

C.    The witness acknowledges that before the U.S. Marshals Service will reimburse him or her for costs of food and lodging during such move, receipts must be presented to the U.S. Marshals Service. This reimbursement will be an account not to exceed $_____ per day.

D.    The witness acknowledges that travel between the relocated area and the place of trial, which is at the request of government attorneys, will be paid for by the U.S. Marshals Service. The mode of travel will be that selected by the U.S. Marshals Service. Before the U.S. Marshals Service will reimburse a witness for costs of food and lodging which may be incurred during such travel, receipts must be presented to the U.S. Marshals Service. This reimbursement will be an amount not to exceed $_____ per day.

WITNESSES HAVING FUNDS FROM OTHER SOURCES MAY NOT RECEIVE SUCH REIMBURSEMENT.

By: _____    _____
     U.S. Marshals Service             Witness Signature

Date: _____    _____
                                  Signature of adult family member(s)

                                 Date: _____

## III.    Pets

A.    Care and feeding of pets is the responsibility of the witness and NOT the United States Marshals Service. Costs for boarding pets will be borne by the witness and witnesses must make such payment from their monthly subsistence.

B.    The witness acknowledges that the United States Marshals Service will pay for the movement of pets as long as such movement can be accomplished by ordinary commercial means, such as by regularly scheduled aircraft, trains, etc. The United States Marshals Service assumes NO responsibility for the care and treatment of such pets while being transported.

## IV.    Statement of Other Sources of Income

The witness acknowledges that he or she must provide the United States Marshals Service with information concerning all sources of income received by them, household members, or held for their account.

                               Initials of Adult Family Members

                                      _____

                                      _____

                                      _____

| AMOUNT OF INCOME | SOURCE | DATE RECEIVED OR ANTICIPATED |
|---|---|---|
| _____ | _____ | _____ |
| _____ | _____ | _____ |
| _____ | _____ | _____ |
| _____ | _____ | _____ |
| _____ | _____ | _____ |

The witness acknowledges that information concerning other sources of income may determine the amount of subsistence which will be paid by the United States Marshals Service. Failure to provide this information or providing false information, may subject the witness to Federal criminal penalties under 18 U.S.C. 641.

By:_____          _____
    U.S. Marshals Service                           Witness Signature

    Date:_____          _____
                                          Signature of adult family member(s)

                                              Date:_____

## V.  Subsistence Payments

A.  The witness acknowledges that subsistence payments may be at a daily or monthly rate and the amount thereof will be determined from Bureau of Labor statistics tables. The method of payment will be determined by the United States Marshals Service.

B.  The witness acknowledges that subsistence payments may end sixty (60) days after permanent relocation or upon obtaining employment.

C.  The witness acknowledges that subsistence payments may be terminated sooner for reasons stated in the attached Memorandum of Understanding.

D.  The witness further acknowledges that he/she must confine spending to the amounts of subsistence authorized and received through the United States Marshals Service.

By:_____          _____
    U.S. Marshals Service                           Witness Signature

    Date:_____          _____
                                          Signature of adult family member(s)

                                              Date:_____

## VI.  Outstanding Debts/Liens

A.  The witness acknowledges that the following debts are presently outstanding.

| CREDITOR | BALANCE OWED |
|----------|--------------|
| _____ | _____ |
| _____ | _____ |
| _____ | _____ |
| _____ | _____ |
| _____ | _____ |
| _____ | _____ |

B.   The witness acknowledges that outstanding liens exist on the following goods.

| DESCRIPTION OF GOODS | LIENHOLDER | ADDRESS |
|----------------------|------------|---------|
| _____ | _____ | _____ |
| _____ | _____ | _____ |
| _____ | _____ | _____ |
| _____ | _____ | _____ |

Have you ever filed for bankruptcy?_____.
If so, give name of court, location, and status of the proceeding.

By:_____         _____
        U.S. Marshals Service                            Witness Signature

    Date: _____         _____
                                                         Signature of adult family member(s)

                                                         Date:_____

## VII.   Outstanding Court Orders and Appointment of Private Counsel

A.   The witness acknowledges that the following court orders exist which direct him or her to perform the following acts.

| COURT | ACTIONS DIRECTED | DATE |
|-------|------------------|------|
| _____ | _____ | _____ |
| _____ | _____ | _____ |

B.   The witness acknowledges that he or she has appointed the below named person to receive service of process and act in his or her behalf in all matters, and that this person has been so notified and retained. THE WITNESS CONSENTS TO THE PERSONAL JURISDICTION OF ANY COURT IN WHICH A CIVIL ACTION MAY BE BROUGHT AGAINST HIM OR HER.

| NAME | ADDRESS |
|------|---------|
| _____ | _____ |

C. The witness acknowledges that if private counsel is not appointed to receive service of process, the General Counsel, U.S. Marshals Service will receive and forward all process to him or her. The witness must then take those steps necessary to respond to said process. The Marshals Service will neither represent nor pay for private counsel to represent a witness' interest in such matters.

By:_____
     U.S. Marshals Service         Witness Signature

Date:_____

                           Signature of adult family member(s)

                           Date: _____

## VIII.   Release of Medical Records

I do hereby request that Dr._____,
                                  (Doctor's Name)

_____, _____,
          (Street Address)                       (City)

_____, release to a representative of the United
      (State and Zip Code)

States Marshals Service (upon proper identification) a copy of any and all medical records in his/her possession pertaining to my family and myself.

                           _____
                                  (Signature)

                           _____
                                  (Date)

NOTE:   The witness shall complete this document and leave it in the package. Separate forms are to be completed for each doctor concerned.

## IX.   Release of School Records

I do hereby authorize and request that_____
                                            (School)

_____
                        (Location)

release to a representative of the United States Marshals Service (upon proper identification) school records pertaining to my child_____.

_____
(Signature of Parent or Guardian)

_____
(Date)

NOTE:   The witness shall complete this document and leave it in the package. Separate school releases are required for each child and school involved.

## X.   Release for Social Security Information

I do hereby authorize the Social Security Administration to release any and all information regarding my social security application to the United States Marshals Service.

On my behalf, I authorize the United States Marshals Service to process, through the Social Security Administration, all legal claims and benefits to which I am entitled.

_____
(Applicant's Signature (New Name)

_____
(Date)

Old Social Security Number:_____

NOTE:   The witness and each family member shall complete this document and leave it in the package. The witness and each family member shall also complete an "Application for a Social Security Number" (Form SS-5) and attach to this package as described in USM Order on "Revised Identity."

If the witness or any member of his family cannot remember his old number, or if a member of the family is over 10 years of age and states that he has never had a Social Security number, provide on a separate piece of paper: True name, place of birth, mother's true maiden name, and father's true name.

## XI.   Revised Identity Agreement

"The undersigned_____ hereby acknowledges that the Department of Justice, by providing me with any documentation which reflects a new identity, has done so only for my protection and safekeeping. I understand that this documentation may not be used for my own personal gain and that any obligations which I incur by utilizing this documentation are my liabilities and not those of the United States government. I further understand that these documents remain the property of the United States government and must be surrendered at its request. Such return request would be predicated upon my misuse of these documents fraudulently or for personal gain."

_____
(Signature of Witness)

_____
(Signature of Adult Family Members)

_____

By:_____    _____
(U.S. Marshals Service)                            (Date)

_____
(Date)

## XII.    Request for Court-Ordered Name Change

I do hereby request that the United States Marshals Service obtain for me and my family a court-ordered name change.

| (True Name) | (New Name) | (DOB) |
|---|---|---|
| (True Name) | (New Name) | (DOB) |
| (True Name) | (New Name) | (DOB) |
| (True Name) | (New Name) | (DOB) |
| (True Name) | (New Name) | (DOB) |

### (USE FULL NAMES, NO INITIALS)

_____
(Signature of Witness)

_____
(Signature of Adult Family Members)

_____

_____

_____

By:_____
(U.S. Marshals Service)

Date:_____

NOTE:    Upon receipt of this form at METRO, a decision will be made on whether a name change is required. If deemed appropriate, a formal petition will be prepared and returned for additional signatures. It is important that this form be filled out and returned to METRO as soon as possible.

## XIII.   Summary

The witness acknowledges having read and understood the foregoing Memorandum of Understanding and accompanying Subsections consisting of twenty (20) pages. All provisions of the Witness Security Program are contained in the foregoing twenty (20) pages. A copy of this Memorandum is not being furnished the witness for security reasons. However, this document may be reviewed by contacting the United States Marshals Service. No amendment to this Agreement is effective and binding unless approved by the Chief, Witness Security Division, and Legal Counsel, United States Marshals Service.

_____
(Signature of Witness)

_____
(Signature of Adult Family Members)

_____

_____

_____
(Date)

By: _____
(U.S. Marshals Service)

Date: _____

# APPENDIX E

## Federal Statutes Dealing with Organized Crime: Hobbs Act and 1970 Organized Crime Control Act (edited)

### CHAPTER 95—RACKETEERING

### Amendments

1970—Pub. L. 91–452, title VIII, § 803(b), Oct. 15, 1970, 84 Stat. 938, added item 1955.

1962—Pub. L. 87–420, § 17(f), Mar. 20, 1962, 76 Stat. 43, added item 1954.

1961—Pub. L. 87–228, § 1(b), Sept. 13, 1961, 75 Stat. 499, added item 1952.

Pub. L. 87–218, § 1, Sept. 13, 1961, 75 Stat. 492, added item 1953.

§ 1951. INTERFERENCE WITH COMMERCE BY
THREATS OR VIOLENCE

(a) Whoever in any way or degree obstructs, delays, or affects commerce or the movement of any article or commodity in commerce, by robbery or extortion or attempts or conspires so to do, or commits or threatens physical violence to any person or property in furtherance of a plan or purpose to do any-

282

thing in violation of this section shall be fined not more than $10,000 or imprisoned not more than twenty years, or both.

(b) As used in this section—

(1) The term "robbery" means the unlawful taking or obtaining of personal property from the person or in the presence of another, against his will, by means of actual or threatened force, or violence, or fear of injury, immediate or future, to his person or property, or property in his custody or possession, or the person or property of a relative or member of his family or of anyone in his company at the time of the taking or obtaining.

(2) The term "extortion" means the obtaining of property from another, with his consent, induced by wrongful use of actual or threatened force, violence, or fear, or under color of official right.

(3) The term "commerce" means commerce within the District of Columbia, or any Territory or Possession of the United States; all commerce between any point in a State, Territory, Possession, or the District of Columbia and any point outside thereof; all commerce between points within the same State through any place outside such State; and all other commerce over which the United States has jurisdiction.

(c) This section shall not be construed to repeal, modify or affect section 17 of Title 15, sections 52, 101–115, 151–166 of Title 29 or sections 151–188 of Title 45.

(June 25, 1948, ch. 645, 62 Stat. 793.)

§ 1952. INTERSTATE AND FOREIGN TRAVEL OR TRANSPORTATION IN AID OF RACKETEERING ENTERPRISE

(a) Whoever travels in interstate or foreign commerce or uses any facility in interstate or foreign commerce, including the mail, with intent to—

(1) distribute the proceeds of any unlawful activity; or

(2) commit any crime of violence to further any unlawful activity; or

(3) otherwise promote, manage, establish, carry on, or facilitate the promotion, management, establishment, or carrying on, of any unlawful activity,

and thereafter performs or attempts to perform any of the acts specified in subparagraphs (1), (2), and (3), shall be fined not more than $10,000 or imprisoned for not more than five years, or both.

(b) As used in this section "unlawful activity" means (1) any business enterprise involving gambling, liquor on which the Federal excise tax has not been paid, narcotics, or controlled substances (as defined in section 102(6) of the Controlled Substances Act) or prostitution offenses in violation of the laws of the State in which they are committed or of the United States, or (2) extortion, bribery, or arson in violation of the laws of the State in which committed or of the United States.

(c) Investigations of violations under this section involving liquor shall be conducted under the supervision of the Secretary of the Treasury.

(Added Pub. L. 87–228, § 1(a), Sept. 13, 1961, 75 Stat. 498, and amended Pub. L. 89–68, July 7, 1965, 79 Stat. 212; Pub. L. 91–513, title II, § 701 (i)(2), Oct. 27, 1970, 84 Stat. 1282.)

## § 1953. INTERSTATE TRANSPORTATION OF
### WAGERING PARAPHERNALIA

(a) Whoever, except a common carrier in the usual course of its business, knowingly carries or sends in interstate or foreign commerce any record, paraphernalia, ticket, certificate, bills, slip, token, paper, writing, or other device used, or to be used, or adapted, devised, or designed for use in (a) bookmaking; or (b) wagering pools with respect to a sporting event; or (c) in a numbers policy, bolita, or similar game shall be fined not more than $10,000 or imprisoned for not more than five years or both.

(b) This section shall not apply to (1) parimutuel betting equipment, parimutuel tickets where legally acquired, or parimutuel materials used or designed for use at racetracks or other sporting events in connection with which betting is legal under applicable State law, or (2) the transportation of betting materials to be used in the placing of bets or wagers on a sporting event into a State in which such betting is legal under the statutes of that State, or (3) the carriage or transportation in interstate or foreign commerce of any newspaper or similar publication, or (4) equipment, tickets, or materials used or designed for use within a State in a lottery conducted by that State acting under authority of State law.

(c) Nothing contained in this section shall create immunity from criminal prosecution under any laws of any State, Commonwealth of Puerto Rico, territory, possession, or the District of Columbia.

(Added Pub. L. 87–218, § 1, Sept. 13, 1961, 75 Stat. 492, and amended Pub. L. 93–583, § 3, Jan. 2, 1975, 88 Stat. 1916.)

## § 1954. OFFER, ACCEPTANCE, OR SOLICITATION
### TO INFLUENCE OPERATIONS OF
### EMPLOYEE BENEFIT PLAN

Whoever being—

(1) an administrator, officer, trustee, custodian, counsel, agent, or employee of any employee welfare benefit plan or employee pension benefit plan; or

(2) an officer, counsel, agent, or employee of an employer or an employer any of whose employees are covered by such plan; or

(3) an officer, counsel, agent, or employee of an employee organization any of whose members are covered by such plan; or

(4) a person who, or an officer, counsel, agent, or employee of an organization which, provides benefit plan services to such plan

receives or agrees to receive or solicits any fee, kickback, commission, gift, loan, money, or thing of value because of or with intent to be influenced with respect to, any of the actions, decisions, or other duties relating to any question or matter concerning such plan or any person who directly or indirectly gives or offers, or promises to give or offer, any fee, kickback, commission, gift, loan, money, or thing of value prohibited by this section, shall be fined not more than $10,000 or imprisoned not more than three years, or both: *Provided,* That this section shall not prohibit the payment to or acceptance by any person of bona fide salary, compensation, or other payments made for goods or facilities actually furnished or for services actually performed in the regular course of his duties as such person, administrator, officer, trustee, custodian, counsel, agent, or employee of such plan, employer, employee organization, or organization providing benefit plan services to such plan.

As used in this section, the term (a) "any employee welfare benefit plan" or "employee pension benefit plan" means any employee welfare benefit plan or employee pension benefit plan, respectively, subject to any provision of title I of the Employee Retirement Income Security Act of 1974, and (b) "employee organization" and "administrator" as defined respectively in sections 3(4) and (3)(16) of the Employee Retirement Income Security Act of 1974. (Added Pub. L. 87–420, § 17(e), Mar. 20, 1962, 76 Stat. 42, and amended Pub. L. 91–452, title II, § 225, Oct. 15, 1970, 84 Stat. 930; Pub. L. 93–406, title I, § 111(a)(2)(C), Sept. 2, 1974, 88 Stat. 852.)

Sec.
1965. Venue and process.
1966. Expedition of actions.
1967. Evidence.
1968. Civil investigative demand.

## § 1961. DEFINITIONS

As used in this chapter—
(1) "racketeering activity" means (A) any act or threat involving murder, kidnaping, gambling, arson, robbery, bribery, extortion, or dealing in narcotic or other dangerous drugs, which is chargeable under State law and punishable by imprisonment for more than one year; (B) any act which is indictable under any of the following provisions of title 18, United States Code: Section 201 (relating to bribery), section 224 (relating to sports bribery), sections 471, 472, and 473 (relating to counterfeiting), section 659 (relating to theft from interstate shipment) if the act indictable under section 659 is felonious, section 664 (relating to embezzlement from pension and welfare funds), sections 891–894 (relating to extortionate credit transactions), section 1084 (relating to the transmission of gambling information), section 1341 (relating to mail fraud), section 1343 (relating to wire fraud), section 1503 (relating to obstruction of justice), section 1510 (relating to obstruction of criminal investigations), section 1511 (relating to the obstruction of State or local law enforcement), section 1951 (relating to interference with commerce, robbery, or extortion), section 1952 (relating to racketeering), section 1953 (relating to interstate transportation of wagering paraphernalia), section 1954 (relating to unlawful welfare fund payments), section 1955 (relating to the prohibition of illegal gambling businesses), sections 2314 and 2315 (relating to interstate transportation of stolen property), sections 2421–24 (relating to white slave traffic), (C) any act which is indictable under title 29, United States Code, section 186 (dealing with restrictions on payments and loans to labor organizations) or section 501(c) (relating to embezzlement from union funds), or (D) any offense involving bankruptcy fraud, fraud in the sale of securities, or the felonious manufacture, importation, receiving, concealment, buying, selling, or otherwise dealing in narcotic or other dangerous drugs, punishable under any law of the United States;

(2) "State" means any State of the United States, the District of Columbia, the Commonwealth of Puerto Rico, any territory or possession of the United States, any political subdivision, or any department, agency, or instrumentality thereof;

(3) "person" includes any individual or entity capable of holding a legal or beneficial interest in property;

(4) "enterprise" includes any individual, partnership, corporation, association, or other legal entity, and any union or group of individuals associated in fact although not a legal entity;

(5) "pattern of racketeering activity" requires at least two acts of racketeering activity, one of which occurred after the effective date of this chapter and the last of which occurred within ten years (excluding any period of imprisonment) after the commission of a prior act of racketeering activity;

(6) "unlawful debt" means a debt (A) incurred or contracted in gambling activity which was in violation of the law of the United States, a State or political subdivision thereof, or which is unenforceable under State or Federal law in whole or in part as to principal or interest because of the laws relating to usury, and (B) which was incurred in connection with the business of gambling in violation of the law of the United States, a State or political subdivision thereof, or the business of lending money or a thing of value at a rate usurious under State or Federal law, where the usurious rate is at least twice the enforceable rate;

(7) "racketeering investigator" means any attorney or investigator so designated by the Attorney General and charged with the duty of enforcing or carrying into effect this chapter;

(8) "racketeering investigation" means any inquiry conducted by any racketeering investigator for the purpose of ascertaining whether any person has been involved in any violation of this chapter or of any final order, judgment, or decree of any court of the United States, duly entered in any case or proceeding arising under this chapter;

(9) "documentary material" includes any book, paper, document, record, recording, or other material; and

(10) "Attorney General" includes the Attorney General of the United States, the Deputy Attorney General of the United States, any Assistant Attorney General of the United States, or any employee of the Department of Justice or any employee of any department or agency of the United States so designated by the Attorney General to carry out the powers conferred on the Attorney General by this chapter. Any department or agency so designated may use in investigations authorized by this chapter either the investigative provisions of this chapter or the investigative power of such department or agency otherwise conferred by law.

(Added Pub. L. 91–452, title IX, § 901(a), Oct. 15, 1970, 84 Stat. 941.)

### Liberal Construction of Provisions;
### Supersedure of Federal or State Laws;
### Authority of Attorneys Representing United States

Section 904 of Pub. L. 91–452 provided that:

"(a) The provisions of this title [enacting this chapter and amending sections 1505, 2516, and 2517 of this title] shall be liberally construed to effectuate its remedial purposes.

"(b) Nothing in this title shall supersede any provision of Federal, State, or other law imposing criminal penalties or affording civil remedies in addition to those provided for in this title.

"(c) Nothing contained in this title shall impair the authority of any attorney representing the United States to—

"(1) lay before any grand jury impaneled by any district court of the United States any evidence concerning any alleged racketeering violation of law;

"(2) invoke the power of any such court to compel the production of any evidence before any such grand jury; or

"(3) institute any proceeding to enforce any order or process issued in execution of such power or to punish disobedience of any such order or process by any person."

### § 1962. PROHIBITED ACTIVITIES

(a) It shall be unlawful for any person who has received any income derived, directly or indirectly, from a pattern of racketeering activity or through collection of an unlawful debt in which such person has participated as a principal within the meaning of section 2, title 18, United States Code, to use or invest, directly or indirectly, any part of such income, or the proceeds of such income, in acquisition of any interest in, or the establishment or operation of, any enterprise which is engaged in, or the activities of which affect, interstate or foreign commerce. A purchase of securities on the open market for purposes of investment, and without the intention of controlling or participating in the control of the issuer, or of assisting another to do so, shall not be unlawful under this subsection if the securities of the issuer held by the purchaser, the members of his immediate family, and his or their accomplices in any pattern or racketeering activity or the collection of an unlawful debt after such purchase do not amount in the aggregate to one percent of the outstanding securities of any one class, and do not confer, either in law or in fact, the power to elect one or more directors of the issuer.

(b) It shall be unlawful for any person through a pattern of racketeering activity or through collection of an unlawful debt to acquire or maintain, directly or indirectly, any interest in or control of any enterprise which is engaged in, or the activities of which affect, interstate or foreign commerce.

(c) It shall be unlawful for any person employed by or associated with any enterprise engaged in, or the activities of which affect, interstate or foreign commerce, to conduct or participate, directly or indirectly, in the conduct of such enterprise's affairs through a pattern of racketeering activity or collection of unlawful debt.

(d) It shall be unlawful for any person to conspire to violate any of the provisions of subsections (a), (b), or (c) of this section.
(Added Pub. L. 91–452, title IX, § 901(a), Oct. 15, 1970, 84 Stat. 942.)

### § 1963. CRIMINAL PENALTIES

(a) Whoever violates any provision of section 1962 of this chapter shall be fined not more than $25,000 or imprisoned not more than twenty years, or both, and shall forfeit to the United States (1) any interest he has acquired or maintained in violation of section 1962, and (2) any interest in, security of, claim against, or property or contractual right of any kind affording a source of influence over, any enterprise which he has established operated, controlled, conducted, or participated in the conduct of, in violation of section 1962.

(b) In any action brought by the United States under this section, the district courts of the United States shall have jurisdiction to enter such restraining orders or prohibitions, or to take such other actions, including, but not limited to, the acceptance of satisfactory performance bonds, in connection with any property or other interest subject to forfeiture under this section, as it shall deem proper.

(c) Upon conviction of a person under this section, the court shall authorize the Attorney General to seize all property or other interest declared forfeited under this section upon such terms and conditions as the court shall deem proper. If a property right or other interest is not exercisable or transferable for value by the United States, it shall expire, and shall not revert to the convicted person. All provisions of law relating to the disposition of property, or the proceeds from the sale thereof, or the remission or mitigation of forfeitures for violation of the customs laws, and the compromise of claims and the award of compensation to informers in respect of such forfeitures shall apply to forfeitures incurred, or alleged to have been incurred, under the provisions of this section, insofar as applicable and not inconsistent with the provisions hereof. Such duties as are imposed upon the collector of customs or any other person with respect to the disposition of property under the customs laws shall be performed under this chapter by the Attorney General. The United States shall dispose of all such property as soon as commercially feasible, making due provision for the rights of innocent persons.

(Added Pub. L. 91–452, title IX, § 901(a), Oct. 15, 1970, 84 Stat. 943.)

## Transfer of Functions

All offices of collector of customs, comptroller of customs, surveyor of customs, and appraiser of merchandise in the Bureau of Customs of the Department of the Treasury to which appointments were required to be made by the President with the advice and consent of the Senate were ordered abolished, with such offices to be terminated not later than Dec. 31, 1966, by Reorg. Plan No. 1 of 1965, eff. May 25, 1965, 30 F.R. 7035, 79 Stat. 1317, set out in the Appendix to Title 5, Government Organization and Employees. All functions of the offices eliminated were already vested in the Secretary of the Treasury by Reorg. Plan No. 26 of 1950, eff. July 31, 1950, 15 F.R. 4935, 64 Stat. 1280, set out in the Appendix to Title 5.

## Section Referred to in Other Sections

This section is referred to in section 2516 of this title.

§ 1964. Civil remedies

(a) The district courts of the United States shall have jurisdiction to prevent and restrain violations of section 1962 of this chapter by issuing appropriate orders, including, but not limited to: ordering any person to divest himself of any interest, direct or indirect, in any enterprise; imposing reasonable restrictions on the future activities or investments of any person, including, but not limited to, prohibiting any person from engaging in the same type of endeavor as the enterprise engaged in, the activities of which affect interstate or foreign commerce; or ordering dissolution or reorganization of any enterprise, making due provision for the rights of innocent persons.

(b) The Attorney General may institute proceedings under this section. In any action brought by the United States under this section, the court shall proceed as soon as practicable to the hearing and determination thereof. Pending final determination thereof, the court may at any time enter such restraining orders or prohibitions, or take such other actions, including the acceptance of satisfactory performance bonds, as it shall deem proper.

(c) Any person injured in his business or property by reason of a violation of section 1962 of this chapter may sue therefor in any appropriate United States district court and shall recover threefold the damages he sustains and the cost of the suit, including a reasonable attorney's fee.

(d) A final judgment or decree rendered in favor of the United States in any criminal proceeding brought by the United States under this chapter shall estop the defendant from denying the essential allegations of the criminal offense in any subsequent civil proceedings brought by the United States.
(Added Pub. L. 91–452, title IX, § 901(a), Oct. 15, 1970, 84 Stat. 943.)

§ 1965. VENUE AND PROCESS

(a) Any civil action or proceeding under this chapter against any person may be instituted in the district court of the United States for any district in which such person resides, is found, has an agent, or transacts his affairs.

(b) In any action under section 1964 of this chapter in any district court of the United States in which it is shown that the ends of justice require that other parties residing in any other district be brought before the court, the court may cause such parties to be summoned, and process for that purpose may be served in any judicial district of the United States by the marshal thereof.

(c) In any civil or criminal action or proceeding instituted by the United States under this chapter in the district court of the United States for any judicial district, subpenas issued by such court to compel the attendance of witnesses may be served in any other judicial district, except that in any civil action or proceeding no such subpena shall be issued for service upon any individual who resides in another district at a place more than one hundred miles from the place at which such court is held without approval given by a judge of such court upon a showing of good cause.

(d) All other process in any action or proceeding under this chapter may be served on any person in any judicial district in which such person resides, is found, has an agent, or transacts his affairs.
(Added Pub. L. 91–452, title IX, § 901(a), Oct. 15, 1970, 84 Stat. 944.)

§ 1966. EXPEDITION OF ACTIONS

In any civil action instituted under this chapter by the United States in any district court of the United States, the Attorney General may file with the clerk of such court a certificate stating that in his opinion the case is of general public importance. A copy of that certificate shall be furnished immediately by such clerk to the chief judge or in his absence to the presiding district judge of the district in which such action is pending. Upon receipt of such copy, such judge shall designate immediately a judge of that district to hear and determine action. The judge so designated shall assign such action for hearing as soon as practicable, participate in the hearings and determination thereof, and cause action to be expedited in every way.

(Added Pub. L. 91–452, title IX, § 901(a), Oct. 15, 1970, 84 Stat. 944.)

### § 1967. EVIDENCE

In any proceeding ancillary to or in any civil action instituted by the United States under this chapter the proceedings may be open or closed to the public at the discretion of the court after consideration of the rights of affected persons.

(Added Pub. L. 91–452, title IX, § 901(a), Oct. 15, 1970, 84 Stat. 944.)

### § 1968. CIVIL INVESTIGATIVE DEMAND

(a) Whenever the Attorney General has reason to believe that any person or enterprise may be in possession, custody, or control of any documentary materials relevant to a racketeering investigation, he may, prior to the institution of a civil or criminal proceeding thereon, issue in writing, and cause to be served upon such person, a civil investigative demand requiring such person to produce such material for examination.

(b) Each such demand shall—

(1) state the nature of the conduct constituting the alleged racketeering violation which is under investigation and the provision of law applicable thereto;

(2) describe the class or classes of documentary material produced thereunder with such definiteness and certainty as to permit such material to be fairly identified;

(3) state that the demand is returnable forthwith or prescribe a return date which will provide a reasonable period of time within which the material so demanded may be assembled and made available for inspection and copying or reproduction; and

(4) identify the custodian to whom such material shall be made available.

(c) No such demand shall—

(1) contain any requirement which would be held to be unreasonable if contained in a subpena duces tecum issued by a court of the United States in aid of a grand jury investigation of such alleged racketeering violation; or

(2) require the production of any documentary evidence which would be privileged from disclosure if demanded by a subpena duces tecum issued by a court of the United States in aid of a grand jury investigation of such alleged racketeering violation.

(d) Service of any such demand or any petition filed under this section may be made upon a person by—

(1) delivering a duly executed copy thereof to any partner, executive

officer, managing agent, or general agent thereof, or to any agent thereof authorized by appointment or by law to receive service of process on behalf of such persons, or upon any individual person;

(2) delivering a duly executed copy thereof to the principal office or place of business of the person to be served; or

(3) depositing such copy in the United States mail, by registered or certified mail duly addressed to such person at its principal office or place of business.

(e) A verified return by the individual serving any such demand or petition setting forth the manner of such service shall be prima facie proof of such service. In the case of service by registered or certified mail, such return shall be accompanied by the return post office receipt of delivery of such demand.

(f)(1) The Attorney General shall designate a racketeering investigator to serve as a racketeer document custodian, and such additional racketeering investigators as he shall determine from time to time to be necessary to serve as deputies to such officer.

(2) Any person upon whom any demand issued under this section has been duly served shall make such material available for inspection and copying or reproduction to the custodian designated therein at the principal place of business of such person, or at such other place as such custodian and such person thereafter may agree and prescribe in writing or as the court may direct, pursuant to this section on the return date specified in such demand, or on such later date as such custodian may prescribe in writing. Such person may upon written agreement between such person and the custodian substitute for copies of all or any part of such material originals thereof.

(3) The custodian to whom any documentary material is so delivered shall take physical possession thereof, and shall be responsible for the use made thereof and for the return thereof pursuant to this chapter. The custodian may cause the preparation of such copies of such documentary material as may be required for official use under regulations which shall be promulgated by the Attorney General. While in the possession of the custodian, no material so produced shall be available for examination, without the consent of the person who produced such material, by any individual other than the Attorney General. Under such reasonable terms and conditions as the Attorney General shall prescribe, documentary material while in the possession of the custodian shall be available for examination by the person who produced such material or any duly authorized representatives of such person.

(4) Whenever any attorney has been designated to appear on behalf of the United States before any court or grand jury in any case or proceeding involving any alleged violation of this chapter, the custodian may deliver to such attorney such documentary material in the possession of the custodian as such attorney determines to be required for use in the presentation of such case or proceeding on behalf of the United States. Upon the conclusion of any such case or proceeding, such attorney shall return to the custodian any documentary material so withdrawn which has not passed into the control of such court or grand jury through the introduction thereof into the record of such case or proceeding.

(5) Upon the completion of—

(i) the racketeering investigation for which any documentary material was produced under this chapter, and

(ii) any case or proceeding arising from such investigation, the custodian shall return to the person who produced such material all such material other than copies thereof made by the Attorney General pursuant to this subsection which has not passed into the control of any court or grand jury through the introduction thereof into the record of such case or proceeding.

(6) When any documentary material has been produced by any person under this section for use in any racketeering investigation, and no such case or proceeding arising therefrom has been instituted within a reasonable time after completion of the examination and analysis of all evidence assembled in the course of such investigation, such person shall be entitled, upon written demand made upon the Attorney General, to the return of all documentary material other than copies thereof made pursuant to this subsection so produced by such person.

(7) In the event of the death, disability, or separation from service of the custodian of any documentary material produced under any demand issued under this section or the official relief of such custodian from responsibility for the custody and control of such material, the Attorney General shall promptly—

(i) designate another racketeering investigator to serve as custodian thereof, and

(ii) transmit notice in writing to the person who produced such material as to the identity and address of the successor so designated.

Any successor so designated shall have with regard to such materials all duties and responsibilities imposed by this section upon his predecessor in office with regard thereto, except that he shall not be held responsible for any default or dereliction which occurred before his designation as custodian.

(g) Whenever any person fails to comply with any civil investigative demand duly served upon him under this section or whenever satisfactory copying or reproduction of any such material cannot be done and such person refuses to surrender such material, the Attorney General may file, in the district court of the United States for any judicial district in which such person resides, is found, or transacts business, and serve upon such person a petition for an order of such court for the enforcement of this section, except that if such person transacts business in more than one such district such petition shall be filed in the district in which such person maintains his principal place of business, or in such other district in which such person transacts business as may be agreed upon by the parties to such petition.

(h) Within twenty days after the service of any such demand upon any person, or at any time before the return date specified in the demand, whichever period is shorter, such person may file, in the district court of the United States for the judicial district within which such person resides, is found, or transacts business, and serve upon such custodian a petition for an order of such court modifying or setting aside such demand. The time allowed for compliance with the demand in whole or in part as deemed proper and ordered by the court shall not run during the pendency of such petition in the court. Such petition shall specify each ground upon which the petitioner relies in seeking such relief, and may be based upon any failure of such demand to comply with the provisions of this section or upon any constitutional or other legal right or privilege of such person.

(i) At any time during which any custodian is in custody or control of any documentary material delivered by any person in compliance with any such demand, such person may file, in the district court of the United States for the judicial district within which the office of such custodian is situated, and serve upon such custodian a petition for an order of such court requiring the performance by such custodian of any duty imposed upon him by this section.

(j)  Whenever any petition is filed in any district court of the United States under this section, such court shall have jurisdiction to hear and determine the matter so presented, and to enter such order or orders as may be required to carry into effect the provisions of this section.

(Added Pub. L. 91–452, title IX, § 901(a), Oct. 15, 1970, 84 Stat. 944.)

# Bibliography

ADAMS, NATHAN M.
1977 "America's Newest Crime Syndicate—The Mexican Mafia." *Reader's Digest* (November): 97–102.

ALBINI, JOSEPH L.
1971 *The American Mafia: Genesis of a Legend.* New York: Appleton-Century-Crofts.

ALLSOP, KENNETH
1968 *The Bootleggers: The Story of Prohibition.* New Rochelle, N.Y.: Arlington House.

ANDERSON, ANNELISE GRAEBNER
1979 *The Business of Organized Crime: A Cosa Nostra Family.* Stanford, Ca.: Hoover Institution Press.

ANDERSON, ROBERT T.
1965 "From Mafia to Cosa Nostra." *American Journal of Sociology 71* (November): 302–310.

ANDREWS, WAYNE
1941 *The Vanderbilt Legend.* New York: Harcourt, Brace & Co.

ARONSON, HARVEY
1978 *Deal.* New York: Ballantine Books.

ASBURY, HERBERT
1928 *Gangs of New York.* New York: Alfred A. Knopf.
1936 *The French Quarter.* New York: Alfred A. Knopf.
1942 *Gem of the Prarie: An Informal History of the Chicago Underworld.* Garden City, N.Y.: Knopf.

ASCHMANN, HOMER
1975 "The Persistant Guajiro." *Natural History 84* (March): 28–37.

AUDETT, JAMES HENRY
1954 *Rap Sheet: My Life Story.* New York: William Sloane Associates, Inc.


BACHERACH, SAMUEL B. AND EDWARD J. LAWLER
1976 "The Perception of Power." *Social Forces 55* (September): 123–134.

BAKER, RUSSELL
1977 "Galente Can Have It." *New York Times Magazine* (March 13): 8.

BARRETT, LAWRENCE AND JOHN TOMPKINS
1977 "The Mafia: Big, Bad and Booming." *Time* (May 16): 32–42.

**294**

BARZINI, LUIGI
1965    *The Italians.* New York: Atheneum.
1977    "Italians in New York: The Way We Were in 1929." *New York Magazine* (April 4): 34–38.

BEIGEL, HERBERT AND ALLAN BEIGEL
1977    *Beneath the Badge: A Story of Police Corruption.* New York: Harper and Row.

BELL, DANIEL
1963    "The Myth of the Cosa Nostra." *The New Leader 46* (December 23): 12–15.
1964    *The End of Ideology.* Glencoe, Illinois: The Free Press.

BELL, ERNEST A., ED.
1909    *War on the White Slave Trade.* Chicago: The Charles C Thompson Co.

BERGER, MEYER
1935    "Schultz Reigned on Discreet Lines." *New York Times* (October 25): 17.
1940    "Gang Patterns: 1940." *New York Times Magazine* (August 4): 5, 15.
1944    "Lepke's Reign of Crime Lasted Over 12 Murder-Strewn Years." *New York Times* (March 5): 30.
1950    "Gross Won't Name Police Associates." *New York Times* (September 21): 1, 20.
1957    "Anastasia Slain in a Hotel Here; Led Murder, Inc." *New York Times* (October 26): 1, 12.

BEQUAI, AUGUST
1978    "Organized Crime in the Computer Area." *Police Chief* (October): 24–29.
1979    *Organized Crime: The Fifth Estate.* Lexington, Mass.: D. C. Heath and Co.

BISHOP, JIM
1971    *The Days of Martin Luther King, Jr.* New York: G. P. Putnam's Sons.

BISHOP, WAYNE H.
1971    "L.E.I.U.: An Early System." *The Police Chief* (September): 30.

BLAKEY, G. ROBERT
1967    "Aspects of the Evidence Gathering Process in Organized Crime Cases: A Preliminary Analysis." Pages 80–113 in Task Force Report: Organized Crime. President's Commission on Law Enforcement and Administration of Justice. Washington, D.C.: U.S. Government Printing Office.
1967    "Organized Crime in the United States." *Current History 52:* 327–333, 364–365.

BLAKEY, G. ROBERT, RONALD GOLDSTOCK AND CHARLES H. ROGOVIN
1978    *Rackets Bureaus: Investigation and Prosecution of Organized Crime.* Washington, D.C.: U.S. Government Printing Office.

BLAU, PETER M.
1964    *Exchange and Power in Social Life.* New York: John Wiley and Sons.

BLOCH, HERBERT A. AND GILBERT GEIS
1962    *Man, Crime, and Society.* New York: Random House.

BLOCK, ALAN A.
1975    *Lepke, Kid Twist and the Combination: Organized Crime in New York City,* 1930–1944. Ph.D. dissertation, University of California at Los Angeles.
1978    "History and the Study of Organized Crime." *Urban Life 6* (January): 455–474.
1979    *East Side-West Side: Organizing Crime in New York, 1930–1950.* Swansea, United Kingdom: Christopher Davis, Publishers.

BLOK, ANTON
1974    *The Mafia of a Sicilian Village, 1860–1960: A Study of Violent Peasant Entrepreneurs.* London: William Clowes Sons, Ltd.

BLUM, HOWARD
1977    "New York Gang Reported to Sell Death and Drugs." *New York Times* (December 16): 1, D12.

BLUM, HOWARD AND JEFF GERTH
1978    "The Mob Gambles on Atlantic City." *New York Times Magazine* (February 5): 10–51.

BLUM, HOWARD AND LEONARD BUDER
1978    "The War on 138th Street." *New York Times* (Six articles appearing on page one from December 18 through December 23).

BOISSEVAIN, JEREMY
1974    *Friends of Friends: Networks, Manipulators and Coalitions.* Oxford: Basil Blackwell.

BOYD, KIER T.
1977    *Gambling Technology.* Washington, D.C.: U.S. Government Printing Office.

BRASHLER, WILLIAM
1977    *The Don: The Life and Death of Sam Giancana.* New York: Harper and Row. Paper edition in 1977 by Ballantine Books, N.Y.

BRECHER, EDWARD M. AND THE EDITORS OF CONSUMER REPORTS
1974    *Licit and Illicit Drugs.* Boston: Little, Brown and Co.

BRILL, STEVEN
1978    *The Teamsters.* New York: Simon and Schuster.

BUENKER, JOHN D.
1973    *Urban Liberalism and Progressive Reform.* New York: Charles Scribner's Sons.

BULLOUGH, VERN L.
1965    *The History of Prostitution.* New Hyde Park, N.Y.: University Books.

BURNHAM, DAVID
1970   "Graft Paid to Police Here Said to Run Into Millions." *New York Times* (April 25): 1.
1970   "Police Corruption Fosters Distrust in the Ranks Here." *New York Times* (April 27): 1.
1970   "How Corruption Is Built Into the System—And a Few Ideas For What to Do About It." *New York Magazine* (September 12): 30–37.

BUSE, RENÉE
1965   *The Deadly Silence.* Garden City, N.Y.: Doubleday.


CALIFORNIA BOARD OF CORRECTIONS
1978   *Prison Gangs in the Community.* Sacramento.

CAMPBELL, RODNEY
1977   *The Luciano Project.* New York: McGraw-Hill.

CAPECI, JERRY
1978   "Tieri: The Most Powerful Mafia Chieftain." *New York Magazine* (August 21): 22–26.

CAPUTO, DAVID A.
1974   *Organized Crime and American Politics.* Morristown, N.J.: General Learning Press.

CARTEY, DESMOND
1970   "How Black Enterprisers Do Their Thing: An Odyssey Through Ghetto Capitalism." Pages 19–47 in the *Participant Observer: Encounters with Social Reality.* Edited by Glenn Jacobs. New York: George Braziller.

CHAFETZ, HENRY
1960   *Play the Devil: A History of Gambling in the United States from 1492 to 1955.* New York: Clarkson N. Potter.

CHALIDZE, VALLERY
1977   *Criminal Russia: Crime in the Soviet Union.* New York: Random House.

CHAMBLISS, WILLIAM
1971   *Law, Order and Power.* Reading, Mass.: Addison-Wesley.
1972   *Box-Man: A Professional Thief's Journey.* New York: Harper and Row.
1973   *Functional and Conflict Theories of Crime.* New York: MSS Modular Publications.
1976   "Vice, Corruption, Bureaucracy, and Power." Pages 162–183 in *Whose Law? What Order?* Edited by William Chambliss and Milton Mankoff. New York: John Wiley and Sons.
1978   *On the Take: From Petty Crooks to Presidents.* Bloomington: Indiana University Press.

CHANDLER, DAVID LEON
1975   *Brothers in Blood: The Rise of the Criminal Brotherhoods.* New York: E. P. Dutton and Co.

CLARK, ALFRED E.
1950 "Erickson's Records of Gambling Bare Underworld Links." *New York Times* (May 18): 1, 19.

CLARK, RAMSEY
1970 *Crime in America.* New York: Simon and Schuster.

CLARKE, THURSTON AND JOHN J. TIGUE, JR.
1975 *Dirty Money: Swiss Banks, the Mafia, Money Laundering, and White Collar Crime.* New York: Simon and Schuster.

CLOWARD, RICHARD A. AND LLOYD E. OHLIN
1960 *Delinquency and Opportunity.* New York: The Free Press.

COFFEY, THOMAS M.
1975 *The Long Thirst: Prohibition in America: 1920-1933.* New York: W. W. Norton.

COHEN, ALBERT K.
1965 "The Sociology of the Deviant Act: Anomie Theory and Beyond." *American Sociological Review 30* (February): 5–14.

COHEN, MICKEY
1975 *Mickey Cohen: In My Own Words.* Englewood Cliffs, N.J.: Prentice-Hall.

COLEMAN, J. WALTER
1969 *The Molly Mcguire Riots.* New York: Arno Press. Originally published in 1936.

COLLINS, RANDALL
1975 *Conflict Sociology.* New York: Academic Press.

COMMITTEE ON THE OFFICE OF ATTORNEY GENERAL
1974 *Prosecuting Organized Crime.* Raleigh: National Association of Attorneys General.
1977 *State Grand Juries.* Raleigh: National Association of Attorneys General.
1978 *Witness Immunity.* Raleigh: National Association of Attorneys General.

CONNABLE, ALFRED AND EDWARD SILBERFARB
1967 *Tigers of Tammany: Nine Men Who Ran New York.* New York: Holt, Rinehart and Winston.

COOK, FRED J.
1972 "Purge of the Greasers." Pages 89–109 in *Mafia, U.S.A.* Edited by Nicholas Gage. New York: Dell Publishing Co.
1973 *Mafia!* Greenwich, Conn.: Fawcett Publications, Inc.
1979 "Shaking the Bricks at the FBI." *New York Times Magazine* (March 25): 31–32, 34, 36, 38, 40.

CORAM, ROBERT
1978 "The Colombian Gold Rush of 1978." *Esquire* (September 12): 33–37.

CRANE, MILTON, ED.
1947 *Sins of New York.* New York: Grosset and Dunlap.

CRESSEY, DONALD R.
  1967  "The Functions and Structure of Criminal Syndicates." Pages 25–60 in Task Force Report: Organized Crime. President's Commission on Law Enforcement and Administration of Justice, Washington, D.C.: U.S. Government Printing Office.
  1967b  "Methodological Problems in the Study of Organized Crime as a Social Problem." *The Annals of the American Academy of Political and Social Science 374* (November): 101–112.
  1969  *Theft of the Nation.* New York: Harper and Row.

CROUSE, RUSSEL
  1947  "The Murder of Arnold Rothstein: 1928." Pages 184–200 in *Sins of New York.* Edited by Milton Crane. New York: Grosset and Dunlap.

CURTIS, CHARLOTTE
  1972  "Pal Joey: A Study in Gangster Chic." Pages 251–255 in *Mafia, U.S.A.* Edited by Nicholas Gage. New York: Dell Publishing.


DAHL, ROBERT A.
  1968  "Power." *International Encyclopedia of the Social Sciences.* New York: The Free Press.

DALEY, ROBERT
  1978  *Prince of the City.* Boston: Houghton Mifflin.

DEFFUS, R. L.
  1928  "The Gunman Has An Intercity Murder Trade." *New York Times* (July 8): XX3.

DE FRANCO, EDWARD J.
  1973  *Anatomy of a Scam: A Case Study of a Planned Bankruptcy by Organized Crime.* Washington, D.C.: U.S. Government Printing Office.

DEMARIS, OVID
  1969  *Captive City.* New York: Lyle Stuart, Inc.

DEMMA, JOE AND TOM RENNER
  1973  "The Mafia in the Supermarket." Pages 303–315 in *Mafia, U.S.A.* Edited by Nicholas Gage. New York: Dell Publishing.

DEPARTMENT OF JUSTICE
  1975  Report of the National Conference on Organized Crime. Washington, D.C.: U.S. Government Printing Office.

DEPARTMENT OF JUSTICE AND DEPARTMENT OF TRANSPORTATION
  1972  *Cargo Theft and Organized Crime.* Washington, D.C.: U.S. Government Printing Office.

DOBYNS, FLETCHER
  1932  *The Underworld of American Politics.* New York: Fletcher Dobyns, Publisher.

DORMAN, MICHAEL
  1972  *Payoff: The Role of Organized Crime in American Politics.* New York: David McKay Co.

1978   "The Mob Wades Ashore in Atlantic City " *New York Magazine* (January 30): 40–44.

DORSETT, LYLE W.
1968   *The Pendergast Machine.* New York: Oxford University Press.

DURK, DAVID AND IRA SILVERMAN
1976   *The Pleasant Avenue Connection.* New York: Harper and Row.

DURKHEIM, EMILE
1951   *Suicide.* New York: The Free Press.

ENGELMANN, LARRY
1979   *Intemperence: The Lost War Against Liquor.* New York: The Free Press.

EPSTEIN, EDWARD J.
1977   *Agency of Fear: Opiates and Political Power in America.* New York: G. P. Putnam's Sons.

FEDER, SID AND JOACHIM JOESTEN
1954   *The Luciano Story.* New York: David McKay.

FEIDEN, DOUG
1979   "The Great Getaway: The Inside Story of the Lufthansa Robbery." *New York Magazine* (June 4): 37–42.

FEINBERG, ALEXANDER
1944   "Lepke Is Put to Death, Denies Guilt to Last; Makes No Revelation." *New York Times* (March 5): 1, 30.
1950   "A Who's Who of New York's Gambling Inquiry." *New York Times* (October 29): 1V6.
1959   "Genovese Is Given 15 Years in Prison in Narcotics Case." *New York Times* (April 18): 1, 15.

FERRETTI, FRED
1977   "Mister Untouchable." *New York Times Magazine* (June 5): 15–17, 106, 108–109.

FITZGERALD, F. SCOTT
1925   *The Great Gatsby.* New York: Charles Scribner's Sons.

FOONER, MICHAEL
1973   *Interpol: The Inside Story of the International Crime-Fighting Organization.* Chicago: Henry Regnery Co.

FOWLER, FLOYD J., JR., THOMAS MANGIONE AND FREDERICK E. PRATTER
1978   *Gambling Law Enforcement in Major American Cities: Executive Summary.* Washington, D.C.: U.S. Government Printing Office.

FRANKS, LUCINDA
1977   "An Obscure Gangster Is Emerging As the New Mafia Chief in New York." *New York Times* (March 17): 1, 34.

FREEMAN, IRA HENRY
1957   "Anastasia Rose in Stormy Ranks." *New York Times* (October 26): 12.

FREUD, SIGMUND
  1974    *Cocaine Papers.* New York: Stonehill Publishing Co.

FRIED, JOSEPH P.
  1979    "New Trial to Begin Over Drug Charges." *NYT* (September 2): 23.

FRIEDMAN, LAWRENCE M.
  1973    *A History of American Law.* New York: Simon and Schuster.

FURSTENBERG, MARK H.
  1969    "Violence and Organized Crime." Appendix 18 in *Crimes of Vio-
          lence, Vol. 13* (A Staff Report Submitted to the National Commis-
          sion on the Causes and Prevention of Violence). Washington, D.C.:
          U.S. Government Printing Office.


GAGE, NICHOLAS
  1971a   *The Mafia Is Not An Equal Opportunity Employer.* New York:
          McGraw-Hill.
  1971b   "Gallo-Colombo Feud Said to Have Been Renewed." *New York
          Times* (June 29): 21.
  1974    "Questions Are Raised on Lucky Luciano Book." *New York Times*
          (December 17): 1, 28.
  1975    "Latins Now Leaders in Hard-Drug Trade." *New York Times*
          (April 21): 1, 26.
  1976    "Five Mafia Families Open Rosters to New Members." *New York
          Times* (March 21): 1, 40.

GALLIHER, JOHN F. AND JAMES A. CAIN
  1974    "Citation Support for the Mafia Myth in Criminology Textbooks."
          *The American Sociologist 9* (May): 68–74.

GAMBINO, RICHARD
  1974    *Blood of My Blood: The Dilemma of the Italian-Americans.*
          Garden City, N.Y.: Doubleday.
  1977    *Vendetta.* Garden City, N.Y.: Doubleday.

GARDINER, JOHN A.
  1967    "Public Attitudes Toward Gambling and Corruption." *Annals of the
          American Academy of Political and Social Science 374* (Novem-
          ber): 123–134.
  1970    *The Politics of Corruption: Organized Crime in an American City.*
          New York: Russell Sage Foundation.
  1973    "The Stern Syndicate." Pages 159–175 in *The Crime Establishment.*
          Edited by John E. Conklin. Englewood Cliffs, N.J.: Prentice-Hall.

GASPER, LOUIS C.
  1969    *Organized Crime: An Economic Analysis.* Ph.D. dissertation, Duke
          University.

GEISS, GILBERT
  1966    "Violence and Organized Crime." *Annals of the American Acad-
          emy of Political and Social Science 364* (March): 86–95.
  1974    *One-Eyed Justice: An Examination of Homosexuality, Abortion,
          Prostitution, Narcotics, and Gambling in the United States.* New
          York: Drake Publishers.

GODDARD, DONALD
    1974    *Joey*. New York: Harper and Row.
    1978    *Easy Money*. New York: Farrar, Straus and Giroux.

GODFREY, E. DREXEL, JR. AND DON R. HARRIS
    1971    *Basic Elements of Intelligence*. Washington, D.C.: U.S. Government Printing Office.

GODWIN, JOHN
    1978    *Murder U.S.A.: The Ways We Kill Each Other*. New York: Ballantine.

GOLDSTOCK, RONALD AND DAN T. COENEN
    1978    *Extortionate and Usurious Credit Transactions: Background Materials*. Ithaca, N.Y.: Cornell Institute on Organized Crime.

GOSNELL, HAROLD FOOTE
    1937    *Machine Politics: Chicago Model*. New York: Greenwood Press. Republished in 1968.

GOTTFRIED, ALEX
    1962    *Boss Cermak of Chicago*. Seattle: University of Washington Press.

GRAHAM, FRED
    1977    *The Atlas Program*. Boston: Little, Brown and Co.

GRINSPOON, LESTER AND JAMES B. BAKALAR
    1976    *Cocaine: A Drug and Its Social Evolution*. New York: Basic Books.

GROSSO, SONNY AND PHILIP ROSENBERG
    1978    *Point Blank*. New York: Grosset and Dunlap.

GRUTZNER, CHARLES
    1969    "Genovese Dies in Prison at 71; 'Boss of Bosses' of Mafia Here." *New York Times* (February 15): 1, 29.

GUSFIELD, JOSEPH
    1963    *Symbolic Crusade: Status Politics and the American Temperance Movement*. Urbana: University of Illinois Press.


HAGERTY, JAMES A.
    1933    "Assassin Fires Into Roosevelt Party at Miami; President-elect Uninjured; Mayor Cermak and 4 Others Wounded." *New York Times* (February 16): 1.

HALLER, MARK H.
    1971–1972–W    "Organized Crime in Urban Society: Chicago in the Twentieth Century." *Journal of Social History* 5: 210–234.

HAMMER, RICHARD
    1975    *Playboy's Illustrated History of Organized Crime*. Chicago: Playboy Press.

HAND, F. D.
    1978    "The Role of the Organized Crime Prevention Council." *FBI Law Enforcement Bulletin* (March): 20–23.

HARKER, R. PHILLIP
    1977    "Sports Wagering and the 'Line.'" *FBI Law Enforcement Bulletin* (November): FBI Reprint.

1978    "Sports Bookmaking Operations." *FBI Law Enforcement Bulletin* (September): FBI Reprint.

HAWKINS, GORDON
1969    "God and the Mafia." *The Public Interest 14* (Winter): 24–51.

HERNDON, BOOTON
1969    *Ford: An Unconventional Biography of the Men and Their Times.* New York: Weybright and Talley.

HESS, HENNER
1973    *Mafia and Mafiosi: The Structure of Power.* Lexington, Mass.: D. C. Heath. Translated from the German.

HIBBERT, CHRISTOPHER
1966    *Garibaldi and His Enemies.* Boston: Little, Brown and Co.

HILLS, STUART L.
1969    "Combating Organized Crime in America." *Federal Probation 33* (March): 23–28.

HINDELANG, MICHAEL J.
1971    "Bookies and Bookmaking: A Descriptive Analysis." *Crime and Delinquency 17* (July): 245–255.

HOBSBAWM, ERIC
1959    *Social Bandits and Primitive Rebels.* Glencoe, Illinois: The Free Press.
1969    "The American Mafia." *The Listener 82* (November 20): 685–688.
1971    *Bandits.* New York: Dell Publishing Co.

HOFFMAN, PAUL
1973    *Tiger in the Court.* Chicago: Playboy Press.
1979a    "Calabria University Studying Mafia 'Businessmen.'" *New York Times* (March 4): 4.
1979b    *Courthouse.* New York: Hawthorn Books.

HOFFMAN, PAUL AND IRA PECZNICK
1976    *To Drop a Dime.* New York: G. P. Putnam's Sons.

HOGAN, WILLIAM T.
1976    "Sentencing and Supervision of Organized Crime Figures." *Federal Probation 40* (March): 21–24.

HOLBROOK, STEWART H.
1953    *The Age of Moguls.* Garden City, N.Y.: Doubleday.

HOMANS, GEORGE C.
1961    *Social Behavior: Its Elementary Forms.* New York: Harcourt, Brace and World.

HOMER, FREDERIC D.
1974    *Guns and Garlic.* West Lafayette, Ind.: Purdue University Press.

HORNE, LOUTHER
1932    "Capone's Trip to Jail Ends a Long Battle." *New York Times* (May 8): IX 1.

IANNI, FRANCIS A. J.
1970    "Mafia and the Web of Kinship." Pages 1–22 in *An Inquiry Into Organized Crime*. Edited by Luciano J. Iorizzo. The American Italian Historical Association Proceedings of the Third Annual Conference, October 24.
1972    *A Family Business: Kinship and Social Control in Organized Crime*. New York: Russell Sage Foundation.
1973    *Ethnic Succession in Organized Crime*. Washington, D.C.: U.S. Government Printing Office.
1974    *Black Mafia: Ethnic Succession in Organized Crime*. New York: Simon and Schuster.

IANNI, FRANCIS A. J. AND ELIZABETH REUSS-IANNI, EDS.
1976    *The Crime Society*. New York: New American Library.

INBAU, FRED E., JAMES R. THOMPSON AND JAMES B. ZAGEL
1974    *Criminal Law and Its Administration*. Mineola, N.Y.: The Foundation Press.

INCIARDI, JAMES A.
1975    *Careers in Crime*. Chicago: Rand McNally Publishing Co.

INCIARDI, JAMES A., ALAN A. BLOCK AND LYLE A. HALLOWELL
1977    *Historical Approaches to Crime*. Beverly Hills, Ca.: Sage Publications.

INTERNATIONAL ASSOCIATION OF CHIEFS OF POLICE COMMITTEE ON ORGANIZED CRIME
1975    *The Police Executive's Organized Crime Enforcement Handbook*. Gaitherburg, Md.: IACP.

IREY, ELMER L. AND WILLIAM T. SLOCUM
1948    *The Tax Dodgers*. Garden City, N.Y.: Doubleday.


JACOBS, JAMES B.
1977    *Statesville*. Chicago: University of Chicago Press.

JEFFREYS-JONES, RHODRI
1978    *Violence and Reform in American History*. New York: New Viewpoints.

JENNINGS, DEAN
1967    *We Only Kill Each Other*. Englewood Cliffs, N.J.: Prentice-Hall.

JOHNSON, EARL, JR.
1963    "Organized Crime: Challenge to the American Legal System." *Criminal Law, Criminology, and Police Science 54* (March): 1–29.

JOHNSON, MALCOLM
1972    "In Hollywood." Pages 325–338 in *Mafia, U.S.A.* Edited by Nicholas Gage. New York: Dell Publishing Co.

JOSEPHSON, MATTHEW
1934    *The Robber Barons*. New York: Harcourt, Brace and Co.

KAPLAN, LAWRENCE J. AND DENNIS KESSLER, EDS.
1976   *An Economic Analysis of Crime.* Springfield, Illinois: Charles C Thomas.

KATCHER, LEO
1959   *The Big Bankroll: The Life and Times of Arnold Rothstein.* New York: Harper and Brothers.

KEFAUVER, ESTES
1968   *Crime in America.* New York: Greenwood Press.

KELTON, HAROLD W. JR. AND CHARLES M. UNKOVIC
1971   "Characteristics of Organized Criminal Groups." *Canadian Journal of Corrections 13* (January): 68–78.

KENNEDY, ROBERT F.
1960   *The Enemy Within.* New York: Popular Library.

KIDNER, JOHN
1976   *Crimaldi: Contract Killer.* Washington, D.C.: Acropolis Books.

KIHSS, PETER
1978   "Mob's Role Discounted in Gambling." *New York Times* (June 26): 1, D11.
1979   "John Dioguardi (Johnny Dio), 64, A Leader in Organized Crime, Dies." *New York Times* (January 16): B6.

KING, RUFUS
1963   "The Fifth Amendment Privilege and Immunity Legislation." *Notre Dame Lawyer 38* (September): 641–654.
1969   *Gambling and Organized Crime.* Washington, D.C.: Public Affairs Press.

KIRK, DONALD
1976   "Crime, Politics and Finger Chopping." *New York Times Magazine* (December 12): 60–61, 91–97.

KLOCKARS, CARL B.
1974   *The Professional Fence.* New York: The Free Press.

KOBLER, JOHN
1971   *Capone: The Life and World of Al Capone.* Greenwich, Conn.: Fawcett Publications.

KNAPP, WHITMAN, ET AL.
1972   *Report of the Commission to Investigate Alleged Police Corruption.* New York: George Braziller.

KWITNY, JONATHAN
1979   *Vicious Circles: The Mafia in the Marketplace.* New York: W. W. Norton and Co.
1979   "New Jersey Files Indictment That Alleges Mafia Exists, Outlines Group's Operation." *Wall Street Journal* (May 25): 6.


LAMOUR, CATHERINE AND MICHAEL R. LAMBERTI
1974   *The International Connection: Opium From Growers to Pushers.* New York: Pantheon Books. Translated from the French.

LANDESCO, JOHN
   1929   *Organized Crime in Chicago*. Chicago: University of Chicago Press.
          Reprinted in 1969.
   1932   "Crime and the Failure of Institutions in Chicago's Immigrant
          Areas." *Journal of Criminal Law and Criminology 23* (July): 238–
          248.
   1933   "Life History of a Member of the Forty-Two Gang." *Journal of
          Criminal Law and Criminology 24* (March): 964–998.

LANGLAIS, RUDY
   1978   "Inside the Heroin Trade: How a Star Double Agent Ended Up
          Dead." *Village Voice* (March 13): 13–15.

LASSWELL, HAROLD D. AND JERIMIAH B. MCKENNA
   1972   *The Impact of Organized Crime on an Inner-City Community*. New
          York: Policy Sciences Center, Inc.

LEE, HENRY
   1963   *How Dry We Were: Prohibition Revisited*. Englewood Cliffs, N.J.:
          Prentice-Hall.

LEWIS, ARTHUR H.
   1964   *Lament for the Molly Maguires*. New York: Harcourt Brace and
          World.

LEWIS, MERLIN, WARREN BUNDY AND JAMES L. HAGUE
   1978   *An Introduction to the Courts and Judicial Process*. Englewood
          Cliffs, N.J.: Prentice-Hall.

LEWIS, NORMAN
   1964   *The Honored Society*. New York: G. P. Putnam's Sons.

LIGHT, IVAN
   1977   "The Ethnic Vice Industry, 1880–1944." *American Sociological
          Review 42* (June): 464–479.
   1977   "Numbers Gambling Among Blacks: A Financial Institution."
          *American Sociological Review 42* (December): 892–904.

LINDESMITH, ALFRED R.
   1941   "Organized Crime." *Annals of the American Academy of Political
          and Social Science 217* (September): 119–127.

LIPPMAN, WALTER
   1962   "The Underworld As Servant." Pages 58–69 in *Organized Crime in
          America*. Edited by Gus Tyler. Ann Arbor: University of Michigan.
          Article originally published in 1931.

LLOYD, HENRY DEMAREST
   1963   *Wealth Against Commonwealth*. Edited by Thomas C. Cochran.
          Englewood Cliffs, N.J.: Prentice-Hall.

LOGAN, ANDY
   1970   *Against the Evidence: The Becker-Rosenthal Affair*. New York:
          McCall Publishing Co.

LUNDBERG, FERDINAND
   1968   *The Rich and the Super-Rich: A Study in the Power of Money
          Today*. New York: Lyle Stuart.

MAAS, PETER
  1968   *The Valachi Papers*. New York: G. P. Putnam's Sons.
  1974   *Serpico*. New York: Bantam.

MACDOUGALL, ERNEST D., ED.
  1933   *Crime for Profit: A Symposium on Mercenary Crime*. Boston: The
         Stratford Co.

MACK, JOHN A.
  1973   "The 'Organised' and 'Professional' Labels Criticised." *Interna-
         tional Journal of Criminology and Penology 1* (May): 103–116.

MAITLAND, LESLIE
  1979   "U.S. Air Cargoes Inquiry Is Seeking Link to Crime." *New York
         Times* (May 30): B1, B2.

MALCOLM, ANDREW H.
  1977   "Police in Osaka Develop a New Anticrime Method: A Drive to
         'Shame' Gangsters from Lawless Ways." *New York Times* (March
         17): 8.

MALCOLM, WALTER D. AND JOHN J. CURTIN, JR.
  1968   "The New Federal Attack on the Loan Shark Problem." *Law and
         Contemporary Problems 133:* 765–785.

MALTZ, MICHAEL D.
  1975   "Policy Issues in Organized Crime and White-Collar Crime." Pages
         73–94 in *Crime and Criminal Justice*. Edited by John A. Gardiner
         and Michael A. Mulkey. Lexington, Mass.: D. C. Heath.
  1976   "On Defining 'Organized Crime.'" *Crime and Delinquency 22*
         (July): 338–346.

MARSHALL, ELIOT
  1978   "State Lottery." *The New Republic* (June 24): 20–21.

MARTIN, RAYMOND V.
  1963   *Revolt in the Mafia*. New York: Duell, Sloan and Pearce.

MERTON, ROBERT
  1938   "Social Structure and Anomie." *American Sociological Review 3:*
         672–682.
  1967   *On Theoretical Sociology*. New York: The Free Press.

MESKIL, PAUL
  1973   *Don Carlo: Boss of Bosses*. New York: Popular Library.
  1977   "Meet the New Godfather." *New York Magazine* (February 28):
         28–32.

MESSICK, HANK
  1967   *The Silent Syndicate*. New York: Macmillan.
  1973   *Lansky*. New York: Berkley Publishing Co.
  1979   *Of Grass and Snow: The Secret Criminal Elite*. Englewood Cliffs,
         N.J.: Prentice-Hall.

MILLER, JUDITH
  1978   "Bankers Gird for More Nasty Questions." *New York Times* (May
         27): E4.

MILLER, WALTER B.
1958 "Lower Class Culture as a Generating Milieu of Gang Delinquency." *Journal of Social Issues 14:* 5–21.

MOCKRIDGE, NORTON AND ROBERT H. PRALL
1954 *The Big Fix.* New York: Henry Holt and Co.

MOQUIN, WAYNE AND CHARLES VAN DOREN, EDS.
1976 *The American Way of Crime.* New York: Praeger.

MORRI, CESARE
1933 *The Last Struggle With the Mafia.* London: Putnam and Co. Translated from the Italian.

MORRIS, NORVAL AND GORDON HAWKINS
1970 *The Honest Politician's Guide to Crime Control.* Chicago: University of Chicago Press.

MURPHY, PATRICK V. AND THOMAS PLATE
1977 *Commissioner: A View From the Top of American Law Enforcement.* New York: Simon and Schuster.

MYERS, GUSTAVUS
1936 *History of Great American Fortunes.* New York: Modern Library.

MCCONAUGHY, JOHN
1931 *From Caine to Capone: Racketeering Down the Ages.* New York: Bretano's.

MCLAUGHLIN, JOHN B.
n.d. *Sicilian and American Mafia.* Police Training Institute of Illinois.

MCPHAUL, JACK
1970 *Johnny Torrio: First of the Gang Lords.* New Rochelle, N.Y.: Arlington House.

NAGEL, JACK H.
1968 "Some Questions About the Concept of Power." *Behavioral Science 13:* 129–137.

NASH, JAY ROBERT
1975 *Bloodletters and Badmen: Book 3.* New York: Warner Books.

NATIONAL ADVISORY COMMISSION ON CIVIL DISORDERS
1968 *Report.* New York: Bantam.

NATIONAL ADVISORY COMMISSION ON CRIMINAL JUSTICE STANDARDS AND GOALS
1975 *A National Strategy to Reduce Crime.* New York: Avon Books.

NELLI, HUMBERT S.
1969 "Italians and Crime in Chicago: The Formative Years; 1890–1920." *American Journal of Sociology 74* (January): 373–391.
1976 *The Business of Crime.* New York: Oxford University Press.

NEW YORK STATE COMMISSION OF INVESTIGATION
1970 *Racketeer Infiltration Into Legitimate Business.* New York.
1978 *A Report on Fencing: The Sale and Distribution of Stolen Property.* New York.

NORTH CAROLINA ORGANIZED CRIME PREVENTION COUNCIL
n.d.  *Organized Crime in North Carolina.* Raleigh: Department of Justice.

NOVAK, MICHAEL
1978  *The Guns of Lattimer.* New York: Basic Books.

O'CONNOR, RICHARD
1958  *Hell's Kitchen.* Philadelphia: J. B. Lippincott Co.
1962  *Gould's Millions.* Garden City, N.Y.: Doubleday.

OPOLOT, JAMES S. E.
1979  "Organized Crime in Africa." Paper presented at the Annual Meeting of the Academy of Criminal Justice Sciences, Cincinnati.

OVERLY, DON H. AND THEODORE H. SCHELL
1973  *New Effectiveness Measures for Organized Crime Control Efforts.* Washington, D.C.: U.S. Government Printing Office.

PACKER, HERBERT L.
1968  *The Limits of the Criminal Sanction.* Stanford, Ca.: Stanford University Press.

PANTALEONE, MICHELE
1966  *The Mafia and Politics.* New York: Coward and McCann.

PASLEY, FRED D.
1931  *Al Capone: The Biography of a Self-Made Man.* Freeport, N.Y.: Books for Libraries Press. Reprinted in 1971.

PETACCO, ARRIGO
1974  *Joe Petrosino.* New York: Macmillan. Translated from the Italian.

PETERSON, VIRGIL
1962  "The Career of a Syndicate Boss." *Crime and Delinquency 8* (October): 339–349.
1963  "Chicago: Shades of Capone." *Annals of the American Academy of Political and Social Science 347* (May): 30–39.
1969  *A Report on Chicago Crime for 1968.* Chicago: Chicago Crime Commission.

PHILCOX, NORMAN W.
1978  *An Introduction to Organized Crime.* Springfield, Illinois: Charles C Thomas.

PILEGGI, NICHOLAS
1972  "The Godfather's New Recruits." Pages 82–83 in *Mafia at War.* Edited by Thomas Plate. New York: New York Magazine Press.

PITKIN, THOMAS MONROE AND FRANCESCO CORDASCO
1977  *The Black Hand: A Chapter in Ethnic Crime.* Totawa, N.J.: Littlefield, Adams.

PLATE, THOMAS AND THE EDITORS OF NEW YORK MAGAZINE, EDS.
1972  *The Mafia at War.* New York: New York Magazine Press.

PRALL, ROBERT H. AND NORTON MOCKRIDGE
1951    *This Is Costello*. New York: Gold Medal Books.

PRESIDENT'S COMMISSION ON LAW ENFORCEMENT AND ADMINISTRATION OF
JUSTICE
1968    *The Challenge of Crime in a Free Society*. New York: Avon Books.


QUINNEY, RICHARD
1974    *Critique of the Legal Order*. Boston: Little, Brown & Co.


RAAB, SELWYN
1978    "4 Gang-Type Killings in Brooklyn Linked to Feud Over Narcotics."
        *New York Times* (February 14): 39.
1979    "Marijuana Vessels Come to Northeast." *New York Times* (March
        4): 34.

RECKLESS, WALTER
1969    *Vice in Chicago*. Montclair, N.J.: Patterson Smith.

REID, ED
1970    *The Grim Reapers*. New York: Bantam Books.

REID, ED AND OVID DEMARIS
1964    *The Green Felt Jungle*. New York: Cardinal Paperbacks.

REISMAN, W. MICHAEL
1979    *Folded Lies: Bribery, Crusades, and Reforms*. New York: The Free
        Press.

REPETTO, THOMAS A.
1978    *The Blue Parade*. New York: The Free Press.

RICHARDSON, JAMES F.
1975    "The Early Years of the New York Police Department." Pages 15–
        23 in *Police in America*. Edited by Jerome H. Skolnick and Thomas
        C. Gray. Boston: Little, Brown & Co.

ROME, FLORENCE
1975    *The Tattooed Men*. New York: Delacorte Press.

ROSEN, CHARLES
1978    *Scandals of '51: How the Gamblers Almost Killed College Basket-
        ball*. New York: Holt, Rinehart and Winston.

ROYKO, MIKE
1971    *Boss: Richard J. Daley of Chicago*. New York: E. P. Dutton and
        Co.

RUBINSTEIN, JONATHAN
1973    *City Police*. New York: Farrar, Straus, and Giroux.

RUBINSTEIN, JONATHAN AND PETER REUTER
1977    *Numbers: The Routine Racket*. New York: Policy Sciences Center,
        Inc. (Preliminary, unpublished draft).

1978a  "Fact, Fancy, and Organized Crime." *The Public Interest 53* (Fall): 45–67.
1978b  *Bookmaking in New York.* New York: Policy Sciences Center, Inc. (Preliminary, unpublished draft).

SALERNO, RALPH AND JOHN S. TOMPKINS
1969   *The Crime Confederation.* Garden City: Doubleday.

SANN, PAUL
1971   *Kill the Dutchman: The Story of Dutch Schultz.* New York: Popular Library.

SATCHELL, MICHAEL
1979   "Atlantic City's Great Gold Rush." *Parade* (June 10): 8–10.

SCHELLING, THOMAS C.
1971   "What Is the Business of Organized Crime." *American Scholar 40* (Autumn): 643–652.

SCHIAVO, GIOVANNI
1962   *The Truth About the Mafia and Organized Crime in America.* New York: The Vigo Press.

SCHNEPPER, JEFF A.
1978   *Inside IRS.* New York: Stein and Day.

SCHORR, MARK
1978   "Gunfight in the Cocaine Corral." *New York Magazine* (September 25): 48–57.
1979   "The .22 Caliber Killings." *New York Magazine* (May 7): 43–46.

SCHUMACH, MURRAY
1977   "30 Indicted in Queens Heroin Crackdown." *New York Times* (April 15): 1, 37.

SCHUR, EDWIN M.
1965   *Crimes Without Victims.* Englewood Cliffs, N.J.: Prentice-Hall.
1969   *Our Criminal Society.* Englewood Cliffs, N.J.: Prentice-Hall.

SCHWARTZ, HERMAN
1968   "The Wiretapping Problem Today." Pages 156–168 in *Criminological Controversies.* Edited by Richard D. Knudten. New York: Appleton-Century-Crofts.

SCHWENDINGER, HERMAN AND JULIA SCHWENDINGER
1977   "Social Class and the Definition of Crime." *Crime and Social Justice 7* (Spring-Summer): 4–13.

SEEDMAN, ALBERT A.
1974   *Chief!* New York: Arthur Fields.

SEIDL, JOHN M.
1968   *Upon the Hip—A Study of the Criminal Loanshark Industry.* Ph.D. dissertation, Harvard University.

SEIDMAN, HAROLD
1938   *Labor Czars: A History of Labor Racketeering.* New York: Liveright Publishing Corp.

SEIGEL, MAX H.
  1977    "14, Including Alleged Charter Member of Purple Gang, Charged
          in Heroin Conspiracy." *New York Times* (December 20): 27.

SERAO, ERNESTO
  1911a   "The Truth About the Camorra." *Outlook 98* (July 28): 717–726.
  1911b   "The Truth About the Camorra: Part Two." *Outlook 98* (August
          5): 778–787.

SERVADIO, GAIA
  1976    *Mafioso: A History of the Mafia From Its Origins to the Present
          Day*. Briarcliff Manor, N.Y.: Stein and Day.

SHAW, CLIFFORD AND HENRY D. McKAY
  1942    *Juvenile Delinquency and Urban Areas*. Chicago: Chicago Univer-
          sity Press. Republished in 1972.

SHERIDAN, WALTER
  1972    *The Fall and Rise of Jimmy Hoffa*. New York: Saturday Review
          Press.

SHERMAN, LAWRENCE, ED.
  1974    *Police Corruption: A Sociological Perspective*. Garden City: Dou-
          bleday.

SICILIANO, VINCENT
  1970    *Unless They Kill Me First*. New York: Hawthorn Books.

SILBERMAN, CHARLES E.
  1978    *Criminal Violence, Criminal Justice*. New York: Random House.

SIMPSON, ANTHONY E.
  1977    *The Literature of Police Corruption*. New York: The John Jay
          Press.

SINCLAIR, ANDREW
  1962    *The Era of Excess: A Social History of the Prohibition Movement*.
          Boston: Little, Brown & Co.

SKOLNICK, JEROME H.
  1978    *House of Cards: Legalization and Control of Casino Gambling*.
          Boston: Little, Brown & Co.

SMITH, ALSON J.
  1962    "The Early Chicago Story." Pages 138–146 in *Organized Crime in
          America*. Edited by Gus Tyler. Ann Arbor: University of Michigan
          Press.

SMITH, DWIGHT C., JR.
  1975    *The Mafia Mystique*. New York: Basic Books.
  1976    "Mafia: The Prototypical Alien Conspiracy." *Annals of the Ameri-
          can Academy of Political and Social Science 423* (January): 75–88.
  1978    "Organized Crime and Entrepreneurship." *International Journal of
          Criminology and Penology 6*: 161–177.

SMITH, DWIGHT C. AND RALPH SALERNO
  1970    "The Use of Strategies in Organized Crime Control." *Journal of
          Criminal Law, Criminology and Police Science 61*: 101–111.

SONDERN, FREDERIC, JR.
  1959   *Brotherhood of Evil: The Mafia.* New York: Farrar, Straus and Cudahy.

SPERGEL, IRVING
  1964   *Racketville, Slumtown, Haulberg.* Chicago: University of Chicago Press.

SPIERING, FRANK
  1976   *The Man Who Got Capone.* Indianapolis: Bobbs-Merrill.

SUPREME COURT OF THE STATE OF NEW YORK, COUNTY OF KINGS
  1942   *A Presentment Concerning the Enforcement by the Police Department of the City of New York of the Laws Against Gambling.* Arno Press Reprint, 1974.

SUTHERLAND, EDWIN H.
  1972   *The Professional Thief.* Chicago: University of Chicago Press. Originally published in 1937.
  1973   *Edwin H. Sutherland: On Analyzing Crime.* Edited by Karl Schuessler. Chicago: University of Chicago Press.

SUTTLES, GERALD D.
  1968   *The Social Order of the Slum.* Chicago: University of Chicago Press.

SWANBERG, W. A.
  1959   *Jim Fisk: The Career of an Improbable Rascal.* New York: Charles Scribner's Sons.


TALESE, GAY
  1965   *The Overreachers.* New York: Harper and Row.
  1971   *Honor Thy Father.* New York: World Publishing Co.

TASK FORCE ON ORGANIZED CRIME
  1967   *Task Force Report: Organized Crime.* Washington, D.C.: U.S. Government Printing Office.
  1976   *Organized Crime.* Washington, D.C.: U.S. Government Printing Office.

TAYLOR, IAN, PAUL WALTON AND JOCK YOUNG
  1973   *The New Criminology.* New York: Harper and Row.

TERESA, VINCENT WITH THOMAS C. RENNER
  1973   *My Life in the Mafia.* Greenwich, Conn.: Fawcett Publications.

THOMAS, JUDY M., ET AL.
  1978   *A Report on Fencing.* State of New York: Commission of Investigation.

THOMPSON, CRAIG AND ALLAN RAYMOND
  1940   *Gang Rule in New York.* New York: Dial.

THRASHER, FREDERIC MILTON
  1968   *The Gang: A Study of 1,313 Gangs in Chicago.* Abridged version. Chicago: University of Chicago Press.

TOBY, JACKSON
　　1958    "Hoodlum or Business Men; An American Dilemma." Pages 542–
　　　　　　550 in *The Jews: Social Patterns of an American Group*. Edited by
　　　　　　Marshall Sklare. Glencoe, Ill.: Free Press.

TOUHY, ROGER
　　1959    *The Stolen Years*. Cleveland: Pennington.

TRAIN, ARTHUR
　　1912    "Imported Crime: The Story of the Camorra in America." *Mc-
　　　　　　Clure's Magazine* (May): 83–94.
　　1922    *Courts and Criminals*. New York: Charles Scribner's Sons.

TUITE, JAMES
　　1978    "Would Benefits of Legalized Betting on Sports Outweigh the Draw-
　　　　　　backs?" *New York Times* (December 19): B21.

TURKUS, BURTON B. AND SID FEDER
　　1951    *Murder, Inc.: The Story of "The Syndicate."* New York: Farrar,
　　　　　　Straus and Young.

TYLER, GUS, ED.
　　1962    *Organized Crime in America*. Ann Arbor: University of Michigan
　　　　　　Press.
　　1975    "Book Review (of Ianni's Black Mafia).' *Crime and Delinquency
　　　　　　21* (April): 175–180.


UNITED STATES SENATE SUBCOMMITTEE ON ADMINISTRATIVE PRACTICE AND
PROCEDURE
　　1978    Hearings on Oversight of the Witness Protection Program. Wash-
　　　　　　ington, D.C.: U.S. Government Printing Office.


VILLANO, ANTHONY
　　1978    *Brick Agent*. New York: Ballantine Books.

VIRGINIA STATE CRIME COMMISSION
　　1972    Report of the Organized Crime Detection Task Force. Richmond:
　　　　　　Department of Purchases and Supply.

VOLSKY, GEORGE
　　1979    "Indictment in Miami Depicts Rise and Fall of Narcotics-Smuggling
　　　　　　Gang." *New York Times* (May 6): 26.

VOLZ, JOSEPH AND PETER J. BRIDGE, EDS.
　　1969    *The Mafia Talks*. Greenwich, Conn.: Fawcett Publications.


WALL, JOSEPH FRAZIER
　　1970    *Andrew Carnegie*. New York: Oxford University Press.

WALSH, MARILYN E.
　　1977    *The Fence*. Westport, Conn.: Greenwood Press.

WASSERSTEIN, BRUCE AND MARK J. GREEN, EDS.
　　1970    *With Justice for Some*. Boston: Beacon Press.

WEBER, MAX
    1949   *The Methodology of the Social Sciences.* Glencoe, Illinois: The Free Press.

    1958   *Protestant Ethic and the Spirit of Capitalism.* New York: Charles Scribner's Sons.

    1968   *Economy and Society.* Edited by Guenther Roth and Claus Wiltich. New York: Bedminster Press.

WENDT, LLOYD AND HERMAN KOGAN
    1943   *Lords of the Levee,* Indianapolis: Bobbs-Merrill Co.

WESSEL, MILTON R.
    1963   "The Conspiracy Charge as a Weapon Against Organized Crime." *Notre Dame Lawyer 38* (September): 689–699.

WHITE, FRANK MARSHALL
    1908   "The Bands of Criminals of New York's East Side." *New York Times* (November 8): V9.

WHYTE, WILLIAM FOOTE
    1961   *Street Corner Society.* Chicago: University of Chicago Press.

WILLIAMS, T. HARRY
    1969   *Huey Long.* New York: Bantam Books.

WILSON, JAMES Q.
    1978   *The Investigators: Managing FBI and Narcotics Agents.* New York: Basic Books.

WINICK, CHARLES AND PAUL M. KINSIE
    1971   *The Lively Commerce.* Chicago: Quadrangle.

WOETZEL, ROBERT K.
    1963   "An Overview of Organized Crime: Mores Versus Morality." *Annals of the Academy of Political and Social Science 347* (May): 1–11.

WOLF, ERIC R.
    1966   "Kinship, Friendship, and Patron-Client Relations in Complex Societies." Pages 1–22 in *The Social Anthropology of Complex Societies.* Edited by Michael Banton. London: Tavistock Publications.

WRIGHT, MICHAEL
    1979   "Phenix City, Ala., Leaves Ashes of Sin in the Past." *New York Times,* June 18: 14.

WRONG, DENNIS
    1968   "Some Problems in Defining Social Power." *American Journal of Sociology 73* (May): 673–681.

X, MALCOLM
    1973   *The Autobiography of Malcolm X.* New York: Ballantine Books.

YEAGER, MATTHEW G.
    1973   "The Gangster as White Collar Criminal: Organized Crime and Stolen Securities." *Issues in Criminology 8* (Spring): 49–73.

ZEIGER, HENRY A., ED.
   1970   *Sam the Plumber.* New York: New American Library.

ZILG, GERARD COLBY
   1974   *DuPont: Behind the Nylon Curtain.* Englewood Cliffs, N.J.: Prentice-Hall.

ZIMMER, ROBERT B.
   1979   "Origins of 'Organized Crime': A Comparative Study." Paper presented at the Annual Meeting of the Academy of Criminal Justice Sciences, Cincinnati.

# INDEX

# AUTHORS